THE TRIUMPH OF PLEASURE

The Triumph of
PLEASURE

*

Louis XIV &
the Politics of Spectacle

GEORGIA J. COWART

The University of Chicago Press   Chicago & London

PUBLICATION OF THIS BOOK HAS BEEN AIDED
BY A GRANT FROM THE BEVINGTON FUND

GEORGIA J. COWART is professor of music
at Case Western Reserve University.

The University of Chicago Press, Chicago 60637
The University of Chicago Press, Ltd., London
© 2008 by The University of Chicago
All rights reserved. Published 2008
Printed in the United States of America

17 16 15 14 13 12 11 10 09 08   1 2 3 4 5

ISBN-13: 978-0-226-11638-9 (cloth)
ISBN-10: 0-226-11638-7 (cloth)

Library of Congress Cataloging-in-Publication Data

Cowart, Georgia.
The triumph of pleasure : Louis XIV and the politics of spectacle / Georgia J. Cowart.
p.   cm.
Includes bibliographical references and index.
ISBN-13: 978-0-226-11638-9 (cloth : alk. paper)
ISBN-10: 0-226-11638-7 (cloth : alk. paper)
1. Louis XIV, King of France, 1638–1715.   2. Music—Social aspects—
France.   3. Music—Political aspects—France.   4. Ballet—France—History—
17th century.   5. Ballet—France—History—18th century.   6. Musical theater—
France—History—17th century   7. Musical theater—France—History—18th
century   8. France—Court and courtiers—History—17th century.   9. France—
Court and courtiers—History—18th century.   I. Title.
ML3917.F5C69 2008
780.94409'032—dc22
2008019417

♾ The paper used in this publication meets the minimum requirements of
the American National Standard for Information Sciences—Permanence of Paper
for Printed Library Materials, ANSI Z39.48-1992.

*For my daughter Rachel Victoria &
in memory of my mother Jewel*

Contents

List of Illustrations ix   Acknowledgments xiii

Introduction xv
The Allure of Spectacle and the Prerogative of Pleasure

*

1 * Muses of Pleasure 1
Louis XIV's Early Court Ballet, 1651–1660

2 * Muses of Memory 41
Louis XIV's Late Court Ballet, 1661–1669

3 * Muses of Satire 84
Le bourgeois gentilhomme *& the Utopia of Spectacle*

4 * Tragic Interlude 120
Reversals at the Paris Opéra, 1671–1697

5 * Sappho, Cythera & the Triumph of Love 161
The Ballet at the Paris Opéra, 1700–1713

6 * Carnival, Commedia dell'arte & the Triumph of Folly 191
The Ballet at the Paris Opéra, 1699–1718

7 * Watteau's Cythera, the Opéra-Ballet &
the Staging of Pleasure 222

*

Bibliography 253   Index 281

Illustrations

Figures

1.1. *Ballet des fêtes de Bacchus*, allegorical figure Mirth *(un Ris)*   2

1.2. *Ballet des fêtes de Bacchus*, Morpheus   3

1.3. *Ballet des fêtes de Bacchus*, allegorical figure Gaming *(le Jeu)*   4

1.4. *Ballet des fêtes de Bacchus*, knights of the Round Table   5
being entertained

1.5. *Ballet des fêtes de Bacchus*, musician performing a *musique*   22
crotesque

1.6. *Les noces de Pélée et de Thétis*, costume of Louis XIV as Apollo   36

1.7. *Les noces de Pélée et de Thétis*, costume of Henriette   37
d'Angleterre as the Muse Erato

6.1. Monsieur Debreil, a dancer of the Paris Opéra, costumed   197
as Scaramouche

6.2. Frontispiece, Michel de La Barre, *La vénitienne*   199

6.3. Frontispiece, André Campra, *Les fêtes vénitiennes*   216

7.1. Claude Gillot, *L'embarquement pour l'île de Cythère*   228

7.2. Bernard Picart, *L'isle de Cythère*   229

7.3. Jean Berain, stage design for *Marthésie, reine des Amazons*   233

7.4. Frontispiece, Michel de La Barre, *Le triomphe des arts* (1700)   239

7.5. Frontispiece, Jacques de La Beaune, *Panegyricus*   241

7.6. Frontispiece, La Barre, *Le triomphe des arts* (1703)   243

7.7. Frontispiece, Thomas Bourgeois, *Les amours déguisés*   244

Musical Examples

1.1. Jean-Baptiste Lully, *Ballet de l'impatience,* snuff-takers 24
chorus, LWV 14/23

1.2. Jean-Baptiste Lully, *Alcidiane,* burlesque dancers, LWV 9/16 28

1.3. Jean-Baptiste Lully, *Alcidiane,* noble dancers, LWV 9/22 31

2.1. Jean-Baptiste Lully, *Ballet des amours déguisés,* followers 60
of Athena and Venus, LWV 21/2

2.2. Jean-Baptiste Lully, *Ballet des amours déguisés,* lament 64
of Armida, LWV 21/20

2.3. Jean-Baptiste Lully, *Ballet des Muses,* chorus of Muses, 68
LWV 32/3

3.1a. Jean-Baptiste Lully, *Le bourgeois gentilhomme,* student 96
composition scene, LWV 43/2

3.1b. Jean-Baptiste Lully, *Le bourgeois gentilhomme,* final 99
version of student composition, LWV 43/2

3.2. Jean-Baptiste Lully, *Le bourgeois gentilhomme,* "Ballet des 106
nations," "Dialogue des gens qui en musique demandent des
livres," opening, LWV 43/23

3.3a. Jean-Baptiste Lully, *Le bourgeois gentilhomme,* "Ballet des 108
nations," "Dialogue des gens qui en musique demandent des
livres," noble ladies and gentlemen

3.3b. Jean-Baptiste Lully, *Le bourgeois gentilhomme,* "Ballet des 109
nations," "Dialogue des gens qui en musique demandent des
livres," Swiss

3.3c. Jean-Baptiste Lully, *Le bourgeois gentilhomme,* "Ballet des 109
nations," "Dialogue des gens qui en musique demandent des
livres," old bourgeois

4.1. Jean-Baptiste Lully, *Isis,* opening chorus, LWV 52/2 129

4.2. Louis Lully, *Orphée,* act 2, scene 2 147

5.1. Michel de La Barre, *Le triomphe des arts,* apotheosis of Sappho 184

5.2. Thomas Bourgeois, *Les amours déguisés,* "L'Amitié," pastoral 185
scene

6.1. André Campra, *Le carnaval de Venise,* act 3, scene 8 ("Orfeo 205
nell'inferi")

6.2. André Campra, *Le carnaval de Venise,* act 3, scene 2 ("Le bal, 207
dernier divertissement")

6.3. André Campra, *Les fêtes vénitiennes,* act 3, scene 2 ("Le bal") 209

Tables

2.1. Structure of Entries in the *Ballet des Muses*   76

3.1. Comparison of the Structure of the *Ballet des Muses* and   104
 Le bourgeois gentilhomme

5.1. Ballets produced at the Paris Opéra, 1675–1713, comparison   174

6.1. Comparison of the *Ballet des Muses, Le bourgeois gentilhomme,*   214
 and *Les fêtes vénitiennes*

Plates following page 136

1. *Ballet des fêtes de Bacchus,* Apollo and the Muses

2. *Ballet de la nuit,* costume of Jean-Baptiste Lully as a beggar

3. *Ballet de la nuit,* costume of Louis XIV as the Rising Sun

4. Antoine Watteau, *Pilgrimage to Cythera* (Paris), 1717

5. Antoine Watteau, *Pilgrimage to Cythera* (Berlin), c. 1718–19

6. Detail of plate 5, *Pilgrimage to Cythera,* ship

7. Detail of plate 5, *Pilgrimage to Cythera,* statue of Venus
 and cupids

8. Antoine Watteau, *L'isle de Cythère,* c. 1708

※

Acknowledgments

My engagement with the ideas of this book, as well as its very conception, grew out of the gift of conversation and intellectual exchange with several close friends over many years, namely, Buford Norman, Patricia Leighten, Mark Antliff, and Mary Davis. The work itself has brought me into long-standing dialogues with other colleagues, now friends, who have guided my research, nurtured my instincts, and corrected my mistakes. These include musicologists Jann Pasler, Geoffrey Burgess, Kate Van Orden, Susan McClary, Wendy Heller, Donald Fader, Rose Pruiksma, Olivia Bloechl, Catherine Gordon-Seifert, and Catherine Cole; art historians Sarah Cohen, John Beldon Scott, and Charlotte Vignon; literary historians/theorists Jean-Marie Apostolidès, Downing Thomas, Lewis Seifert, Stephen Fleck, and David Levin; and baroque dance specialist Catherine Turocy. I am grateful to Kathleen Hansell, music editor at the University of Chicago Press, who has advised the project for a number of years, and to the readers who offered detailed written reports, both formal and informal, including Davitt Moroney, Orest Ranum, Thomas Christensen, and Rebecca Harris-Warrick. It is hardly necessary to add that the responsibility for any error of fact or judgment remains with the author.

I am also grateful for a wealth of institutional support, most especially from the American Council of Learned Societies, the National Endowment for the Humanities, Case Western Reserve University, and the Metropolitan Museum of Art in New York, where I am currently serving as Sylvan C. Coleman and Pamela Coleman Memorial Fund Fellow in Art History. My work was further supported by music librarian Stephen Toombs and the music department staff at Case Western Reserve University, and by the staff of the Bibliothèque nationale in Paris and the Thomas J. Watson Library at the Metropolitan Museum of Art. It has also been furthered by the fruitful exchange with many members of scholarly societies before whom I have presented my work, including the American Musicological Society, the Society for Seventeenth-Century Music, the North American Society for Seventeenth-Century French Literature, the British Society for Seventeenth-Century Studies, the Société d'Étude du XVIIe Siècle, the American Society for Eighteenth-Century Studies, the Society for Dance History Scholars, and the conferences "God, Men, and Monsters" at New College, Oxford, and "Le plaisir musical" at the University of Burgundy in Dijon. My ideas were also shaped in visits to the departments of music and musicology at Stanford University, Princeton University, the University of New Hampshire, the University of California at Los Angeles, and the University of California at Santa Barbara; the humanities centers at Stanford, the University of New Hampshire, and Case Western Reserve University (CWRU); the Program for Critical Studies and Experimental Practices at the University of California at San Diego; and the ongoing research project "Power *mise-en-scène,*" sponsored by the University of Oslo and the Norwegian Research Council. A critical but tolerant audience has included the students in a succession of graduate seminars at CWRU, and I wish to acknowledge both the students in those classes and those who have served as research assistants over the years. I am also appreciative of the stimulating exchanges with my colleagues on the faculty at CWRU and at the Met. Finally, I wish to acknowledge the *Journal of the American Musicological Society* and the *Art Bulletin,* for permission to rework articles published in 2001, and the Bevington Subvention Endowment of the University of Chicago Press.

This book is dedicated to the memory of my mother, Jewel, whose last years coincided with its completion and whose pleasure in the "smaller things" infused its spirit; and to my daughter Rachel, whose love and friendship have always provided deep support and continuing joy.

New York, 2008

‎❊‎

Introduction

The Allure of Spectacle and
the Prerogative of Pleasure

This book considers spectacle as a kaleidoscopic reflection of a complex and changing society, where images and ideologies met, commingled, and competed over the seventy-two years (1643-1715) of Louis XIV's reign as king of France. Its aims are threefold: to examine the overlapping, interdependent, and at times oppositional politics of power and pleasure as they were performed within this festive space; to observe the strategies of artists as they created and at times deliberately undermined a propaganda of kingship; and to reveal the forces that effectively transformed the celebration of the monarch into the utopian celebration of public entertainment as a new societal model. It is offered to the reader in the belief that the contested ground of spectacle, especially as it moved from the court to the Parisian public sphere in the late seventeenth and early eighteenth centuries, opens new dimensions for an understanding of fundamental shifts in ideology occurring in ancien-régime France, and the central role of the arts in reflecting and contributing to those changes.

In Louis XIV's time, the term *spectacle* referred to almost any genre of theater, or to public events with a strong visual element, such as public hangings. In relation to theater in the ancien régime, the English term "spectacle" generally refers more specifically to events produced on a grand scale, especially those containing the element of dance. These include not only the diverse manifestations of the ballet, but also opera, with its dance-based divertissements. They can also include the entertainments of the French *commedia dell'arte* and the *théâtre de la foire*, which—along with acrobatics, magic tricks, and transformation scenes—also include an important

component of music and dance. To understand the term as a simple designator, however, is to miss the charged meanings it has held throughout history. In the leisured society of the French court, being entertained was one
of the highest privileges, and the ability to produce entertainment one of the
highest signifiers of power. For the theater-going public as well, spectacle—
especially the ballet and opera, with their courtly associations—signaled a
mystique of allure, fashionability, and prestige.

At the same time, a virulent antitheatricalist discourse, emanating from
the Gallican church and especially the Jansenist stronghold of Port-Royal,
circulated widely in France during this period. Paralleling the Puritan opposition to the theater in England and sharing its aversion to pleasure (with
which theatrical entertainment was considered virtually synonymous), the
French antitheatrical movement was distinguished by a high level of eloquence and the enlistment of some of the finest writers in France, such as
Jacques-Bénigne Bossuet and Pierre Nicole. A strong discomfort with theater and theatrical pleasures also infiltrated to some degree the upper reaches
of the aristocracy, the class most identified with a hedonistic way of life, and
eventually reached to the queen, and even the king himself in his later years.
The theater also had its defenders, however, whose voices could be heard
not only in theoretical tracts such as Samuel Chappuzeau's *Le théâtre français*
(Paris, 1674), but also from the stage itself, where a number of playwrights
wove a defense of theater into the fabric of their plays.

Controversies over spectacle have not been limited to the early modern
period, but rather have characterized practically every period of vibrant
theatrical activity from the time of the ancient Greeks. In more recent times
the idea of spectacle has been attacked from the more radical end of the political spectrum. The effects of Guy Debord's *La société du spectacle* (1967),[1]
for example, a scathing critique of late twentieth-century capitalist culture,
were so strong as to have contributed to the Parisian student uprisings of
1968. Debord's metaphorical use of the term coincided with a longstanding
tendency, in the English-speaking world, to equate "spectacle" with superficiality and emptiness of meaning. More recently, the term has been somewhat recuperated by an interest, influenced by Roland Barthes and the new
historicists, in the ephemeral, the contingent, and the performative. As it
applies to the early modern period, to date such a critical interest has focused mostly on the English masque, but an emerging body of work has

---

1. Trans. Donald Nicholson-Smith as *The Society of the Spectacle* (Boston: Zone Books/
MIT Press, 1995).

also begun to consider, for example, the French court ballet, opera parody, and *parade*.

The book's methodology was developed gradually and pragmatically, in response to the difficulties posed by the illusory nature of spectacle and the various systems of propaganda for which it served as vehicle. Throughout the process I have been guided by the belief that the inclusive—not to mention theatrical—nature of spectacle demands treatment as a textured dialogue consisting of a heterogeneity of discourses, rather than as the reflection of a monochromatic, absolutist culture. This has forced me to consider a wider array of genres and individual works, across a greater variety of disciplines, than I had originally intended. At the same time it has allowed me both to discover and to analyze more fully the mechanisms of spectacle as they operate on two levels: 1) as a complex polyphony of ideological voices within single theatrical works, and 2) as an intertextual or dialogic system in which individual pieces and genres engaged with each other, over time, through a variety of means including allusion, parody, satire, and tribute.[2]

In this way, for example, the court ballet (discussed in chaps. 1 and 2) and the *tragédie en musique,* both of which have been cited as iconic representations of the king's power, can also be seen to reflect tensions between the king and his nobility, between factions of the nobility, and at times between the king and his own image-makers.[3] Likewise, *Le bourgeois gentilhomme,* to take only one of the *comédie-ballets* of Lully and Molière, can be interpreted not only as ridicule of a bourgeois and a Turkish ambassador, but also—as I suggest in chapter 3—as a parody of Louis XIV's *Ballet des Muses.* As such it functions as a trenchant commentary on an absolutist ideology of the arts, and—in the seldom-performed ballet that serves as its epilogue—as a glorification of the arts, artists, and audience of the public theater as a new societal utopia. In these genres, as in the later *opéra-ballet* and related theaters of the Parisian *commedia dell'arte* and the *foire,* there is evidence that a system of imagery centered on pleasure and its artistic expression at times resisted, challenged, and undermined an iconography of sovereign power. Absent from conventional historical narratives, this process has been largely

2. On the concept of the dialogic, see Mikhail Bakhtin, "Discourse and the Novel," in *The Dialogic Imagination: Four Essays by M. M. Bakhtin,* ed. Michael Holquist, trans. Michael Holquist and Caryl Emerson, 259–422 (Austin: University of Texas Press, 1981); and *Problems of Dostoevsky's Poetics,* ed. and trans. Caryl Emerson, Theory and History of Literature, 8 (Minneapolis: University of Minnesota Press, 1984).

3. These tensions were not new to the period of Louis XIV, nor to the genre of the ballet (see below, chapters 2 and 3).

overlooked because of the ephemeral nature and presumed superficiality of spectacle. Ironically, possibly because censors tended to overlook the frivolous, much of the ideological import of these works resides in their peripheral divertissements rather than in their more central plot structure.

While frivolity could be an end in itself, the locus of pleasure also motivated more serious philosophies and aesthetic systems. In the early seventeenth century, the ancient doctrine of Epicurus was revived by Pierre Gassendi and a loose circle known as the *libertins érudits*. Later in the century, the designation *libertin* was applied to a wide variety of individuals who combined in varying degrees a personal hedonism, the ideal of sexual freedom, and a dangerous brand of political free thought anticipating the Enlightenment. Many of the artists discussed in this book have some association with libertine behaviors and beliefs. Molière, who had connections to Gassendi's circle, incorporated strands of libertine thought into his comedies and the *comédie-ballets* he produced with Lully; as I have indicated above, through parody techniques the *comédie-ballet* could serve as a trenchant commentary on the ideology of the court ballet. In his last years, Lully collaborated with another libertine writer, Jean de Campistron, who like the composer frequented the libertine community of the Temple. Recent archival evidence attests to the degeneration of Lully's reputation with the king in these late years,[4] and in chapter 4 I attribute that degeneration not only to Lully's libertine conduct, but also to a subversive current in these late works. The theater in general and especially the Paris Opéra served as a refuge for libertinism, especially in the *opéra-ballets* of André Campra and his contemporaries (discussed in chaps. 5 and 6), at a time of severe moral conservatism in both the church and the monarchy. Antoine Watteau, who is believed to have worked at the Opéra as a stage painter around 1702, has been connected with a later group of freethinkers (*libertins d'esprit*).[5] As I show in chapter 7, his *Pilgrimage to Cythera*, based directly on the imagery and ideology of two ballets produced at the Opéra and related works at the *théâtre de la foire*, may be seen as the most complete expression of an operatic, proto-Enlightenment vision of an alternative, utopian society.

Throughout the reign of Louis XIV, the ideal of pleasure was also associated with a court aristocracy, for whom the delicate, erotically charged aesthetic of *galanterie* defined a noble identity and way of life. Especially as

---

4. Jérôme de La Gorce, *Jean-Baptiste Lully* (Paris: Fayard, 2002), 305–40.

5. François Moureau, "Watteau libertin?" in *Antoine Watteau (1684–1721): Le peintre, son temps et sa légende*, ed. François Moureau and Margaret Morgan Grasselli (Paris: Champion, 1987), 17-22.

a young man, Louis XIV shared with this noble elite a propensity for a bold hedonism clothed in a refined sensibility of manners and taste. The long tradition of the king's two bodies, developed in England and France, held that the king, like Jesus, inhabited not only the divine body of kingship, but also a physical body in his capacity as man, lover, courtier, etc.[6] Therefore, at least theoretically, Louis could partake (and, through his dancing roles, literally embody) the pleasures of his court. On the other side, the music and dance of spectacle were seen not only to reflect, but also to emanate from his royal divinity much as sacred music emanated from and announced the presence of God. Donald Chae speaks of the seventeenth-century understanding of royal music as a sonic presence that "swelled forth" around Louis XIV, effacing his personal, physical body while simultaneously reconstituting the eternal body of the office of kingship.[7]

This quasi-mystical view of music in the service of kingship was beginning to break down as older theories mingled with and eventually gave way to newer systems of representation. As they had evolved over time, notions of kingship grew from and depended on the identity of the king with the power of the state. In a complex interaction of aesthetics and politics, the artistic and the political enactment of this power became mutually reinforcing and highly interdependent. Court ritual both influenced and was influenced by official portraiture, which incorporated theatrical gestures, elaborate costuming, and sophisticated backdrops to stage the omnipotence of the king/state. But over the course of the seventeenth century, the identity of the king with the state—related to his identity with mythological gods, Roman emperors, and legendary heroes—began to be questioned. As Louis Marin has theorized, these modes of representation produced the composite "portrait of the king," a fictionalized ideal based on visual, aural, and narrative images and descriptions, holding great persuasive power but little substance. This composite ideal is easily taken for the king, yet behind the "portrait" may be found, instead of the presence of the king himself, only a gaping absence. Marin takes the example of Paul Pellison's proposal, successfully presented to Louis XIV's finance minister Jean-Baptiste Colbert in 1670, to write a history of Louis's reign. Pellison's description projected a historical narrative that would unfold not as an accurate rendering of

6. Ernst H. Kantorowicz, *The King's Two Bodies: A Study in Mediaeval Political Theology* (1957; Princeton: Princeton University Press, 1997).

7. Donald Chae, "Music, Festival, and Power in Louis XIV's France: Court Divertissements and the Musical Construction of Sovereign Authority and Noble Identity, 1661–1674" (Ph.D. dissertation, University of Chicago, 2003), 124–25.

events but in a dramatic, idealized manner as if for a theater audience. Its central motivation would be to memorialize present deeds for future memory. The overriding role of the historian, therefore, would be not to report facts but rather to position the king as actor in a performative reshaping of history. In this enterprise the writer himself would also play an important role in the staging of the king's power. It is not coincidental, then, that Pellison, as ghostwriter for Louis XIV's *Mémoires*, helped to shape what was known to posterity as the king's own "voice."[8]

Following Marin, a number of writers have explored the semiotic emptiness of Louis XIV's representation.[9] Nicholas Henshall's *The Myth of Absolutism*,[10] Jeroen Duindam's *Myths of Power*,[11] and works in a similar vein have dismissed the concept of absolute power. The king, as these authors argue, was in fact limited in a number of ways by his relationships with various institutions and factions, all requiring continual negotiation. Jean-Marie Apostolidès's *Le roi-machine* traces the disappearance of the actual person of Louis XIV into the theatrical "imaginary king" of the court spectacle. As Apostolidès hypothesizes, the eventual result of this process, in the 1680s and 1690s, was a "machine-king," identified only with the lifeless mechanisms of the state.[12] Peter Burke's *The Fabrication of Louis XIV* explores the artificial construction of the king's image, as well as the deconstruction of that image in the underground pamphlet literature arising in France over the course of the seventeenth century.[13] This body of revisionist work, while questioning the concept of absolutism (at least in its narrow sense) as a political reality, confirms its applicability to royal imagery

8. Louis Marin, *The Portrait of the King*, trans. Martha Houle (1981; Minneapolis: University of Minnesota Press, 1988), 39–50. An account of Pellison as historiographer may be found in Orest Ranum's *Artisans of Glory: Writers and Historical Thought in Seventeenth-Century France* (Chapel Hill: University of North Carolina Press, 1980), 233–77.

9. These theories derive to some extent from Michel Foucault's writings on representation, the most useful of which, in this context, is *Les mots et les choses: Une archéologie des sciences humaines* (Paris: Gallimard, 1966).

10. Nicholas Henshall, *The Myth of Absolutism: Change and Continuity in Early Modern European Monarchy* (London: Longman, 1992).

11. Jeroen Duindam, *Myths of Power: Norbert Elias and the Early Modern European Court*, trans. Lorri S. Granger and Gerard T. Moran (Amsterdam: Amsterdam University Press, 1994).

12. *Le roi-machine. Spectacle et politique au temps de Louis XIV* (Paris: Minuit, 1981).

13. New Haven: Yale University Press, 1992. See also Nicole Ferrier-Caverivière, *L'image de Louis XIV dans la littérature française de 1660 à 1715* (Paris: Presses universitaires de France, 1981).

constituting the king's representation; in fact, it was in that imagery that the concept came to exist.

Almost all the terminology we would use to describe the processes by which royal imagery was promulgated—propaganda, publicity, marketing, advertising, public relations, public opinion (indeed even the term "public" itself in the modern sense)—remains anachronistic to the early modern period. The term "propaganda" came about only in the late eighteenth century, in the context of the Revolution. Before that, there was no need to sway the minds of the populace; to rulers like Louis XIV, such a concept would have seemed a sign of weakness. As John B. Wolf has noted, early modern image-making, which sought to brand an iconography of power onto the living memory of the upper classes, foreign dignitaries, and—most important—posterity, had its motivation more in impression than persuasion. This process was understood as the fostering of reputation or, as it was most commonly expressed, the *gloire* of the monarch.[14]

If it is true, as Marin, Apostolidès, and others have argued, that the king's absolute power resided in its representation, then it follows that the control of that representation resided not only with Louis, but also with his artists, who, like the king's historiographer, created theatrical images on which the opinions of posterity depended. It also follows that at least some of Louis XIV's image-makers, charged with his "fabrication" and the mechanisms of his glory, would have had the opportunity to expose the rupture between the portrait they were charged with creating and the essential reality it was supposed to signify. One of the tasks of this book, then, is to explore the implications of artists' awareness as well as their control of the mechanisms of glory, including a potential for resistance that shaded at times into subversion. Another is to explore a deeper layer, seldom acknowledged, of artists' own self-representation, under a variety of tragic and comic masks, vis-à-vis the king. The most venerable of these artists' personae is the group of nine Muses, who appear a number of times, either together or as individuals, in the court ballet, *tragédie en musique,* and *opéra-ballet.* Others are based on artist figures of mythology and legend, including for example Orpheus and Sappho, as they stand in relationship either to absolutist tyrants or to future utopian rulers. Another category of artist representation includes the nameless, comic "masters," all related, that appear and reappear, offering a

---

14. John B. Wolf, *Louis XIV* (New York: Norton, 1968), 44; Peter Burke, *The Fabrication of Louis XIV* (New Haven: Yale University Press, 1992), 4–5; Ranum, *Artisans of Glory,* 252.

commentary on and defense of the theatrical arts as they pass from the court to the public sphere: Quinault's "director of the masquerade" and "writer of the comedy" in *Les poètes,* an inserted entertainment in the *Ballet des Muses;* the masters of many arts in *Le bourgeois gentilhomme,* and the music and dance masters in Campra's *Les fêtes vénitiennes.*

Finally, while the staging of Louis XIV's power has received extensive critical consideration, less attention has been devoted to the staging of pleasure in the form of a noble *galanterie,* nor has adequate attention been paid to the patronage and consumption of pleasure as a form of power in itself. In the 1660s and 1670s, Louis's prerogative of dispensing court entertainment had been equally if uneasily matched by the courtiers' prerogative of receiving them. In the late years of the seventeenth century, this balance was upset in two ways: by the weakening of the king's hold on the nobility and by the concomitant rise to prominence of elite public forms of entertainment. Significantly, the composer André Campra and the painter Antoine Watteau, unlike their predecessors Lully and Charles Lebrun, worked outside the king's patronage and could therefore shape their production more directly to the taste of their public audience. That taste was largely formed by a noble aesthetic of the chic and pleasurable as it had it had arisen at court and in mid-seventeenth-century Parisian salons. The *opéra-ballet* of Campra and the related genre of the *fête galante* of Watteau, both introduced around the turn of the eighteenth century, updated that older aesthetic for a new public.

In the late seventeenth century, an aesthetic of *galanterie* had been overshadowed—though never displaced—by the rhetoric of absolutism. In the early eighteenth century, it reasserted itself for a commercial marketplace in a profusion of cupids, lovers, flutes and musettes, carnival masks and *commedia dell'arte* costumes. This imagery, derived from the old court ballet and the pastoral divertissements of opera, can be more directly traced to two counterutopias of the opéra-ballet, the carnival of Venice and Venus's sacred island of Cythera, as extended metaphors for a new society shaped by the festive arts. In these works, depictions of the commercial stage and the *fête galante* serve as metonymic signifiers of a more egalitarian community chararacterized by public spectacles and intimate, private entertainments. As such they emphasize a flamboyant musical *italianisme* and a pastoral *galanterie,* respectively, in contradistinction to the adulatory choruses, militaristic fanfares, and massed orchestral forces characterizing the power of the king.

Until 1686, operas were generally premiered first at court, during carnival, and later in the spring at the Paris Opéra. This rhythm of operatic production was disrupted by Louis XIV's failure to mount Lully's *Armide* (1686) and *Acis et Galathée* (1687) at court, for reasons discussed in chapter 4. Between 1687 and the end of Louis's reign, the center of operatic production shifted from the court to the Opéra, while its audience, including a number of the court nobility for whom Versailles had lost its former appeal, became a de facto countercourt. During this period, as a contemporary observer noted, the road from Paris to Versailles was crowded in the early morning hours with the carriages of courtiers returning from an evening in town.[15] Well before the end of the reign, taste was no longer set by Versailles but by Paris, in a process that would be symbolically completed when the duc d'Orléans, who served as regent (1715–1723) for Louis XV, moved his residence to the Palais-Royal, also the home of the Paris Opéra. This taste is most clearly observed in the *opéra-ballet,* arguably the most representative genre of the upper-class public sphere, but it also influenced the post-Lullian *tragédie en musique,* in which a *galant* aesthetic began to overshadow the increasingly perfunctory trappings of monarchical praise. In effect, by the time of the late, eighteenth-century phase of Louis's long reign, the monarchy had lost the image war to a rising public sphere, influenced by a growing disenchantment with absolutist heroism and dominated by its own collective identity as heir to the prerogative of pleasure.

15. Jean-François Solnon, *La cour de France* (Paris: Fayard, 1987), 314.

CHAPTER ONE

✳

Muses of Pleasure

Louis XIV's Early Court Ballet, 1651–1660

In May 1651, in the midst of the devastating series of civil wars threatening the Regency of Anne of Austria and the young king Louis XIV, the French court gathered to witness an entertainment of unprecedented opulence entitled *Ballet des fêtes de Bacchus*. The prologue, set on a fantastical "Golden Isle," announced the banishment of the allegorical figures of Sobriety, Austerity, and Want. The entries that followed presented a series of noble dancers, dancing masters, and musicians, dressed in magnificent and fanciful costumes, celebrating the hedonism of a young and fashionable court. A climactic entry featured a triumphant Bacchus, garlanded with grapevines, astride a three-headed monster representing the cheerful, furious, and soporific qualities of wine. Further entries depicted Venus with her Graces and the allegorical figures of Mirth (*les Ris*) in her suite (fig. 1.1); Apollo and the Muses (plate 1); Pan with his fauns; and the god of sleep with his dreams (fig. 1.2), all paying obeisance to the god of hedonism. In alternating entries, the noble dancers masqueraded as lower-class members of a contented, picturesque realm, enjoying feasting, wine, and entertainments of all sorts. Many of the entries were comical, such as the one for the allegorical characters of Gaming, Gluttony, and Debauchery, dressed in costumes respectively covered with playing cards, serving plates, and wine goblets. (The first of these, Gaming or *le Jeu*, is shown in fig. 1.3.) In a spoof of chivalric themes, several dancers portraying knights of the Round Table enjoy a feast spread by the god Pan, while being entertained by magicians, cock-fights, and a dancing monkey (fig. 1.4). The young king, at thirteen years of age already a virtuoso dancer, portrayed the roles of a diviner, a bacchante,

Figure 1.1. *Ballet des fêtes de Bacchus*. Allegorical figure Mirth (*un Ris*).
Institut de France/Art Resource.

Figure 1.2. *Ballet des fêtes de Bacchus.* Morpheus.
Bibliothèque nationale de France.

Figure 1.3. *Ballet des fêtes de Bacchus*. Allegorical figure Gaming (*le Jeu*).
Bibliothèque nationale de France.

Figure 1.4. *Ballet des fêtes de Bacchus*. Knights of the Round Table being entertained.
Bibliothèque nationale de France

a Muse, an intoxicated pickpocket, an icicle in the temple of dreams, and a Titan. Equating the court and wider realm with the peace and plenty showcased in the ballet, its artists and image-makers offered reassurance to a kingdom in the midst of armed rebellion and to a court aristocracy in the midst of profound social, political, and cultural change.

At the court of Louis XIV, leisure and pleasure informed a way of life, including activities such as promenades, the hunt, boating, feasting, gambling, and the arts of dance and music making. In addition, a constant round of festive entertainments regularly punctuated the life of the court. These included theatrical productions by imported professional troupes, including the French company of the Hôtel de Bourgogne, the Italian players of the *commedia dell'arte*, and singers of Italian opera. The king's establishment included a large array of professional musicians who performed for the court on a regular basis. Of all these court productions, the most reflective of noble identity—and the most important for an understanding of court society—was the *ballet de cour* or court ballet. This genre drew together the king and the best noble dancers, who performed on temporary stages in the royal palaces of the Louvre, the Palais-Royal, and the Tuileries and in the outlying chateaux of Saint-Germain-en-Laye, Chambord, and Fontainebleau.[1] Based on loose-knit subject matter emphasizing image and spectacle over conventional plots, the ballet was enhanced by lavish stage sets created by the leading exponents of stage design. The combination of the courtiers' skills with the professional support of librettists, dancing masters, musicians, and stage designers set a standard that would pave the way for the founding of an academy of dance in 1661 and for the establishment of the public ballet on the stage of the Paris Opéra in the 1670s.[2]

The court ballet of Louis XIV, staged with regularity during the decades of the 1650s and 1660s, celebrated a vision of the court as a utopia of pleasure, and of the kingdom as a picturesque and contented realm. Beneath the surface of this embracing propaganda of social harmony, however, separate systems of image-making operated in an interdependent fashion. The two most obvious of these represented the respective interests of the king and the high nobility, known as *les grands seigneurs*. A third, less obvious, represented the interests of the artists charged with the creation of spectacle. The ballet of the 1650s, which this chapter takes as its subject, served preponderantly as an icon of an aristocratic class, with which Louis XIV as a young man was primarily identified, and with whose aesthetic of playful *galanterie* the artists of spectacle aligned themselves as well. With rare exceptions, this genre is largely untouched by the propaganda of sovereign power that would begin to appear more prominently in the following decade, as the king reached adulthood and took over the reins of government.

1. Barbara Coeyman, "Theaters for Opera and Ballet during the Reigns of Louis XIV and Louis XV," *Early Music* 18 (1990): 22–37. Venues for first performances are given in Herbert Schneider, *Chronologisch-thematisches Verzeichnis sämtlicher Werke von Jean-Baptiste Lully* (LWV) (Tutzing: Hans Schneider, 1981).

2. On entertainment at Louis XIV's court, see Robert Isherwood, *Music in the Service of the King: France in the Seventeenth Century* (Ithaca: Cornell University Press, 1973), 1–157; and Philippe Beaussant and Patricia Bouchnot-Déchin, *Les plaisirs de Versailles: Théâtre et musique* (Paris: Fayard, 1996). The only book-length study of the court ballet of Louis XIV remains Marie-Françoise Christout, *Le ballet de cour de Louis XIV, 1643–1672: Mises en scène* (Paris: Picard, 1967). The *livrets* may be found in *Benserade: Ballets pour Louis XIV*, ed. Marie-Claude Canova-Green, 2 vols. (Toulouse: Société de littératures classiques, 1997). Two shorter surveys of the ballet over the period of the seventeenth century are Georgie Durosoir, *Les ballets de la cour de France au XVIIe siècle, ou les fantaisies et les splendeurs du baroque* (Geneva: Papillon, 2004), and Philippe Hourcade, *Mascarades et ballets au grand siècle (1643–1715)* (Paris: Éditions Desjonquères/Centre national de la danse, 2002).

Mazarin, the Fronde, and the
Early Ballet of Louis XIV

The court ballet of the 1650s was played out against the backdrop and after-math of the Wars of the Fronde, a series of civil wars that seriously threat-ened the government of the Regency and the young king. Though proceed-ing in waves involving different layers of society from the princes of the blood down to the third estate, these wars may be generally attributed to a pervasive dissatisfaction with the Regency of Louis XIV's mother, Anne of Austria, and her Italian prime minister Jules Mazarin, who continued the consolidation of power begun by his predecessor, Cardinal Richelieu, under Louis XIII. During the years of the Fronde, a flood of anti-Mazarin pam-phlets containing libelous chansons, satires, and political tracts circulated anonymously throughout France. These *Mazarinades,* as they were called, revealed the power of a virulent and irrepressible underground press. Criti-cizing Mazarin for a range of evils including the aggrandizement of his per-sonal fortune at the expense of the lower classes, they implicitly targeted the monarchy as he had shaped it.[3]

One might have expected Mazarin to follow the lead of his predecessors, especially Cardinal Richelieu, who under Louis XIII had exploited the dra-matic court ballet as a means of defending and enhancing the power of the monarchy.[4] Perhaps because of a lack of sensitivity to this innately French genre, Mazarin does not seem to have attempted to control its content or to use it for overt political ends. Instead, he attempted in the 1640s and 1650s to import Italian opera into France. Opera had become a fashionable interna-tional ornament of other royal courts in this period, enhancing the prestige of the monarchy. With its highly political prologues, especially modified for French audiences, it might have done the same in France. Despite Mazarin's

3. On the Fronde, see Orest Ranum, *The Fronde: A French Revolution, 1648–1652* (New York: W. W. Norton, 1993). A more succinct overview may be found in Roger Mettam, *Power and Faction in Louis XIV's France* (Oxford: Basil Blackwell, 1988), 128–74. Lewis Seifert explores the boundaries among gender, sexuality, and politics in "Eroticizing the Fronde: Sexual Deviance and Political Disorder in the Mazarinades," *L'esprit créateur* 35, no. 2 (Summer 1995): 22–36. The term came from the French word for "slingshot," used by protestors to pelt Mazarin's windows with stones.

4. Margaret McGowan, *L'art du ballet de cour en France, 1581–1643,* 2nd ed. (1963; Paris: Éditions du Centre national de la recherche scientifique, 1978), 176–185; Henry Prunières, *Le ballet de cour en France avant Benserade et Lully* (Paris: Henri Laurens, 1914), 123–33.

forceful efforts, the French court never embraced the genre, although compromises were occasionally reached.[5]

Meanwhile the cardinal, intent on solidifying the authority of the crown, allowed the ballet to distract the courtiers and to divert their attention from his own political machinations. He also excluded the king from the avenues of power, leaving Louis to dance with the nobility while he himself attended to the task of ruling France. The early ballets of the 1650s, therefore, reflect the taste of the noble class to whom the creation, performance, and direction of the genre primarily belonged. They are imbued with elements especially identified with this aristocratic elite, and with a young king whose artistic personality had not yet diverged (at least to the public eye) from that of his fellow nobles. This noble taste, centered on pleasure, took expression in chivalric galanterie, comic entertainment, and aristocratic leisure devoted to song, dance, and masquerade.

The *ballet à entrées* differed from the earlier dramatic ballet, which had been organized around a continuous plot. While the heroic plots of Louis XIII's late ballets had served as an ideal vehicle for royal propaganda, the *ballet à entrées*, with its emphasis on episodic spectacle, provided the ideal vehicle for a noble identity. Instead of a plot, its structure involved a parade of personages and dances loosely organized around general themes, such as the seasons, the pleasures, or the arts. The genre took its name from the successive "entries" of groups of dancers. The term *entrée* referred literally to these dancers' entries with their music, and more generally to the group of dances and airs it introduced. The entries were grouped into larger structural sections known as *parties* (generally from one to four, depending on the length and complexity of the ballet), often introduced by a vocal air known as a *récit*. Although *récits* could also be interspersed among the entries, the inclusion of vocal music did not imply any kind of musical continuity or operatic stage action, as it had begun to do in Louis XIII's late ballets, but was merely a simple descriptive setting preparing the atmosphere of the entry.

Another advantage of the *ballet à entrées* was its conduciveness to a high degree of self-reflexivity. A large number of entries portrayed a court nobility—the courtiers performing either as themselves or as idealized noble characters from romance literature, legend, or mythology—all enjoying the privileges and pleasures associated with class distinction. The dramatic de-

---

5. In the *Nozze/Noces de Pélée et de Thétis*, ballet entries were integrated into the action of an Italian opera, and in *L'Amor malato/L'Amour malade*, the ballet followed an opening Italian *comédie en musique* as the "cure" for lovesick Cupid.

vice of entertainments-within-entertainments allowed the ballet to portray the nobility as participants in or as audience for plays, ballets, comedies, pastorals, and costume balls, all within the embracing structure of the court ballet.

The court ballet included a number of professional dancers (known as *maîtres de danse*) who danced alongside the nobility. Members of this profession were also expected to be adept as violinists, providing rehearsal music with their pocket-sized violins. Many were also accomplished composers, supplying much of the instrumental music for the ballet. Pierre Beauchamps (1636–1705), the principal choreographer, also contributed the music for some of the ballet entries.[6] In the 1670s he began to develop a system of dance notation which, published in 1700, would allow for the preservation of a number of dances from the later seventeenth and early eighteenth centuries.[7] Unfortunately, the loss of the choreography of the earlier court ballet makes it impossible to reconstruct the genre. The musical scores, which have only recently begun to appear in modern editions, often lead to as many questions as answers. Nonetheless, combined with the *livrets*, extant descriptions of spectators, plates and sketches of the costumes and stage designs contributed by the Italian machinists Giacomo Torelli, Gaspare Vigarani, and the latter's sons Carlo and Ludovico, and our knowledge of the choreography of a later period, these can help to piece together at least a general idea of its nature.[8]

6. Wendy Hilton, *Dance of Court and Theater: The French Noble Style, 1690–1725* (Princeton: Princeton Book Company, 1981), 24–25.

7. The historical record appears to justify Beauchamps's claim that his system was plagiarized by Raoul Auger Feuillet, after whom it is commonly named, in Feuillet's *Chorégraphie, ou l'art de décrire la danse* (1700). Details are given in Rebecca Harris-Warrick and Carol Marsh, *Musical Theatre at the Court of Louis XIV: The Example of "Le marriage de la grosse Cathos"* (Cambridge: Cambridge University Press, 1994), 83–87. The publication of Beauchamps's notation system allowed for the preservation of choreographies by Beauchamps's successor Louis Pécour; several of these returned to the music of Lully. See Anne L. Witherell, *Louis Pécour's 1700 "Recueil de dances"* (Ann Arbor, MI: UMI Research Press, 1983); Rebecca Harris-Warrick, "Contexts for Choreographies: Notated Dances Set to the Music of Jean-Baptiste Lully," *Jean-Baptiste Lully, Actes du colloque tenu à Saint-German-en-Laye et Heidelberg* (Laaber: Laaber Verlag, 1990), 433–55; and Wendy Hilton, "Dances to Music by Jean-Baptiste Lully," *Early Music* 14 (1986): 51–63. The most important eyewitness account is that of Jean Loret, in *La muze historique* (Paris: C. Chenault, 1650–1665; new ed. in 4 vols., Paris: P. Jannet, 1857–78). The music and *livrets* will be discussed below.

8. On the stage machinery of the ballet, see Per Bjurström, *Giacomo Torelli and Baroque Stage Design*, 2nd ed. (Stockholm: Almquist and Hiksell, 1962), and Jérôme de La Gorce, *Carlo Vigarani, intendant des plaisirs de Louis XIV* (Paris: Éditions Pierre and Château de Versailles, 2005).

The individual primarily responsible for the programmatic content of the court ballet was François de Beauvilliers, comte (later duc) de Saint-Aignan, who served for two decades as its director (*ordinateur*) as well as a principal dancer. Merely a rough outline, this program was fleshed out through the texts of the poet Isaac de Benserade,[9] the main creator of poetry for the vocal airs, *récits*, and choruses of the ballet. Benserade took a special interest in the *vers de personnage*, through which he cleverly linked the noble dancers' roles in the ballet with their personal lives and their roles as courtiers. These *vers* were not performed but rather included in the program to be enjoyed by a noble audience—particularly the women of the court, to whom many verses are addressed. Forging direct links between the dancers and court society, they offer a rare glimpse of the personalities behind the propaganda of the ballet.[10]

Through the unified galanterie of Benserade's *récits* and *vers de personnage*, he was able to mitigate the negative effects of the ballet's loose structure and unwieldy generic inclusiveness. Since the ballet was generally performed by male dancers, Benserade's poetry framed the work as an offering on the part of the noble dancers to the women of the court. This frame allowed him, through the *vers*, to mediate between the roles of the dancers on stage and their roles in the witty gossip of court society. Adding to the structure of the ballet complex layers of masking, Benserade was thus able to construct subtle innuendoes and allusions to the private lives of the courtiers, with ingenious blending of their roles and real-life personalities.

Each year at the court of Louis XIV a new court ballet was performed during the season of carnival (between Epiphany and Ash Wednesday, climaxing in Mardi Gras). The nature of carnival masking allowed courtiers to traverse a wide variety of noble and nonnoble characters, the former characterized by artful elegance, the latter by burlesque distortion. Through contrast with a diverse array of outsiders—gypsies, shopkeepers, Turks, bourgeois, thieves, and so on—the noble dancers and their audience could more fully appreciate their own distinction. Noblemen, including the king, danced these burlesque roles, many characterized by cross-casting and

9. Charles Silin's *Benserade and His Ballets de Cour* (Baltimore: Johns Hopkins University Press, 1940; New York: AMS Press, 1978) is still the standard source for Benserade; Canova-Green *(Benserade: Ballets pour Louis XIV)* also includes a wealth of material in her critical apparatus.

10. Until Canova-Green's recent publication of Benserade's *livrets*, the *vers* have been generally unavailable and therefore overlooked as a major source for understanding the intersection of the arts and court culture.

class reversal.[11] Nonetheless, while the conventions of the ballet allowed courtiers to dance all types of roles, they restricted the actual portrayal of nobility to an elegant galanterie with which they had become identified. Unlike the king, nobles were seldom portrayed as leaders or warriors; unlike the lower classes, they were never characterized by toil, industry, or commerce. The juxtaposition of noble and burlesque parallels the juxtaposition of masque and antimasque at the English court, but rather than separating the two genres, the court ballet presents entries of each type in various forms of alternation. The finale or *grand ballet* was important in this process, as it generally resolved (like the English revels) previous identity reversals in the presentation of the courtiers, half masked, as noble dancers of the court. There is also some overlap of the court ballet and the masked balls given during carnival.[12] In addition, there are a number of less formal ballets that were danced during carnival, particularly from the 1650s, including such impromptus as the *Ballet des proverbes* (1654). This work, apparently hastily produced and resembling a game of charades, belongs to a genre known as the *mascarade*.[13]

The masks and games of carnival reinforced the courtiers' fascination with indirect signs and secret allusions. As in carnival, the artists of the ballet came to use the medium of masks as a way of weaving a counterpoint between what was presented and what was hinted at beneath the surface. In many ways the ballet, like carnival, was a metaphor for the court, where things were always different from the way they appeared, everyone wore a mask, and hedonism was a way of life. The masks of the ballet, like those of carnival, allowed the court, like any gossip circle, to close its ranks

11. Women's roles were most often danced by cross-cast male courtiers. On some occasions they were danced by women of the court, especially roles of a more dignified nature—as in the prologue to *Les noces de Pélée et de Thétis*. There is, interestingly, also a series of roles for young girls, daughters of the dancing masters, who danced especially in the 1650s. On cross-casting, cross-dressing, and gender in the court ballet, see Julia Prest, *Theatre under Louis XIV: Cross-Casting and the Performance of Gender in Drama, Ballet, and Opera* (New York: Palgrave Macmillan, 2006), 77–127.

12. Masking at the court of Louis XIV is a topic still lacking study. Terry Castle's *Masquerade and Civilization: The Carnivalesque in Eighteenth-Century English Culture and Fiction* (Stanford: Stanford University Press, 1986) and Matthew Head's *Orientalism, Masquerade, and Mozart's Turkish Music* (London: Royal Music Association, 2000) treat the topic in a later period. For the English masque, see Stephen Orgel, *The Johnsonian Masque* (Cambridge: Harvard University Press, 1965), and *The Illusion of Power: Political Theater in the English Renaissance* (Berkeley: University of California Press, 1975).

13. On the mascarade, see Hourcade, *Mascarades et ballets au Grand Siècle*, 87–113.

and mock its others. This phenomenon helps to explain why, when faced with the prospect of Italian opera, the courtiers clung to the ballet, and why Mazarin, who was not involved with its production, did not embrace it. In the closed social world of the ballet, with its ridicule of Italians and other foreigners, he remained an outsider.

The Court Ballet as Icon of Noble Pleasure

Through the seventeenth century and especially after the Fronde, as the power of *les grands seigneurs* diminished, the pursuit of pleasure, always a component of French court life, became its defining characteristic. The nobility was no longer as strongly identified with a life at arms as in sixteenth- and early seventeenth-century France,[14] or with the defense and management of feudal estates. In order to obtain advancement, *les grands* were increasingly obliged to live at court for at least a portion of the year, where they were gradually transformed from a powerful group of independent vassals to a more docile breed of courtiers. Norbert Elias, one of the first to trace this development, painted the nobility as the victims of a new, money-based economy and a devalued currency, their inheritances further decimated by the lavish consumption that was the price of their status.[15]

There is some disagreement as to the extent to which the nobility were deprived of their former economic and military strength. Elias's work has been revised and updated by recent scholars, who make a clearer distinction between the small percentage of *les grands,* for whom court life was imperative for social and political advancement, and the lesser nobility who continued to live on their provincial estates, wielding considerable local power. These writers show how, among the aristocrats who did reside at court, not all were impoverished by any means. Nor did the loss of a class identity defined by military service mean the end of fighting; it was the general custom for noblemen to serve, or risk the displeasure of the king. Many of the nobility continued to distinguish themselves on the field of battle, but as firearms—associated with the lower classes—lessened the need for knights

14. Kate Van Orden, *Music, Discipline, and Arms in Early Modern France* (Chicago: University of Chicago Press, 2005).

15. Norbert Elias, *The Court Society,* trans. by E. Jephcott (Oxford: Basil Blackwell, 1983). See also Ellery Schalk, *From Valor to Pedigree: Ideas of Nobility in France in the Sixteenth and Seventeenth Century* (Princeton: Princeton University Press, 1986). Schalk tracks the increasing emphasis on pedigree rather than on action as the basis for a changing noble identity.

in armor, and as the army filled with mercenaries, an increasing number of nobles were able to avoid going to war.[16]

With the loss of their identity as rulers in their own right, the deracinated court nobility turned increasingly to a model of refinement and studied ease deriving from the Italian court tradition of Castiglione's *Il Cortegiano* (The Book of the Courtier) and the feudal ideal of *courteoisie*. They also turned to an aestheticized ideal of pastoral escapism found in the fashionable genres of the chivalric and pastoral novel, the first expressing their nostalgia for the glorious deeds of a dying feudal knighthood, the second, for the rural life they had sacrificed to the gilded cage of a courtly existence. The unprecedented vogue of Honoré d'Urfé's pastoral novel *L'Astrée*, published between 1607 and 1633 but still widely read and imitated throughout the century, has been seen as a clear reflection of the impasse felt by the noble class. Finding it increasingly difficult to oppose the centralization of state power by valorous deeds, they turned to daydreams and bucolic idylls, characterized by the aim of living "more gently and without constraints."[17] The peace and freedom inherent in this way of life provide the context for an idealized love, on which the lengthy plots and story lines of the novel revolve.

The life of Louis XIV's courtiers, modeled to an extent on *L'Astrée* and the pastoral novel, also revolved around the games of love and pleasure. Eschewing the more serious and high-flown sentiments of the old courtly conventions, however, the new fashion took the form of more flirtatious and lighthearted games of love and elaborate self-display. The shift from a valor-centered to a pleasure-centered society, attributable in part to the growth of fashionable salons in the early seventeenth century, gave a larger measure of influence to women and to the fashion of galanterie that gradually supplanted earlier ideals of masculine valor. In its broadest sense, galanterie had to do with love, more in the sense of flirtation or love affair (for which it sometimes served as euphemism) than of marriage. The term itself underwent a

16. On the changing status of the nobility, see Mettam, *Power and Faction;* Donna Bohanan, *Crown and Nobility in Early Modern France* (Houndmills, Basingstoke, Hampshire: Palgrave, 2001); Jonathan Dewald, *The European Nobility, 1400–1800* (Cambridge: Cambridge University Press, 1996); William Beik, *Absolutism and Society in Seventeenth-Century France: State Power and Provincial Aristocracy in Languedoc* (Cambridge: Cambridge University Press, 1985); J. Russell Major, *From Renaissance Monarchy to Absolute Monarchy: French Kings, Nobles, and Estates* (Baltimore: Johns Hopkins University Press, 1994); and Jay M. Smith, *The Culture of Merit: Nobility, Royal Service, and the Making of Absolute Monarchy, 1600–1789* (Ann Arbor: University of Michigan Press, 1996).

17. "Vivre plus doucement et sans contrainte," quoted by Elias, *Court Society*, 261; on *L'Astrée*, see also 246–66.

change over the course of the seventeenth century; in the earlier part of the century it was associated more with valor, gradually taking over associations with love and pleasure around mid-century. It reflected a new adulation of youth as well as a more liberated position for women in society, and it was particularly associated with occasions of ritualized interaction between the sexes, such as balls, picnics, promenades, and the informal social gatherings known as *fêtes galantes*. Its skills comprised elegant comportment, lavish attire, witty conversation, and refined taste, which inclined to the lighter literary genres, such as *lettres galantes, vers galants, jeux,* and *emblèmes*. In all things, a sophisticated dilettantism was prized over intense specialization, but this did not preclude the cultivation of an aesthetic sensibility that began to take the place of military prowess as a class designator. The quality of galanterie served the critical purpose of distinguishing the court nobility from the lesser nobility and above all from the scorned bourgeoisie and professional classes. From the seventeenth century down to the present, aspects of a *galant* way of life have contributed to French taste in culture and the arts, as well as to the French affinity for the chic and stylish.[18]

The fashioning of a noble galanterie in the ballet owes much to the poetic texts of Benserade. Known as the "father of galanterie," he linked its cult at court with a parallel cult in the Parisian salons at mid-century, which he frequented and whose tone he helped to shape. These salons, run by society women known as *précieuses,* fostered an artistic refinement and advancement of feminine tastes that had a profound impact on the court as well as on an emerging reading public.[19] Their ideals were exemplified in the love poetry of Benserade, Vincent Voiture, Jean-François Sarasin, and Jean Renaud de Segrais, and in the chivalric novels of Madeleine de Scudéry and her contemporaries. In some ways, the salon movement reflected the tastes of a new social

18. For a history of the concept of *galanterie,* see Jean-Michel Pelous, *Amour précieux, amour galant* (Paris: Klinksieck, 1980). For a description of music and fashion in the early twentieth century, see Mary E. Davis, *Classical Chic: Music, Fashion, and Modernism* (Berkeley: University of California Press, 2006); and Joan DeJean, *The Essence of Style: How the French Invented High Fashion, Fine Food, Chic Cafés, Style, Sophistication, and Glamour* (New York: Free Press, 2005). The English term "gallantry" does not completely cover the range of meaning associated with the French *galanterie,* for which "politeness" in its eighteenth-century sense or the current term "chic" come closest to capturing the essence.

19. On the salons, see Carolyn Lougee, *Le Paradis des Femmes: Women, Salons, and Social Stratification in Seventeenth-Century France* (Princeton: Princeton University Press, 1976); and Dena Goodman, "Public Sphere and Private Life: Toward a Synthesis of Current Historiographical Approaches to the Old Regime," *History and Theory* 31 (1992): 1–20.

class emerging in the seventeenth century, a "leisured bourgeoisie," empowered through its economic status to imitate the customs and tastes of the nobility. Scudéry's dual status as a member of the minor nobility and a leading light of salon society enabled her to translate the noble aesthetic of galanterie into a commercial form addressing a wider audience. Like Benserade, she moved easily between court and salon, broadcasting to a newly wealthy bourgeoisie the ideals of leisure and pleasure as the appurtenances of a galant style that in itself delineated a new conception of nobility. Simultaneously, her novels inspired the court with renewed pride and enthusiasm for the noble life.[20]

The cult of galanterie was associated, in the literary genres, with the goddess Venus and her son Cupid (in his adult form, known as L'Amour). Venus and Cupid are only two of the many gods, goddesses, and mythological creatures of various sorts that appear in the court ballets, but their appearances—though occasionally contributing to burlesque scenes—are more often treated with a special sensibility. Far from merely an artificial ornament to the ballet, riding above the stage action in her cloud machine (though that too), the figure of Venus held a deep significance for its aristocratic audience. The court ballet had always used classical mythology in a symbolic manner, but before Benserade Athena, the goddess of war and wisdom, also a symbol of France, had received more prominent treatment. In elevating the god and goddess of love, Benserade reached back to the Neoplatonic ideal of universal harmony that had inspired the festivals of the Italian Renaissance. Drawing on Marsilio Ficino's concept of love as the highest goal of artistic achievement, with Venus and Cupid its expression, artists had incorporated these two mythological figures as the tangible symbols of a harmonious, idyllic society. Many festivals, especially those created in celebration of dynastic marriages, held up marriage itself as a further symbol of this idealized society, with reference to Cythera, Venus's island, and her Temple of Love as its sacred sites.[21] From its origins in 1581, the French court ballet had incorporated this Neoplatonic philosophy of universal love, but

20. On Scudéry, see Marlies Mueller, *Les idées politiques dans le roman héroïque de 1630–1670*, Harvard Studies in Romance Languages, 40 (Cambridge: Department of Romance Languages and Literatures of Harvard University, 1984), 65–115; and Joan DeJean, *Tender Geographies: Women and the Origins of the Novel in France* (New York: Columbia University Press, 1991), 78–93. On the function of taste as a bond between nobility and bourgeoisie, see Dewald, *European Nobility*, 51–59.

21. Roy Strong, *Splendor at Court: Renaissance Spectacle and the Theater of Power* (Boston: Houghton Mifflin, 1973), 53. For example, an entertainment entitled *Il tempio d'Amore*, created

in the late 1630s and early 1640s its ideal was overshadowed by the cult of sovereign power engineered by Richelieu. At the same time, an early modern spirit of scientific inquiry began to dismantle the Renaissance adherence to Neoplatonic mysticism.[22] Benserade's *livrets* for Louis XIV's court ballets of the 1650s and 1660s may be seen as prolonging the life of this older philosophy while merging it with the pastoral idealism of *L'Astrée* and the new, more ironic galanterie coming into vogue at mid-century.

The Music of Louis XIV's Court Ballet and the *Air sérieux* before Lully

In the court ballet of the early 1650s, the portions devoted to instrumental music were composed by dancing masters, including Louis de Mollier, M. Verpré, and the violinist Michel Mazuel.[23] Its vocal music, mainly consisting of airs, was provided by the most prominent court composers at mid-century: Jean de Cambefort, Jean-Baptiste Boësset, and Michel Lambert.[24] Boësset and Lambert were associated with the Parisian salons as well as the court, and around mid-century what had been known as the *air de cour* began to be called simply *air* or *air sérieux*. The *récit,* as the air was called in the ballet, aptly expressed the noble aesthetic embraced at court and in the

---

in 1565 to celebrate the marriage of Duke Alfonso of Este to Barbara of Austria, depicted chivalrous knights overcoming evil sorceresses in order to enter the Temple of Love by the paths of Honor and Virtue. Probably devised by Torquato Tasso, its libretto, like his pastoral epic *Gerusalemme liberata,* reflects his success in fusing the themes of classical antiquity and medieval romance within a Neoplatonic tradition.

22. For an interpretation of this paradigm shift and its impact on early opera, see Gary Tomlinson, *Metaphysical Song: An Essay on Opera* (Princeton: Princeton University Press, 1999), 9–71. Chae gives a succinct but useful summary, in the context of French court entertainment, in "Music, Festival, and Power," 294–335.

23. Manuscript scores of the court ballets, copied by Philidor, may be found on the Gallica website of the Bibliothèque nationale de France as PDF files, at http://gallica.bnf.fr. See Jérôme de La Gorce, *Jean-Baptiste Lully* (Paris: Fayard, 2002), 375–80, for a discussion of the problems of attribution in Louis XIV's early court ballet, and 57–102 for a discussion of Lully's first years at court. See David Buch, *Dance Music from the Ballets de Cour, 1575–1651* (Stuyvesant, NY: Pendragon Press, 1993), for an overview and transcriptions of the instrumental music from the earlier court ballet, from Philidor manuscripts containing five-voice scoring for violins.

24. On the *air* before Lully, see Georgie Durosoir, *L'air de cour en France, 1571–1655* (Liège: Pierre Mardaga, 1991); and on Lambert, Catherine Massip, *L'art de bien chanter: Michel Lambert (1610–1696)* (Paris: Société française de musicologie, 1999).

salon. Characterized by flexible rhythms and elegant ornamentation, the air also contributed to a repertoire of chamber music conveying a certain timeless pleasure in the eternal moment of love. According to Pierre Perrin, "The Air proceeds in a free though serious measure and movement and thus is more proper for the expression of honest love and the tender emotions of pain or of joy that it wakens in the heart."[25] This aesthetic suited the court and the salon, which privileged sensuality and pleasure, along with an indirect discursive mode suitable to leisure and the idle passing of time.[26]

Lambert, a well-known composer, lutenist, and dancer, brought the *air sérieux* to its apogee as the emblem of a particularly French art and way of life connected with a noble elite and its bourgeois imitators. His songs in this genre embodied the delicate emotional nuance and compositional elegance found in the *précieux* poetry of Sarasin, Voiture, Segrais, and Benserade, all of whose poems he set. Like those of his contemporaries, Lambert's airs and *récits* exhibit an elegant sensitivity to the union of text and music and an artful simplicity characterized by a supple melodic line, delicately affective harmonies, and discreet ornamentation. The embellishment of the melodic line is shown to particular advantage in the *double,* or ornamented repetition used for the second and succeeding verses. Although ornamented *doubles* were a common feature of performance in this period, Lambert actually incorporated these as a compositional feature. His published and manuscript collections transmit examples affording a glimpse of seventeenth-century performance practice as well as the combination of sophistication and sentiment characterizing both the genre and Lambert's own compositional style.

Lambert was also associated with a technique of singing developed by Pierre Niert, a French nobleman at the court of Louis XIII, who was also a singer and teacher. Niert's method, combining the expressivity of Italian performance with the elegance of the French, also brought the improvised *doubles* of the air into line with the subtleties of the text. Hilaire Dupuis, another student of Niert who became Lambert's sister-in-law and, after the death of his wife, his lifelong companion, was perhaps the most famous exponent of the delicate and sensitive technique taught by Niert and Lambert. Lambert and Dupuis were celebrated at court and in the salons of the *précieuses.* In fact, chamber music became a defining feature of salon enter-

25. Pierre Perrin, *Recueil de paroles de musique*, Bibliothèque nationale MS fr. 2298, 7; quoted by Anthony, *French Baroque Music*, 415.

26. This "timeless" quality has been identified by Susan McClary, "Temporality and Ideology: Qualities of Motion in Seventeenth-Century French Music," *ECHO: A Music-Centered Journal* 2 (Fall 2000): 8–14, available at http://www.humnet.ucla.edu/echo.

tainment, especially as amateur music making began to be facilitated by the dissemination of published anthologies and manuscript collections.[27] The journals of Scudéry, Montpensier, Mme de Sévigné, and others all attest to a rich Parisian concert life, which is confirmed by frequent references in Jean Loret's *Muze historique* and later in the *Mercure galante*. Wealthy bourgeois also held concerts in which they themselves performed and professional musicians performed as their guests. Concerts were also given on a regular basis in the homes of musicians, such as the bass viol player Jean de Sainte-Colombe and the lutenist Jacques Gallot, as well as Lambert and Dupuis. Christian Huygens, traveling in France, described the concerts of "Monsieur Lambert and Mademoiselle Hilaire, his sister-in-law, who sings like an angel."[28] In Scudéry's *Mathilde,* her mention of "the admirable Lambert and the charming Hilaire"[29] links the novel to Parisian musical circles; Lambert also set two of Scudéry's poems to music.[30]

Lully and the Court Ballet[31]

It is a testament to the versatility of the artists of the ballet that the most well known composer of Louis XIV's time, Jean-Baptiste Lully, should have first distinguished himself as a dancer.[32] In 1646 the chevalier de Guise, Roger de Lorraine, younger brother of the duc de Guise, had brought Lully from Italy, to tutor his niece Marie-Louise de Bourbon, the duchesse de Montpensier (La

---

27. A large number of lute publications began to be supplanted by harpsichord collections in the later part of the century. *Airs de cour* were also published in vast quantities from the beginning of the seventeenth century; in the second half of the century, Christophe Ballard issued an important series of published airs.

28. Anthony, *French Baroque Music,* 346–47.

29. Massip, *L'art de bien chanter,* 111: "l'admirable Lambert et la charmante Hilaire."

30. Ibid., 332.

31. Scores of four of Lully's early court ballets (*Ballet du temps, Ballet des plaisirs, Ballet de l'Amour malade,* and *Ballet d'Alcidiane*), as well as ballets composed for the Italian opera *Xerxes,* may be found in Henry Prunières, *Oeuvres complètes de J.-B. Lully (Les Ballets,* vols. 1–2).

32. Lully's early ballets are discussed in La Gorce, *Jean-Baptiste Lully,* 381–413; Philippe Beaussant, *Lully ou le musicien du soleil* (Paris: Gallimard, 1992), 77–440; and Manuel Couvreur, *Jean-Baptiste Lully: Musique et dramaturgie au service du prince* (Paris: Marc Vokar, 1992), 65–139. On the problematic sources for Lully's ballets, see Rebecca Harris-Warrick, "Editing Lully's Ballets: Problems and Responses," *L'oeuvre de Lully: Études des sources: Hommage à Lionel Sawkins,* ed. Jérôme de La Gorce and Herbert Schneider (Hildesheim: Georg Olms, 1999), 23–47.

Grande Mademoiselle), in the Italian language. A connoisseur of music, the chevalier must have also been aware of Lully's impressive talents as a dancer and musician. Although there is no record of Lully's role in Montpensier's musical establishment, the young Italian would have received an education in music and dance simply through his presence there. As first princess of the blood, La Grande Mademoiselle lived in the palace of the Tuileries with an impressive musical establishment of her own, devoted to lavish entertainments on a scale rivaling those of her cousin, the young king. An extraordinary personality, she was one of the so-called "Amazons," high-born women who served as military leaders of the Fronde. With the eventual victory of the king's forces, La Grande Mademoiselle was exiled to her country estate of Saint-Fargeau in Burgundy. Lully accompanied her into exile but was soon called into the service of the king.[33] In 1653, Lully made his court début, dancing several burlesque roles in the *Ballet de la nuit*. (See plate 2 for the costume of Lully as a beggar.) The ballet, an allegorical celebration of the end of the Fronde, also featured the fifteen-year-old king in his well-known role as the Rising Sun, putting an end to the dark forces of civil unrest (plate 3).[34]

Less than a month later, Lully was appointed *compositeur de la musique instrumentale du roi*. Some time after this, he took over direction of the *petits violons*, an instrumental group in the personal service of the king. This group, which performed in the court ballet *La galanterie du temps* (1656), replaced the disorderly ensemble playing and extemporized passagework of the traditional *vingt-quatre violons du roi* with a legendary precision. By 1657 Lully had become the principal composer of both vocal and instrumental music for the court ballet, as well as a principal dancer. As with his instrumental music, his vocal music retained a melodic elegance while moving away from an earlier tendency to florid ornamentation in French music, as seen in Lambert. There was, however, undoubtedly a continual mutual influence between these two musicians, whose acquaintance in the 1650s was to deepen into a close personal and professional relationship over the span of more than three decades; in 1662, with his marriage to Lambert's daughter Madeleine, Lully became Lambert's son-in-law. Lully's vocalists comprised the king's French singers, including Anne de La Barre and Hilaire Dupuis, and a group of Italian singers, including the soprano Anna Bergerotti. These vo-

33. On La Grande Mademoiselle, see Vincent Pitts, *La Grande Mademoiselle at the Court of France, 1627–1693* (Baltimore: Johns Hopkins University Press, 2000), and Joan DeJean, ed., *Against Marriage: The Correspondence of La Grande Mademoiselle Anne-Marie-Louis d'Orléans* (Chicago: University of Chicago Press, 2002).

34. Canova-Green, *Benserade: Ballets pour Louis XIV*, 1: 158.

calists, like the instrumentalists, were drawn from the professional class and drew wages as part of the official royal establishment. The French singers were among those who performed the *récits* of the ballet. Anna Bergerotti would have been imported for Italian airs; and although castrato singing was anathema to the court ballet, the famous Atto Melani once performed the nonsinging role of Cupid in *L'Amour malade* (*L'Amor malato*).

One of Lully's greatest contributions, and a possible explanation for the strong political impact of his compositional output, was his assimilation of various amorphous elements of preexisting repertoires into a distinctive French style. This involved the combination of several elements, including the use of characteristic meters and rhythms of an emerging late seventeenth-century dance repertoire, and the asymmetrical melodic patterns, subtle harmonies, and language-based rhythms of the air. Lully's varied handling of the dotted rhythms of the *entrée* brought to the ballet an atmosphere of importance and sophistication. In the late 1650s, his juxtaposition of this duple-meter dotted style with the lively, triple-meter fugato of the Italians produced the French overture, which along with the French court dances quickly spread to all of Europe. In all his music, his genius was to draw generously on an Italian musical language, while assimilating, framing, and containing it in such a way that the impression of the whole was uniquely French.[35]

Lully's physical knowledge of the dance undoubtedly contributed to the refinement and subtlety he brought to his composition for the ballet and to its subsequent international success. He composed most of his entries in a free manner; in others he incorporated or made reference to contemporary ballroom dances.[36] The manner in which dance types intersected with characteristic roles of the ballet has received almost no scholarly treatment, though the work by Rose Pruiksma on the sarabande and chaconne reveals the possibilities inherent in such study.[37] A preliminary survey of these and several other types, as the court ballet developed over the decades of the 1650s and 1660s, indicates that certain dances, or references to dance types

35. Rose A. Pruiksma, "'Dansé par le roi': Constructions of French Identity in the Court Ballets of Louis XIV" (Ph.D. diss., University of Michigan, 1999), 134–51, discusses the ballet portions of *L'Amour malade* in terms of their containment of the Italian style.

36. On the ball at Louis XIV's court, see Rebecca Harris-Warrick, "Ballroom Dancing at the Court of Louis XIV," *Early Music* 15 (1986): 41–49.

37. Pruiksma, "'Dansé par le roi,'" 180–275. For a general survey of the dances used by Lully, see Meredith Ellis, "Inventory of the Dances of Jean-Baptiste Lully," *Recherches sur la musique française classique* 9 (1969): 21–55.

through characteristic rhythms and meters, were tied to fairly stereotypical roles. Entrances of the dancers were frequently accompanied by music of a stately dotted rhythm conveying dignity and nobility, though this pompous tone could also lend a note of irony to the entrances of burlesque characters. The gavotte was often used for dances of a comic or lighthearted nature. Along with the bourrée, the couple dance par excellence, it was often used to depict the pure dance of ballroom scenes. The quick-paced gigue and canaries tended to depict burlesque characters such as gypsies or the comic masks of the commedia dell'arte. The triple meter with dotted second beat, associated with one of the sarabande types, typically accompanied roles characterized by some form of sensuality, whether the noble galanterie of the young king, the mythic voluptuousness of Venus, or the exotic eroticism associated in this period with Moorish men or Spanish women. The chaconne, based on the instrumental motif of a descending bass line, did not have its origins in the ballroom dances, but like the sarabande, it carried connotations of a mixed sensuality and dignity combined with possibilities for large-scale musical development.

The court ballets of the 1650s contain a high proportion of burlesque (*crotesque*) entries, departing from the standard dance forms and styles. A large number of these early ballets, in fact, may be considered comic works altogether, namely, the *Ballet de Cassandre* (1651), the *Ballet des proverbes* (1654), the *Ballet de la revente des habits* (1655), *L'Amour malade* (1657), the *Ballet de la raillerie* (1659), the *Ballet de l'impatience* (1659), and *Les noces de village* (1663). The last four of these lead directly into the *comédie-ballets* of Lully and Molière. Although a burlesque musical style has yet to be adequately defined, it seems to be characterized primarily by discontinuity in melody, rhythm, and meter and by the use of dissonance, as well as occasional extremes of tempo or affection. Although the comic effect is largely lost without a knowledge of the choreography, it probably also rests on the principle of musical distortion supporting a similar distortion of movement and pantomimic gesture. The burlesque style could also use unusual instruments. In the *Ballet des fêtes de Bacchus*, as an introduction to the entry for Gaming, Gluttony, and Debauchery, three musicians (one of whom was Michel Lambert) performed a *musique crotesque*. Wearing animal headdresses (perhaps corresponding to the three-headed monster representing the three qualities of wine), they performed on instruments resembling marine trumpets. In figure 1.5, the musician is costumed with a boar's head, while the instrument is capped by a doll figure wearing a cape similar to the musician's, leaving the impression that the animal is using the musician himself as an instrument.

Figure 1.5. *Ballet des fêtes de Bacchus*. Musician performing a *musique crotesque*.
Bibliothèque nationale de France.

The *Ballet de l'impatience* and *Les noces de village* also contain isolated scenes of a more extreme comic effect, developed by Lully in the late 1650s, consisting of a broad and humorous Italian style, characterized by pronounced metrical accents, hemiola, fast repeated notes, wide leaps, and simple but sometimes unexpected harmonies. Some of these may be observed in a chorus of snuff takers from the *Ballet de l'impatience* (ex. 1.1). This style reflects the influence of the Italian frottola, along with the comic scenes of contemporary Italian operas by Luigi Rossi and Francesco Cavalli. The ways in which it is deployed, juxtaposed, and contained point toward significant elements of national and class identity in the ballet. It is almost always directed toward nonnoble characters of various guises. Its somewhat manic, extravagant language is used for purposes of more extreme satire or ridicule than is found in the French burlesque. Often targeting foreigners, the lower classes, or persons in the professions such as doctors and pedants, this style particularly delighted a noble elite who held these individuals in the highest contempt. In this example (LWV 14/23), a two-part chorus of snuff takers "impatient for their tobacco," a perpetual eighth-note rhythm moves along in a swinging 6/4 meter, with a shift into hemiola in measure 5. Typical of Lully's appropriation of an Italian burlesque style are the chromatic movement of the bass in measures 2–3, the quick repeated notes and the wordplay involving the repeated word "tobacco," with its rhyming word play "Bacco ch'un sacco ne stacco, ne spacco, m'ammacco, tabacco," etc. These elements provide a strong precedent for Lully's later collaborations with Molière.

These Italian scenes also reveal the influence of the commedia dell'arte, whose players, occasional guests of the French crown since the sixteenth century, had become part of the French theatrical landscape in the 1650s. Performers of opera as well as comedy, they came to France to present Francesco Sacrati's opera *La finta pazza* in 1645 and remained afterward, playing at the court of the regent. Like his Italian grandmother Marie de Médicis, the young Louis was enamored of the Italian players. Their leader, Tiberio Fiorelli, known by his stage name Scaramouche, was said to have dried the tears of the king as a child. With his colleagues Arlequin, Trivelin, Pantalon, the old doctor, and the young lovers to whom these comic characters served as foils, Scaramouche created not only a theater but also a mystique that was to have a pronounced effect on the ballet as well as other French art forms.[38]

---

38. On the commedia dell'arte in France, see Virginia Scott, *The Commedia dell'Arte in Paris, 1644–1697* (Charlottesville: University Press of Virginia, 1990); and Gustave Attinger, *L'esprit de la commedia dell'arte dans le théâtre française* (Paris: Librairie théatrale, 1950). More general studies include Allardyce Nicoll, *The World of Harlequin: A Critical Study of the Commedia dell'arte* (Cambridge: Cambridge University Press, 1963); Roberto Tessari, *La commedia dell'arte nel seicento: Industria e arte giocosa della civiltà barocca* (Florence: L. S. Olschki, 1969); and Nino Pirrotta, "Commedia dell'arte and Opera," in *Music and Culture in Italy from the Middle Ages to the Baroque* (Cambridge: Harvard University Press, 1984), 343–60.

Example 1.1. Lully, *Ballet de l'Impatience*, snuff-takers chorus [Coro di scolari], LW V 14/23. Bibliothèque nationale de France, Collection Philidor, Rés. F 509, 41–42.

* Source: 6/4

Example 1.1. (*continued*)

A dancer of the court ballet, M. Hesselin, reenacted the role of Arlequin in the *Ballet des fêtes de Bacchus* in 1651. In 1655, the *Ballet des plaisirs* included an entry for the "real" Scaramouche, Trivelin, and Pantalon,
who performed an improvised sketch.[39] Scaramouche was again in Paris
during the carnival season of 1656, when Lully and Beauchamps created
an entry of the *Ballet de la galanterie du temps* in imitation of the commedia
dell'arte. Jean Loret, an eyewitness to the event, describes a group of imitation Trivelins (including Lully and Lambert) and Scaramouches (including
Beauchamps), who in their comic gestures, acrobatics, and pantomime were
"an improvement on the original."[40] According to Loret's account, Tiberio Fiorelli appeared unexpectedly, and angered by the parody (or perhaps
feigning anger), took off his belt and cracked it like a whip.[41] Lully mimicked
Scaramouche again the following year in an entry from *L'Amour malade*.

The burlesque of the court ballet reached a high point in *Les noces de village, mascarade ridicule* (1663). As its subtitle indicates, this work is not a
court ballet in the strict sense but rather a *mascarade*. It is also one of a series
of court ballets celebrating the village wedding and one of the last to incorporate a substantial burlesque musical style. From its gentle mocking of the *bons
bourgeois* and the pompous *seigneur de la ville* to the directly farcical treatment
of a charlatan's show and a troupe of gypsy thieves, the *mascarade* as a whole,
in keeping with its genre, treats a distinctly nonnoble segment of society.

The *Ballet d'Alcidiane* and the Noble Ideal of Pleasure

Of all the early court ballets of Louis XIV, the one that most aptly captures
the ideal of a noble class is the *Ballet d'Alcidiane*, performed at the Louvre in
1658. The novel on which the story was based, *Polexandre* by Marin Le Roy,
sieur de Gomberville, was written in 1637 but still widely read at mid-century.
The novel portrays an ideal relationship between monarchy and nobility in
its description of an idyllic island whose queen, Alcidiane, lives in harmony
with a strong noble class, epitomized by the hero Polexandre. The ballet,
saturated like the novel with the perfume of chivalric romance, reflects important elements of a courtly model: an adherence to an aristocratic code
of conduct; a self-reflexive celebration of the ideals of leisure and pleasure
along with their attendant arts of song, dance, and masquerade; and a taste

39. Canova-Green, *Benserade: Ballets pour Louis XIV*, 1: 261: "les veritables Triuelin,
Scaramouche, & Pantalon."

40. *La muze historique*, 2: 157: "Enchéry sur l'Original."

41. Scott, *Commedia dell'Arte in Paris*, 38; Christout, *Le ballet de cour*, 81.

for the burlesque, both as a mode of entertainment and as a way of high-lighting through contrast the refined galanterie of a privileged caste.

With the exception of a few vocal airs by Boësset, most of the music for this ballet was composed by Lully. According to Loret's report, the overture—the first fully developed example of the French overture—was played by eighty-four instruments, including thirty-six strings, in addition to woodwinds, keyboards, guitars, theorbos, and lutes.[42] The ballet consists of three parts, depicting respectively "the delights of the Happy Island, where this beautiful queen held her court," "the principal adventures of Polexandre before his arrival," and "his triumph and glory in possessing Alcidiane." The ballet as a whole affords an opportunity to observe how Benserade and Lully, in one of their first collaborative large-scale works, translate the courtly tone of the chivalric novel to the court ballet. Against this aristocratic standard, burlesque entries create a comic effect. The music of these scenes points to eccentric or comic pantomimes or dances reinforcing through contrast the conventions of courtly behavior and alluding to the musical fabric of everyday life. In *Alcidiane,* these burlesque entries generally represent the *mascarades* and other staged entertainments enjoyed by the members of Alcidiane's court and signify indirectly a noble taste for masking, pantomime, and raillery.

An example of the French burlesque style may be seen in the entry entitled "les baladins ridicules" (LWV 9/16), in which eight dancers, costumed as "four ridiculous dancers and their wives," provide a *mascarade* for the court of Alcidiane. This entry, featuring some of the most virtuoso dancers at Louis XIV's court,[43] was mentioned by Loret as a scene that particularly delighted its audience. A study in discontinuity, its disjunct motion and awkward cadences probably mirrored a series of nonnoble physical gestures (ex. 1.2). The awkward harmonic language includes uncomfortable part-writing and grating dissonances. Perhaps most amusing is the sense of rhythmic irregularity, produced by frequent changes in meter as well as patterns of note values. At measure 16 all forward motion stops completely for six long beats, followed by a bizarre prolongation of the same harmony for another six beats.

This scene is juxtaposed with an entry depicting "the eight best dancers of the court of Alcidiane" (LWV 9/22), whose smooth part writing and continuous dotted rhythms may be seen, in contrast, as a marker of nobility

---

42. Loret, *La Muze historique,* 2: 444–45.

43. These included Lully, Lambert, and Beauchamps.

Example 1.2. Lully, *Alcidiane*, burlesque dancers [4ᵉ entrée. Les baladins ridicules], LWV 9/16. Bibliothèque nationale de France, Collection Philidor, Rés. F 507, 15–16.

Example 1.2. (*continued*)

Example 1.2. (*continued*)

(ex. 1.3). In this entry, a stable harmonic rhythm supports a supple melody that gradually climbs to a single high point, then gently descends to a half cadence at the double bar. This process is elaborated and extended in the second half of the piece. The meter changes in this section support a rhythmic stability lacking in *Les baladins ridicules*. And while a melodic and harmonic prolongation occurs in the upper voices in mm. 8–9, a graceful flowing motion is maintained by the continuing movement in the bass.

To illustrate the entertainments of the court, a mock combat (LWV 9/27-33, labeled *combat crotesque* in a later source) is pantomimed. In the tradition of Clément Janequin and others, this musical battle includes a drumroll and marches, followed by a charge, retreat, attack, combat, and final victory. The stage directions commend its comic nature as the sign of a peaceful society in which war has become obsolete. Likewise, its music mimics military maneuvers through the use of a mix of note values, changing meters, military cadences, fanfares, and occasional "wrong notes." Polexandre's marriage to Alcidiane, celebrated by a group of shepherds, shepherdesses, and fauns, highlights the pastoral landscape of the ballet's idyllic setting. The faun, a mythical animal symbolizing an idealized natural world, was a common figure in the court ballet's pastoral entries. This particular entry featured Lully himself, dressed as a faun, conducting a stage band of twelve woodwind instruments (LWV 9/64-67).

There is evidence that the fantasy represented by *Alcidiane* had its roots in the cultural politics of early seventeenth-century France. The sieur de Gomberville, the author of the original novel *Polexandre*, was a noble at

Example 1.3. Lully, *Alcidiane*, noble dancers [6ᵉ entrée. 8 meilleurs danseurs de la cour d'Alcidiane], LWV 9/22. Bibliothèque nationale de France, Collection Philidor, Rés. F 507, 18–19.

Example 1.3. (*continued*)

Louis XIII's court, serving as counselor-secretary to the king from 1619 to 1621. Marlies Mueller analyzes his *Polexandre* as one of many chivalric novels that, behind a veil of the long ago and far away, represent a growing resistance to a more centralized rule and the passing of noble authority and privilege into the hands of the king under Bourbon rule. The authors of these works—including Gomberville, Madeleine de Scudéry, and Gaultier de Coste, seigneur de La Calprenède—did not oppose the monarchy itself as much as the abuses committed under the ministers Richelieu and Mazarin. Their ideas intersected at times with the aims of the Fronde, and it was said that Le Grand Condé, leader of the Fronde, read *Polexandre* like a Bible. The "inaccessible isle" where Alcidiane held her court, according to Mueller, should be considered not only a dreamy romance but a real blueprint for an ideal society as seen through the eyes of a disenfranchised nobility. Though the monarchy is not abandoned altogether in that society, the queen, essentially weak, depends upon a feudal nobility for her defense and protection. The hero undergoes many trials in her service, but the ideal remains a peaceful realm, free of the urge for war or imperial domination.[44]

Gomberville, whom Tallemant des Réaux called "un grand frondeur," was exiled by Louis XIII for his subversive attitude.[45] His novel and its identification with Condé might therefore seem an unusual choice for the court ballet. Yet it is precisely this view of a utopian noble world that seems to have appealed to the court in the 1650s, when the tone was set not by the king, the prime minister, or the queen mother but rather by the nobility and the artists in their service. It is also a mark of a changing noble identity, as well as an inherent generic distinction from the novel, that the ballet focuses almost exclusively on peaceful pleasures rather than heroic adventures. *Alcidiane* therefore brings together the aesthetics and politics of the court ballet of the early years of Louis XIV, portraying the court—as well as the ballet itself—as a "happy isle" in which the noble prerogative of pleasure is given meaning and definition through the power of spectacle.

Louis XIV, the Muses of Pleasure, and the Goddess of Love

In recent studies of the Old Regime, the king's body has been seen as a site of royal power through its ability to represent the larger body politic. The wide variety of roles he danced, for example, shepherd, Spaniard, slave, knight, drunkard, gypsy, Moor, fury, and nymph, identify him with a variety of elements within a diverse social order.[46] While this is true, it could also be said of the other dancers, whose roles—equally diverse—appear to have been assigned more according to talent than to hierarchical class distinctions. A number of virtuosic roles—a demon, the god of the winds, a bacchante, a fury—demonstrated Louis XIV's physical dexterity and consummate skill. At the same time, Louis's roles often carried nuances associated

44. Mueller, *Les idées politiques*, 24–64.

45. Ibid., 63–64.

46. According to Joseph Roach, the use of the king's natural body to symbolize the body politic may be seen as facilitating the notion of the modern imperial nation-state. See "Body of Law: The Sun King and the Code Noir," in *From Royal to the Republican Body: Incorporating the Political in Seventeenth- and Eighteenth-Century France,* ed. Sara E. Melzer and Kathryn Norberg (Berkeley: University of California Press, 1998), 117. See also Benedict Anderson, *Imagined Communities: Reflections on the Origin and Spread of Nationalism,* rev. ed. (London: Verso, 1991), 47–65.

with the qualities of youth and galanterie, identifying him more with noble values than with the mantle of kingship that as yet fell lightly upon
his shoulders. More feminine roles—a Muse, a nymph, a bridesmaid—
highlighted his physical grace and youthful beauty.[47] The role of a Moor,
a race associated in the seventeenth century with sexual prowess, hints at
the sexual desirability of a king from whom procreation was expected. As a
galant in the *Ballet de la galanterie du temps* (1656), Louis exhibited his considerable talent as a guitarist, presenting a serenade outside the window of
a lady. Such galant roles and themes highlighted the eligibility of the eigh-
teen-year-old king for courtship and marriage, while continuing to display
his talents for dance and music. Other roles danced by Louis support a noble, often allegorical, identity. One of the earliest was that of an allegorical
Golden Age, in the *Ballet du temps* (1654), in which he literally represented
the embodied ideal of the ballet. The embedded entertainments of the *Ballet
des plaisirs* culminated in a court ball at the end of the work, allowing a characteristic *grand ballet* in the noble style. As an introduction to this noble ball,
Louis himself appeared as the "spirit of the dance" (*génie de la danse*).

While Louis's own dancing roles tell us something about his image as it
was projected in the earliest years of his reign, the roles of the Muses can tell
us something about the arts and his relationship to them. The Muses make
two appearances in the early ballet of Louis's court. The first of these, in the
Ballet des fêtes de Bacchus, includes an entry featuring Apollo and the nine
Muses (see plate 1), who pay court to Bacchus. Ignoring the traditional distinction between Apollo, leader of the Muses, and Bacchus, the god of rev-
elry, the poet defends the appearance of the Muses "because of the affinity
they have with Bacchus."[48] In this entry, Louis's role as a Muse identifies
him as a general participant in the court's galant hedonism, undifferenti-
ated from the other noble and professional dancers in that role. As in other,
similar situations, however, Benserade uses the *vers de personnage* to point up
the king's difference. Written in the king's voice, his lines tell the Muses to
ready themselves for the "great and beautiful epic poem" he is preparing for
them, an allusion to his future exploits.[49]

---

47. Louis's role as a coquette in the *Ballet des fêtes de Bacchus*, however, was suppressed
before the ballet was produced, leading Prest (*Theatre under Louis XIV,* 89) to speculate that
there may have been some question as to the propriety of this particular role.

48. Canova-Green, *Benserade: Ballets pour Louis XIV,* 1: 84: "à cause de l'affinité qui est
entre elles & Bacchus."

49. Ibid., 1: 85: "Je medite un hardy projet, / Et vous prepare le sujet / D'un grand &
beau Poëme heroïque."

The second appearance of the Muses occurs in an introductory entry to the ballet-within-a-ballet enclosed within the second part of the *Ballet de la nuit* (1653). In it, Apollo and three of his Muses—Clio, Euterpe, and Erato—are hurrying to the festive wedding of Peleus and Thetis. Carrying an armful of violins, Apollo appears to be a dancing master charged with the music of the fête. The choice of Clio, Muse of history; Euterpe, Muse of pastoral; and Erato, Muse of love, identifies the ballet with historical/mythological, pastoral, and galant subject material. Symbolically, both of these appearances of Apollo and the Muses reflect the aesthetic of Louis XIV's early court ballet, in which the arts were seen as serving the hedonistic pleasures of the court.

By contrast, the Muses' appearance in the Italian opera performed at court in 1654, *Les noces de Pélée et de Thétis*, forecasts a more dignified role for Louis XIV and the arts. The opera is interspersed with ballet entries, and a ballet occurs as part of the larger prologue. In this, Louis as Apollo (see fig. 1.6), surrounded by the nine Muses and flanked by two choirs singing his praise, descends from Parnassus. The nine Muses were danced by high-ranking ladies of the court, creating a strong connection between Apollo's Parnassus and Louis XIV's court. (See fig. 1.7 for a picture of Louis's cousin, Henriette d'Angleterre, as the Muse Erato.)[50] The performance, which took place in April of 1654, occurred in the context of preparations for Louis's coronation, which might also explain the level of dignity displayed in this prologue. This more regal treatment of Louis XIV and the arts, foreshadowing Louis's image as artistic patron and absolute ruler, also foreshadows the more serious praise found in Lully's opera prologues of the 1670s.

Three appearances of Venus in a singing role—in the *Ballet des fêtes de Bacchus* (1651), the *Ballet de la nuit* (1653), and the *Ballet des plaisirs* (1655)—connect Louis and the ballet to the galanterie that shaped the arts in these early years. Two of Venus's *récits* open a major *partie* devoted to the arts of entertainment, pointing up the connection between Venus and the hedonism of spectacle.[51] In each, she appears as a vision of awe and magnificence, descending in a chariot-machine accompanied by members of her retinue: the Graces, the Pleasures, and the Games. In each, Venus delivers the same portentous message that her power is superior to the power of kings. Alluding to

50. Erato was the Muse of lyric poetry, especially erotic poetry, and was thought by some to have invented the lyre, associated in seventeenth-century France with the lute—hence the lute she is holding and the lutes and Cupid's bows on the bottom of her skirt.

51. In the *Ballet de la nuit*, the second *partie* is devoted to the depiction of an evening's entertainments at court. These include a ball, a ballet, and a comedy. In *Ballet des plaisirs*, the second partie is devoted to the entertainments of Paris.

Figure 1.6. *Les noces de Pélée et de Thétis*. Costume of Louis XIV as Apollo.
Institut de France/Art Resource.

Muses. Erato. Madame la Princesse. D'Angleterre.
les autres Huict estoient vestues demesme, distinguées seulement
par les Couleurs des habits.

Figure 1.7. *Les noces de Pélée et de Thétis*. Costume of Henriette d'Angleterre as the Muse
Erato. Institut de France/Art Resource.

the king's destiny as lover and husband, the power of Venus and of love is a common trope in galant poetry. In the 1650s, that trope was more compatible with the ballet than with the opera prologue, which represented a more straightforward gesture of monarchical praise.

Benserade also invests the young king's relationship with the goddess Venus, like his relationship with the Muses, with significance. In the *Ballet de la nuit*, Louis XIV danced the role of a Game (*un Jeu*) in Venus's suite. Benserade's *vers* for Louis in this role adumbrate an ideology of galanterie which, inscribed in the verse and images of his *livrets* over the years, would have the king obedient to the power of Venus and to the arts of love. Later in the same year that this ballet was performed, Louis would take part in his first military campaign, against the rebellious prince de Condé.[52] In his *vers* for Louis as a Game in the service of Venus, Benserade expresses a kind of wistfulness, a regret that the king will soon leave the goddess's side to seek his glory. He casts these verses in his own voice as a prayer to Venus ("À Vénus"). Without abandoning the witty, satirical tone for which he was known, Benserade praises Louis's devotion to Venus and expresses, as a commonplace but also with a clear sincerity, his own fear that Louis will inevitably be won away from her side by the lure of Mars:

> But you [Venus] will hardly keep him,
> His soul, heroic and stern,
> Loves his bloody occupations too much,
> Already his great projects are taking shape,
> And I fear that Honor and Mars
> In the end will lure him away from you.[53]

The significance of this passage is heightened by the fact that, of all Benserade's *vers de personnage*, these are unique in being addressed to the character herself, rather than to a performer enacting the role. Benserade's *vers* may thus be read as a form of invocation to Venus, expressing the fears of the artist that the inevitable occupation of war will distract the king from a true pursuit of the arts, represented by the beauty, love and pleasure embodied in the goddess.

52. Canova-Green, *Benserade: Ballets pour Louis XIV*, 1: 118. Condé, having sided with the Spanish after his defeat in the Fronde, marched into France at the head of a Spanish army. Louis would oppose Condé in the siege of Arras, under the famous general Turenne.

53. Ibid.: "Mais vous ne le garderez guere, / Son ame heroïque & seuere / Ayme trop les sanglans hazards, / Dé-ja ses grands projets s'ébauchent, / Et je crains que L'Honneur & Mars / A la fin ne vous le débauchent."

Benserade sets up a subtle contradiction between the praise of love he speaks in his own voice in the *vers* for Louis as a Game and the praise of glory he puts in the mouth of the king in the *vers* for Louis as a *curieux* in part 3.[54] These introduce a concept that would inform Louis XIV's later propaganda, the coexistence of the opposing qualities of glory and love in the person of the king. Specifically, the idea of glory refers to the heroic performance expected of the young king on the battlefield, the idea of love to his eligibility for courtship and marriage (and sometimes to his love affairs). While both are integral to the king's image, the primacy of glory henceforth becomes a common trope. These *vers* for Louis as a *curieux*, written in the first person for the king, declare for the first time what will be repeated many times over the course of the court ballet, the subordination of passion to the quest for glory:

> I know how to triumph over myself and [my passions]
> As well as over enemies,
> And to count myself among all the rebels
> Fought and vanquished.[55]

This interplay between love and glory serves at once to identify the king with the pleasures of his aristocracy, while at the same time setting him on a higher plane as a military leader responsible for their welfare. Bridging the difference between Louis XIV and his courtiers, at the same time it prepares the way for a more serious tone as Louis comes into his maturity. Benserade's two sets of *vers*, then, for Louis as a Game and as a *curieux*, set out, from two different points of view, the ultimate truth of Louis's dual role: in the end Louis the king must triumph over Louis the galant courtier. From the beginning, the young king is portrayed as accepting this hierarchy unequivocally. Benserade, speaking as an artist on behalf of a noble class, would seem to acknowledge its truth with some reluctance and regret.

Premonitions of Power

Within the noble world of galanterie that constituted the court ballet of the 1650s, one image strikes a dissonant contrast. In the *Ballet de Psyché* (1656),

54. As a "curious one," Louis peers into the devastation left by the monsters and goblins of the night, a metaphor for the Fronde.

55. Canova-Green, *Benserade: Ballets pour Louis XIV*, 1: 140: "Et puis les passions seruiront à ma gloire, / J'en veux subir la Loy, / Pour leur oster après l'empire & la victoire / Qu'elles auroient sur moy. / Je sçauray triompher de ma personne et d'elles / Ainsi que d'ennemis, / Et me conter moy-mesme entre tous mes rebelles / Combatus & soûmis."

Louis was cast as Pluto, ruler of the underworld. In Benserade's *vers*, a rare moment of political directness pulls the veil from the façade of a happy solidarity between king and court. Rather, the king is depicted as drawing on the dark side of his power to reign over the viperous demons of the rebellious court nobility, still fractious after the Fronde. Benserade's *vers* take the form of a political monologue, in which the king fulminates against his courtiers and the difficulties of ruling over the traitors among them:

> The court where I reign is fertile with demons,
> This abyss produces a great quantity of smoke:
> Hate, self-interest, ambition, self-love,
> Sometimes all four together, other times one by one
> Constitute the long and crude pain of these unhappy ones,
> No one under my law is exempt from tribulations,
> Everyone has his misery, and god that I am,
> Do I not have my own inquietude?
> After having conquered the night and the chaos [of the Fronde]
> Which plotted to deprive me of my mastership,
> And just as I was hoping to rejoice in this peace
> As much as possible in Hades,
> I feel in my mind new problems,
> An internal war, and secret combats.[56]

Lully's music included an infernal *concert italien* for chorus and four solo voices, representing the qualities of Fear, Suspicion, Despair, and Jealousy found in Hades and by implication among Louis XIV's courtiers. Though this scene is lost except for the *vers de personnage,* these *vers* point to a political shadow lurking in the recesses of Louis's court. As in the *Ballet de la nuit,* the *Ballet de Psyché* presents Louis as the enemy of the dark forces, but it is a measure of the changes in the three years between the two works that instead of the Rising Sun, he is now depicted as the king of the underworld.

---

56. Ibid., 1: 324–25: "la cour où je regne est fertile en Démons, / Cét Abisme produit quantité de fumée. / La haine, l'interest, l'ambition, l'amour, / Tantost tous quatre ensemble, & tantost tour à tour / Sont de ces Malheureux la peine longue & rude, / Personne sous ma loy n'est exempt des ennuis, / Chacun a sa misere, & tout Dieu que je suis / N'ay-je pas mon inquietude? / Apres auoir vaincu la Nuict, & le Chaos / Qui broüilloient pour m'oster la qualité de Maistre, / Et comme je pensois joüir de ce repos / Où l'Enfer est luy-mesme autant qu'il y peut estre, / Je sens dans mon esprit de nouueaux embaras, / Une guerre intestine, & de secrets combas."

✳

CHAPTER TWO

Muses of Memory

Louis XIV's Late Court Ballet, 1661–1669

In 1660, Louis XIV married Marie-Thérèse, the Infanta of Spain, and, following the death of Mazarin in March of 1661, defied all expectation by
choosing to rule alone rather than to appoint a new prime minister. The
1660s may be considered a transitional period in which the king's image,
while still associated with noble pleasure, began to take on facets of om-
niscience and omnipotence. This transition may be attributed not only to
Louis's passage from youth to adulthood and his personal decision to take
on the responsibilities of government but also to a vast artistic project having certain similarities with the present-day public relations campaign. The
ballet, with its strong ties to aristocratic self-display and the pleasures of
the court at carnival, tended to retain its lighthearted galanterie while other
artistic enterprises, including paintings, sculpture, monuments, urban festivals, military parades, and medals, provided a more serious imagery of
kingship that would define the later phases of Louis XIV's reign. Especially
in the late 1660s, however, images of sovereign power began to penetrate
the ballet's stronghold of galanterie and courtly pleasure.[1]

1. I am grateful to Ståle Wikshåland and the Norwegian research group engaged in a
project entitled "Power *mise-en-scène*" for including me in a seminar on that topic sponsored
under the auspices of the Norwegian Research Council, where I was able to refine ideas developed in this chapter.

The Cult of Empire and the Society of Pleasures

The iconography of sovereignty was derived from a long European tradition of lavish festivals promoting idyllic dreams of good government centered on a strong ruler. Drawing from the ancient Roman model, Renaissance festivals focused particularly on the idea of empire, often depicting the current reign as the return of the Golden Age and the imperial *renovatio* foretold in Virgil's Fourth Eclogue. Imperial imagery, already present in the late medieval period, was given impetus and focus by the sudden reality of empire brought about by the naming of Charles V as Holy Roman Emperor in 1530. After this event all of Europe sought to emulate the mythology of universal empire created in Hapsburg festivals, processions, triumphs, and entries uniting the cult of the monarch with the entertainments of courtly pageantry. In these festivities, fueled by the rediscovery of classical antiquity, Charles and his imitators appeared as Roman emperors wreathed in laurel and accompanied by the ancient panoply of empire, including images of gods, heroes, and subject peoples. The royal entry, formerly a dialogue between the ruler and his urban citizens, now attained the status of an imperial triumph in the Roman style. The ancient Roman practice of emperor worship was not lost on the Renaissance imagination, wracked by a crisis of faith brought about by the fragmentation of the church. The *rex christianissimus*, along with the mythological gods and heroes that were his surrogates, stood ready to represent the hopes and dreams of a people left bereft by the breakdown of the religious order of a united church and the political order of a united medieval Christendom.[2]

Imperial imagery informed the politics of rulers across early modern Europe. Henry VIII justified his break with Rome by defining England as an "empire" standing outside the authority of the pope, and the cult of Elizabeth I, resting on her identity as "most high Mightie and Magnificent Empresse,"[3] equated her with Virgil's Astraea, the virgin whose ad-

---

2. Roy Strong, *Art and Power: Renaissance Festivals, 1560–1650* (Berkeley: University of California Press, 1973), 65–97. See also Alexandre Y. Haran, *Le lys et le globe: Messianisme dynastique et rêve imperial en France à l'aube des temps modernes* (Paris: Champ Vallon, 2000); Marie Tanner, *The Last Descendent of Aeneas: The Hapsburgs and the Mythic Image of the Emperor* (New Haven: Yale University Press, 1993); Mary Beard, *The Roman Triumph* (Boston: Belknap Press of Harvard University Press, 2007); and James Ronald Mulryne and Elizabeth Goldring, *Court Festivals of the European Renaissance: Art, Politics, and Performance* (Aldershot, Hampshire: Ashgate, 2002).

3. The quotation is taken from the dedication page of Spenser's *Fairie Queene* of 1590.

vent foretold an imperial renewal. A propaganda of empire helped to transform the Medici in Florence from a mere banking family into a formidable political dynasty. The Florentine synthesis of neoclassical imperialism and Neoplatonic philosophy, brought to France by Catherine de Médicis, built on the praise of empire in sixteenth-century French historiography. During the reign of Louis XIII in the early seventeenth century, imperialist themes pervaded the imagery of the court ballet, as well as portraits, emblems, medals, engravings, frontispieces, entrées, tapestries, statues, and carrousels.[4]

The mystique of empire was transmitted to Louis XIV through the Hapsburg lineage of his mother, Anne of Austria, and his wife, Marie-Thérèse; through the court ballet of Louis XIII; and through the pervasive imperial iconography that had been absorbed into royal propaganda by the Valois and early Bourbon dynasties. It was also bound up with colonialism as it was developing around the globe. By 1661, French activities related to trade and exploration had diminished. All that remained were a few hundred men in Canada, the beginnings of a settlement in the West Indies, and sporadic trading expeditions along the African coast. Although Colbert launched new colonial ventures in the 1660s and 1670s, as a colonial power France did not yet compete with Spain, Portugal, the Netherlands, or England.[5] Nonetheless, French pretensions to universal empire remained strong, and royal propaganda drew on images of native Africans, Americans, and Asians paying obeisance to Louis XIV. Another manifestation of imperial imagery depicted the deference of other rulers to his sovereignty. For example, a carrousel of 1662 depicted members of the nobility as leaders of quadrilles representing the armies of Persia, Turkey, and Europe, all ceding to the superiority of the French king, costumed as the emperor of Rome. This imagery conflated the imagery of Louis XIV and seventeenth-century France with that of Augustan Rome, and also neatly conflated Louis's authority over rival kings with his authority over leaders of his own nobility. The appearance of the rebellious prince de Condé, now defeated and pardoned, as submissive leader of the Turks held a particular resonance.

This more heroic, imperial face of kingship appears sporadically, but with increasing frequency in the court ballet of the late 1660s. Louis XIV's dancing roles, though contributing to an overall picture of the ballet, cannot

---

4. Ranum, *Artisans of Glory*, 41–49; Françoise Bardon, *Le portrait mythologique à la cour de France sous Henri IV et Louis XIII* (Paris: Picard, 1974). Bardon includes a series of portraits of Henri IV, Louis XIII, and their contemporaries as Roman emperors and as Mars-Emperor, Hercules-Emperor, Jupiter-Emperor, etc.

5. Pierre Goubert, *Louis XIV and Twenty Million Frenchmen*, trans. by Anne Carter (New York: Pantheon Books, 1970), 30–31.

be taken as an accurate gauge of royal propaganda, because—as we have seen in chapter 1—they were only slightly distinguished from the other noble dancers. Cultivated primarily to showcase the body as the site of galanterie, beauty, and noble bearing, the skill of dance enhanced the image of the king, alongside the other nobles with whom he danced, as a living work of art. Viewed with more specificity, however, these roles may be taken as an indication of the transitional nature of his image in his twenties and early thirties, during which time his comic roles decreased dramatically, while galant roles continued and absolutist roles increased. From 1651 to 1660, the roles associated with the king's power numbered only two or three; from 1661 to 1670, about a half dozen (approximately one-third).[6] More important than Louis XIV's dancing roles, in the context of image making, was the depiction of kingship. Almost all heroic and militaristic associations in the ballet, including imperialist themes, depiction of combat, and praise of military victories, were associated (often through the *vers de personnage*) with sovereignty, as were the roles of gods and heroes. In contrast, the nobility was depicted as an idle and fashionable elite. For example, nobles were depicted self-reflexively enjoying courtly entertainments in the *Ballet de la nuit*, the *Ballet d'Alcidiane*, and the *Ballet des plaisirs*. In the *Ballet des arts*, four nobles dance the part of courtiers covered in gold. Here, as elsewhere, the noble dancers are described as handsome, witty, young, adroit, and galant (with the exception of the pockmarked marquis de Genlis, who is mocked for his ugliness). The *vers de personnage* as they relate to the nobility await systematic study, but in general they make very few references to these noble dancers as warriors or heroes or even as possessors of qualities that befit their roles as soldiers. Even given the generic association of the ballet with the pleasures of carnival, this is ironic since a number of the nobles who danced with Louis in the ballets were also military men, and in fact the coordination and grace required by the ballet were thought to enhance soldiers' performance on the battlefield. The duc de Saint-Aignan, by far the eldest of the noble dancers (still dancing in his sixties), had actually been wounded on several occasions in battle. The comte de Guiche is listed in the military histories of France and served in the Holland campaign of 1652, dying at Kreugznach (Creutzenack) in November of 1673. His father was one

6. On theories of the noble body as art, see Domna C. Stanton, *The Aristocrat as Art* (New York: Columbia University Press, 1980). A list of Louis XIV's dancing roles may be found in Beaussant, *Lully ou le musicien du soleil*, 112–15, and in Philippe Hourcade, "Louis XIV travesti," *Cahiers de Littérature de XVIIe siècle* 6 (1984): 257–71. The former also includes a valuable list of Lully's dancing roles, but the latter is more accurate.

of Louis XIII's generals, the maréchal de Grammont, who had produced a ballet in 1659 for the members of the court traveling across the Pyrenees to negotiate the marriage of Louis and the Infanta.[7]

These modes of representation reflect a complex relationship between Louis XIV and his nobility. In his youth, as a noble himself, he shared their galant identity, and for social and political reasons he continued to need an elegant aristocracy to ornament his court. At the same time, the cohabitation of Louis and his court nobility created a certain tension. Never forgetting the Fronde, Louis kept a watchful eye on his courtiers, monitoring their activities with vigilance. On their side, the courtiers enjoyed the prestige and glamour of court life, along with its opportunities for social and political advancement, but some of them chafed against the bars of its gilded cage. In response to the growing control and even surveillance of the monarchy, nobles divided into factions according to their varying degrees of loyalty. Many welcomed a strong king in the wake of the Fronde, but despite Louis XIV's general popularity following the restoration of order in this period, strains of discontent persisted.

A massed rebellion in arms was no longer possible after the Fronde, and in the 1660s some aristocrats began to oppose the king by means of the pen rather than the sword. As noble identity with the military waned, some individuals wrote strongly worded political tracts protesting the wars of the crown and their negative impact on the financial situation of the nobility.[8] One focus of aristocratic discontent was the unfavorable fiscal policy initiated by the finance minister Jean-Baptiste Colbert, which was viewed as oppressive and financially ruinous to their caste. As Lionel Rothkrug has shown, what began as remonstrances against specific situations, mostly economic, gradually developed into more generalized forms of resistance and even protest over the course of the late seventeenth century. Rothkrug and others find the origins of the eighteenth-century French Enlightenment embedded in ideas arising from this resistance.[9]

---

7. Rose Pruiksma, private communication. Even in the *Ballet de Flore*, whose finale incorporates the same kind of military quadrilles as seen in the Carrousel of 1662, along with music in the grandest military style (discussed at the end of this chapter), this military character is associated solely with the tribute paid to Louis XIV by men and women from the four corners of the earth, rather than with any recognition of the nobility in military roles.

8. Lionel Rothkrug, *Opposition to Louis XIV: The Political and Social Origins of the French Enlightenment* (Princeton: Princeton University Press, 1965), 115.

9. Ibid., 86–174; on the objection of the high nobility to war, see 115. See also Arlette Jouanna, *Le devoir de révolte: La noblesse française et la gestation de l'état moderne*

As the king grew older he began to regard court entertainment from the point of view not so much as a participant but as a patron; in this period they served him more as a political gesture than as a personal pleasure (and also as a way to distract his restless nobility). In his *Mémoires*, he claimed that he had created a Society of Pleasures as a sign of his beneficence toward his court and his people, and in itself as a sign of his power:

> But the more I was obligated to limit this excess [the disorder of the Fronde], and by more agreeable remedies, the more it was necessary to preserve and carefully cultivate all that bonded me in affection with my people and especially the nobility, without diminishing my authority and the respect that was due to me, in order to show them in this way that it was not aversion for them, nor affected severity, nor rudeness of spirit, but simply reason and duty, that motivated me in other ways [causing me to be] more reserved and strict toward them. This Society of Pleasures, which gives persons at the court a frank familiarity with us, touches them and charms them more than one realizes. . . . In this way we captivate their minds and their hearts, sometimes more strongly perhaps than by recompenses and gifts; and in regard to foreigners' seeing a state that is flourishing and well regulated, what is consumed in these expenses (which could pass for superfluous) strikes them with a very advantageous impression of magnificence, power, richness and grandeur.[10]

Louis XIV's Society of Pleasures, as depicted in the court ballet of the 1660s, amounted to the noble ideal of the previous decade, still incorporating a voluptuous hedonism, but laced with images of a strong ruler. The galant ideal still defined the genre, and the burlesque continued to appear, though less frequently. Both, however, began to be framed and punctuated by themes and music of a more pompous nature. Since *Alcidiane*, the court ballet had gradually begun to incorporate more vocal music. In the ballets of

---

(1569–1661) (Paris: Fayard, 1989), 8–9; and Fanny Cosandey and Robert Descimon, *L'absolutisme en France* (Paris: Seuil, 2002), 175–180. On the nobility's role and participation in the Enlightenment, see Rothkrug, *Opposition to Louis XIV;* Dewald, *European Nobility,* 183–87; and Mettam, *Power and Faction,* 309–22. It is perhaps significant that Colbert, born into the bourgeoisie, was of the newer *noblesse de robe* rather than the older *noblesse de l'épée;* les grands might have reacted less aggressively to his financial policies had he been one of their "own."

10. Kathryn Hoffman, *Society of Pleasures: Interdisciplinary Readings in Pleasure and Power during the Reign of Louis XIV* (New York: St. Martin's Press, 1997), 13–14.

the late 1660s, one finds occasional passages of recitative, along with large choruses of praise. These, along with increasingly complex formal structures, point toward the tragédie en musique of the 1670s.

As a genre, then, the court ballet continued to embody the pleasure of the king and his court. Clearly, the nobles who served as creators and dancers enjoyed a certain intimacy with Louis XIV, who danced by their side and committed tremendous energy, time, and expense to this common endeavor. The professional creators of the ballet, such as Lully and Benserade, also enjoyed a close relationship with the king, along with rich opportunities for artistic and political advancement. In the decade after the bloody wars of the Fronde, however, it would be naïve to expect that, even at court, the ballet's idealized images of social harmony would reflect a reality unsullied by internecine strife. As Benserade had indicated in the *vers* for the *Ballet de Psyché*, the terror of the Fronde had long tentacles, some reaching into the heart of the court itself. Although after the Fronde it would have been unthinkable to articulate a language of protest—or even mild resistance—at court, there must have been some nobles among *les grands* who remained nostalgic for the autonomous power they felt slipping away from their class. There were probably those, as well, who would not have welcomed the use of the ballet as an absolutist vehicle, as it had been used by Richelieu and Louis XIII in the 1630s and early 1640s.

In the 1660s, the ballet was still the instrument of a court nobility, for whom participation in the pleasures of the court provided almost all of what was left of a class identity. This privileged elite had blocked the attempts of Mazarin to introduce Italian opera as a vehicle for monarchical propaganda, probably out of political motivations as well as for reasons of taste. In the ballet of the 1660s, the appearance of absolutist images, accompanied by *grande musique* and pompous texts, served as a compromise between a court ballet devoted to galanterie and noble pleasure, and the more serious opera used in other European courts to enhance the ruler's prestige. As Louis XIV gained in political strength and military victory, images of a strong ruler pulled against the lighthearted galanterie of the ballet. Rather than moving toward the more politicized propaganda of Louis XIII's ballet in his late reign, the genre would give way in the early 1670s to a new form of French opera as the dominant form of courtly spectacle.

While the ballet continued to serve as entertainment and recreation for the king and court in the 1660s, then, it also reflected some deeply encoded questions as to who would control pleasure, who would be represented, and how. Would it serve a nobility who used pleasure as an icon of its identity? Or would it serve the king, who, as first of the nobility and both purveyor and participant in the pleasures of the court, also perceived them as an instrument of control? Was it possible for the genre to satisfy the need for a propaganda of power and pleasure, each with its own complex meaning for the king and the nobility, itself divided by the fractures of the wars of the Fronde? In a sense, the question was not so much who would partake of pleasure, a given in the ballet as well as in the life of the king and his court, but whose prerogative it would be and whose interest it would serve. A further question arose over how pleasure, like power, would be represented by Louis XIV's artists and to what extent the control of that representation lay in their hands.

These questions were answered in theory, if not always in actual practice, by older Neoplatonic theories of music and dance as they had defined the function of the ballet since its inception, bridging the lines of division between king and nobility, power and pleasure, politics and entertainment. Music, for example, was believed to signify the king through choruses of praise and military gestures borrowed from the battlefield and urban festivals, but it also provided a sonic aura that encompassed both the power of the king and the pleasures of the king and his nobility. In the same way, dancers' response to the power of music could embody the subject's submission to the monarch's command, as well as to a more general universal harmony. Neoplatonic philosophy fostered a view of the arts as both reflecting and participating in that harmony, and in the process drawing it down to earth. Within that system, the goal of the artist was to capture through art the eternal essence of things, in particular the eternal body of the king, the *corpus mysticum*, through its tangible correspondence to the king's temporal image.[11] In the decade of the 1660s these beliefs mingled and competed with newer systems of representation (discussed above, in the introduction), in which the bridge between image and essence was beginning to be ruptured. With that rupture came a profound crisis in the role of the arts vis-à-vis the king, as the arts could now be perceived as serving a degraded form of propaganda in the modern sense, rather than the eternal truth they had been believed to reflect.

---

11. On Neoplatonism in the ballet, see Isherwood, *Music in the Service of the King*, 1–54, and Chae, "Music, Festival, and Power," 15–24. I agree with Chae that Isherwood, constructing his argument from theoretical treatises rather from internal evidence, tends to overstate the importance of Neoplatonism as a philosophical underpinning of the ballet in the period of Louis XIV.

Strains of Resistance in the Artists' Community

Only a few months after taking the reins of government in 1661, Louis XIV
and his court attended a fête at the new home of Nicolas Fouquet, his minister of finance. Accounts of the event indicate that Vaux-le-Vicomte, never
more beautiful than on this evening, dazzled Louis's courtiers with its show
of unprecedented luxury married to the finest of artistic tastes. In seeking
to impress the new king, however, Fouquet had not calculated the cost of
outshining him, nor had he anticipated Louis's determination to subjugate
the inordinate power of bankers and financiers to royal authority. On Mon-
day, September 5, 1661, Louis XIV's twenty-third birthday, he had Fouquet
arrested without warning and thrown into prison. His action, while clearly
based on Fouquet's self-aggrandizement through the use of his office, almost
certainly had to do with other motivations as well. As finance minister, Fouquet had obtained his fortune by questionable means and had falsified the accounts to his own advantage. As he stated in his own defense, however, his
financial practices were no different from those of Mazarin, who had blurred
the distinction between the state treasury and his own personal fortune. In a
larger sense, the arrest of Fouquet signaled Louis XIV's desire to turn from
the old order of Mazarin and the Regency, characterized by fiscal confusion
and political anarchy, toward a new order, associated with the rising star of
his new finance minister, Jean-Baptiste Colbert, and characterized by control
and official authority. On a more personal level, the confidence with which
Fouquet had placed his wealth in the service of art and luxury also had a dramatic effect on the young and impressionable king. It is an irony of history
that the distinctive style of the paintings of Charles Le Brun, the architecture
of Louis Le Vau, the landscapes of André Le Nôtre, and the comédie-ballets
of Molière, all contributing to the artistic identity of the mature Louis XIV,
had already been launched under the direction of the finance minister.

The incarceration of Fouquet prompted widespread protest, epitomized
by an anonymous pamphlet attack entitled *L'innocence persécutée*. Proclaiming Fouquet's innocence, the author portrays him as a victim of Louis
XIV and Colbert and widens the argument to question the very founda-
tions of the French monarchy.[12] Written sometime between 1661 and 1664,

---

12. On the Fouquet affair, see Ranum, *Artisans of Glory*, 246–53; Rothkrug, *Opposition
to Louis XIV*, 193–211; and Marc Fumaroli, "Nicolas Fouquet, the Favourite Manqué," in
J. H. Elliott and L. W. B. Brockliss, eds., *The World of the Favourite* (New Haven: Yale University Press, 1999), 239–55.

this document challenged the image promulgated by official propaganda as Louis XIV consolidated his power after the death of Mazarin. It represents an early example of a series of seditious documents, produced and disseminated in much the same way as the underground pamphlet literature of the Fronde. Defying governmental censorship, this literature circulated in manuscript within France or came off the presses of England, Holland, and Germany. It increased as antimilitaristic sentiments emerged in the late 1660s. Louis XIV's campaign against the Low Countries in 1667–68, although praised in official sources for its discipline and morale, produced a bitter and long-lasting enmity in that region. It also provoked criticism within France. The widely disseminated *Bouclier d'Etat* (1667), criticizing Louis's insatiable ambition and warning of his pernicious intention to dominate Europe, set a model for the protest of "universal empire." The annexation of Flanders, celebrated in a week-long fête at Versailles in 1668, coincided with sentiments of pacifism among the populace and a breakdown of military discipline in the army, which in 1671 lost ten thousand men to desertion.[13]

There is evidence that Louis XIV's political self-aggrandizement in the 1660s widened the resistance of a community of writers and artists associated with the disgraced finance minister. In the 1650s, at the beginning of Louis XIV's reign, members of this community apparently hoped that Fouquet would become Louis XIV's prime minister, guiding the monarch in shaping a kingdom inspired by the loftiest ideals of freedom and the arts. The arrest and trial of the finance minister and the concomitant consolidation of Louis's power in the 1660s shattered these hopes and served to intensify a discourse of innuendo and ambiguity paralleling the more blatant pamphlet literature. Involving the subtle manipulation of mythology and allegory within the boundaries of officially sanctioned genres, this strain has only begun to attract scholarly attention. Mild in comparison with the pamphlet literature, it avoided direct critique, while presenting alternatives to

13. Burke, *Fabrication of Louis XIV*, 135–50; Joseph Klaits, *Printed Propaganda under Louis XIV: Absolute Monarchy and Public Opinion* (Princeton: Princeton University Press, 1976), 17–26; Ferrier-Caverivière, *L'image de Louis XIV*, 306–50; Mueller, *Les idées politiques*, 187–89. Dunlop, *Louis XIV*, 156–57, following the chevalier de Quincy, author of *Maximes et instructions sur l'art militaire*, cites positive reviews of Louis XIV's treatment of the troops in the Low Countries campaign, but see Mueller, *Les idées politiques*, 189–93, for a different account of low morale and desertions. Negative perceptions of the campaign were exacerbated by the fact that Louis made his quarters in the greatest luxury and brought his wife and mistresses.

the absolutist program embedded within superficially innocent *loci amoeni*. Two of the most important of these were the mythological sites of Parnassus, home of the Muses, and Cythera, home of Venus and her cult of love. Both of these, fostered in the salons of mid-century Paris and in the fashionable chivalric novel, were common tropes familiar to a wide audience. They held the potential for opposition, however, in their implied protest against official control of the arts, and more specifically as it affected the artistic expression of personal sentiment and individual passion.

Marc Fumaroli's recent book on Jean de La Fontaine places the poet and fabulist at the center of this movement, along with the writers Madeleine de Scudéry, her brother Georges, and Paul Pellison in his early career.[14] Unlike the authors of the underground pamphlet literature, these writers, especially La Fontaine and Pellison, enjoyed a close personal relationship with the king, as well as official recognition. Their resistance operated in a complicated manner, at times incorporating effusive praise of the king while subtly challenging the imagery of royal propaganda from within. For example, whereas royal propaganda depicted the king as Apollo and the arts as his Muses, loyal in their devotion to his glory, La Fontaine calls on their sacred mountain of Parnassus as a symbol of the gulf between the king and the artistic community. Nostalgically recalling the reign of the Valois, he laments the separation of Parnassus and Olympus (respectively, the domains of the arts and political rule). From ancient times the sacred home of the Muses had been regarded as the site of poetic and artistic inspiration, and, since Dante, the image of Parnassus had represented an artistic community devoted to the highest principles of the arts and humanist thought. In the Renaissance, the image of Parnassus signified a refuge for poets and artists, a sanctuary for those creative spirits excluded from the avenues of power. La Fontaine's reference, despite royal propaganda to the contrary, clearly alludes to the alienation of the artists' community under Bourbon rule.[15]

The other site of resistance, Venus's island home of Cythera, may have originated with the Italian poet Giambattista Marino. Marino addressed his last poem, *Adone* (1623), written in France, to Marie de Médicis and her son Louis XIII. In a preface to his French version of the poem, its translator, Jean Chapelain, provides an important key to the poem's political meaning. Identifying Venus's island home of Cythera as a timeless symbol of transcendental beauty, he explains the death of Adonis, the mortal lover of

14. Fumaroli, *Le poète et le roi: Jean de La Fontaine et son siècle* (Paris: Fallois, 1997).

15. Ibid., chap. 1 ("L'Olympe et le Parnasse"), 41–105.

Venus, as a reflection on the tragic fragility of art amidst a world of human insensitivity. Chapelain goes on to interpret Marino's *Adone* as an invitation to Marie and Louis to bring to the barbaric kingdom of France a renewal of the civilized Epicureanism associated with Venus and the island of Cythera, and indirectly with Marino's own native country.[16] Marino's literary style, full of *concetti* or syntactic distortions for surprise effect, had a profound effect on his French followers, whose florid circumlocutions, known as *marinisme,* contributed to a vogue abating only under the onslaught of a classicizing reaction in the 1660s.

Marino's imagery, if not his manneristic idiom, was taken up by La Fontaine. In *L'Adonis* (1658), a long poem dedicated to Fouquet (and the sole copy of which was held in Fouquet's library), La Fontaine brings a shadowy Cytherean mystique into the French language. The work was directly modeled on Marino's *Adone,* and according to Fumaroli, anyone versed in literature would have recognized it as a renewal of Marino's aim after thirty years of what La Fontaine considered the political failure of the Bourbon regime. More specifically, the eventual triumph of Psyche and her union with Cupid would herald the future of France under the guidance of Fouquet as prime minister.[17]

The cult of love as espoused by La Fontaine and Scudéry has linkages with a more serious philosophy of pleasure developed by an early seventeenth-century group of philosophers and men of letters known as *libertins érudits,* or freethinkers. Returning by way of Montaigne and Rabelais to the authority of ancient Epicurean writers, they gathered around Pierre Gassendi (1592–1655), a Catholic priest and scientific thinker who blended a philosophy of Epicurean pleasure with the tenets of an Augustinian Christianity. These writers expressed a defiance of political authority and religious dogma bordering on heresy. Taking as their bible *De rerum natura* of the Hellenistic philosopher Lucretius, they couched an opposition to political violence in a devotion to the principle of love embodied in the goddess Venus.[18] Pellison, a friend of La Fontaine and one of Fouquet's closest associates, equated Venus with God as the source of love dwelling in all things. In addition to this ideological hedonism, Pellison also embraced a radical

16. Ibid., 210–11.

17. Ibid., 172–73; see also Marc Fumaroli, "Politique et poëtique de Venus: *L'Adone* de Marino et l'*Adonis* de La Fontaine," *Le fablier, revue des amis de Jean de La Fontaine* 5 (1993): 11–16.

18. At the beginning of *De rerum natura*, Lucretius invokes the goddess as the nurturing mother and the ultimate pleasure of mankind and the gods.

pantheism opposing the narrow interpretations of traditional Catholicism.[19] Later, Pellison was imprisoned for a time alongside Fouquet. After his release, he underwent a conversion to more conventional paths, and as Louis XIV's historiographer and author of his *Mémoires*, he served as one of the king's most enthusiastic panegyrists.

It made sense that those who opposed the king's ruthlessness in his treatment of Fouquet and those who regretted the loss of an artistic sensibility independent of monarchical aggrandizement would do so under the auspices of the goddess of love. Ancient philosophy had seen Aphrodite, and later Venus, as a symbol for the uniting of opposites, in contrast to her nemesis Discord, the goddess of separation and war. She did not figure much in Virgil's song of "arms and the man," and in Homer's *Odyssey* she intervened on the side of Paris, Helen, and the peace-loving Trojans in opposition to Athena and the warlike Greeks.[20] In addition, the celebration of Venus implied the advancement of a new form of art devoted to a softer aesthetic ideal. The goddess of love, more than any of the other deities of the pantheon, was associated with the essence of feminine beauty, and pilgrims came to her shrines not only as devotees of the goddess but also as devotees of art. Indeed, the two were inseparable, for the image of Venus had inspired some of the most renowned art of the ancient world. Associated with the cult of art that followed the goddess was the cult of sacral prostitution; in fact, prostitutes often served as models for ancient portraits of Venus. This art was condemned for its indecency by the Church Fathers. In its historical context, however, it represented an art of devotion to a legitimate matriarchal ideal.

In the early seventeenth century, both Venus and Orpheus figure in a mystical strain of libertine poetry drawing on hermetic Renaissance philosophies with links to pantheism and magical practices. Within a complex, veiled system this poetry subtly denounces all forms of uncontrolled force, whether as a result of political tyranny or of offensive militarism. The role played by Venus in this body of work, while sometimes couched in flippant allusions to carefree love, more deeply reflects a systematic philosophy linked to the force of love uniting all things in nature. Tristan L'Hermite's novel *Le page disgracié* suggests that the page's disgrace was due to a philosophy related to the cult of Venus and guided by a discourse of pleasure

---

19. Fumaroli, *Le poète et le roi*, 177.

20. Geoffrey Grigson, *The Goddess of Love: The Birth, Triumph, Death, and Return of Aphrodite* (London: Constable, 1976), 83–100.

as it challenged royal power.[21] His long poem *Orphée*, influenced by Marino's *Orfeo*, constitutes an apology for music as an occult thread promoting the secret unity of all things. It may also be seen as a defense of the artist as peacemaker, "giving birth to peace where formerly there was always war"[22] and as victim in the uneven struggle between art and power. Nonetheless Tristan describes the poet's role as a persistent effort to materialize the spiritual, thereby recovering the lost power of his ancestor Orpheus.[23]

Another critique of the monarchy in the early years of Louis XIV's reign may be found in the chivalric novel, which enjoyed a wide readership in seventeenth-century France.[24] An essentially aristocratic genre coming of age with the Fronde, the novel often combined a celebration of love with an implied critique of the policies of Mazarin and the king. Some novelists, including the sieur de Gomberville, Madeleine de Scudéry, and the seigneur de La Calprenède, turned from the glorification of battle during the Fronde to a more pacific tone at its close and, after the imprisonment of Fouquet, to a veiled criticism of Louis XIV. The most widely read and discussed novel of this genre was Scudéry's ten-volume *Artamène, ou le grand Cyrus* (1649–53). Written during the height of the Fronde, Scudéry's work follows the adventures of the Persian king Cyrus, a hero who has been compared to Le Grand Condé, uncle of Louis XIV and leader of the rebellion. The last volume of the work, whose publication coincided with the end of the war, included an inserted story entitled *L'histoire de Sapho*. On one level the story refers to the historical Sappho, the ancient poet of feminine passion and historical leader of a cult of Venus. On another, it represents a quasi-autobiographical portrayal of Scudéry herself, who inscribed in her work a discourse not only of passionate expression but also of implied resistance to the patriarchy of the crown. Scudéry sets her story on Sapho's island domain, characterized by a continual series of fêtes galantes involving promenades in pleasure

21. Doris Guillumette, *La libre pensée dans l'oeuvre de Tristan L'Hermite* (Paris: A. G. Nizet, 1972).

22. Tristan L'Hermite, "Orphée," in *Les amours et autres poésies choisies*, ed. Pierre Camo (Paris: Garnier frères, 1925), 146: "Faisoient naistre la paix où fut tousjours la guerre."

23. Hélène Albani, "Tristan L'Hermite, poète mariniste," *Revue des études italiennes* 13 (1967): 331–46; Cecilia Rizza, "L'*Orphée* di Tristan e l'*Orfeo* del Cavalier Marino," *Convivium* 22 (1954): 429–39; Guillumette, *La libre pensée*, 59, 91, 104, 141. On the connection between music and Renaissance hermetic practices, see Gary Tomlinson, *Music in Renaissance Magic: Toward a Historiography of Others* (Chicago: University of Chicago Press, 1993).

24. Discussed above in chapter 1.

boats, divertissements in wooded grottos by the sea, and disquisitions and conversations about love. In contrast to a world of death and dry desolation surrounding "those who follow the god Mars," Scudéry invests her island fantasy with images of life-giving water, reflecting the regenerative force of feminine pleasure, love, and diversion. Criticizing heroic, masculine talk of battle, wars, and great events as too lofty for human concern, she advocates the "little things," including love, pleasure, and diversion, and an art characterized by delicate emotion and sensitive nuance.[25]

Joan DeJean has interpreted Scudéry's novels in the period of the 1650s as a prescription for those women who formed part of a feminist opposition to the government of Louis XIV and the regent in the Fronde. No longer able to fight actively or to speak out against the crown, these women would find their only satisfaction in retirement (*repos*) from the artificial, pernicious life of the court. Like Sapho on her island retreat, they would retreat to their private salons, where they would keep alive the pleasures of the fête galante, of song and dance and conversation symbolizing a world of pleasure endangered by official control.[26]

Another figure who fits the archetypal model of revolutionary-turned-writer is the duchesse de Montpensier, La Grande Mademoiselle. Pardoned by Louis XIV, she had returned to Paris to live in the Luxembourg palace, the old home of Marie de Médicis, who was her grandmother and the king's. There she wrote two short novels, *La relation de l'isle imaginaire* and *La princesse de Paphlagonie*, both published in 1658, which pursued the utopian imagery initiated in the *Histoire de Sapho*. Just as Scudéry painted her own portrait as Sapho in *Artamène*, Montpensier (according to a key published at the end of the original edition of *L'isle imaginaire*) painted herself as queen of the Amazons, a similarly autobiographical role and one with direct reference to her own leadership in the Fronde. This role also intersects with Scudéry's *Story of Sapho*, in which Sapho is given shelter by the Queen of the Amazons, and thus indicates the solidarity of these two women utopians. Considering her own love of entertainment and her lav-

---

25. Scudéry, *The Story of Sapho*, ed. and trans. by Karen Newman, Other Voice in Early Modern Europe (Chicago: University of Chicago Press, 2003). Other writings of Scudéry have also been recently edited and translated by Jane Donawerth and Julie Strongson as *Selected Letters, Orations, and Rhetorical Dialogues*, Other Voice in Early Modern Europe (Chicago: University of Chicago Press, 2004). The original French version of *The Story of Sapho*, in the context of the larger novel, may be found as *L'histoire de Sapho*, in *Artamène ou le Grand Cyrus* (Paris, 1649–53; reprint, Geneva: Slatkine Reprints, 1972), 333.

26. DeJean, *Tender Geographies*, 60–66.

ish patronage before the Fronde, it is not surprising that Montpensier makes music, dance, and diversion de rigueur. More radically than her noble contemporaries, moreover, she especially promotes the low-culture arts of the people. Like other utopian novelists, she likens her imaginary island to an idealized republic, which she compares to the natural communities of the ants and the bees.[27]

In the novels of Scudéry and some of her contemporaries, the obsessive presence of metaphors of love and war far exceed the boundaries established by literary convention, reinforcing the possibility of a political interpretation equating the imagery of love with a political resistance to the policies of Richelieu, Mazarin, and later Louis XIV.[28] These novelists combine an emphasis on the games and strategies of love with a critique of historical figures known for their abuse of power, such as the Roman emperor Tarquinius in Scudéry's *Clélie* (1654–61). In other works, the most illustrious historical figures, standard surrogates for the king in royal publicity, are depicted as villains. In *Cassandre* (1642–58), La Calprenède depicts the conqueror Alexander as a vicious tyrant. Similarly, his *Cléopatre* (1647–58) depicts Augustus Caesar, the first Roman emperor and a model for French kings, as a hypocritical and cruel ruler, hated by a noble class in rebellion against imperial authority.[29] In other works, particularly those following in the aftermath of the Fronde, these authors turn from a more heroic orientation to decry the horrors of war and, through subtle allusion, defend a program characterized by an implied protest of the unnecessary use of force.[30]

In the early years of Louis XIV's court, the cult of the romanesque novel had paralleled and even served as the model for a seventeenth-century cult of chivalry. In fact, Louis himself, who had enjoyed these novels as a teenager, shared his contemporaries' enthusiasm for the fashion of love, convenient to his amorous propensities and those of a young, pleasure-loving court. He never completely divested himself of this mystique, but in the 1660s his own political identity shifted away from its path. Meanwhile, as we have seen in Scudéry's *Sapho* and in La Grande Mademoiselle's *Relation de l'isle imaginaire*, certain novelists who had previously glorified war and bat-

27. Mlle de Montpensier, *La relation de l'isle imaginaire* (Amsterdam: François Changuion, 1723), 46.

28. Mueller, *Les idées politiques*, 101.

29. Ibid., 127–48.

30. La Calprenède's *Faramond* (1661–70), written at the time of Louis XIV's invasion of the Low Countries, carries a particularly pacific tone. See Mueller, *Les idées politiques*, 189–93.

tle had by now moved in the opposite direction, deemphasizing the mythology of glory in order to foster a renewed, and in some cases oppositional, mythology of love and pleasure.

Disguised Cupids and the Contest between Love and Glory

Weaving through the rich texture of the court ballet, the dual voices of love and glory engage in a dialogue that ranges in tone from comfortable compatibility to shrill competition. Introduced in Benserade's *vers* for Louis XIV as a *curieux* in the *Ballet de la nuit*, the continuing juxtaposition of love and glory at times knits together and at other times opposes the patriarchal virtues of heroism, power, valor, and militarism and the galant virtues of beauty, love, pleasure, and refinement. The tragedies of Pierre Corneille had established *la gloire* as a synonym for duty and moral will; his noble protagonists had struggled between its claims and those of love and family responsibility. On the other side, the ideal of *l'amour* had drawn on the Neoplatonic celebration of love as the apex of spiritual attainment as well as political and cultural harmony. In the court ballet, as we have seen, the topos of glory served the royal image exclusively, while that of love served both royal and aristocratic interests. As a young man, Louis XIV took pride in his galanterie, his *politesse,* and his conquests in love, and in the larger sense of *l'amour* he took pride in the achievements of the arts and culture under his reign. The combination of glory and love in the person of the king, then, broadcast a kingdom that was at once powerful and civilized.

The construct of absolutism incorporated the virtues of love, along with its softer, more feminine qualities, as a way of humanizing the king and perhaps also of affirming the king's fertility after the anxiety-ridden barren years of Louis XIII and Anne of Austria, who took twenty-two years of marriage to produce a living male heir. At the same time, by its nature constrained to dominance, that construct demanded the subordination of love to glory. Therefore, Louis XIV's image came to incorporate love and pleasure but included the necessity of triumphing over them (perhaps also as a necessary antidote to Louis's actual sexual behavior). In a complex way, the triumph of glory over love broadcast the king's self-discipline and mastery over his emotions. In a larger sense it represented his dominance over his courtiers and the ultimate privileging of royal power over noble pleasure.

In the *Ballet des amours déguisés* (1664), these polarities find expression in the introductory dialogue between Venus, goddess of love, and Athena, goddess of wisdom and war. The anomalous tone of this work may perhaps be attributed to its librettist, the abbé de Perigny, tutor of the Dauphin and a newcomer to the ballet.[31] The prologue imported actors from the public theater of the Hôtel de Bourgogne, representing Venus and Athena in spoken declamation rather than in the customary musical *récit*. Anticipating the later opera prologues, the dialectic represented by Venus and Athena finds its synthesis at the end of the prologue, when both unite to praise the king. Here, however, the polarization is extreme and the unity is reluctant. Venus's denunciation of Athena is couched in strong language:

> This immortality paraded before our eyes
> Creates carnage and death everywhere,
> And among your warriors this cruel virtue,
> This noble fury that appears so beautiful to you,
> This bitter avidity for the blood of the unfortunate,
> It is by this that the epithet of "valorous" is acquired,
> Or by which, to put it more clearly, as many crimes are committed
> As at your bloody altars victims are offered;
> But all your conquerors, so idly vaunted,
> For all their long travails, for all their impiety,
> For all the blood spilled on an oppressed land,
> What can they show, except a bit of nothing called Renown?[32]

The ballet proper consists of a series of entries in which Venus displays to Mercury a panorama of the covert activities of her cupids, masked in various disguises, in the service of the goddess and other gods, including her lover Mars, her husband Vulcan, and Pluto. In the first entry, in the employ of the blacksmith god Vulcan, they are seen forging cupids' arrows rather than other armaments, with their headbands protecting their ears from the

31. There is some confusion over the distribution of responsibility for the texts of this ballet. Benserade probably wrote the *vers*, and the abbé Buti—the librettist for Rossi's *Orfeo* and Cavalli's *Ercole amante*—may have contributed the Italian portions. See Harris-Warrick, "Introduction" to Lully, *Oeuvres complètes*, ed. Jérôme de La Gorce and Herbert Schneider (Hildesheim: Georg Olms, 2001), 1: xxvii.

32. Canova-Green, *Benserade: Ballets pour Louis XIV*, 2: 648: "Cette immortalite qu'on estale a nos yeux / Fait porter le carnage & la mort en tous lieux, / Et parmy vos guerriers cette vertu cruelle, / Cette noble fureur qui vous paroist si belle, / Cette aspre auidite du sang des malheureux, / C'est par ou l'on acquiert le nom de valeureux, / Ou par qui, pour mieux dire, on fait autant de crimes / Qu'a vos sanglans autels on offre de victimes; / Mais tous ces conquerans, si flement vantez, / Pour de si longs trauaux, pour tant d'impietez, / Pour tant de sang verse sur la terre opprimee, / Qu'ont-ils ? qu'un peu de vent, qu'on nomme Renommee?"

noise of the anvils. In the second and third entries, disguised as oarsmen, they turn the heart of Mark Anthony from military ambition to love, as he retreats with his lover Cleopatra from their sea battle with Augustus Caesar. In the entries that follow, Pluto, fearing that his demons will not show proper respect, borrows the cupids to aid in the abduction of Persephone. Later, they assume the guise of marine gods and nymphs in order to aid Jason's abandoned lover Isiphile. Disguised as musicians/shepherds, the cupids perform a *récit* fashioned to prevent the hero Rinaldo (Renaut) from abandoning the sorceress Armida (Armide). Finally, a group of cupids actually mutiny against the interest of Venus, in aiding Menelaus and the Greeks against the goddess's favored Trojans. This event brings the entry, and the finale of the work, back to the traditional theorem of the supremacy of *la gloire* over *l'amour*, and its corollary of the supremacy of Western patriarchy over eastern exoticism. The ending thus echoes the ultimate victory of Augustus Caesar over the lovers Anthony and Cleopatra and that of the hero Rinaldo over the sorceress Armida.

The music of the ballet reflects its ideological polarities. The prologue (LWV 21/2), a "combat between different [types of] music," introduces a face-off between fourteen musicians representing the followers of Athena and eight representing the followers of Venus. The larger group is identified as "the Virtues and the Arts," appropriate to Athena's association with chastity and her patronage of the household arts; the smaller group is identified as the "Graces and the Pleasures," allegorical companions to Venus. Each group consisted of string players from *les petits violons*, supplemented by three wind players.[33] Although information as to the precise instruments of these wind players is lacking, the score does specify "flûtes" (a term generally referring to recorders in this period) for Venus's followers, reflecting a time-honored association of Venus and Cupid with both the recorder and the transverse flute.[34] Athena's followers perform a lively passage in 3/4, alternating with a slower, sarabande-like rhythm performed by Venus's followers (see ex. 2.1). Venus's music also contains the exoticism of

33. Rebecca Harris-Warrick, "Notes on Performance," in Lully, *Oeuvres complètes*, ed. Jérôme de La Gorce and Herbert Schneider (Hildesheim: Georg Olms, 2001), 1: xxxiii.

34. Edward E. Lowinsky traces the historical connection between Venus and the flute in *Cipriano de Rore's Venus Motet: Its Poetic and Pictorial Sources* (Provo, UT: College of Fine Arts and Communications, Brigham Young University, 1986), 22–29. For associations of Venus with the "pipe" (also probably a recorder) in England, see Amanda Eubanks Winkler, "'O ravishing delight': The Politics of Pleasure in *The Judgment of Paris*," *Cambridge Opera Journal* 15 (2003): 22.

Example 2.1. Lully, *Ballet des amours déguisés*, followers of Athena and Venus [Symphonie des Arts, des Grâces & des Plaisirs], LWV 21/2. Bibliothèque nationale de France, Collection Philidor, Rés. F 511, 2–3, mm. 1–17.

an upward-climbing chromatic line, in contrast to the diatonic simplicity of Athena's music. In a rare indication of dynamics, Athena's music, a tutti of sorts, is designated as "the louder" of the two ensembles, with Venus's music, performed by the smaller, concertino-like group, as "the softer."[35]

35. Canova-Green, *Benserade: Ballets pour Louis XIV*, 2: 643: "The scene opens with a combat between two different types of music: the louder is composed of the Arts and Virtues who follow Minerva [Pallas]; and the softer, of the Graces and Pleasures who accompany Venus" (Le Theatre s'ouure par vn combat de deux differentes Harmonies; La plus forte est composée des Arts & des Vertus qui suiuent Pallas; & la plus douce, des Graces & des Plaisirs, qui accompagnent Venus).

Example 2.1. (*continued*)

6   *Les Grâces & les Plaisirs (à parties simples)*

Les Arts (tout le monde)

In the entry of Rinaldo and Armida, the cupids disguised as shepherds present a pastoral *concert des bergers* (LWV 21/15) to persuade Rinaldo and his warriors to turn to the side of love. This divertissement featured eighteen of Louis XIV's court musicians (twelve strings and six woodwinds, probably double-reed instruments),[36] costumed as shepherds and performing onstage. Later in this entry, an instrumental air (LWV 21/24) accompanies a dance for *les petits amours* (the little cupids, as opposed to the adult form of the god in the other entries), frightened by the destruction of Armida's palace. Scored for four recorders in different registers, this air was one

36. Harris-Warrick, "Notes on Performance," xxxiv.

Example 2.1. (*continued*)

of a suite of dances performed by children of the court. To the pastoral innocence of this entry, with its shepherds and child-cupids, the spectacular
destruction of the palace provides a stark contrast. In the final entry (LWV
21/33), martial fanfares announce the victory of the Greeks over the Trojans
and the final victory of Athena over Venus.

Reflecting the ideological intensity of the *livret*, the entries of Anthony
and Cleopatra and of Armida and Rinaldo represent unprecedented climactic expressions of love in the face of glory. In the first, a reenactment of the
battle of Actium, Mark Anthony abandons the field of battle in order to follow Cleopatra in retreat. His *récit* makes a poignant defense of *l'amour* at the
expense of *la gloire*:

To my love I have sacrificed my glory,
Never was a lover so transported,
I have done more, in making you believe it,
And to that end I have divested myself
Of empire and victory.[37]

The duet of Anthony and Cleopatra, composed by Lambert (LWV 21/7),[38] at once laments their political fate and celebrates their personal victory. This piece, employing the supple lines and subtle rhythms of the *air sérieux*, creates an emotional peak in its passionate tone. Its descending chromatic bass and melodic dissonance underscore Cleopatra's words, "Hélas qu'avez-vous fait, / Amant fidelle, Amant parfait!"

In entries 6–9, the refusal of the hero Rinaldo to give in to Armida's love provides a turning point and climax of the work as a whole, culminating in the spectacular destruction of her palace. Whereas Lambert's dialogue air for Anthony and Cleopatra exemplifies French expressiveness, Lully's multipartite *récit italien* for Anna Bergerotti as Armida employs an Italian style contributing to a passionate rhetoric of desire (ex. 2.2). The opening lament (LWV 21/20), structured as a da capo aria, contrasts an A section in G minor, passing through B-flat and C minor, with a B section in B-flat. The A section opens with a chromatically inflected octave descent, over which the melody, set to the text "Ah, Rinaldo, e dove sei?" first droops to the dominant, then sighs into a downbeat rest followed by a whole note tied over the bar line. The phrase is repeated twice, first climbing to a high point on f, then, after an octave leap into a 7-6 suspension, descending again to G minor. The B section climbs chromatically, first in the voice, then in the bass line as the melody reaches its climax in Armida's realization that even her pain cannot keep her beloved with her. The lament ends with an exact return of the A section. Together with the following series of arias punctuated by recitative-like sections, the *récit* demonstrates a mastery of the mid-century Italian cantata style, which—hardly extreme by Italian standards—stands in stark contrast to the French idiom of the remainder of the ballet.

Les amours déguisés, then, points up the antagonism of love and glory as they serve the propaganda of the king. The final victory of Rinaldo and, at the

---

37. Canova-Green, *Benserade: Ballets pour Louis XIV*, 2: 659: "A mon amour j'ay fait ceder ma gloire, / Jamais Amant ne fut si transporté, / I'ay fait plus, je vous l'ay fait croire, / Et par la me suis raquite / De l'Empire & de la Victoire."

38. Massip, *L'art de bien chanter*, 249, supports Lecerf de la Viéville's attribution of the handful of airs containing *doubles* in the court ballet to Lambert.

Example 2.2. Lully, *Ballet des amours déguisés*, lament of Armida [Récit italien chanté par la Signora Anna], LWV 21/20. Bibliothèque nationale de France, Collection Philidor, Rés. F 511, 43–45, mm. 16–62.

Example 2.2. (*continued*)

end of the ballet, of the Greeks reassured its audience that, combining both qualities in his royal person, Louis would not allow the softness of love to intrude on the demands of glory. Nevertheless, the conflicting ideologies of the ballet, while still yoked together in their service to the king, take on an intensity unmatched in any of the other court ballets Perhaps as an antidote to this intensity, the ballet of the following year, *La naissance de Vénus* (LWV 27), brings the aims of the king more into alignment with the goddess of love and with the noble galanterie that served as the aesthetic and ideological basis of the court ballet. The focus on Venus and love may be explained in part by the ballet's celebration of Henriette d'Angleterre, Louis's sister-in-law and current object of his affections, who danced the role of Venus. In a more political

sense, the realignment of monarchical interests with a mythology of galanterie could also be seen as healing the rift between noble love and absolutist
glory. In a striking scene change toward the end of the work, the temple of
Venus at Paphos appeared, and its doors opened to reveal a statue of the goddess. Priests scattered rose petals on her altar, before which six poets of antiquity knelt, offering their books and laurel crowns in dedication to Venus.

In *La naissance de Vénus*, Louis XIV danced the role of Alexander the
Great paying tribute to the goddess of love, a role allowing him to be depicted as the perfect lover without sacrificing the ideals of heroism and glory.
According to the *vers* written by Benserade, the galant finesse for which
Louis's court was famous included a willingness, unknown to the ancients,
to use the fruits of war for the purposes of peace. Throughout the ballet, the
masculine authority of Alexander is softened by the sensual world of Venus, Cupid, and their pastoral pleasures. The propaganda of the ballet had
a twofold purpose. On the one hand, it presented a balanced image of Louis
as both military conqueror and chivalrous lover. On the other, it justified
Louis's propensity for extramarital affairs. The effectiveness of the role of
a galant Alexander in accomplishing this purpose may have influenced Racine's play *Alexandre le grand*, first produced at the end of the same year.[39]
The heavy dose of galanterie in Racine's play has also been interpreted as an
attempt on the part of Louis XIV's own artists to remind the king of his responsibilities to a more civilized culture.[40]

The Muses of Memory

The following year's *Ballet des Muses*, first produced at Saint-Germain-en-
Laye on December 2, 1666, received many performances in widely differing
versions before the carnival season ended on February 19, 1667. The work,

39. The relationship of the two works deserves study. The ballet was first produced in
January 1665, the play in the following December. However, *Alexandre le grand* was well under way by January 1665, when Racine read three and a half acts aloud at the salon of Mme du
Plessis Guénégaud at the Hôtel de Nivers. It is possible that the two works, simultaneously in
progress in late 1664 and early 1665, had some mutual influence, though given the association
of Louis XIV with Alexander since birth, and the vogue of the *tragédie galant*, the character-
ization seems almost inevitable. See Georges Forestier's preface to *Alexandre le grand* (Racine, *Oeuvres complètes*, vol. 1 [Paris: Gallimard, 1999], 1277), for a summary of the propagandistic advantages it afforded. See also his *Jean Racine* (Paris: Gallimard, 2006), 229–33, for a
discussion of its *héroïsme galant*.

40. Fumaroli, *Le poète et le roi*, 114–16.

representing the apex of the court ballet and a tour de force of French theatrical entertainment, frames courtly pleasure with sovereign praise in a complex structure representing a compendium of different artistic genres.[41] It is introduced as a living memorial to Louis XIV's glory by the character Mnemosine (Memory), whose daughters, the Muses, have forsaken Parnassus for his court. The imposing opening dialogue between Mnemosine and the Muses (LWV 32/2, ex. 2.3) states the theme of the ballet, the role of the arts and artists in the service of Louis's propaganda. Mnemosine (sung by the soprano Hilaire Dupuis) sets out the awesome responsibility of the Muses for publishing that propaganda to the ends of the earth:

> Living under his leadership,
> Muses, in your concerts,
> Sing what he has done, sing what he contemplates,
> And carry the sound of it to the end of the universe.
> In this delightful *récit* unceasingly make the French Empire understand
> What it has to hope for,
> Make the whole world understand what it has to admire,
> Make kings understand what they have to learn.[42]

In response, the four-part choir of nine Muses (composed of pages from the king's Musique de la Chambre and Musique de la Chapelle) voice an idealized acceptance of this charge. Their chorus (LWV 32/3) is based on multiple repetitions of two basic textual premises, corresponding to the two musical sections of the work. The first, "Let us submit to his laws,/It is good to follow them" (Rangeons-nous sous ses loix/Il est beau de les suivre) represents an acceptance of Mnemosine's charge, and of the "laws" of Louis's propaganda which the Muses are bound to follow. The music of this section, introduced by voices and continuo alone and repeated with string accompaniment, proceeds in stately syllabic homophony, dotted rhythms, and grounded root-position triads centered on a tonality of G minor. The second section, a musical extension of the first in G major, sets out the reward promised

41. The performance history and editorial problems resulting from its many versions are discussed in James Anthony, "More Faces than Proteus: Lully's *Ballet des Muses,*" *Early Music* 15 (1987): 336–44.

42. Canova-Green, *Benserade: Ballets pour Louis XIV*, 2: 736: "Vivant sous sa conduite, / Muses, dans vos Concerts / Chantez ce qu'il a fait, chantez ce qu'il médite, / Et portez-en le bruit au bout de l'Univers. / Dans ce récit charmant faites sans cesse entendre / A l'Empire François ce qu'il doit esperer, / Au monde entier ce qu'il doit admirer, / Aux Roys ce qu'ils doiuent aprendre."

Example 2.3. Lully, *Ballet des Muses,* chorus of Muses, LWV 32/3. Bibliothèque nationale de France, Collection Philidor, Rés. F 521, 7–14.

by this contract with the king: "Nothing is so sweet as to live at the court of Louis XIV, the most perfect of kings" (Rien n'est si doux que de vivre/À la cour de Louis le plus parfait des Roys). This text—like the first, a series of regular dactylic feet set in an emphatic triple meter—is stated first by the *basses,* then by all four parts in alternation with the strings. The section, gathering momentum with repetitions of the last line of text, reaches a high

Example 2.3. (*continued*)

point in m. 42 at the final repetition of the words, "most perfect of kings." Throughout this section, the words "cour" and "Roys," along with the second syllable of "Lou-is," are repeatedly emphasized, underscoring the identity of Louis's name with the court and with kingship. The melody of the entire chorus traverses a narrow range that, along with the artful use of dactylic rhythms adhering to a comparatively regular phrase structure, can be

Example 2.3. (*continued*)

Example 2.3. (*continued*)

Example 2.3. (*continued*)

easily comprehended and retained. Given the repetition within each section, not to mention a full repeat of the entire chorus, there is little doubt that this chorus would have indelibly branded the tangible name, as well as the more ineffable *gloire* of the monarch, on the collective memory of its audience.

Jean-Marie Apostolidès, in a discussion of what he calls *le mythistoire*, has tracked a shift in Louis XIV's propaganda in the 1660s, from an emphasis on

Example 2.3. *(continued)*

classical imperial imagery, as seen in the carrousel of 1662, to a new awareness of the supremacy of French culture over the ancient heritage of Greece
and Rome. That supremacy had been debated since the sixteenth century,
most notably in the quarrels of the Ancients and the Moderns, and in the
1660s the king's image-makers exploited the "modern" position to propa-
gandize how France under Louis XIV had progressed beyond the models of

Example 2.3. (*continued*)

the ancients.[43] The *Ballet des Muses,* therefore, draws not so much on classical imperial imagery as on the image of a French empire, superior to both
ancient and contemporary European powers and cultures. The Muses' cho-

43. Apostolidès, *Le roi-machine,* 66–92. On the quarrel of the Ancients and the Moderns,
see Georgia Cowart, *The Origins of Modern Musical Criticism: Quarrels over French and Italian
Music, 1600–1750* (Ann Arbor: UMI Research Press, 1981), 27–48.

Example 2.3. (*continued*)

rus sets up the imperial supremacy of Louis XIV and France, while the entries, showcasing the art of each of the nine Muses respectively (see table
2.1), constitute a panoramic spectacle representing the supremacy of the arts
in seventeenth-century France. The work therefore represents a model for
understanding the place of the arts at Louis XIV's court, especially in their
relationship to Louis XIV's "modern" imperialist agenda. In the portion
of the ballet devoted to Clio (History), the role of Alexander, danced by

TABLE 2.1. Structure of Entries in the *Ballet des Muses*

Muse	Entry
Urania (astronomy)	Noble dancers' costume parade (reflects brilliance of stars)
Melpomene (tragedy)	Pantomime of tragic myth of Pyramus and Thisbe
Thalia (comedy)*	Inserted comédie-ballet by Molière and Lully: *Mélicerte* (later replaced by *La pastorale comique*)
Euterpe (pastoral, music)	Pastoral danced by king and courtiers as shepherds and shepherdesses
Clio (history)	Pantomime of Alexander's victory over, and mercy to, Porrus
Calliope (poetry)*	Inserted comedy *Les poètes* by Philippe Quinault. Includes Spanish masquerade by Spanish troupe, Louis XIV, and courtiers
Erato (love poetry)	King and nobles appear as heroes of chivalric novels
Polymnia (rhetoric)*	Comic actors from Comédie-Italienne and Hôtel de Bourgogne, spoof on ancient Greek philosophers and Latin orators
Terpsichore (dance)	Dance of fauns and Amazons
Epilogue: *Le Sicilien**	Comédie-ballet by Molière and Lully

NOTE: asterisk signifies inserted entertainment.

Beauchamps, again illustrates the qualities of the king as ruler.[44] The entry, drawing on the historical Alexander's mercy toward Porrhus and his Indian forces, illustrates both the military might of Louis/Alexander and his magnanimity.

The ballet as a whole demonstrates Louis XIV's rule over an empire of the arts as a natural corollary to his rule over the political empire of Europe and the Indies. Within this imperialistic program, the Muses are reduced to royal flatterers, with the arts they represent—like the imperial conquests of Louis XIV's ambitions—subject to a policy of conquest, control, and containment. In order to illustrate this artistic imperialism, the creators of the ballet augmented the traditional entries with guest appearances of the

44. Rose Pruiksma suggests, in a private conversation, that since Beauchamps was also Louis's personal dancing master, he served as a double of the king's body in a certain sense.

major theater companies of France, all now under royal patronage. One of these featured Scaramouche and his colleagues Arlequin and Valerio from the Parisian theater of the commedia dell' arte, in an improvised farce with French actors of the Hôtel de Bourgogne. Lully joined forces with Molière to produce two inserted comédie-ballets: *La pastorale comique* (LWV 33)[45] and *Le Sicilien* (LWV 34). All these widely varied imported entertainments— from whimsical to burlesque to galant—are loosely contained in the framework of absolutist praise provided by the Muses.

In these early years of his reign, Louis XIV was still identified with Apollo, leader of the Muses, and his propaganda drew on two important facets of that mythology. One was the association of his image with artistic patronage, a primary attribute of sovereign power. The other had to do with the Muses' lineage as daughters of Jupiter and Mnemosine, which made them the ideal vehicle for memorializing the deeds of kings. At the end of the *Ballet des Muses*, a contest between the Muses and the Pierides underscores the victory of the arts of absolutism over other types of art. The scene is based on the myth in which the Pierides, daughters of Pierius living near the sacred mountain of the Muses, challenge the Muses to an artistic contest. In this symbolic contest between human and divine, the Muses defeat the Pierides and transform them into croaking magpies as a punishment for their temerity. The ballet draws on the same symbolism, representing the Pierides as "human" agents—that is, artists not affiliated with official propaganda—who might challenge that official agenda.

As in the *Ballet des amours déguisés*, a voice of lament may also be heard in the *Ballet des Muses*, in a remarkable *concert et récit d'Orphée* (LWV 32/19-20) that featured Lully as Orpheus and Hilaire Dupuis (who had also sung the role of Mnemosine) as a nymph witnessing his distress.[46] As Orpheus, Lully spills out his passion in an expressive, chromatically inflected lament for violin. Based on an Italianate lyricism combined with the rhythms of the sarabande, associated with erotic desire, this remarkable piece also anticipates the violin concerto in its extensive juxtaposition of passages for the soloist, accompanied by continuo, with the larger orchestra. The stage di-

---

45. *La pastorale comique* apparently replaced Molière's unfinished comédie-ballet, *Mélicerte*, originally planned for the work.

46. This piece is discussed by La Gorce, *Jean-Baptiste Lully*, 448–51; and Beaussant, *Lully ou le musicien du soleil*, 332–41. Beaussant, quoting Robinet who asserts that "Lully dances while playing" (Lully danse en jouant), believes that Lully would have pantomimed the action of the scene while performing on the violin (338).

rections directly allude to the emotional quality of this scene, proclaiming a range of emotion extending from "languishing sadness" to "violent anger." Though Orpheus speaks only through the passionate tones of his instrument, the nymph voices his inner thoughts in an embedded air attributed to Lambert, in which the violin part continues as an obbligato. The text portrays Orpheus's distress in not being able to express his love, and in being torn between a Cupid who is too indiscreet and a duty that is too demanding. The *double* copied by Philidor as an appendix presents a lavish variation of the vocal part.[47] The text of the *double* underlines the theme of stifled expression, ending with the words, "It is the greatest pain to love when one cannot say [express] it" (Le plus grand des malheurs c'est d'aymer quand on ne le peut dire).

Referring enigmatically to the "secrets of his heart,"[48] the stage directions for this scene describe Orpheus's emotions as intense and passionate, in stark contrast to the remainder of the work. Benserade's *vers* for Lully as Orpheus are unusual, not only in being addressed to a nonnoble, but also in their division into two completely different sets of verses. One presents a more conventional *vers de personnage,* the other an impassioned "unsung" text, serving as an interpretation of Lully's solo performance. This "unsung" text represents a dramatic voicing of the anguished desire to be rescued by Cupid as the ruler of a parallel, benign universe and, failing that, an intention to remain silent in the face of force and violence. In all, these *vers* reinforce a view of Lully as one constrained to silence, or to the translation of the passionate "secrets of his heart" into a transcendent wordless music:

> Alas, what I wish is not so difficult,
> I only wish to touch a heart and make it tender.
> No, I do not pretend that Cupid through my voice
> Will come to constrain nature and its laws,

47. The *Ballet des Muses* may be found in the Philidor collection of the Bibliothèque nationale, Rés. 521, pp. 68–76 (with the *double* included as an appendix on p. 104), and on the Gallica Web site at http://gallica.bnf.fr/ark:/12148/bpt6k103673d. The *livret* of the ballet is generally attributed to Benserade; however, Manuel Couvreur, in "La collaboration de Quinault et Lully avant la Psyché de 1671" (*Recherches sur la musique française classique* 27 [1992]: 9–34), attributes the text of the air and other portions of the ballet to Quinault. A manuscript at the Bibliothèque municipale de Versailles (manuscrit musical 86) names Lully as Orphée.

48. Canova-Green, *Benserade: Ballets pour Louis XIV,* 2: 766.

:nce are necessary,

ilence.[49]

a tribute to the power of music, isolated
point of the *Ballet des Muses,* and also
lly as Orphic oracle—hinted at in the
composer and performer. Probably the
for this strikingly unusual passage was
1s, following his difficulties with bring-
ed the love of women and was tradition-
troduced sodomy into Greece.[50] Lully's
nce with a group of libertine writers and
<ness as their trademark will be discussed
Ballet des Muses, Orpheus's *récit* presents
a salient contrast to the opening chorus of the Muses. Whereas the chorus
affirms the Muses' identity as the disseminators of royal propaganda, based
on the word, Orpheus's music represents a noumenal, wordless ideal. Combined with the expressive, ornamental nature of the nymph's *double,* it may
be understood in two ways. On one side, it fulfills the premise of the *Ballet
des Muses,* by demonstrating the achievements of the arts under Louis XIV
and by exhibiting the power of music, which according to Neoplatonic theory was thought to align the aims of the ruler with his kingdom and with a
beneficent world harmony. At the same time, however, it strains against that
older conception through its representation of the artist's aims, centered on
a private subjectivity, as essentially different from the exigencies of royal
propaganda. Indeed, Orpheus's claim to silence in a world of force and violence may be seen as undermining, if not defying, Mnemosine's directive to
"Sing what he has done, sing what he contemplates,/And carry the sound
of it to the ends of the universe." Further significance may be found in the
reversal of gender roles in these two entries of the ballet. While the Muses
speak through a chorus of male voices (though written for pages, the four
parts include the standard lower voices of *basse* and *taille*), Orpheus/Lully
speaks not only through the feminine voice of the nymph, but also through

49. Ibid., 2: 788: "Helas ce que je veux n'est pas si difficile, / Ie ne veux que toucher un
coeur & l'atendrir. / Non je ne prétens point que l'Amour par ma voix / Vienne contraindre
icy la Nature & ses loix, / S'il y faut de la force & de la violance, / J'ayme mieux le Silence."

50. Judith Peraino, *Listening to the Sirens: Musical Technologies of Queer Identity from
Homer to Hedwig* (Berkeley: University of California Press, 2006), 24–25.

an ornamented style that in this period held associations with the feminized space of the salon.[51]

The Gardens of Flora

The pompous tone of the prologue to the *Ballet des Muses* is maintained and even heightened in portions of the *Ballet de Flore* (LWV 40, 1669), the last of the series of court ballets in the late 1660s. In the spirit of image making brought to an apogee by the artists of the ballet, the work cast the king in the role of the Sun, the beneficent source of fruition and abundance. This role itself served as a climax to the succession of sun-related roles Louis had danced and to the long history of the association of kings of France (including Henry II, Henry IV, and Louis XIII) with an iconography of the sun. The prologue of the work proclaims its message from the outset: "This ballet taken in its allegorical sense marks the peace that the king has recently given to Europe, the abundance and happiness with which he crowns his subjects, and the respect that all peoples of the earth have for His Majesty."[52] The following entries of the ballet begin with festivities honoring Flora, moving into a series of disparate scenes with a common topos of flowers. The work culminates in a grand ballet (LWV 40/33–39), in which native Americans, Asians, and Europeans pay homage to the fleur-de-lis, emblem of the Bourbon kings. The performance of this multimovement finale, a prototype for the *grande musique* of the future opera, featured forty-four stringed instruments, eight woodwinds, and two *trompettes allemandes*. Both the king's string groups were deployed in the four quadrilles that represented the four corners of the earth, the *grands violons* as the European and Persian quadrilles, the *petits violons* as the African and American.[53]

The external structure of this ballet, more conventional than the sprawling succession of stages-within-stages of the *Ballet des Muses*, still moves beyond the earlier court ballet in its large quantity of vocal music. In addi-

51. For a discussion of the split between voice and logos found in wordless singing and its association with both Orpheus and a specifically feminine voice, see Carolyn Abbate, *In Search of Opera* (Princeton: Princeton University Press, 2001), "Orpheus: One Last Performance," 1–54, 70–71. I am indebted to Susan McClary (private conversation) for the image of the composer clothed in the ornamental filigree of salon preciosity.

52. Ibid., 2: 829: "Ce Ballet pris en son sens allégorique marque la Paix que le Roy vient de donner à l'Europe, l'abondance & le bonheur dont il comble ses sujets, & le respect qu'ont pour sa Majesté tous les Peuples de la Terre."

53. Harris-Warrick, "Notes on Performance," xxxiii.

tion to its dances, a series of airs, vocal ensembles, and choruses points toward the tragédie en musique of the following decade. This prototype, like its operatic counterpart, relies on an increased textuality that, while not replacing visual spectacle, provided a different kind of avenue for monarchical propaganda. The *Ballet de Flore*, operatic in its scope and in its verbal message, was the last ballet in which Louis XIV appeared in a dancing role and indeed the last of the series of court ballets until the genre was revived sporadically, beginning in the 1680s.[54]

In the midst of its paean to Louis XIV, the *Ballet de Flore* contains another extraordinary lament, sung by Venus for her mortal lover Adonis (LWV 40/23). Based on a French text, it weaves the musical language of the Italian lament, replete with chromatic bass, dissonant melodic intervals, and affective rests, into the fabric of the French style. Like the earlier *récit* of Armida, this passage is multipartite and contains Italianate inflections, but the language and structure remain French. The ornamented *double* of the work (probably by Lambert) represents a florid style increasingly out of fashion in the classicizing atmosphere of the late court ballet. Set against its syllabic choruses and *récits*, like the laments of the *Ballet des amours déguisés* and the *Ballet des Muses*, this *double* contributes melismatic floridity to a musical language of passionate intensity.

The Triumph of Glory and the Laments of Love

Emerging out of the kaleidoscopic world of the ballet, then, a new lamenting voice is heard in three works produced between 1664 and 1669. This voice—occurring at rare moments of heightened emotional intensity—draws on two very different musical sources: an Italian chromatic idiom, dramatic and filled with dissonance, and a more delicate idiom based on the florid ornamentation of the *air sérieux* of Lambert, by now rare in the court ballet. It belongs primarily to vocalists representing lovers. There are four examples of this style, which hold in common an intense expressive passion absent from the remainder of these ballets: the love duet of Anthony and Cleopatra (*Ballet des amours déguisés*) and the laments of Armida (*Ballet des amours déguisés*), Orpheus (*Ballet des Muses*), and Venus (*Ballet de Flore*). Cleopatra, Armida, and Venus represent a feminine voluptuousness and softness either repudiated by or subordinated to more patriarchal virtues by

---

54. Apostolidès, *Le roi-machine*, 60, sees the beginning of this process in the heightened emphasis on text in the *livrets* of Benserade in the beginning of Louis XIV's reign.

Louis in the 1660s. Two of these women are victimized by a specific figure representing patriarchal glory: Anthony and Cleopatra by Augustus Caesar, and Armida by Rinaldo. Further, Venus's lament for Adonis in the *Ballet de Flore* recalls Marino and La Fontaine, who earlier presented Venus's love for Adonis as the earthly manifestation of a Neoplatonic love amidst a world of violence and destruction. In that sense, the lament of Venus—the emotional climax of the ballet—resonates with the symbolic loss of a world of art and beauty upon the advent of Bourbon rule. This entry, a celebration of the iconic metamorphosis of Adonis into the blood-red anemone, stands in sharp contrast to the final *grand ballet* celebrating the white fleur-de-lis of the Bourbon dynasty. Finally, the figure of Orpheus, as discussed above in regard to the poetry of Tristan, embodied the quintessential artist/peacemaker and simultaneous victim of political oppression.

All of these characters bear features of an eastern, orientalizing character setting them apart from the Roman model of imperial domination to which the Bourbon dynasty aspired. As Geoffrey Burgess calls the sorceress in later operatic settings, these figures may be seen as the Other of sovereignty.[55] The potent combination of exoticism, eros, and lament hints at a potential political opposition that is powerfully felt but lacks clear definition. In this regard, the roles of Cleopatra and Armida are prototypical, but Venus and Orpheus, too, were associated with eastern exoticism. The worship of Aphrodite had arisen with the importation of the Sumerian Inanna, who entered Greece via the Babylonians, the Assyrians, and finally the Phoenicians. Venus, more eastern in origin than the rest of the Olympian pantheon, was always associated with a flavor of exoticism, unlike such deities as Apollo and Athena, embodiments of moderation and reason.[56] Likewise, the cult of Orpheus had originated in the eastern region of Thrace. The ecstatic inspiration integral to its origins and dissemination made Orpheus a symbol of expressive passion embodying an ideal directly opposed to Greek rationalism.

The use of these potentially oppositional figures in Louis XIV's court ballet reflects strategies overlapping with those of the contemporary literature discussed above. As we have seen, in contemporary poetry and the novel, the topos of love, a common literary trope, had at times begun to take

---

55. "Ritual in the Tragédie en musique: From Lully's *Cadmus et Hermione* (1673) to Rameau's *Zoroastre* (1749)" (Ph.D. diss., Cornell University, 1999), 359–429.

56. Grigson, *Goddess of Love*, 27. The association of Venus with the attribute of the dove derives from Inanna.

on a political dimension. In the court ballet, love and glory were deployed most commonly as two facets of the royal image, but the imagery and ideology of the court ballet paralleled and at times intersected those of the literature discussed above. Therefore, to represent Venus, Orpheus, Cleopatra, and Armida as victims of characters identified with the monarchy could serve both the interests of the king and those of his critics. From the official point of view, the submission of love to glory represented the king as adhering to superior patriarchal values. At the same time, the defeat of these archetypal lovers at the hands of rulers and warriors could represent the threatening encroachment of absolutist ideals, echoing the novel's critique of the crown.

Both these points of view reflected and responded to an increasing politicization and centralization of the arts, largely through the mechanism of royal academies, through which the king and his ministers had begun to wield an unprecedented artistic control. That process had begun earlier in the century with the founding of the Académie française in 1634 and the Académie royale de peinture et de sculpture in 1648. In 1661 the Académie royale de danse appeared, to be followed shortly by the Académie royale de musique in 1669 and the Académie royale d'architecture in 1671. In 1663, the Petite académie (later the Académie royale des médailles et des inscriptions) was formed as a means of controlling the king's image across a wide spectrum of artistic enterprises. Like the Muses in the prologue to the *Ballet des Muses*, the academies dictated taste in the service of the king's *gloire*. These vast projects of centralization in Paris resonate with Benserade's depiction of the Muses as having left Parnassus to live at the court of Louis XIV. Like the Muses, the work of the actual artists in Louis's service was to create for posterity the image of "the most perfect of kings," with the promise of opportunities and compensations that came with serving the arts that flourished at court. In the commerce of that exchange, however, artists would accrue to themselves an unprecedented potential not only for shaping that image but also for undermining it. In the ballets surveyed in this chapter, that potential may be seen primarily in the vehicle of the lament. In the years immediately following, as well as throughout the remainder of the century, it would be seen primarily in the vehicle of satire and parody.

❊

Muses of Satire

Le bourgeois gentilhomme
& the Utopia of Spectacle

The genre of the *comédie-ballet* was born at Fouquet's fête at Vaux-le-Vicomte on the fateful evening of Louis XIV's visit in August 1661.[1] After a lavish dinner, Fouquet's guests enjoyed a performance of *Les fâcheux*, a play by Molière, intermingled with dance and music by Pierre Beauchamps. The genre was said to have originated in the practical need for the actors to rest and change costumes between acts, with the musical portions originating as interludes that later became interspersed throughout the spoken play. Conceived as ballet as much as comedy, the comédie-ballet bore many similarities to the burlesque entries of the court ballet. Though taken up soon afterward at court by Molière and Lully, however, the comédie-ballet was never bound up, as was the court ballet, with either a royal or a courtly identity. Instead it addressed the interests and concerns of a public audience, primarily composed of the bourgeoisie and nobility who attended Molière's theater at the Palais-Royal (the Grande Salle of Richelieu's old palace opposite the Louvre, which was now outfitted as a public theater). Critics exploring the multivalent or "bifocal" quality of the comédie-ballets in light of their dual audience have suggested ways in which Molière constructed them to be read differently at court and in town.[2] At court, their satire could be understood

1. For a modern edition of the music of this ballet, see George Houle, ed., Le ballet des fâcheux: *Beauchamp's Music for Molière's Comedy* (Bloomington: Indiana University Press, 1991).

2. Charles Mazouer, *Molière et ses comédies-ballets* (Paris: Klinksieck, 1993), 49–65 ("Les deux publiques"), and W. D. Howarth, *Molière: A Playwright and His Audience* (Cambridge: Cambridge University Press, 1982), 35–46.

as an extension of the lighthearted mockery that had always informed the burlesque entries of the court ballet. In town, it could be seen as challenging the social boundaries that the court ballet had sought to maintain, as well as the court ballet's ideology of praise. *Les fâcheux*, for example, took as its subject a series of courtiers, not as idealized exemplars of their social class as in the court ballet, but rather bores from whom the protagonist is trying to escape. Extending the burlesque techniques of interruption, fragmentation, and delay of the court ballet, *Les fâcheux* also took those themes as its overt subject matter. Despite the ostensibly innocent content of the play, the constant postponement and diversion of meaning—along with the burlesque treatment of courtiers—suggest the possibility of resistance to the straightforward propaganda of the court ballet.

Until the decade of the 1990s, the comédie-ballets of Molière and Lully were treated as spoken plays, both in performance and in the critical literature, with their ballet portions generally ignored or misunderstood. Recently, several writers have begun to treat music and dance in the genre. Jérôme de La Gorce's and Philippe Beaussant's recent biographies of Lully offer excellent surveys of the music, and Stephen H. Fleck's *Music, Dance, and Laughter* treats the divertissements and their music in the context of comedy.[3] Claude Abraham has studied the structure of the comédie-ballet with special attention to its ballet entries,[4] and Robert McBride has focused on the centrality of the ballet in Molière's theater.[5] Manuel Couvreur sets the comédie-ballet within the cultural politics of mid-seventeenth-century France, with a reading of *Le bourgeois gentilhomme* as a roadmap to the state of music in 1670.[6] Despite this welcome attention to music and dance, however, there has been little exploration of the relationship of the comédie-ballet to Louis XIV's court ballet, and almost no attempt to compare the social and political structures of the two genres. Partly because the court ballet itself has been inadequately studied, commentators have not recognized how it provided an important artistic and ideological model profoundly influencing the conception and development of the new genre, which at once

3. *Music, Dance, and Laughter: Comic Creation in Molière's Comedy-Ballets*, Biblio 17, 88 (Paris: Papers on French Seventeenth-Century Literature, 1995).

4. *On the Structure of Molière's Comédie-ballets*, Biblio 17, 19 (Paris: Papers on French Seventeenth-Century Literature, 1984).

5. *The Triumph of Ballet in Molière's Theatre* (Lewiston, NY: Edwin Mellen Press, 1992); "Ballet: A Neglected Key to Molière's Theater," *Dance Research* 2 (Spring 1984): 3–18.

6. Couvreur, *Jean-Baptiste Lully*, 141–209; the discussion of *Le bourgeois gentilhomme* is found on pp. 192–209.

absorbed and reacted to its conventions. In fact, much of the ideological content of the comédie-ballet may be traced to the song and dance of its ballet entries, what Molière called "the ornaments of fête."[7] A study focusing on the spectacle of these works, then, can yield important insights into the connections of their burlesque nature with the aesthetic and ideology of the court ballet, and thus illuminate a side of the comédie-ballet that remains obscure to a study of the spoken text alone, or even to a study of the divertissements in isolation.

The Politics of the Burlesque

Even in the court ballet, the burlesque had always held a multivalent potential. Mark Franko argues that under the reign of Louis XIII, a series of burlesque court ballets, produced between 1620 and 1636, contain allusions to the impotence of courtiers and to threats of violence lurking beneath their ludic pleasure. Franko hypothesizes that whereas the traditional forms of courtly dance were created as praise to be "read" by the king and his court, the more individual, improvised forms of the burlesque undermine that propagandistic legibility. Dissolving into a world of carnivalesque madness, these burlesque works—constituting a category apart from the later "political" ballets aggrandizing Louis XIII and his ministers—represent a feigned insanity seeking to escape domination.[8]

The burlesque was an age-old component of carnival celebration. It had figured in courtly entertainments at least since the Burgundian fêtes of the fifteenth century, where comic masks mingled among the revelers. In the seventeenth century, the burlesque, like carnival itself, was welcomed at court not only as an occasion for pleasure but also as a means of containing political pressures. At the same time, it also harbored a potential for political resistance, as a fashionable satirical mode encountered the claims of royal propaganda. Seventeenth-century satire targeted a variety of social phenomena, including manners, superstitions, institutions, and authority of all kinds, including that of the crown. The ballet had originated, and continued

---

7. Mazouer, *Molière et ses comédies-ballets*, 191.

8. *Dance as Text: Ideologies of the Baroque Body* (Cambridge: Cambridge University Press, 1993), 63–107. Franko, making a case for the origins of the burlesque ballet in the nobility's resistance to the crown, takes issue with Margaret McGowan, who attributes the phenomenon instead to the rise of the bourgeoisie in the early seventeenth century.

to function, as carnival entertainment, and in that sense it retained a sense of license and a tendency toward a carnivalesque undermining of the status quo.[9] In the courts of both Louis XIII and Louis XIV, the burlesque flourished in the ballet of the early reign under a strong nobility, declining with the centralization of power in the crown.

The burlesque can also be related to a more radical group of libertine writers, indirectly associated with the *libertins érudits*, who pushed the more abstract philosophy of Gassendi and his circle to its outer extremes. This group, including poets and novelists such as Théophile de Viau, Tristan L'Hermite, Charles Sorel, Charles Coypeau (known as D'Assoucy), and Cyrano de Bergerac, produced works characterized by religious unorthodoxy, political subversion, and social rebellion. Proponents of a radical free thought as well as of a freedom in manners, these writers wore their lack of conformity as a badge of personal and political resistance to authority. Adhering to theories of Epicureanism and anticipating the naturalism of Jean-Jacques Rousseau, they advocated love as an alternative to social convention and nature as an alternative to the intrigues of court life. Ignoring a repressive code of religious orthodoxy, they tended to espouse a paganism drawing on ancient mythology as well as on the nature deities of their Celtic ancestors. One of their hallmarks was the use of a single name (Théophile, Tristan, Cyrano) as the sign of a radical abandonment of tradition. Another was an extravagant language that defied the increasing clarity mandated by the Académie française as a reflection of royal taste. Following Marino, they incorporated surprising turns of phrase and bold literary conceits.[10] In the seventeenth century it was dangerous to write or publish libertine works; a strict censorship prevented any acknowledgment of atheism or even religious uncertainty. Théophile was condemned to the stake and later burned in effigy when he escaped to the estate of his protector, the prince de Condé. Faced with the dilemma of censorship and harsh punishment, especially in the period beginning with the 1660s, libertine

9. The connections among carnival license, insurgence, and rebellion in early modern France are discussed by Natalie Z. Davis, *Society and Culture in Early Modern France* (Stanford: Stanford University Press, 1975); Emmanuel Le Roy Ladurie, *Carnival in Romans*, trans. by Mary Feeney (New York: G. Braziller, 1979); Daniel Fabre, *Carnaval ou la fête à l'envers* (Paris: Gallimard, 1992); and Yves-Marie Bercé, *Fête et révolte: Des mentalités populaires du XVIe au XVIIIe siècle* (Paris: Hachette, n.d.).

10. On the literary burlesque, see Joan DeJean, *Libertine Strategies: Freedom and the Novel in Seventeenth-Century France* (Columbus: Ohio State University Press, 1981).

authors often clothed their protest in veiled allusions to silence, secrecy, and darkness.[11]

Burlesque novels challenged traditional literary forms and ideologies through an art of fragmentation, experimentalism, and comic irreverence. Sorel's *Francion*, for example, treats its eponymous protagonist as a new, antiheroic symbol of France and inverse of the politicized image of the king. Francion, though a nobleman like Sorel himself, engages in picaresque, antiheroic adventures that tend to flatten social hierarchies. In one scene, Francion gains entrance to a public performance of the king's ballet at the Petit-Bourbon, the theater used for many of the ballets of Louis XIII.[12] Instead of the orderly movement of the ballet itself, Sorel depicts the frenzied chaos of its audience. This burlesque game of reversal upsets the intended purpose of the court ballet, demoting it to a mere backdrop for the burlesque antics of Francion. The contrast between this antihero and the king is taken to its extreme at the climax of the scene, when Francion, unable to find a seat, kneels to disguise himself as a human music stand—thus becoming the lowest of servants of the ballet, in opposition to the king its master.[13]

Alongside the egalitarian "everyman" approach of Sorel's *Francion*, libertine novelists also disguised their critique by using exotic or historical settings. Roger de Rabutin, comte de Bussy, sets his *Histoire amoureuse des Gaules*, a critical treatment of Louis XIV's court, in early medieval France. Other works, like Cyrano's *Voyage dans la lune*, use the tales of benevolent societies in remote or science-fiction settings to point up the contrast to current politics. In both cases, burlesque techniques of disjunction, fragmentation, and multiple plots and subplots serve as a veil for implicit political

11. Harriet Dorothea MacPherson, *Censorship under Louis XIV, 1661–1715: Some Aspects of Its Influence* (New York: Publications of the Institute of French Studies, 1929), 13–26.

12. The early seventeenth-century practice of offering performances of the court ballet to the public had ceased under the reign of Louis XIV. The theater of the Petit-Bourbon faced the Seine near the present site of the Cour Carrée of the Louvre. Molière's troupe was allowed to use it until 1660, when it was destroyed to allow for expansion of the Louvre.

13. The passage is found in Sorel, *Francion*, ed. Yves Giraud (Paris: Garnier-Flammarion, 1996), 397–401. It did not appear in the original 1623 edition, but rather in the second edition from 1626. For a recent discussion of Sorel's *Francion* in its relationship to the libertine literature, see Michel Jeanneret, *Eros rebelle: Littérature et dissidence à l'âge classique* (Paris: Seuil, 2003), 81–88.

resistance. Libertine writers and their followers, already persecuted by Louis XIII and his minister Richelieu, went underground as Louis XIV's reign became increasingly antagonistic. They continued, however, to move covertly within the social, political, and philosophical spheres of late seventeenth-century France.

Molière has been linked to this group of libertines in several ways, including his one-name pseudonym (he was born Jean-Baptiste Poquelin). He began his career in service to the rebellious prince de Condé, who had brought a libertine current of thought into the high nobility, and to Fouquet. Early in his career, his translation of Lucretius's *De rerum natura* was censored for its emphasis on anti-authoritarian passages, and his *Dom Juan* and *Tartuffe* both stirred controversy as libertine models. The latter, a satirical portrait of a religious hypocrite, was suppressed from 1664 to 1669, when Molière was forced to soften what was considered its shocking immorality. Unlike Lully, Molière never became exclusively identified with the entertainments of the court, and his Paris theater, unlike the Académie royale de musique, remained independent of royal image making. In 1663, Molière's plays were criticized for their subversive orientation by Jean Donneau de Visé, a contemporary critic. Donneau de Visé, who lambasted these works for ridiculing the kingdom and throwing suspicion on persons worthy of respect, interpreted Molière's turn to the comédie-ballet as a result of the king's decreasing support for his straight dramas on account of their libertine orientation.[14]

The burlesque, as it was excised from the court ballet in the 1660s, was simultaneously picked up in the new genre of the comédie-ballet. Because of the chronological parallel of the collaboration between Molière and Lully (1661–70) with Louis XIV's late court ballet (1661–69), it is possible to view these two genres as participating in a kind of dialogue, in which the comédie-ballet parodies the pretensions of its courtly models. In this process may be seen a general destabilization and in some cases an actual deconstruction of courtly self-fashioning. Whereas the court ballet used the burlesque as a foil to enhance the image of an idealized court, the comédie-ballet uses the burlesque (among other purposes, including social satire targeting almost everyone) as a means of reversing the content of the court ballet, offering instead a metatheatrical celebration of the theater itself, with its professional performers and public audience, as a new social and political model.

14. John Cairncross, *Molière: Bourgeois et libertin* (Paris: A. G. Nizet, 1963), 47, 103.

The *Ballet des Muses* and Its Comic Counterparts

Given Molière's and Lully's contribution of several comédie-ballets to the larger structure of Louis XIV's *Ballet des Muses*, as well as Lully's creation of the music for the entire production, it is surprising that the inserted comédie-ballets have rarely been discussed in terms of their relationship to the massive parent work. Structurally the most complex of all the court ballets, the *Ballet des Muses* had enclosed within itself a plethora of theatrical entertainments of all sorts. In addition to its regular entries, as described in chapter 2, the work in its various manifestations embraced not only the comédie-ballets performed by Molière's troupe but also *Les poètes*, a spoken play performed by the Hôtel de Bourgogne; a comic masquerade performed by the queen's Spanish troupe; and an improvised sketch by members of the French and Italian theaters. All of these interpolated works illustrated various aspects of Louis XIV's empire of the arts, in which comedies, masquerades, pastorals, and improvised theater, colonized artistic territories exploited for their potential to serve royal ends, acknowledge Louis XIV's imperious Muses. For the third entry, in honor of the comic Muse Thalia, Molière contributed the pastoral *Mélicerte*, performed in a truncated version that he never completed. For later performances of the *Ballet des Muses* in 1667, he substituted a comédie-ballet, *La pastorale comique*, for which only the divertissements remain (LWV 33). From what we can tell from these works, *La pastorale comique* far surpasses *Mélicerte*—a more conventional pastoral based on a novel by Madeleine de Scudéry—in its burlesque orientation. Molière also contributed a more extended comédie-ballet, *Le Sicilien*, as an epilogue to the work.[15]

Though carefully contained within the imperialist framework of the *Ballet des Muses*, all of these inserted entertainments attest to a radically different orientation from the court ballet. Much of this difference may be attributed to simple generic distinctions arising from the new aesthetic and social functions of the comédie-ballet. At the same time, the clear manipulation of

---

15. Georges Couton, preface to *La pastorale comique*, in Molière, *Oeuvres complètes*, 2 vols. (Paris: Gallimard, 1956), 2: 264. According to Couton, *La pastorale comique* was substituted for *Mélicerte* on January 5, 1667, and *Le Sicilien* was added on February 14. There is some disagreement as to how, when, and if all of Molière's works were used; Virginia Scott, in *Molière: A Theatrical Life* (Cambridge: Cambridge University Press, 2000), 154, maintains that *Mélicerte* might never have been performed at all, and Anthony ("More Faces than Proteus," 338) speculates on the possibility that *Mélicerte* and *La pastorale comique* may have been performed concurrently.

the conventions of the court ballet, as well as its specific content, indicates at times an intention to use these generic distinctions as a means of highlighting ideological differences. These differences lead, in turn, to a celebration of the comédie-ballet itself as the antithesis of the courtly genre. All offered in the spirit of carnivalesque, "world-turned-upside-down" good fun, none of these works defy ideological propriety; as David Culpin has pointed out, a certain amount of political commentary was tolerated and even expected within the conventions of *raillerie,* especially in the early reign of Louis XIV.[16] The common denominator of the ballet, however, allowed a particular resonance between the court ballet and comédie-ballet, the subtle handling of which could allow a new kind of political innuendo. The comédie-ballet, favored at court and in fact growing out of the courtly genre, enjoyed the impunity associated with a favored child or with the court fools that Louis XIV's wife had brought from Spain.

Les poètes, a comedy added to the *Ballet des Muses* in tribute to Calliope, Muse of poetry, was probably contributed by the playwright Philippe Quinault.[17] Like the added works of Molière, it turns its satire on the court nobility and on the court ballet itself, rather than on the lower classes. Obviously self-reflexive, the work presents two characters charged with producing a masquerade for the king at his chateau at Saint-Germain-en-Laye, the actual performance venue for the *Ballet des Muses.* One of these—Ariste, a nobleman—bears similarities to the duc de Saint-Aignan, the director of the king's ballets (an aristocrat, as the name implies). The character playing his friend Silvandre, charged with "a little comedy to add to the ballet," probably refers to Quinault as the author of *Les poètes,* or possibly Molière. "Silvandre," the name of the shepherd-protagonist in many pastoral settings including *L'Astrée,* contrasts the natural and elegant world of D'Urfé's pastoral to the bizarre, ridiculous world of the court. Though the actual dialogue is no longer extant, the summary included in the manuscript of the *Ballet des*

---

16. "*Raillerie, honnêteté,* and 'les grands sujets': Cultured Conflict in Seventeenth-Century France," in *Culture and Conflict in Seventeenth-Century France and Ireland,* ed. Sarah Alyn Stacey and Véronique Desnain (Dublin: Four Courts Press, 2004), 133–34: "*Railler* and *entendre raillerie* are indispensable elements of the discourse on *honnêteté* practiced 'viva voce' in the salons. . . . All those who are '*honnêtes gens*' (including '*les grands*' and the sovereign himself) should, at least on a good day, be able to *entendre raillerie* and not censure those who call them to account."

17. Couton, preface to *La pastorale comique,* in Molière, *Oeuvres complètes,* 2: 264; Manuel Couvreur, "La collaboration de Quinault et Lully," *Recherches sur la musique française classique* 27 (1992): 21–22.

Muses indicates that the plot ridicules the courtiers' amateur efforts at poetry and their ludicrous attempts to control the content of the ballet. The Spanish masquerade (LWV 32/14–17) also highlights the artists of the court ballet by casting Saint-Aignan himself and Pierre Beauchamps, choreographer of the ballet, as "two directors of the *mascarade.*" The dancers included the king, with Henriette d'Angleterre and ladies and gentlemen of the court as Spanish dancers, accompanied by members of the queen's Spanish troupe. The comic difficulties and frustrations of Ariste and Silvandre are mirrored in the content of the song texts, all having to do with love's bizarre pains. In all, the content of *Les poètes* reverses the content of the *Ballet des Muses:* the courtiers are ridiculed for their lack of taste, the king of France and his court are cast as foreigners, and the artists lament the exigencies of working in such an unfavorable setting. Without an extant script for *Les poètes,* it is impossible to know the content of the dialogue between its artist-protagonists, but it is clear from the summary that the point of view promulgated in this work is not that of the court but that of the artists in its service.

Typical of the burlesque in the court ballet, *Les poètes* and Molière's inserted comédie-ballets serve the traditional role of foil, setting off and enhancing the more dignified royal and noble personae of the *Ballet des Muses.* This system begins to break down, however, when the satire is turned on the court itself and when the lower-class types of the comédie-ballets emerge as sympathetic protagonists rather than as mere objects of ridicule. At times the reversal of royal image making is immediate and specific. Molière's pastoral *Mélicerte,* for example, preceded the pastoral entry ("Euterpe") of the *Ballet des Muses,* in which Louis danced the dignified role of a shepherd, symbol of the leadership of France. *Melicerte,* in contrast, praises the country life at the expense of "scepters" and "crowns," and the wild burlesque of *La pastorale comique* privileges its rustic swain above those of a superior social station.

While these references may be seen as standard conventions of the contemporary comedy and pastoral, a different strategy characterizes the more developed *Le Sicilien,* the final comédie-ballet of the *Ballet des Muses.* This work presents a complex system of reversals that may be seen as actually challenging the aesthetic, and indirectly the ideology, of its parent work. Taking as its subject the arts in the service of love and freedom, it involves the freeing of Isidore, a Greek slave with whom the protagonist Adraste has fallen in love, from the clutches of a tyrannical Sicilian grandee, Dom Pedre. Adraste's servant Haly leads a band of musicians who perform two divertissements. The first, a ruse to bring Isidore to the window of Dom

Pedre's home, presents a mock lesson in musical aesthetics, with two shepherds performing lugubrious airs and a third mocking them with his bright celebration of carpe diem (LWV 34/1–3). Perhaps alluding to the litany of love's pains in the Spanish entry of *Les Muses,* this musical scene sets up the important theme of the ability of the arts to turn pain into pleasure. Haly's second entertainment is a heavily rhythmic, Italianate musical setting of a text in the lingua franca—a hodge-podge of Italian, French, and Turkish used by traders of the Mediterranean. Its strophic form, accented 6/4 meter, repeated notes, and syncopations represent an intensification of the Italianate burlesque developed in the early court ballet. Through the intervention of this nonsensical, high burlesque entertainment, and later, through the masking of Adraste as a portrait painter, Isidore is freed and the villain is foiled.

As the alternative, then, to an empire of the arts with their common goal of subservient flattery, *Le Sicilien* presents a world turned upside down. In this world, representatives of the lower-class foreigner (Isidore, Haly, and his Turkish musicians), ridiculed in the court ballet, become the sympathetic protagonists of the play, and the arts serve as a vehicle of inclusion and liberation rather than of exclusion and flattery. As in *Les poètes,* a spotlight is placed on the arts and artists of fête, and in this finale to the *Ballet des Muses,* festive entertainment serves not to flatter its patron but rather to create a carnivalesque world of comic celebration and liberation.

Music and the Burlesque in *Le bourgeois gentilhomme*

True to the ability of Molière and Lully to produce multivalent readings addressing the comédie-ballet's dual audience, *Le bourgeois gentilhomme,* the product of their last collaboration in 1670, may be read in at least two different ways. For the court, Molière acquiesced to Louis XIV's desire for revenge on a Turkish ambassador.[18] In that sense, the burlesque of *Le bourgeois gentilhomme* is directed at the Turkish foreigner and at the bourgeois himself, two standard targets of the court ballet. The town audience, however, might have read this comédie-ballet in a different way, not only as a parody of the content, themes, and strategies of the court ballet in general, but more

18. Couton, "Notice," in Molière, *Oeuvres complètes,* 2: 695–98; John S. Powell and Claudia Jensen, "'A Mess of Romans Left Us But of Late: Diplomatic Blunder, Literary Satire, and the Muscovite Ambassador's Visit to Paris Theaters in 1668," *Theatre Research International* 24, no. 2 (1999): 131–44.

specifically as a continuation of the direct commentary on Louis XIV's artistic program as set out in the *Ballet des Muses,* with particular reference to the system of reversals already adumbrated in *Le Sicilien.*

In the same way that the *Ballet des Muses* presented a panorama of the arts in the service of the king, *Le bourgeois gentilhomme* presents a panorama of the arts in the service of the nouveau-riche bourgeoisie. The play consists of a series of attempts by the artists in the service of M. Jourdain to commodify a courtly style for his consumption, while the bourgeois—played by Molière in the original production—constantly subverts their efforts in an extravagant travesty of that style. In that travesty, the work points up the parallel with Louis XIV, whose artists must (in a different way, but just as rigorously) subordinate their artistry to the whims of patronage. Both works take image making as their subject. In the *Ballet des Muses,* the arts serve the glorious image of the king; in *Le bourgeois gentilhomme,* they seek to raise the status of the bourgeois and ultimately serve to anoint him as a king of fools. Produced in 1670, one year after the effective demise of the court ballet with the double retirements of Louis XIV from the stage and of Benserade as poet of the ballet, *Le bourgeois gentilhomme* self-reflexively comments on the transformation of the ballet as it moves from the court into the hands of the bourgeoisie.

The world of *Le bourgeois gentilhomme* is one of multiple layers of satire, directed both at the conventions of the court and at M. Jourdain's attempts to imitate them. In the court ballet, class distinction was conveyed through costume, music, stage design, and (presumably) choreography. In all these, stylistic elegance set the court aristocracy apart as a privileged class. In the ballet as in real life, a fashionable galanterie designated this privileged elite. At the same time, the salons of the *précieuses* and the novels of Madeleine de Scudéry at mid-century had shaped the notion of upward social mobility through an appropriation of that galant style. By 1670, economic conditions had led to a dramatic increase of wealth among the bourgeoisie, whose aspirations became a reality through marriage into the nobility. But wealth and even marriage could not bestow the successful assimilation of a galant style that had become perhaps the most important signifier of nobility in an age when the old bloodlines were losing their meaning. Thus the ideal of galanterie, available to the nobility and to members of the wealthy bourgeoisie alike, began to overshadow and even usurp the ideal of *noblesse* as a quality that could be commodified and delivered to those who would stop at nothing for the social benefits it provided. The arts, especially music and dance, were integral to this process as prized commodities. In 1670, while a small portion of the bourgeoisie had actually assimilated the chic fashionability advertised by the purveyors of a noble lifestyle, a larger number had become laughingstocks, satirized in Molière's *Les précieuses ridicules* and *Le bourgeois gentilhomme*. Nonetheless, a process had begun whereby the ideal of noble galanterie would eventually be assimilated by a public culture that would supersede the court in setting standards of taste. And while Molière mocks M. Jourdain, he also uses bourgeois pretensions as a wormhole into a utopian vision of that public culture.

Beginning with the court ballet's dialectic between the galant and the burlesque, *Le bourgeois gentilhomme* ends with a radically different synthesis. In this process, a burlesque style associated with M. Jourdain and his pretensions to power engages and challenges a galant style associated with the court and bourgeois pretensions, as well as a monarchical style associated with the pomp and dignity of the king. On the surface, *Le bourgeois gentilhomme* grows directly out of the court ballet's use of the burlesque to ridicule the bourgeoisie. Here, however, the courtly style can be an object of amusement as well—a mode of expression representing not only an unattainable goal but also a futile and inappropriate one for M. Jourdain. As in the court ballet, these two styles engage in dialogue, but without the sense of hierarchy inherent in the courtly genre. *Le bourgeois gentilhomme* may be seen, then, as turning the court ballet inside out. In the earlier genre, the burlesque was used as a foil to point up noble galanterie; in the comédie-ballet, the burlesque becomes the point of reference against which courtly galanterie is contrasted. The piece begins with a French overture in the grand style (LWV 43/1), such as had been developed in the late court ballets. From the beginning, its solemn gravitas causes the listener to wonder, as Fleck comments, why a bourgeois should merit royal ceremonial music.[19] Instead of opening onto an imposing *récit,* however, as in the court ballet, the curtain rises to reveal a student composer in the act of bungling an *air sérieux* he has been assigned by the music master, to whom he serves as apprentice (LWV 43/2). The comic effect of this prologue is produced by its repetition, lack of structure and harmonic direction, and *ou ou*s and *ta la tay*s in place of text (ex. 3.1a). The juxtaposition of the burlesque style in the butchered air and the "corrected" version, sung by Mme Hilaire shortly thereafter as the *chanteuse*, reminds one of a similar juxtaposition of styles in the dances

19. Fleck, *Music, Dance, and Laughter*, 98.

Example 3.1a. Lully, *Le bourgeois gentilhomme*, student composition scene, LWV 43/2. Bibliothèque nationale de France, Collection Philidor, Rés. F 578, 4–5.

Example 3.1a. (*continued*)

-ris,   qui vous ay - me,

ta - ta - tay   qui vous ay - me,   hé - las,   hé -

- las,   que pour - riez-vous fe - ra,   fe - ra,   hé -

- las,   que pour - riez - vous fai - re   à   vos en - ne - mis?

ou - ou   ou - ou - ne - mis,   ta -

- ta - la la   la la lay,   si vous trait-tez ain - si,   belle I -

Example 3.1a. (*continued*)

for the noble dancers and the burlesque dancers in the court ballet *Alcidiane*. This new version (ex. 3.1b), besides being performed by one of France's finest singers, is also compositionally much tighter. Rather than wandering aimlessly, the material is shaped into a succinct binary form. The melody peaks elegantly on the word *extrème*, then settles in the second phrase to F major. The accompanying harmony leads from D minor to an intermediate cadence on A major, with the second phrase cadencing on the mediant of F major. The twenty-eight measures of the first half are condensed into a cogent ten measures in the revision; the fifty-two measure of the second half into a mere eighteen. The meaning of this juxtaposition, however, has different consequences than it would in a court ballet. In the world of the comédie-ballet, the air is a commodity produced on demand, even by an inexperienced student. What might have served as a contrast between noble and burlesque in the court ballet is now set adrift in the new social construct of the comédie-ballet. Yet this opening air may be seen as a microcosm of *Le*

Example 3.1b. Lully, *Le bourgeois gentilhomme*, finished version of student composition, LWV 43/2. Bibliothèque nationale de France, Collection Philidor, Rés. F 578, 10.

bourgeois gentilhomme as a whole, which stands in the same parodic relationship to the court ballet as the burlesque version of the air stands in relation
to the conventional opening *récit* of the courtly genre.

The following scene, a conversation between the music master and the
dance master, alludes to *Les poètes*, the inserted comedy in the *Ballet des
Muses*. Like Ariste and Silvandre in that work, the music and dance masters
of *Le bourgeois gentilhomme* voice the dilemma of the arts in 1670, faced with
the task of providing the bourgeois an unattainable artificial identity. Despite the difference in method and result, the implication is the same for the
court ballet, whose propaganda sought to create an artificial identity for the
king and his court. In the second part of this scene, the exhibitions arranged
by the music and dance masters display the different affections in their
disciplines. The music master's contribution to this exhibition, the miniature pastoral in act 1 (LWV 43-46), expands on the affections of the major
and minor airs of Haly's musicians in *Le Silicien*, demonstrating happy and
sad emotions in love. Each of the three airs performed by its *musicienne* and
two *musiciens* explores a different facet of love. The first, a simple air, extols
freedom from attachment. The second, set to a descending chromatic bass
line, argues that pleasure is not possible without amorous desires; the third,
in effect a prototype of the recitative with quick, speechlike rhythms, repeated notes, meter changes, and frequent rests, insists that love is in vain
because all women ("shepherdesses") are unfaithful. The trio that ends this
demonstration of musical affection begins in contrapuntal disagreement,
but gradually the voices find harmonious accord as they sing together, "Ah,
how sweet it is when two hearts love each other."

Not only do many of the scenes feature the same categories of the arts being exhibited before the bourgeois as were exhibited before the king in the
Ballet des Muses, but the original production of *Le bourgeois gentilhomme* also
featured many of the same singers and dancers. Hilaire Dupuis, who had
sung the opening *récit* of the *Ballet des Muses*, is the singer of the (corrected)
opening "*récit*" of *Le bourgeois gentilhomme*. The musical pastoral, with its
singers dressed as shepherds and shepherdesses, has clear parallels with the
pastoral in the *Ballet des Muses*, most obviously in the connecting presence
of its singers, all of whom performed in both works. The following scene, an
exposition of noble dance parallel to the entry for Terpsichore in the *Ballet
des Muses*, also included two of the dancers, M. Saint-André and M. Favier,
who had danced in that scene. This literal overlap between the performers
of these two works, trying to please the bourgeois in the comédie-ballet as

they had tried to please the king in the court ballet, would have heightened the parody for those who witnessed performances of both.[20]

The next entry features M. Jourdain's well-known travesty of the minuet (LWV 43/8). As the dancing master issues futile instructions, M. Jourdain careens awkwardly around the stage. A touchstone of noble *galanterie*, the minuet serves as the most effective of all the measurements by which the bourgeois fails to attain to the class status he so desires. A similar use of parody occurs in the tailor scene, in which M. Jourdain, dressed in his ridiculous new clothes, struts pompously across the stage to the solemn rhythms and flourishes of a formal entry. This scene represents an escalation of M. Jourdain's delusions of nobility. The forms of address used by the tailors (the bourgeois equivalent of the king's image-makers) increase in respect as M. Jourdain continues to pour money into their hands, escalating from *mon gentilhomme* to *Monseigneur* to *Votre Grandeur* as he empties his purse. Reflecting a patronage system based on the exchange of flattery for gold, then, the bourgeois, through the signs of outward appearance, quickly ascends by stages to the highest of noble stations.

The role of M. Jourdain has been interpreted as a satire of Colbert, whose life exhibits a number of similarities to that of the bourgeois.[21] A few allusions, beginning with the overture noted above, may also be seen to target M. Jourdain as a satirical portrait of the king. His distressed discovery that the flowers on his new dressing gown are upside down may allude to the carnivalesque game of reversal in which a burlesque character becomes an "upside down" version of the king's fleur-de-lis. So may Mme Jourdain's horrified misunderstanding of M. Jourdain's new status of *paladin*, or knight, which she mistakes as *baladin*, or ballet dancer. "At your age?" she gasps, alluding to the recent retirement of Louis XIV from the ballet stage, according to some because of his age. The music for Jourdain's awkward minuet was actually taken from *Les amants magnifiques*, the last work in which the king was supposed to have performed. Given this evidence, Fleck believes that Jourdain is aping not only the nobility but "the very highest of all pos-

---

20. Performers are listed by name in the *livrets* of both works; a cast list for *Le bourgeois gentilhomme* is also given by Herbert Schneider, introduction to Lully, *Le bourgeois gentilhomme*, trans. by Vincent Giroud, in *Oeuvres complètes*, series 2, vol. 4 (Hildesheim: Georg Olms, 2006), xlv–xlix.

21. The comparison was first made by Antoine Adam, cited by Herbert Schneider, "Introduction" to Lully, *Le bourgeois gentilhomme*, xli–xlii.

sible nobility, the king himself."[22] These reversals build to a climax in the Turkish ceremony, a plot resolution in which M. Jourdain finally gives the hand of his daughter to the man she loves, disguised as a Turkish prince.

In a more general way, this scene may be seen as a celebration of the Feast of Fools. This medieval burlesque tradition, ultimately derived from the Greek Chronia and the Roman Saturnalia, overturned traditional distinctions of rank and status in an orgy of festive satire, ruled over by a King of Fools drawn from the populace. The Turkish ceremony, in which M. Jourdain, dressed as a Turkish prince, is ceremoniously outfitted with a sword and turban (complete with tiers of lit candles), may then also be seen as the coronation of M. Jourdain as a fool king. With Lully as the Turkish "Mufti," it directly parallels the Turkish scene in *Le Sicilien,* Molière's epilogue to the *Ballet des Muses,* in which the Turkish slave Haly leads a group of musicians in subverting the status quo. In both of these ultraburlesque Turkish scenes, the lovers are reunited through the aid of the festive arts.

Like the Turkish scene in *Le Sicilien,* the Turkish ceremony also uses a lingua franca text accompanied by an extreme Italianate burlesque. Lully led this burlesque investiture ceremony in his bass voice with "contortions and grimaces," ridiculously dressed, along with six dancers, four dervishes, and musicians, *à la turque* (LWV 43/14-22). Like novels of this and a later period, set in exotic locales to disguise political critique (Montesquieu's *Persian Letters* is an obvious example), the Turkish ceremony employs a wider, more complex form of satire than the court ballet's ridicule of the nonnoble. The festivities of the divertissement provide a denouement by which the lovers are freed from the fetters of a patriarchal tyrant under cover of the masquerade. In addition, the roles featuring Lully, as the master of the fête, and Molière, as the fool king submitting to its reign of universal comic madness, may be seen as an echo of the roles of Ariste, the director of the fête, and Silvandre, the creator of the comedy, in *Les poètes.* On one level, they play the parts of the Mufti and M. Jourdain, but on another level they represent the role of the artist in this theatrical Feast of Fools and the power of the arts to create a reign of burlesque festivity exploding all the premises of conventional reality. Whereas at court the extravagant burlesque of *Le bourgeois gentilhomme* could still be read as a condemnation of the pretensions of the

22. Ibid., 115. For Louis XIV's retirement from the ballet stage, see Canova-Green, *Benserade,* 2: 187. It is not clear whether or not the king danced in *Les amants magnifique* of 1670, as originally planned, or whether his last performance would have been in the *Ballet de Flore* of the preceding year.

bourgeois, in town it could be read as a praise of the role of the arts in the service of a new society, as represented by the professional theater.

Table 3.1 shows that almost every entry of the *Ballet des Muses* has its parody or comic counterpart in *Le bourgeois gentilhomme*. As the table indicates, *Le bourgeois gentilhomme*, a comédie-ballet concluded by a full-length mock court ballet, represents a photographic negative of the *Ballet des Muses*, a court ballet concluded by a full-length comédie-ballet. Like the inserted entertainments of the *Ballet des Muses*, particularly *Les poètes* and *Le Sicilien*, *Le bourgeois gentilhomme* may also be seen as a parody of the *Ballet des Muses*, and a reversal of its premises on both a structural and an ideological level. Like *Le Sicilien*, its Turkish entertainment allows the lovers' happy denouement. And finally, just as *Le Sicilien*, standing at the close of the *Ballet des Muses*, presents an alternative, positive view of the arts in the service of love and freedom, so does the "Ballet des nations," standing at the end of *Le bourgeois gentilhomme*, present an alternative, positive view of the arts in the service of a public audience.

The "Ballet des nations," alluded to earlier as a "king's ballet" but having nothing to do with the king, may be interpreted as a court ballet offered to the bourgeois as fool king.[23] It is presented to a stage audience consisting of M. Jourdain and all the characters of the Turkish ceremony, still dressed in their outlandish Turkish garb, as well as the other members of M. Jourdain's household. The work harks back to earlier treatments of the "nations" subgenre, used in the early seventeenth century as a ploy for acknowledging the superiority of France and its king.[24] In this comic work, however, the "nations" refer instead to the entertainments at different public theaters, the arts composing them, and the audience of different social classes in attendance. Depicting the same "nations" as the *Ballet des Muses*, but substituting a new public ideal in the place of royal propaganda, the "Ballet des nations" forms an ideological reversal and climax to the comédie-ballet.

Whereas galant and burlesque styles have been sharply defined from one divertissement to another up until this point, the clear distinction breaks down in this long epilogue, in which the dialogue fragments and escalates. In the first entry (LWV 43/23), a prologue of sorts to this large epilogue,

---

23. It is introduced by the lines, "Let's see our ballet, and offer it as a divertissement to His Turkish Highness" (Voyons notre ballet, et donnons-en le divertissement à Son Altesse Turque). Molière, *Oeuvres complètes*, ed. Georges Mongrédien (Paris: Garnier-Flammarion, 1965), 4: 134.

24. The chorus of nations in the *grand ballet* of the *Ballet de Flore*, discussed in chapter 2, may be seen as a derivative of this genre.

TABLE 3.1. Comparison of the Structure of the *Ballet des Muses* and *Le bourgeois gentilhomme*

Muse	ENTRY (*Ballet des Muses*)	ENTRY (*Bourgeois gentilhomme*)
Prologue	Mnemosine, mother of Muses, sings *récit* in praise of Louis XIV	Imposing *récit* of court ballet parodied by music student's bungled air
Urania (astronomy)	Noble dancers' costume parade (reflects brilliance of stars)	Act 2, tailor scene: M. Jourdain parades in his new costume
Melpomene (tragedy)	Pantomime of tragic myth of Pyramus and Thisbe	Frame plot of star-crossed lovers but with happy ending
Thalia (comedy)	Inserted comédie-ballet by Molière and Lully: *Mélicerte* (later replaced by *Pastorale comique*)	celebrates comedic universe
Euterpe (pastoral, music)	Pastoral performed by king and courtiers as shepherds and shepherdesses	Act 1: pastoral dialogue as exhibition of noble style in music, sung by king's singers as shepherds and shepherdesses
Clio (history)	Pantomime of Alexander's battle with Porrus	Act 2: scene of master at arms, mock duel as spoof on arts of war
Calliope (poetry)	Inserted comedy *Les poètes;* self-reflexive depiction of creators of the entertainment: Ariste and Sylvandre in the frame of *Les poètes;* the duc de Saint Aignan and Beauchamps in the Spanish masquerade of *Les poètes*	Act 1: music master and dance master as spokespersons for the arts, parallel with characters from *Les poètes*
Erato (love poetry)	King and nobles appear as heroes of chivalric novels	Act 3: M. Jourdain's ridiculous infatuation with Dorimène (banquet scene)
Polymnia (rhetoric)	Comic actors from Comédie-Italienne and Hôtel de Bourgogne, spoof on ancient Greek philosophers and Latin orators	Act 2: master of philosophy: lesson on consonants and vowels

TABLE 3.1. *(continued)*

Muse	ENTRY (*Ballet des muses*)	ENTRY (*Bourgeois gentilhomme*)
Terpsichore (dance)	Dance of fauns and Amazons as exhibition of noble dance	Act 1: dance master produces exhibition of "the most beautiful noble dance"
Epilogue	*Le Sicilien*, a comédie-ballet by Molière and Lully, serves as epilogue to the *Ballet des Muses*, a court ballet	*Ballet des nations*, a mock court ballet, serves as epilogue to *Le bourgeois gentilhomme*, a comédie-ballet. Turkish ceremony alludes to Turkish entertainment of *Le Sicilien*

a multiplicity of musical styles confront each other, phrase by phrase, at the gathering of a public audience comprising nobles, bourgeois, provincials, and foreigners assembled to view a "king's ballet." The scene is familiar, not from any performance under Louis XIV's reign, but from the early seventeenth-century ballet depicted in Sorel's *Francion*. As in the novel, the breakdown of the distinction between a noble galanterie and an ignoble burlesque signifies the disintegration of class distinctions, symbolized (as in Sorel's novel) by the mad crush and commingling of theater patrons trying to find a seat. The allusion to *Francion* is reinforced by a passage in the Turkish scene, excised in the final version, in which M. Jourdain is forced to kneel to allow his back to be used as a stand for the Koran.[25] The incident recalls the way Francion had kneeled to allow his back to be used for a music stand in the "king's ballet" in Sorel's novel. In this way, Francion as French Everyman and M. Jourdain as fool king both represent the reversal of the king's high place in the ordination of entertainment.

Like the king's ballet in *Francion*, the "Ballet des nations" is introduced from the fragmented, even chaotic points of view of its public audience. The opening chorus exhibits the burlesque characteristics of simple harmonic progressions, repeated notes, and repeated phrases, as the entire assemblage breathlessly compete with one another to gain the attention of the distributor of libretti for the ballet (ex. 3.2). The chaos of the scene is conveyed in

25. Couton, "Notice," in Molière, *Oeuvres complètes*, 2: 701.

Example 3.2. Lully, *Le bourgeois gentilhomme*, "Dialogue des gens qui en musique de-mandent des livres," opening, LWV 43/23. Bibliothèque nationale de France, Collection Philidor, Rés. F 578, 146-47, mm. 1–10.

Example 3.2. (*continued*)

this passage through a pseudocontrapuntal setting in a perpetual rhythm, with the vocal parts serving little more purpose than to outline the underlying chords in paired alternation producing repeated eighth notes. The effect of the rhythm is one of constant movement, going nowhere. This is combined with harmony that modulates up from G major to E major, intensifying the increasing pressure of the crowd.

Example 3.3a. Lully, *Le bourgeois gentilhomme*, "Ballet des nations," "Dialogue des gens qui en musique demandent des livres," noble ladies and gentlemen, LWV 43/23. Bibliothèque nationale de France, Collection Philidor, Rés. F 578, 148–49, mm. 27–35.

The competition for libretti and seats represents a social leveling through which representatives of all social classes and ethnicities are equally frustrated. All of the participants, fellow victims of the pressing crowd, the heat, and a shortage of seats and libretti, voice their complaints in turn. Their solo phrases all retain some character of the opening, but gradually different personalities begin to emerge within the context of a complex, recitative-like texture. The aristocratic ladies and gentlemen sing in short phrases containing more rhythmic complexity (ex. 3.3a). Gascon country bumpkins and an inebriated Swiss run on at greater length in their dialects and quick repeated notes (ex. 3.3b). A garrulous old bourgeois (echoing the eponymous bourgeois of the play) breaks away entirely from the cut time of the piece to sing in broader, more accented rhythms of a swinging 6/8 meter his frustration

Example 3.3b. Lully, *Le bourgeois gentilhomme*, "Ballet des nations," "Dialogue des gens qui en musique demandent des livres," a Swiss, LWV 43/23. Bibliothèque nationale de France, Collection Philidor, Rés. F 578, 150, mm. 60–64.

Example 3.3c. Lully, *Le bourgeois gentilhomme*, Rés. F 578, "Ballet des nations," "Dialogue des gens qui en musique demandent des livres," a garrulous old bourgeois, LWV 43/23. Bibliothèque nationale de France, Collection Philidor, Rés. F 578, 150, mm. 64–70.

with the situation (ex. 3.3c); later he declares his disgust at being relegated to the worst seats, next to provincials from Lantriguet (in Brittany), and his intention never again to attend "either ballet or comedy."

Finally this motley assemblage settles down to watch the ballet-within-a-ballet. Carlo Vigarani's complex stage design for this finale had to accommodate two stage audiences: the mock public audience of the "Ballet des nations," and the audience consisting of M. Jourdain, his family, and his entourage of mock Turks. This finale confirms that the closing ballet, earlier

referred to as "the king's ballet," now belongs not the king but to the carnivalesque fool king. These two stage audiences, moreover, neatly point to
the actual public and courtly audiences that, in town and at court respectively, would *also* be witnessing the work. The entries of the ballet (LWV
43/25–38), depicting the "nations" of Europe, actually represent typical
scenes of the Spanish, French, and Italian theaters of Paris, and more specifically, the same theaters showcased in the *Ballet des Muses*. The entry
entitled "A Night at the Italian Theater" affords a unique glimpse of the entertainments at the Comédie-Italienne, including (like the *Ballet des Muses*) the
actual participation of the leader of that troupe, Domenico Biancolelli as Arlequin in the original performance of the work. Because of the lack of extant
documentation of the entertainments of the Italian players until the 1690s,
Molière's depiction of the "Night" provides a valuable glimpse into the nature
of their divertissements around 1670. An Italian aria, sung by Mlle Hilaire
representing the troupe's *cantarina*, is a unique combination of the Italian
language and musical style, with its sequences and chromaticism, and the
binary form of the French air and *double*. Unlike the French *double*, however, with its dotted rhythms and complex syncopations, this one displays
the regular rhythms, more metrical setting, and typical ornamentation of
the Italian style. The use of the quintessentially French *double* as the vehicle
for a quasi-Italian style, and its performance by Mlle Hilaire, perhaps the
most well-known exemplar of French singing, could also be understood as
an indication that these representatives of the "nation" of Italy are really the
members of a troupe that, having lived in France for almost two decades,
had begun—like Lully himself—to take on a French style and character.
Like the lament of Flora in Lully's *Ballet de Flore*, it is an early example of *les
goûts-réunis,* well before the term was coined by François Couperin.

The Spanish entry, similar in character to the Spanish entry in the *Ballet
des Muses,* imitates the mock anguish of its songs. Unlike its model, though,
the Spanish scene in the "Ballet des nations" ends with a celebration of festive entertainment as the means of turning pain into pleasure. In doing so,
this entry stands at the beginning of a long line of works placing comedy
and satire above tragedy, the icon of royal power, in the hierarchy of genres.
Also conspicuous is the use in the "Ballet des nations" of the same professional singers and dancers who had performed beside the king in the *Ballet
des Muses*.

The "Ballet des nations" may therefore be seen as alluding to the interpolated Spanish, Italian, and French entries of the *Ballet des Muses,* much as
the Turkish scene alludes to Molière's own *Le Sicilien,* that work's appended

finale, and as the main acts of *Le bourgeois gentilhomme* proper allude to the parade of the arts in its main entries. All of these parallels point up even further the transfer of praise from the real king to the fool king and his ecstatic kingdom of folly. The "Ballet des nations" represents festive theater as a utopian experience shared by an audience of diverse social classes and performers of different nations—the primary objects of ridicule in the court ballet. Each of these entertainments, like the miniature pastoral performed earlier in *Le bourgeois gentilhomme*, presents its own conflict of various views of love and life; each resolves these in a festive celebration of theater.

In the final scene (LW V 43/39), the stage audience and the participants of the "Ballet des nations" join together, in homophonic agreement sharply contrasting with the sociomusical clashes of the opening scene, to praise the blissful experience of witnessing entertainment as sweet as that tasted by the gods—perhaps an allusion to the king and his court, the gods of Olympus. Once again, the exoticism and social condescension formerly associated with the burlesque in the court ballet have been inverted to depict this utopian highest good, in which the harmonious bliss of a socially stratified theater audience represents the harmonious workings of an ideal society. As in the musical dialogue in act 1 and the final resolutions of the Spanish, Italian, and French theatrical demonstrations, this final chorus resolves all previous tensions in a celebration of theater. Its slower, quarter-note rhythms and simple harmonies, along with a pervasive homophony indicating consonance and agreement, contrast completely with the chaos of the opening chorus, now reflecting an awed appreciation of the magic of theater. Presumably this delighted and awed stage audience, moreover, represents the town audience of *Le bourgeois gentilhomme* itself, a musical transformation of the *Ballet des Muses* into a public work.

Just as early seventeenth-century versions of the "Ballet des nations" celebrated the power of the king throughout the world, the "Ballet des nations" of *Le bourgeois gentilhomme*, with its international audience and acts, extends the comic madness of M. Jourdain to the entire universe and ensures his triumph as fool king. Resolving the dialectic of noble and burlesque, reason and madness, it represents a triumph of folly over conventional wisdom, and the substitution of a higher wisdom of festive celebration.[26] The ending of the "Ballet des nations," and of the work as a whole, reassures us that the ridiculous pretensions of M. Jourdain lead into a higher world of

26. Gérard Defaux, *Molière et les metamorphoses du comique: De la comédie morale au triomphe de la folie* (1980; Paris: Klinksieck, 1992), 280.

a unifying harmony offered and represented by the shared experience of spectacle. The "Ballet des nations," then, transforms the empire of the arts into an inclusive utopia of festive theater, in which the "nations," far from representing the subject peoples of Louis XIV's empire or the colonized arts, represent instead the arts of the public sphere in the service of a new social order.

As with other burlesque works, the initial impression of the "Ballet des nations" is one of confusion and fragmentation, but the work falls into perspective when one begins to take into account not only the content of the ballet but also the audience. The seventeenth-century theater was one of the few public venues where the social classes met and commingled. Molière's audience would have provided an apt symbol for a new society built on more fluid class distinctions. While the *premières loges* were reserved for persons of quality, the other loges and amphitheater were also available to wealthy members of the bourgeoisie and their families. Lackeys and servants (usually in attendance on the wealthier patrons in the loges) tended to occupy the standing-room male preserve of the less expensive floor or *parterre*, but this area was mainly peopled by male members of the bourgeoisie, who were often joined by gentlemen taking a break from their loges.[27] The seating arrangement, fluid but still hierarchical, fits nicely with the political aims of certain reformers who wished to see a society that transcended rather than destroyed class distinctions.

The Turkish ceremony and the "Ballet des nations," then, standing back-to-back at the end of *Le bourgeois gentilhomme,* hold within themselves the resolution of the conflict between noble and ignoble that has characterized the play. This resolution, lost in any performance of the spoken play alone, lies in a view of theatrical spectacle, defined by its "ornaments" of music and dance, as a utopia of social leveling and harmony bridging the difference of nationality and social class, where common mortals may view entertainment as sweet as that tasted by kings. The Turkish ceremony presents a carnivalesque utopia, in which the substitution of the fool for the king suggests an ecstatic celebration of folly. The inversion by which the bourgeois supplants the king is also the inversion by which the comédie-ballet supplants the court ballet and the prerogative of patronage passes into the public sphere. Molière's parody of the *Ballet des Muses,* then, represents a symbolic moment in which the memorializing Muses of Louis's absolutism move

27. Howarth, *Molière,* 35–36.

to the sphere of the bourgeoisie. The main body of *Le bourgeois gentilhomme* depicts them under the awkward private patronage of the bourgeois. The Turkish ceremony, in which the bourgeois is crowned as fool king, opens a window into a more visionary understanding of the Muses' new role, culminating, via the apotheosis of the "Ballet des nations," in the artistic and social world of an idealized public theater.

Utopias and Counterutopias

This utopia of folly grew directly or indirectly out of a tradition of utopian fiction that can be indirectly traced to two early sixteenth-century works, the *Utopia* (1516) of Thomas More and *The Praise of Folly* (1509) by More's friend and fellow humanist Erasmus. These works are related; in fact, Erasmus's Latin title, *Moriae encomium*, was conceived as a pun on More's name. Erasmus's Folly, while ostensibly criticizing the follies or vices of humankind, actually praises a higher folly of ecstatic creativity and extravagant satire. More's *Utopia* had represented an idealized society in which social equality was paramount and totalitarianism and war abhorrent.[28] More dedicated his *Utopia* to Erasmus, and like *The Praise of Folly*, his book glorified the fool as the childlike exemplar of the utopian state and celebrated the "topsy-turvy" world in which fools could be regarded as kings and kings as fools. Both More's and Erasmus's works have important political dimensions; indeed, it has always been the function of the fool, whether male or female, to speak truth under the guise of foolishness, especially in the presence of kings.

The utopian visions of More and Erasmus both served as critiques of contemporary society under the respective masks of fantasy and comic extravagance. Along with the carnivalesque utopias of Rabelais from the late sixteenth century, they served as a model for fictional protests of the Bourbon dynasty in the seventeenth century. Both of their works circulated in French translation and influenced the utopian visions of Rabelais and Montaigne in the sixteenth century, as well as a series of French novels in the seventeenth. Stimulated by Cyrano's lunar and solar voyages, which extended utopian thought into the realm of science fiction, and Sorel's *Francion*, celebrating the bourgeois picaresque hero as a countermonarchical symbol of France, the

---

28. This is hinted at in the full title, *A Fruitful and Pleasant Work of the Best Republic and of the New Isle Called Utopia.*

production of utopian novels climaxed in the late seventeenth century. In fact, never did such a plethora of utopias proliferate in any country, or in any period, as during the reign of Louis XIV. Played out in a consistent frame of anti-authoritarianism, the utopias of Gabriel de Foigny, Denis Veiras, Claude Gilbert, and Bernard le Bovier de Fontenelle were variously stamped with republican, atheistic, and/or libertine overtones.[29]

Under the guise of a fictional utopia, authors could offer at once a vision of a future society and a critique of the present regime. Two ideals common to their utopian visions are a financial redistribution of wealth and a redistribution of pleasure and entertainment. The second is as critical to the reformist vision as the first. It is this latter condition that Molière presents in the epilogue to *Le bourgeois gentilhomme* as the emblem of a new society. This resolution, moreover, represents an appropriate antidote to the theatrical utopia of Louis XIV's court as presented in the court ballet. In contrast to the imperial model presented there, Molière's staging of a public utopia also indirectly hails the commercial marketplace as the reflection of a new society based on a redistribution of wealth.

Molière and the Libertines

Seventeenth-century utopian novelists, intellectual heirs of More, Erasmus, and Rabelais, provided a link between Renaissance humanism and the eighteenth-century Enlightenment. Molière would certainly have known the popular novels of Cyrano and his contemporaries, and perhaps the French translation of Erasmus's *Praise of Folly* that appeared in 1670, the same year as the *Bourgeois*. A common model for all these writers was the second-century Epicurean philosopher Lucian, whose ideal of the Saturnalia became a prototype for an exalted conception of fête. More and Erasmus together, and later Molière, translated his work and absorbed elements of his

29. On the subject of utopian protest during the period of Louis XIV, see Robert C. Elliott, *The Shape of Utopia: Studies in a Literary Genre* (Chicago: University of Chicago Press, 1970); Lise Leibacher-Ouvrard, *Libertinage et Utopies sous le règne de Louis XIV* (Geneva: Droz, 1989); and Myriam Yardeni, *Utopie et révolte sous Louis XIV* (Paris: Nizet, 1980). Though occasionally criticized for use beyond More's novel, the term "utopian" is extended by most writers to various fictional works positing the image of a better world. This usage is the basis for the dossier "Utopie" of the on-line Gallica site of the Bibliothèque nationale, comprising utopian fiction of the period; see http://gallica.bnf.fr/utopie/. See also Lise Leibacher-Ouvrard, "Sauvages et utopias (1676–1715): L'exotisme-alibi," *French Literature Series* 13 (1986): 1–12.

thought, especially the skeptical vision of his *Satires* that served as a libertine bible in the seventeenth century. The libertine faction descended from Lucian and the Renaissance humanists was driven underground by successive waves of repression, beginning with the burning at the stake of the Italian Giulio Cesare Vanni at Toulouse in 1619 and the condemnation of Théophile de Viau to the stake in 1623. The repression continued with the influence of the devout party led by the mother of Louis XIV, and later Louis's own policies. In 1662 a young libertine writer named Claude Le Petit was seized, imprisoned in the Châtelet, and burned at the stake in the Place de Grève for his pornographic novel *Le bordel des Muses, ou les neuf pucelles putains* (The Brothel of the Muses, or the nine virgin-whores). The portions of *Le bordel des muses* that escaped extinction show it to be an extended celebration of sex as the energy propelling all living things, and a call for art to reflect and participate in a universal symphony of desire. To illustrate this aim, Le Petit depicts Parnassus as the site of the transgression of all taboos, including incest, sodomy, and bestiality.

In *Éros rebelle: Littérature et dissidence à l'âge classique,* Michel Jeanneret reveals how later writers learned to occupy a "gray zone," in which they masked a strong libertine/erotic discourse in an elegant, galant language. These included Théophile himself, who after his escape wrote poetry that remained sensual, but in a less violent manner than in his previous works, as well as Benserade, Racine, La Fontaine, and Molière.[30] Another strategy that libertines employed was an unannounced intertextuality allowing them to satirize the status quo and at the same time pay homage to other libertine works while avoiding the dangers of overtly associating themselves with the movement. This strategy might help to explain *Le bourgeois gentilhomme* not only as a satire on Louis XIV's *Ballet des Muses* but also, perhaps, as a tribute to the martyred Le Petit's *Bordel des Muses*. In addition, aside from the cabaret, the most important haven of libertinism was the theater, which attracted the vituperative disapproval of the devout party. It was the custom in France, in contrast to other countries, to deny actors and playwrights burial in sanctified ground, and actresses of the public stage, like singers and dancers of a slightly later period, were routinely condemned as prostitutes. The celebration of fête at the end of *Le bourgeois gentilhomme,* besides setting out the ideal of the theater audience as a model for a new society, undoubtedly also represented a defense of the libertine theater in response to Molière's critics.

30. Jeanneret, *Eros rebelle,* 277–302.

This reading of the play, while confirming Molière's identification with a libertine orientation, stands in direct contradiction to Lully's reputation as dictatorial director of the Académie royale de musique. After 1670, the path of the "two Baptistes" parted forever, as Lully rose in royal favor and Molière fell from royal grace. Lully, like Benserade, is naturally associated with the propaganda of absolutist image making par excellence. In the careers of both these artists, however, there are links with the libertine community in Paris. The connections of Lully with this circle will be discussed more fully in chapter 4. In Benserade's poetry, the intersection of a libertine attitude with the more delicate fashion of preciosity and galanterie has been recognized for some time.[31] Both Lully and Benserade frequented the libertine salon of the courtesan Ninon de Lenclos, a haven of subversive artistic discussion. Herself a fine musician, Ninon espoused the cause of sentiment in music, a favorite libertine theme. Lully and Benserade also frequented certain cabarets, such as the Croix de Lorraine and the Bel-Air, known for a libertine clientele.[32] The Bel-Air cabaret, whose proprietor was Hilaire Dupuis's father and Lambert's father-in-law, was known as a haven for libertine gatherings. According to documents unearthed by Catherine Massip, there was a change in tone at the Bel-Air around mid-century, when it became associated more with a galant, lighthearted libertinism than with the more serious older style.[33] Because of censorship, subversive movements depended on private conversation more than the written word. For this reason, the cabaret, like the later coffee house, provided an ideal gathering place.

Lully's reputation, of course, rests on his later works, his tragédies en musique composed for the king at the height of his power. Taken together, the evidence suggests that in his earlier works, at least through his collaborations with Molière and Benserade, Lully provided the music for texts that are open to multivalent interpretation. Lecerf de la Viéville's designation of Lully as "un peu libertin" in 1702 came at a time when the meaning

31. Antoine Adam, *Histoire de la littérature française au XVIIe siècle*, vol. 3 (Paris: Del Duca, 1962), 168–70.

32. On the association of Lully and Benserade with Ninon de Lenclos, see René Pintard, *Le libertinage érudit dans la première moitié du dix-septième siècle* (Paris: Boivin, 1943), 131. On Benserade's connections with libertine circles, see F[rançois T[ommy] Perrens, *Les libertins en France au XVIIe siècle* (1896; New York: Burt Franklin, 1973), 173, 192–96, 218–20, 271–74; and Silin, *Benserade and His Ballets de Cour*, 158. On the intersections of libertinism with cabaret life, see Perrens, *Les libertins*, 72–73, 151, 218–19, 227–34, 327–45, 407.

33. Massip, *L'art de bien chanter*, 43–55.

of that term was still entrenched in seventeenth-century usage emphasizing a political outlook (*libertinage d'esprit*), while also beginning to take on an eighteenth-century usage more concerned with personal manners (*libertinage de moeurs*).[34] From the beginning, however, personal and political uses of the term overlapped, and seventeenth-century *libertinage*, especially as it referred to the poets and writers of burlesque novels in the circles of Cyrano, Théophile, and Tristan, often flaunted its rebelliousness against societal norms. Lully's practice of sodomism was well known to his contemporaries.[35] It is possible that the connections that Joan DeJean finds among libertinism, sodomy, and political free thought, connections that lay behind novelistic techniques of fragmentation and the burlesque, might have a bearing on our understanding of Lully's biography and his early works.

Before his creation of the tragédie en musique, then, Lully participated in the production of two separate bodies of work, each with its own political implications. In the court ballet, he created music displaying a refined galanterie as well as a pompous magnificence, dignity, and grandeur. Working alongside his father-in-law, Lambert, he deployed the tender and sensuous *air sérieux*, as well as more Italianate extremes of emotion that could be interpreted as a passionate, and at times dissonant, counterdiscourse. In the comédie-ballet, together with Molière, he parodied elements of the structure and the ideology of the court ballet. Because of the greater fame of his later oeuvre, Lully's comic genius has not been fully recognized as the equal of Molière's and an important component of a satirical ideological strategy that would be taken up by composers in future generations.

Louis XIV's initial response to *Le bourgeois gentilhomme* was one of total silence, and the courtiers spent several days in fear of passing judgment themselves lest they contradict the king. The later, positive reception of the work at court, after a delay in which Louis seemed to be making up his mind what to make of it, indicates that it was finally enjoyed there with impunity and praise. Molière's biographer, however, relates that "never had a play been more unfortunately received [at court] than that one; and none of those of Molière had given him so much trouble."[36] This apparent contradic-

---

34. Jean-Laurent Lecerf de la Viéville, *Comparaison de la musique italienne et de la musique française*, 3 vols. (1704–6; Geneva: Minkoff, 1972).

35. Seventeenth-century sodomism as part of a wider libertine movement will be discussed in chapter 4.

36. Jean-Léonor Le Gallois, sieur de Grimarest, *La vie de M. de Molière*, ed. Georges Mongrédien (Paris: Centre National de la Recherche Scientifique, 1955), 112–13.

tion may only be understood within the larger picture of official response to the more general literature of protest emerging in the decade of the 1660s. Throughout his reign, the king's deified image dictated against answering his critics, and to the end he maintained a lofty, aloof silence in the face of escalating criticism. His ministers, on the other hand, actively sought to counteract the effects of the growing oppositional literature. Colbert, in particular, waged a two-pronged campaign, adroitly using the popular print media to garner support for the king's policies, while increasing surveillance and censorship. Finding it easier to control production than distribution, he and his associates put a large number of publishers out of business, allowing the *privilège* only to a trusted few.

Still, oppositional literature continued to flourish, even increasing through the decades of the late seventeenth century despite ever more stringent attempts at suppression. In this period, political pamphlets, known as *gazettes à la main*, were becoming so much of a problem that in 1670 a law forbade the selling of libelous writings. The first offense was punished by flogging and banishment, the second by consignment to the galleys. Even well-known writers were not immune to the threat of censorship and banishment. Charles de Marguetel de Saint-Denis, seigneur de Saint-Evremond, for example, was exiled from France, probably for his critique of the monarchy and his libertine connections. The ultimate failure to stem this tide has been used as evidence either of the limits of Louis XIV's power or of his choice not to exert it in certain situations. In the end, accepting the difficulty of suppression and the fact that the notoriety of censorship could inflame rather than deter the public, Colbert and his successors opted for a pragmatic policy balancing strict regulation and stringent punishment with discreet acquiescence.[37]

Censorship in the seventeenth-century theater is still a subject lacking thorough investigation, but it is clear that the official attitude to subversion in the early part of Louis XIV's reign was more relaxed than in the late years of the century, when censorship was strict and theatrical works could disappear without a trace after only a few performances. In his early years, Louis's anticlerical sentiments were not wholly incompatible with those of the libertines, and at times he protected Molière against the *dévôts* in the quarrels over *Tartuffe*. From all the evidence, it appears that the king, as well as his censors, was prepared to overlook much of the innuendo, and even out-

---

37. Nicholas Hensall, *The Myth of Absolutism: Change and Continuity in Early Modern European Monarchy* (London: Longman, 1992), 71; Klaits, *Printed Propaganda*, 43.

right critique, that transpired in the official theater, especially before the mid-1670s. This was particularly true of his attitude toward Molière, for whom he held a genuine fondness and profound respect.

Finally, it is impossible to know for sure what effect the satirical, utopian vision of *Le bourgeois gentilhomme* would have had on the king. We may turn here to Donneau de Visé's comment that Molière took refuge, in the genre of the comédie-ballet, from the king's growing distaste for his spoken plays. In 1670, Molière had just endured a painful period of four years (1665–69) in which *Tartuffe* had been withdrawn by censorship. In *Le bourgeois gentil-homme*, he found a brilliant way to combine the utopianism of Cyrano, Foigny, and Veiras with the impunity of the fool and the upside-down world of carnival folly. Within this framework, Molière's ecstatic celebration of the *fête publique* contained only an indirect critique of the *fête monarchique*, handled lightly and deftly. The success of this strategy is confirmed by the use of *Le bourgeois gentilhomme* as an acknowledged model by playwrights and composers of a future era, particularly those of the *opéra-ballet* around the turn of the century.

It is clear that Molière did experience the cooling of the king's admiration, along with the betrayal of Lully. That the composer, more attuned to the winds of change, abandoned the playwright to take over the monopoly of the Opéra is well known. Louis XIV fully supported Lully's illegal seizure of the operatic *privilège*, as well as his stricture on the musical productions of other theaters, despite its devastating effect on Molière's career. Whatever Lully's involvement in the politics of the comédie-ballet, his decision to seek the Opéra *privilège* would have led him away from the Muse of satire and into the service of the Muse of tragedy in the 1670s.

✳

CHAPTER FOUR

Tragic Interlude

Reversals at the Paris Opéra, 1671–1697

In 1669 the poet Pierre Perrin founded the Académie royale de musique, commonly known as the Opéra, for which he and the composer Robert Cambert produced the pastoral *Pomone* in March of 1671.[1] In the following year, Perrin went to debtor's prison, causing the Académie to close its doors until January 1672, when it reopened for the performance of a second pastoral by Cambert, *Les peines et les plaisirs de l'Amour.* Set to a text by Gabriel Gilbert, this work continues the glorification of love that had always characterized the pastoral and linked it to the court ballet. It also throws into question the system of praise embodied in the imagery of the Muses as flatterers, as it had been developed in the *Ballet des Muses* (1666). In the prologue, Apollo, commanded by the Muses to follow the rule of a totalitarian Jupiter, deserts the Muses and joins with the Graces who defend love. This betrayal enrages the Muses, who castigate the fruits of love as pains and denigrate the deadly powers of Cupid. The Graces, companions of Venus, voice their disagreement, praising the fruits of love as pleasures. The prologue ends with the defeat of the Muses and with the descent of a throne of love, accompanied by Venus, Apollo, cupids, the Graces, Pan, and all the characters of the ballet praising the supreme power of love to transform pains into pleasures.

The prologue, in which Venus and Fame join together to praise Louis XIV as a "new Apollo," identifies the king with Apollo in the pursuant plot. The cruel treatment of Apollo by Jupiter, however, would seem to point up

---

1. On Perrin, see Louis E. Auld, *The Lyric Art of Pierre Perrin* (Henryville, Ottawa: Institute of Medieval Music, 1986).

a split between Louis XIV's roles as patron of the arts and as political ruler, and between an allegorical "Parnassus" and "Olympus," as La Fontaine identified the respective realms of the arts and the seat of Bourbon political power in this period (see chap. 2 above). It could also point to his usurpation of the role of patron from private individuals and perhaps more specifically to his cruel treatment of Fouquet. Produced only six years after the *Ballet des Muses*, it implicates that work in its alignment of the Muses with Jupiter's ruthless authority. It would also seem to echo the parody of the *Ballet des Muses* found in *Le bourgeois gentilhomme*, produced only two years earlier, as well as that work's foundational metaphor of the transformation of pain into pleasure as the means by which a utopia of spectacle could serve as the model for a new society. Altogether, the triumph of pleasure in this work suggested that the offerings of the fledgling Académie would move away from the dictates of the Muses of absolutism, and towards an unmitigated celebration of love and pleasure. It also hinted that leadership of the arts, banished from "Olympus," was now passing into the Parnassus of the public sphere. In 1672, it would have appeared that, with the demise of the court ballet in 1669, the festive arts had indeed been banished from the "Olympus" of Louis XIV's court, and that the new Académie might represent this new Parnassus.

Almost immediately, however, with Lully's well-known confiscation of the *privilège* from Perrin in 1672, the new opera house became an official theater in more than name only. Because of its double status as entertainment for the court as well as for the public, the new genre of French opera, created by Lully and his librettist Philippe Quinault, now reverted somewhat to the formula of the late court ballet in superimposing monarchical praise on a genre consisting of ravishing music, rhetorical eloquence and emotional power. The new opera, like the comédie-ballet of Lully and Molière, carefully negotiated the tastes of its dual audience. It was the genius of Lully and Quinault to balance praise and pleasure, tragedy and pastoral, heroism and *galanterie* in a manner that assured the success of the genre with the king and at court, as well as with the Parisian public. This success would continue until the period of Lully's disgrace with Louis XIV around 1685, ushering in a new era at the Paris Opéra.

The Triumph of the Tragic Muse: The *Tragédies en musique* of Lully and Quinault

The first of Lully's works for the Opéra, a pastoral prepared hastily for his début there, was a pastiche from his comédie-ballets with Molière, entitled

Les fêtes de l'Amour et de Bacchus. For the prologue to this work (LWV 47/2), Lully and Quinault modified the *livret* scene that had served as the prologue to the "Ballet des nations" from *Le bourgeois gentilhomme*. Instead of depicting a utopia of theater, however, as in the original comédie-ballet, the scene is revised to bring it into line with a more serious depiction of its royal patron. The action takes place in a majestic room instead of an ordinary public theater, and there is a "superb palace" depicted on the backdrop. The initial chorus, instead of accelerating in its burlesque confusion, is halted abruptly by the imperious recitative of Polymnia, Muse of theatrical gesture, who insists that the audience cease their common squabbling and speak in the high style more appropriate to a glorious king.[2] Melpomene, Muse of tragedy, and Euterpe, Muse of pastoral, then descend on cloud machines. In their music, respectively "very loud" (*très-forte*) and "very soft" (*très-doux*), Melpomene's dotted rhythms and recitative-like style contrast with Euterpe's simpler song in triple meter.

Polymnia awards the highest status to Melpomene, indicating that the pastoral, though present in the new form of spectacle, would be subordinate to tragedy. For the remainder of the prologue, these three Muses command the rambunctious, lively, and diverse audience of *Le bourgeois gentilhomme* to sing a stilted, artificial tribute to the king, which they teach them line by line like schoolchildren. This scene, written in the year of Molière's death, marks the demise of the comédie-ballet and the manifesto of a new kind of monarchical entertainment emphasizing tragedy and heroism. Inaugurating the direct intervention of monarchical propaganda in the affairs of the Académie royale de musique, it reflects an intention to stamp the king's identity on this new public venue, to silence the collective voice of a heteroglot public, and to continue to use the Muses—the united arts and artists of the new Paris Opéra—as a mouthpiece for royal flattery. The text of the prologue can be read as an intention on the composer's part to turn from the comédie-ballet of Thalia to the more dignified entertainments of Melpomene and Euterpe and to silence the burlesque and Italianate voices of his own compositional past. At the same time, through a different lens, the prologue can also be read as a satirical treatment of Louis XIV's absolutist Muses, now policing a public audience, and as a ironic commentary on the process whereby public entertainment was now constrained to praise the king through the genre of tragedy.

2. Michel de Pure, ed., *Recueil général des opéras représentés par l'Académie royale de musique depuis son établissement*, 3 vols. (1703–46; Geneva: Slatkine, 1971), 1: 40.

The effective victory of Melpomene in the prologue, though not apparent in the burlesque pastiche that followed, was prophetic. In 1674, with *Cadmus et Hermione* (LWV 49), Lully embarked on a series of works variously known as the *tragédie lyrique, tragédie en musique,* or (in the sense of "works") opera. This genre was shaped by his long and fruitful collaboration with Quinault, whose career as a playwright was at its zenith in 1673. Typically, operas were produced every year at court during the period of carnival and then at the Académie royale de musique in the spring around Easter. After *Cadmus,* the Académie was located at the Palais-Royal, Molière's old theater, which the king had granted to Lully. The genre elicited a new sense of status on the part of the Parisian public, now having access to the most privileged form of monarchical entertainment. Despite its structure of five acts and a tragic plot, the tragédie en musique scarcely resembled the spoken tragedies of Corneille and Racine. In some respects, the genre grew out of the late court ballet—especially the *Ballet de la naissance de Venus,* the *Ballet des Muses,* and the *Ballet de Flore*—which had provided a laboratory for its music, dance, stage design, and spectacular machine effects. Each act of the tragédie en musique generally included a divertissement, similar to the ballet but integrated into the action of the whole. While substituting plots of greater cohesiveness and dramatic tension for the ballet's loose succession of entries, the tragédie en musique operated on a different set of principles from those of classical drama, which demanded verisimilitude and the unities of time, place, and action.[3]

The tragédie en musique, like the court ballet, represented an amalgam of heroism and galanterie, but with a more serious tone. Like the more heroic images of the court ballet, the genre was identified with Louis XIV as the touchstone of his taste and reflection of his power. Its roles and imagery, however, were less tangibly tied to the figure of the king. Though setting a heroic, idealistic tone, it did not conform to a specific referent or any one norm of heroic behavior but rather constructed a composite image of heroism, one that through its immensity set a new standard of greatness by which Louis XIV could be measured. Drawn from mythology and legend, its plots are set in a world of adventure and danger filled with gods, dragons, monsters, enemies, armies, warriors, infernal deities, demons, serpents, and

3. Catherine Kintzler, in *Poétique de l'opéra français de Corneille à Rousseau* (Paris: Minerva, 1991), shows how the genre works according to an alternative set of principles that, despite their differences from those of classical theater, maintain an internal integrity and consistency.

Furies. Though the individual heroes of the operas often fall victim to the pitfalls of lesser humans, this fallibility serves only to enhance the image of Louis XIV, who in the prologues retains none of the individual flaws but only the abstract virtues associated with the "greatest hero." The tone of these operas and their prologues, the logical outgrowth of the late superimpositions of absolutism on the court ballet, convey this idea of heroism and seriousness of purpose, now inseparable from the image, if no longer the actual body, of the king. Although utopian imagery occasionally figures in the prologue of the tragédie en musique (that of *Phaéton* takes as its theme the return of the Golden Age), this genre sought to represent not so much fruitful abundance, luxury, and pleasure as awesome danger faced and overcome. The result is a portrayal of Louis XIV as the grand hero of military victories and an almost complete abandonment of any references to his artistic patronage.[4]

The hero of the tragédie en musique is usually either a knight of legend such as Amadis, Rinaldo, or Orlando or a mythological figure such as Theseus, Perseus, or Hercules—all possessing qualities from which the abstract *héros* of the opera prologue is constructed. The operas of Lully and Quinault, especially those of the 1680s, emphasize patriarchal power at the expense of their female characters. *Isis* and *Perséphone* both revolve around abductions as their central plot device, exemplifying the tendency to use rape as a positive symbol for imperial domination.[5] In *Isis*, Quinault conflates European and Egyptian mythology to identify Isis, a central figure in the Egyptian pantheon, with Io, the nymph abducted by Jupiter/Louis as Europa. The opera thus subordinates the matriarchal eastern goddess to the European patriarchal ideal. In *Atys*, the goddess Cybele, a figure of great feminine power from Greek mythology, is portrayed as a victim of helpless love and a villain in her own right as she perpetrates her vengeance on Atys and his beloved.

The late court ballet had represented the overlapping interests of a noble elite class identified with leisure, pleasure, and love, and a king who

4. On the changing image of Louis XIV, see Apostolidès, *Le roi-machine*, 59–65. See also Buford Norman, *Touched by the Graces: The Libretti of Philippe Quinault in the Context of French Classicism* (Birmingham, AL: Summa Publications, 2001), for an analysis of Quinault's *livrets*, primarily from an aesthetic point of view but with some astute observations regarding the ideological content of the prologues and their relationship to the operas.

5. Norman, *Touched by the Graces*, 228. In that sense they stand as theatrical versions of the *parterre d'eau* at Versailles, representing four rapes from classical mythology as the celebration of world order through the use of force.

was beginning to be identified with heroism and military victory. The tragédie en musique inherited the voluptuousness that had characterized the court ballet, for which it was harshly criticized by clerics and other members of the devout party. At the same time, it represents a further shift toward heroism and glory, especially in the frame provided by the prologue, for a king approaching the zenith of his career. In order to create this genre out of the materials of the court ballet, Quinault and Lully had to negotiate the amalgam of the burlesque and the galant in that earlier genre, onto which they had begun to graft a propaganda of power. The burlesque, already on the wane in the late court ballet, continued to decline in the tragédie en musique.

Before coming to opera, Quinault had incorporated an aesthetic of galanterie into the genre of the *tragédie galante* with great success. Quinault sensed the taste of the Parisian public, which—like salon society—seemed to have an insatiable interest in love's conventions and games, and his emphasis on galanterie in his collaboration with Lully created a veritable craze for opera. Quinault's aesthetic owes a debt to both the galant poets of the salon and to the pastoral novel. His affinity for galant maxims and poetic forms,[6] along with Lully's affinity for the underlying structure of galant dances and airs that had characterized the ballet, ensured that love and pleasure would still remain at the heart of the genre's artistic conception. The success of these qualities was assured by their appeal to a primarily upper-class audience, identified with galanterie, along with an upwardly mobile bourgeoisie who sought to imitate them.[7] There is also no reason to doubt Louis XIV's taste for the combination of heroism and romance, as it had developed in the chivalric novel, nor would he have rejected the incorporation of themes of pleasure as a means of strengthening the "hero's" association with nobility, refinement, and taste. Nonetheless, in almost all of Lully's

6. Marilyn K. Browne, "Opera and the *Galant homme:* Quinault and Lully's *Tragédie en musique, Atys,* in the Context of Seventeenth-Century Modernism" (M.A. thesis, University of North Texas, 1994), 35–61.

7. On French opera audiences in the late-seventeenth and early-eighteenth centuries, see Arianne Ducrot, "Les representations de l'Académie de musique au temps de Louis XIV (1671–1715)," *Recherches sur la musique française classique* 10 (1970):19–55; La Gorce, *L'Opéra à Paris* and "Opéra et son public au temps de Louis XIV," *Bulletin de la Société de l'histoire de Paris et de l'île de France* 108 (1981): 27–46; John Lough, *Paris Theatre Audiences in the Seventeenth and Eighteenth Centuries* (London: Oxford University Press, 1957); Paul Lacroix, *The Eighteenth Century: Its Institutions, Customs, and Costumes* (New York: Ungar, 1963); and Pierre Mélèse, *Le théâtre et le public à Paris sous Louis XIV, 1659–1715* (1934; Geneva: Slatkine, 1976).

operas a tension exists, as in the late court ballet, between the demands of pleasure and power, love and glory.

The prologues of Lully and Quinault occasionally take this tension for their actual subject. The question is generally resolved—as in the prologues to *Atys, Proserpine,* and *Phaéton*—through the image of Louis triumphant imposing peace. Louis XIV's warlike imperialism is justified because it bestows glory on the state, while also making possible the return of fruition, abundance, and pleasure. Melpomene, Muse of tragedy, takes precedence as the repository of the memory of Louis's glorious deeds, while pastoral scenes often have their motivation in a celebration of peace gained through heroic conflict rather than of pleasure as its own reward.

In general, the tragédie en musique succeeds in yoking together the demands of love and glory, or at least resolving their difference by the end of the prologue. In some cases, however, the limits placed on pleasure are tested as the artists of the tragédie en musique become its declared advocates. Quinault's first two libretti present the persona of the artist pleading with Louis to turn from the glory of war to the pleasures of peace. The dedication of *Cadmus*, written in the midst of the war with Holland declared in 1672, complains that the poet "comes in vain to offer you the charms [of opera]; you do not take your eyes off war."[8] He adds that "the empire over which you rule, without seeking to expand, / Finds enough greatness in having you for its master, / Your reign suffices for its felicity / Allow it to rejoice in tranquility."[9] Finally, in a passage directly opposing the mythology of love to Louis XIV's military campaigns, he pleads, "No longer be content to be the terror of the world, / And reflect that heaven answers our desires by giving you to us / To be the Cupid and the Pleasures of humanity."[10]

The dedication of *Alceste* (1674), written another year into the Dutch wars when the fortunes of France were on the wane, declares that "a frightful season lays waste the earth enough / Without adding still the horrors of war" and ends by begging the king, "despite the heat of your noble de-

---

8. Philippe Quinault, *Livrets d'opéra*, ed. Buford Norman (Toulouse: Société de Littératures Classiques, 1999), 1: 2: "Mais je viens vainement vous en offrir les charmes; / Vous ne tournez les yeux que du côté des armes."

9. Ibid: "L'Empire où Vous régnez, sans chercher à s'accroître, / Trouve assez de grandeur à Vous avoir pour Maître, / Votre règne suffit à sa félicité, / Souffrez qu'il en jouisse avec tranquillité."

10. Ibid., 3: "Ne Vous contentez plus d'être l'Effroi du Monde, / Et songez que le Ciel Vous donne à nos desires / Pour être des humains l'Amour et les Plaisirs."

sires / Endure [a period of] respite and allow the pleasures."[11] The prologue of *Alceste* (LWV 50/2) picks up this theme, clothing it in mythological garb. Entitled "Le retour des Plaisirs," it is set against the backdrop of the gardens of the Tuileries, where the nymph of the Seine, fearing the extended absence of "the hero," greets with dismay the martial fanfare ("bruit de guerre") of Glory (La Gloire). "He [Louis] follows you too much into the horror of combat," she complains; "Leave his triumphant valor in peace for a moment."[12] The prologue climaxes with a chorus, which alternates strings and bucolic oboes with military fanfares of trumpets and drums, and ends with a general celebration of the return of the Pleasures.

In the prologue to *Thésée* (1675, LWV 51/2–15), a chorus of cupids, Graces, Pleasures, and Games—set against a backdrop of the façade of the palace of Versailles—complains that Louis XIV, loving only victory, has neglected the Pleasures. One of the Pleasures laments that Venus hoped in vain to establish her court in the gardens of Versailles. Venus calls upon her retinue to reanimate the gardens with love, and as Venus's lover, Mars uses his powers to overcome Bellona, goddess of war. Venus and Mars then celebrate the coexistence of pleasure and glory under Louis XIV, who is to be both loved and feared. The prologue ends with Mars, Venus, Bacchus, and Ceres praising the presence of peace and plenty, even in the midst of war.

In the dialogue between Melpomene and Flora in the prologue of *Atys* (1676, 53/2–12), followers of the imperious Melpomene, insisting on dominance over the goddess of peace and pleasure, ask Flora to yield as they sing, "Let the rustic charms / of Flora and her games / Cede to the magnificent trappings / Of the tragic Muse / And her pompous spectacles."[13] Through the mediation of the goddess Iris, however, who extends her rainbow of peace in the sky, the two groups rejoin, symbolizing that tragedy and pastoral both have a place in the tragédie en musique. In effect the voice of the artist in Quinault's two dedications, pleading with Louis to turn his attention to the arts and leisure, merges with the voice of Flora, begging Melpomene to share the tragic stage with the divertissements of pleasure. This strategy,

11. Ibid., 54, 55: "Une affreuse saison desole assez la Terre, / Sans y mêler encor les horreurs de la guerre"; "Et malgré la chaleur de Vos Nobles Désires, / Endurez le repos & souffrez les plaisirs."

12. Ibid., 59: "Il ne te suit que trop dans l'horreur des combats; / Laisse en paix un moment sa Valeur triomphante."

13. Ibid., 174–75: "Que l'agrément rustique / De Flore & de ses jeux, / Cede à l'appareil magnifique / De la Muse tragique, / Et de ses spectacles pompeux."

flattering Louis XIV's artistic patronage, allies the arts with the goddess Flora, symbol of spring and abundance. It also presents the artists' program, couched within the time-honored language of flattery, as desirable to Louis himself and to France. Finally, it aligns tragedy with the king's militarism and pastoral with the advocacy of peace and pleasure.

Praise of the king in the prologue to *Isis* (1677) begins with a particularly spectacular chorus (LWV 54/2, see ex. 4.1). The curtain opens onto the palace and the throne of Fame, where this deity, accompanied by her retinue and a crowd of followers, is seated with her trumpet. A throng of allegorical Rumors and Noises, all likewise holding trumpets, arrive from the corners of the earth and join the retinue of Fame. All these forces join together to form a large chorus, introduced and punctuated by a military fanfare for strings, five trumpets, and continuo. (A timpani part, which would also have been included, has been added editorially.) Its march-like rhythm and meter, diatonic C-major harmony, and syllabic homophony, along with an easily retained melody, illustrate this text: "Declare everywhere / The triumphant valor of the greatest of heroes; / Let the earth and the heavens / Resound with the sound of his magnificence."[14] This passage recalls the fanfares and marches that Lully, Philidor, and others had composed for Louis XIV's military campaigns and also for the victory celebrations that marked their successful conclusion. As Robert Isherwood has shown, given the frequency of war during Louis XIV's reign, these military celebrations were the most numerous and pompous of all ceremonies; even when the fortunes of France were on the wane, they redirected attention to the glory and grandeur of the king. Lully was one of several composers contributing martial airs for the king's wind band and trumpet calls and drum signals for military maneuvers. These were frequently recycled among the battlefield and various royal parades and ceremonies. Such a ceremony, staged by officers and musicians of the Écurie, had marked the conquest and occupation of Franche-Comté three years earlier, in 1674. Under a triumphal arch in the Place du Palais-Royal, the allegorical figure of Victory had crowned a statue of the king. Accompanied by Felicity, Abundance, and the Pleasures, against the backdrop of fountains flowing with wine, dancers

14. Quinault, *Livrets d'opéra*, 2: 1: "Publions en tous lieux, / Du plus grand des heros, la valeur triomphante, / Que la Terre & les Cieux / Retentissent du bruit de sa gloire éclatante." I am grateful to Lionel Sawkins for an advance copy of the score to *Isis*, which will appear in Lully, *Oeuvres complètes*, series 3 (Opéras), vol. 6 (Hildesheim: Georg Olms, forthcoming).

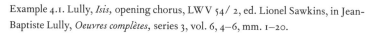

Example 4.1. Lully, *Isis*, opening chorus, LWV 54/ 2, ed. Lionel Sawkins, in Jean-Baptiste Lully, *Oeuvres complètes*, series 3, vol. 6, 4–6, mm. 1–20.

* The parts for Trompettes 3, 4 and 5 are derived from the parts for
  Haute-Contre de Violon, Taille de Violon and Quinte de Violon.
** The part for Timballes is editorial.

Example 4.1. (*continued*)

Example 4.1. (*continued*)

Example 4.1. (*continued*)

15

represented nations submitting to Louis's authority, while choruses praised his victories.[15]

As in many of Lully's operas, the prologue to *Isis* consists of a dialogue between the forces of glory and those of pleasure. The final scene presents the nine Muses, the liberal arts, and Apollo, in conversation with Fame, Neptune, and their retinues. Calliope, Muse of poetry, calls for a cessation of the terrible noise of war and joins with Clio, Melpomene, Thalia, and Urania in pleading that it not interfere with the sounds of their "divine harmonies." The Muses then join Apollo in begging Fame to speak not only of "cruel war" but also of pleasures and games, and the prologue ends, like that of *Alceste*, with an invitation of the allegorical Pleasures.

A dialectical pattern, then, emerges in the operas composed during the period of the Dutch wars (1672–78). In *Cadmus* and *Alceste*, Quinault speaks for the artists of the opera in rhetorically begging Louis to turn his attention from war to the pleasures of peace. The plots of the operas composed throughout the 1670s frequently involve the tension between glory and love. The prologues to *Thésée*, *Atys*, and *Isis* are based, likewise, on a dialogue between the forces of glory and war on one side, and on the other, the pleasures of peace, including the arts, and more specifically opera itself. This dialogue typically involves a complaint—from characters such as Venus, Flora, and the Muses—that Louis XIV's wars are usurping the place of love, the pleasures, and the arts. After some disagreement, the dialogue ends with a reconciliation between these forces and an agreement—from balancing characters such as Mars, Melpomene, and Fame—to love as well as to fear Louis XIV, to invite the allegorical Pleasures, and more generally, to partake of the pleasures of peace even in the midst of war. While the rhetorical strategy changes little throughout the decade of the 1670s, the role of the Muses evolves. In *Les fêtes de l'Amour et de Bacchus*, the Muses (recalling their absolutist models in the *Ballet des Muses* and their more cruel counterparts in the slightly earlier *Peines et plaisirs de l'Amour*) imperiously force a public audience to praise Louis XIV. In *Alceste*, Melpomene and Flora represent the opposing sides of glory and pleasure. Finally, in *Isis*, all the Muses, together with the liberal arts, join together to protest glory and to champion pleasure.

Though prominent in the prefaces and divertissements of the early cycle of tragédies en musique, pleas for peace and the invitations of the Pleasures abate in the operas after *Isis*. This change may be attributed to the peace

---

15. Isherwood, *Music in the Service of the King*, 281–87.

resulting from the treaty of Nijmegen (1678), praised in the prologues to *Bellerophon* (LWV 57) in 1679 and *Proserpine* (LWV 58) in 1680, which provided a respite from the exigencies of war. It may also be attributed to a different view of love and pleasure in the decade of the 1680s. Coinciding with the secret marriage of Louis XIV to the morally upright Mme de Maintenon, the operas of the 1680s reflect Louis's own turn from marital infidelity to a monogamous piety and religious austerity accompanying the increasing political control of his later years. The late operas emphasize the dangers of the excess of love. Thus, in *Roland* (LWV 65, 1685), Orlando's neglect of reason leads to madness; and in *Armide* (LWV 71, 1686), the sorceress Armida's amorous witchcraft represents the opposite of the hero Rinaldo's heroism. Patricia Howard argues that the pastoral scenes of these late works, rather than celebrating the galant aspects of love as before, now tend to signal its perverse, pernicious aspects.[16] In addition, the late operas often represent a *heroisme manqué,* using the tragic flaws of their characters as a negative reinforcement of the perfection of Louis XIV as the "greatest hero."

In these late works, the claims of love most often lose out to the claims of glory, but not in any simplistic manner. In 1686, Louis XIV's choice of the legend of Armida and Rinaldo, in which the hero overcomes the magic of the enchantress, has been read as a final commitment of the king to the path of glory and duty and a renunciation of love and the arts.[17] In *Armide,* however, the role of the eponymous heroine is so vividly and sympathetically drawn that the audience is reluctant to welcome the ultimate victory of the hero, Rinaldo. On the contrary, through the emotional power of Lully's music, the listener tends to share Rinaldo's passionate desire more than his sense of duty. The power of music to serve love, as opposed to duty and reason, had been introduced in the *Ballet des amours déguisés,* where a group of court musicians, costumed as shepherds and representing the cupids in disguise, sought to persuade Rinaldo to remain with Armida. From the beginning, then, the artists of the ballet had been subtly identified with the side of love, and that identification continued in Quinault's prefaces and perhaps ultimately in the portrayal of human passion, nowhere more evident than in *Armide.*

16. Patricia Howard, "Quinault, Lully, and the *Précieuses:* Images of Women in Seventeenth-Century France," in *Cecilia Reclaimed: Feminist Perspectives on Gender and Music,* ed. Susan C. Cook and Judy S. Tsou (Urbana: University of Illinois Press, 1994), 70–89; and "The Influence of the *Précieuses* on Content and Structure in Quinault's and Lully's *Tragédies Lyriques,*" *Acta musicologica* 63 (1991): 57–72. See also Norman, *Touched by the Graces,* 305–51.

17. Couvreur, *Jean-Baptiste Lully,* 401–2.

La Fontaine's Letter on Opera as Political Critique

The performance of Lully's *Isis* in 1677 provoked Jean de La Fontaine to pen a document in which opera criticism is colored by politics. The letter to his trusted friend Pierre Niert, the singer and pedagogue who had taught Michel Lambert and Hilaire Dupuis, remained unpublished until the year of the death of Louis XIV. Even that publication continued to omit the most politically sensitive passages of La Fontaine's long letter in verse, which did not appear until 1765.[18] In the strongest of these passages, La Fontaine criticizes the bombast and grandiosity of the tragédie en musique. Comparing the king's operas with his military campaigns, he equates Lully's large choruses with the shouts of soldiers, and the ballets with the gladiator games of ancient Rome:

> Grand in everything, he wants to make everything grand,
> War constitutes his joy and his greatest passion;
> His divertissements all resemble war,
> His concerts of instruments are characterized by the noise of thunder,
> And his vocal concerts resemble the outbursts
> Made by the shouts of soldiers in a day of combat.
> The dancers, by their number, dazzle the sight,
> And the ballet appears as a [military] exercise, review,
> Gladiator game on the field of Mars,
> Such as the Caesars would hold on their days of triumph.[19]

Ignoring the intimate and voluptuous passages of the work, as well as the ideological dialectic complicating the dialogue between Fame and the Muses in its prologue, La Fontaine clearly targets the heroic and militaristic aspects of Lully's opera, more specifically the laudatory verses of Fame and her followers that open the work.

---

18. The piece was first printed, with omissions, in *Nouveau choix de pièces de poésie*, ed. Duval de Tours (Paris, 1715). It was reprinted in the same form in *Oeuvres diverses de La Fontaine* (Paris, 1758), and published complete for the first time in the Abbé Sablier, *Variétés sérieuses et amusantes* (Paris, 1765). On Niert, see chapter 1 above.

19. La Fontaine, *Oeuvres diverses*, ed. Pierre Clarac (Paris: Bibliothèque de la Pléiade, 1958), 618: "Grand en tout, il veut mettre en tout de la grandeur; / La guerre fait sa joie et sa plus forte ardeur; / Ses divertissements ressentent tous la guerre; / Ses concerts d'instruments ont le bruit du tonnerre, / Et ses concerts de voix ressemblent aux éclats / Qu'en un jour de combat font les cris des soldats. / Les danseurs, par leur nombre, / éblouissent la vue, / Et le ballet paroît exercice, revue, / Jeu de gladiateurs, et tel qu'au champ de Mars / En leurs jours de triomphe en donnoient les Césars."

La Fontaine, writing during the period of Louis XIV's war on Holland, makes a clear distinction between Lully's operatic language and a genre and style of singing, developed by Niert, that had earlier combined the expressivity of the Italians with the delicacy of the French. In contrast to the massed violins and harpsichords and the warlike trumpets and drums of *Isis*, La Fontaine favors pieces designed to be performed in smaller, private, more intimate venues. These pieces can range from the flute and oboe of amorous shepherds to more sophisticated chamber airs for voice and lute. Nostalgically recalling the chamber music concerts Lambert and Dupuis had presented in their home, he also speaks with nostalgia of the airs of Lambert, Sébastien Le Camus, and Jean-Baptiste Boësset; the harpsichord music of Jacques Champion de Chambonnières; and the lute music of Denis Gaultier.

La Fontaine's preference for the air and chamber music of an earlier period may also have political implications. The air was most commonly accompanied by the lute, specifically the long-necked bass lute known as the theorbo (*théorbe*), while the eleven-string baroque lute was the solo instrument of choice. The early seventeenth-century lute repertoire of Ennemond and Denis Gaultier and their contemporaries was characterized by a vaporous, improvisatory style filled with ornaments, arpeggios, and unexpected melodic and harmonic turns. It influenced the harpsichord music of Chambonnières, Louis Couperin, and Jean Henry D'Anglebert, a repertoire eagerly embraced by salon society. Much of this music, both vocal and instrumental, had an effect of discontinuity and timelessness, undermining any clear sense of tonal direction or rhythmic drive. Its aesthetic suited the salon, which valued sensuousness and pleasure for their own sake. Its indirect discursive mode was suitable to the passing of time without pressing goals or need for forceful or pointed rhetoric, as opposed to the direct, overpowering discursive mode of monarchical propaganda—an opposition implicit in La Fontaine's wistful comparison of the lone voice of a lute, sounding in the *ruelle* of a salon,[20] with the thunderous forces of the opera.

This nostalgia for a dying musical sensibility had already been treated by La Fontaine, in his *Songe de Vaux* (1671), as an evocation of the fragile world shaped by Fouquet and later shattered by his imprisonment and the resulting dislocation of the artists under his patronage. The *Songe* represents the poet's memory of Fouquet's chateau at Vaux-le-Vicomte as a latter-day

---

20. Since the early seventeenth century, it had been fashionable for women to hold salons in their bedrooms, where the *ruelle*, or private corridor beside the bed, represented the most intimate access to the hostess.

1. *Ballet des fêtes de Bacchus*, Apollo and the Muses, Bibliothèque nationale de France.

2. *Ballet de la nuit*, costume of Jean-Baptiste Lully as a beggar. Art Resource.

3. *Ballet de la nuit*, costume of Louis XIV as the Rising Sun. Art Resource.

4. Antoine Watteau, *Pilgrimage to Cythera* (Paris: Louvre), oil on canvas, 1717. Art Resource.

5. Antoine Watteau, *Pilgrimage to Cythera* (Berlin: Charlottenburg Palace), oil on canvas, c. 1718–19. Art Resource.

6. Detail of figure 5, *Pilgrimage to Cythera*, ship. Art Resource.

7. Detail of figure 5, *Pilgrimage to Cythera*, Venus term. Art Resource.

8. Antoine Watteau, *L'isle de Cythère*, oil on canvas. Städelschen Kunstinstitut, Frankfurt.

conflation of Arcadia, Parnassus, and Cythera, celebrating Venus and Cupid as rulers over a utopian world of love and peace. A remarkable passage in this work describes the competition between Lambert and a dying swan. In this passage, the speaker, wandering through the grounds of Vaux, is drawn by the sound of a lute and learns that Lambert has been brought by carriage to compete with a dying swan on the lake. After tuning his lute, Lambert sings one of his airs, and all are astonished at its beauty. Compared to Orpheus and Amphion, the musician is said to have walked the grounds of Vaux with Fouquet, the sound of his voice causing the stones to spring into the architecture of its chateau without need of machines or human hands. The company assembled are afraid the dying swan will be afraid to compete with Lambert, but finally it too sings its song, which is judged to be far inferior to the composer's. This passage may be interpreted as a "swan song" not only for Fouquet and his world but also for the dream of a society built on the aesthetic of the delicate air and the lute. As Catherine Massip points out, it implies that Lambert may have at some point enjoyed the patronage of Fouquet.[21] Whether or not that is true, clearly the figure of Lambert—as singer, lutenist, and composer of airs—was for La Fontaine a swan-like icon of a dying social, political, and musical era.

From at least the early seventeenth century, the *air de cour* and other chamber music was associated with a courtly music of peace and leisure, a respite for the king and his court after the labors of war, as opposed to the warlike trumpets and drums. As François Richard (c. 1585–1650) wrote in the dedication to Louis XIII of his *Airs de cour à quatre parties* of 1637, "I know that after the sounds of the trumpets and drums, those of lute and voices do not displease you."[22] Louis XIII and Louis XIV both kept a dynamic *musique de chambre* as a division of their musical establishments, and both excelled as soloists, on the lute and guitar, respectively. Louis XIV also enjoyed chamber music and the airs of Lambert. The air had a prominent role as the foundation for the *récits* and other vocal music of the court ballet and served as the basis for Lully's compositional style in the tragédie en musique.

La Fontaine's critique in this passage fails to account for either the king's love of chamber music or the more intimate moments of the tragédie en musique. Instead, the poet seems to be expressing a preference not only for a quieter, pastoral chamber style but also for a galant literary style that he himself had developed in the previous decade, in his *Les amours de Psyché*

21. Massip, *L'art de bien chanter*, 113–14.

22. Quoted in Anthony, *French Baroque Music*, 412.

et de Cupidon (1669) and *Le songe de Vaux* (1671). More immediately, he is probably also advocating a pastoral operatic style that he also had developed in the mid-1670s. It has been noted that *Les amours de Psyché et de Cupidon* in many ways resembles an opera *livret*,[23] and the love-drenched *tragédie-ballet* entitled *Psyché*, produced by Louis and Thomas Corneille at the Opéra in 1671, was directly influenced by La Fontaine's novel.[24]

There is a possibility that Lully invited La Fontaine to write a *livret* for his use or at least that La Fontaine believed he could persuade Lully to accept one. In September 1674, La Fontaine presented the *livret* for the pastoral *Daphné* to the composer, who famously rejected it, ostensibly because the pastoral had fallen out of favor with the public. The disappointed poet subsequently composed a diatribe in verse against Lully, entitled *Le Florentin*, but the antipathy was resolved in later years. In 1674 or 1675, he began another *livret*, *Galatée*, which was never completed. Finally, in 1691, his *L'Astrée* was produced at the Opéra, with music by Pascal Collasse. All of these works look back to the cult of love codified in D'Urfé's *L'Astrée* and in the salons, taken to its most poetic extreme. Though ultimately unsuccessful commercially, these *livrets* represent the transfer of La Fontaine's aesthetic, as set forth in his letter to Niert, to his own attempts at opera. Their pastoral settings, perhaps influencing Lully's own turn to the pastoral in his *Acis et Galatée*, may have also influenced a pastoral vogue at the Opéra in the 1690s.

La Fontaine's *Lettre* follows up on Madeleine de Scudéry's advocacy, in *L'histoire de Sapho*, for the fête galante as the ideological counterpart to the *fête monarchique* (see chap. 2 above). La Fontaine was a friend of Scudéry, and his opposition of chamber music to the tragédie en musique parallels her praise of *les petites choses* of love and the pleasures of the salon as an alternative to *les grandes choses* of wars and great events. Neither author seems to have been disturbed by the fact that Louis XIV also presented fêtes galantes to his courtiers. The message they both convey is rather that the salon, with its emphasis on elegant behavior and the artful life rather than noble birth, could now serve as the iconic signifier of a new way of life and a new society. In this sense, La Fontaine's nostalgic homage to the *air* supports and adds another layer to a growing aesthetic and ideology of the fête galante.

23. Geoffrey Burgess, "La Fontaine Sets the Stage . . . and Waits in the Wings: *Les Amours de Psyché et de Cupidon* and the Production and Politics of Opera in Seventeenth-Century France," paper delivered at a meeting of the American Musicological Society, Houston, 2003.

24. In 1678 a new version of this work was produced as a tragédie en musique. Both versions will be discussed further in chapter 5.

Lully, the Libertines, and the Grand Dauphin

Lully's *Acis et Galatée* (LWV 73), with a *livret* by Jean Galbert de Campistron, represents a striking new direction for the composer, which details of his life help to explain. At the beginning of 1685, it came to the attention of Louis XIV that Lully had engaged in illicit relations with a page named Brunet. In an earlier time the king might have condoned such behavior, but unfortunately for Lully, the incident occurred during the height of the influence of the *parti des dévôts* and the devout Mme de Maintenon. It also came just after an upsetting scandal surrounding the debauchery and death of the comte de Vermandois, Louis XIV's son by Louise de La Vallière, and during the period of Louis's health crisis with a painful anal fistula. Probably for all these reasons, Louis reacted to this incident with extreme displeasure. A letter written by Rodolphe Reuss, dated January 24, 1685, mentions that the monarch had forbidden Lully to appear in his presence. According to the *Nouvelles ecclésiastiques* a few days later, Lully was warned that a repeat offense would carry the punishment of burning at the stake, and the journalist predicted that the Opéra would "soon go up in smoke" as well. Although probably exaggerated, these claims reflect the seriousness of Lully's position.[25]

During this period, Louis XIV's interest in Lully's music began to wane. Although the composer retained his official position at court, his major works of this period were composed for other patrons. The Dauphin took charge of the creation and execution of Lully's ballet *Le temple de la paix*, going so far as to oversee rehearsals of the work. In 1686, Louis suspended the usual practice of presenting Lully's operas at court before they appeared at the Opéra. Despite the public success of *Armide*, it was never staged at Versailles. Concert versions were produced at court for the Dauphin, the Dauphine, and the princesse de Conti, but there is no evidence that Louis XIV ever attended a performance. When Lully approached the king to ask for his support for a new opera, Louis is said to have responded that the funds would be better employed in the service of the poor.[26]

At this time, Lully found a protector in his friend the duc de Vendôme (1654–1712) and in the libertine community led by the duc's brother Philippe (1655–1727), the "Grand Prieur" of the knights of the order of the Hospitaliers de Saint-Jean de Jérusalem dating back to the thirteenth century. Philippe de Vendôme lived in the massive old fortress in the Marais, still

25. La Gorce, *Jean-Baptiste Lully*, 317.
26. Ibid., 331, citing a quotation from the *Nouvelles ecclésiastiques* of February 18, 1686.

known today as "the old Temple," that had sheltered this order for centuries. The Temple and the surrounding community, standing outside Parisian police jurisdiction, had become a refuge for oppressed people of all kinds. The size of the community was probably already large; documents from 1759 show that at that time it numbered approximately four thousand. La Fontaine and later Fontenelle were habitués there, as well as the libertine poets Guillaume Amfrye de Chaulieu[27] and Charles Antoine de La Fare, the composer Henri Desmarets, and the courtesan Ninon de Lenclos.[28]

The community of the Temple was one of unbridled and illicit pleasures. The duc, who stayed at the Temple when in Paris, was widely known as a sodomite, and the Grand Prieur shared a mistress, a *musicienne* at the Opéra, with the Abbé Chaulieu and the marquis de La Fare. According to La Fare's memoirs, Lully was a "friend to all."[29] Campistron, the librettist of *Acis et Galatée,* was employed by the duc de Vendôme as his secretary. Saint-Simon said of him, "Campistron was one of those dirty poets, dying of hunger, who will do anything to survive. The Abbé Chaulieu picked him up—God knows where—and took him to the home of the Grand Prieur, which . . . he [later] left like a rat from a sinking ship and burrowed into the home of M. de Vendôme. Although his handwriting was not legible, he made him his secretary."[30] A chanson of the day, making reference to his equal taste for ugly women and pretty boys, called him "the greatest bugger of all humans."[31] These comments probably say at least as much about the

27. Chaulieu was a close friend of Jean-Baptiste Lully; his letters attest to occasions when the composer and the poet vied in writing compliments to the singer Mlle Rochois, and Chaulieu was known to have improvised verses to Lully's music at private dinners. See Robert Finch, *The Sixth Sense: Individualism in French Poetry, 1686–1760* (Toronto: University of Toronto Press, 1966), 68.

28. On Ninon's association with libertinism, see Jeanneret, *Eros rebelle,* 179–85. Lully's connections with this libertine circle have been a subject of fascination but, until La Gorce's recent biography, little hard evidence. Unfortunately, information from Henry Prunières's fictionalized biography of Lully (*La vie illustre et libertine de Jean-Baptiste Lully* [Paris: Plon, 1929]) has confused the issue by being occasionally cited as fact. See for example Scott, *Molière: A Theatrical Life,* 309, note 25.

29. Perrens, *Les libertins en France,* 346–51; La Gorce, *Jean-Baptiste Lully,* 332–33.

30. La Gorce, *Jean-Baptiste Lully,* 333: "L'abbé de Chaulieu l'avait ramassé je ne sais où et l'avait mis chez le grand prieur, d'où, sentant que la maison croulait, il en était sorti comme les rats et s'était fourré chez M. de Vendôme. Quoique son écriture ne fût pas lisible, il était devenu son secrétaire."

31. Ibid., 334: "Du plus bougre des humains."

contemporary reaction to libertine morality as about the librettist's biography. In fact, Campistron was the highly regarded author of two tragedies that had recently been well received on the Parisian stage, and in general his plays found more success with the Parisian public than any playwright's since the death of Racine.[32]

The duc de Vendôme lived in a chateau in the country at Anet. In September of 1686 he and his brother sponsored a magnificent, week-long fête there in honor of the Dauphin, who spent four or five days at the estate. It was for this occasion that Lully and Campistron were commissioned to produce *Acis,* which was also performed at the Opéra later in the year. Its *livret* represents a radical turn away from the pompous heroism and praise of the tragédie en musique. The prologue, self-reflexively set at the chateau d'Anet, lavishly praises the Dauphin and the duc de Vendôme's chateau. Though lip service is paid to Louis XIV and his glory, the prologue represents a paean to Comus, the god of entertainment, and to the reconvening of the Games and Pleasures under the direction of the Dauphin at the chateau d'Anet. The three acts of the pastoral may be read as a critique of Louis XIV and as a thinly veiled account of his treatment of Lully. The plot revolves around the love of the shepherd Acis for the water nymph Galatée. The latter, fearing the wrath of the monster Polyphemus, has acquiesced to the monster's offer of prestige and power despite her love for Acis. On behalf of the nymph, and of free love against tyrannical power, Acis confronts the monster. In a stage action of unsurpassed violence, Polyphemus, infuriated, kills the "traitor" by crushing him with a rock. The work can be read as an autobiographical account of Lully as the shepherd Acis, crushed under the cruel authority of Louis XIV. If so, it would follow in a line of libertine novels by D'Assoucy, Cyrano, Tristan, and others, who present their autobiographical antiheroes as victims of their difference in a manner that borders on paranoia.[33]

The fête at Anet was attended not only by the Dauphin but also by most of the court nobility, many of whom partook of its pleasures over the course

32. On Campistron, see Dorothy F. Jones, *Jean de Campistron: A Study of His Life and Work* (University, MS: Romance Monographs, 1979). His relationship to the Vendômes is discussed in the chapter "The Vendômes," 88–102. Campistron's plays have never been studied in the light of their ideological content. Since at least one was withdrawn because of censorship, such an investigation might bring to light patterns similar to those in the *livrets.*

33. DeJean, *Libertine Strategies,* 101–56.

of several days. Its festivities included five performances of *Acis et Galatée*, performed by musicians from the Paris Opéra at great expense to the duc. The piece was staged by Jean Berain, stage designer of the Opéra, and it starred Marthe le Rochois and Louise and Françoise Moureau, mistresses of Chaulieu, La Fare, and the Grand Prieur, respectively. According to La Fare's memoirs, Louis XIV was not pleased about this event. He did not allow the performance of *Acis et Galatée* at court, even in concert version, and he began to commission other composers, including Desmarets, Jean-Baptiste Boësset, and Michel-Richard de Lalande (favored by the *dévôts* because of his role in the king's sacred music) in Lully's place. Shortly after the production of *Acis* closed at the Opéra at the end of 1686, Louis XIV evicted Lully and his company from the Palais-Royal, in order to house the duc de Chartres there. In March of 1687, the composer purchased property on the rue Saint-André-des-arts, with the intention of building a new opera house, but these arrangements were interrupted by his untimely death from gangrene on March 22.[34]

At the time of Lully's death he was working on another opera, *Achille et Polixène* (LWV 74), with a *livret* by Campistron. Collasse, Lully's student and secretary, completed the score. The first act of this work treats the story of Achilles and Patroclus, in which Patroclus's bravery and death set an example for the reluctant Achilles. Despite the dedication of the remainder of the work to Achilles' love for Polyxena, daughter of Priam, the fact that the relationship between the two warriors was traditionally considered a locus classicus for homoerotic love would not have been lost on the libertine community to which the librettist belonged.[35] Lecerf de la Viéville recounts an interesting anecdote concerning *Achille et Polixène*. At the beginning of 1687, when Lully believed that he was going to die, a confessor refused to give him absolution unless he burned his unfinished opera.

34. La Gorce, *Jean-Baptiste Lully*, 334–37; *L'Opéra à Paris*, 66–79; Jones, *Jean de Campistron*, 94.

35. On the homoerotic dimension of the myth of Achilles and Patroclus, see Bernard Sergent, *Homosexuality in Greek Myth*, trans. by Arthur Goldhammer (Boston: Continuum/Athlone, 1986), 250ff.; Wendy Heller, "Reforming Achilles: Gender, 'Opera Seria,' and the Rhetoric of the Enlightened Hero," *Early Music* 26 (1998): 562–81; Kenneth James Dover, *Greek Homosexuality* (1978; rev. ed, Cambridge: Harvard University Press, 1989), 197–99; David M. Halperin, *One Hundred Years of Homosexuality and Other Essays on Greek Love* (New York: Routledge, 1990), 179 n. 3; and Carol Ockman, "Profiling Homoeroticism: Ingres's *Achilles Receiving the Ambassadors of Agamemnon*," *Art Bulletin* 75 (June 1993): 259–74.

Lully acquiesced, but a short time later, believing himself out of danger, he claimed that he had saved another copy of this work.[36]

In April of the same year, Campistron's tragedy *Phraate* was removed from the boards after only two performances, probably because of censorship. The author was quoted as saying, "They did not say I was a poor poet. They said that I was imprudent and I would get myself thrown into the Bastille."[37] Campistron later wrote another *livret, Alcide,* set to music by Lully's son Louis and Marin Marais. After Lully's death he continued his association with the duc de Vendôme, becoming a member of his retinue and serving under his command at the battle of Steinkirchen in 1692.[38] The duc de Vendôme continued to serve as a commander in the king's army until 1710, when he himself fell into disgrace.[39]

With a knowledge of these background connections and secret intrigues, it is possible to link Lully to a cabal around the Dauphin, just beginning to arise in Lully's last years. This prince, a lover of the arts, was admired by members of the nobility and by artists, particularly those of the Paris Opéra. From the 1680s until his death in 1711, he served as monarch of a veritable countercourt that gathered there.[40] His faction included princes and princesses of the blood, excluded from power by Louis XIV and Mme de Maintenon. It became increasingly powerful as Louis XIV aged and as courtiers anticipated the transition of power from the king to his son. The Dauphin's chateau at Meudon became known as "the court of Meudon," and in the late years of the century courtiers found it necessary, as it was said, to "mix visits to Marly [Louis XIV's chateau] with visits to Meudon." Before his own disgrace, the duc de Vendôme was a leader of this cabal, later known as the "cabal de Vendôme." Though factions were fluid and diverse during the late reign of Louis XIV, the Dauphin found many supporters among the nobility, who appreciated his hedonistic spirit and connoisseurship at a time of

36. Lecerf de La Viéville, *Comparaison de la musique italienne et de la musique française,* 2: 192.

37. Jones, 97: "On ne disoit pas que je faisois mal les vers. . . . On disoit que j'étois un imprudent et que je me ferois mettre à la Bastille."

38. Spire Pitou, *The Paris Opéra: An Encyclopedia of Operas, Ballets, Composers, and Performers,* vol. 1: *Genesis and Glory, 1671–1715* (Westport, CT: Greenwood Press, 1983), 189–90.

39. Wolf, *Louis XIV,* 555–58.

40. The Dauphin's frequent attendance at the Opéra is documented in the "Journal de l'Opéra," a manuscript held by the Bibliothèque de l'Opéra, detailing performances and mentioning the presence of luminaries in attendance.

austerity and artistic retrenchment.[41] With the duc de Vendôme at the head of this faction, it would have also found support in the libertine community and among the artists the duc supported.

In the last years of Lully's life, then, as he fell out of favor with the king, the libertine, pro-Dauphin community provided a haven. In the same period, the Paris Opéra provided a haven for a disenfranchised social elite, where they could escape the watchful eye of the Sun King. As head of this de facto countercourt, the Dauphin attended the Opéra more than ever during the period of Lully's disgrace. He also came personally to the composer's support, attending at least eight performances of *Armide* in Paris, besides the productions he sponsored at court. There is also documentation of his obtaining special permission from the king for himself and his wife to attend *Acis*, and he apparently interceded unsuccessfully with the king on behalf of the composer in attempting to have *Acis* performed at court.[42]

Tragic Reversals at the Opéra

Between 1685 and Louis XIV's death in 1715, a series of devastating military defeats, an unprecedented deficit, crippling taxation, and the loss of over a million inhabitants to emigration and death by starvation intensified a literature of protest. The king's revocation of the Edict of Nantes in 1685 and the ensuing dislocation of thousands of Huguenots to England, Germany, and the Low Countries increased the flow of seditious literature from those countries as well as from clandestine presses within France. Of the latter group, one of the most famous was *Les soupirs de la France esclave* (1689), which posited the relationship of France to Louis as that of a slave to a tyrannical master. In general, targets of criticism included the unbridled ambition of the king, his immorality, tyranny, impiety, militarism, and propensity to self-flattery. Many of these criticisms were presented in a mode of satirical reversal. For instance, one medal shows the laurel wreath, a common signifier of victory, being removed from the head of the king. Reversing the title *roi très chrétien*, Louis is referred to as "Le Mars très chrétien" and "Le Turc très chrétien."[43] In addition to this pamphlet literature, a chanson literature

41. Emmanuel Le Roy Ladurie, *Saint-Simon and the Court of Louis XIV*, trans. by Arthur Goldhammer (Chicago: University of Chicago Press, 2001), 135–59. See also Fumaroli, *Le poète et le roi*, 484, who dates the Dauphin's cabal from c. 1685.

42. La Gorce, *Jean-Baptiste Lully*, 317–39.

43. Burke, *Fabrication of Louis XIV*, 138–39.

arose, as in the time of the *Maʒarinades* during the Fronde. As Catherine Gordon-Seifert has shown, the manuscript Chansonnier Maurepas contains fifty opera parodies, dating from 1673 to 1696, which satirize Louis XIV and his propaganda through the use of a crude, erotic imagery.[44]

There is evidence that, by means of a system of ideological reversals, a subversive political libertinism gained strength within the Opéra around the time of the death of Lully. In contrast to the blatant satire of the pamphlet literature, the Opéra, being an official theater, could incorporate only a milder system of reversal and innuendo. Difficult to identify with certainty within any one work, a dense network of intertextual allusions nonetheless reveals a clear, sophisticated pattern of opposition to the politics of Louis XIV. These seem to have begun with Lully's *Acis et Galatée* and to have continued with a pair of tragédies en musique composed by two of his sons: *Zéphire et Flore* (1688), by Louis and Jean-Louis Lully, and *Orphée* (1690), by Louis Lully. Their librettist, the musician and poet Michel du Boulay, served, like Campistron, as secretary to the duc de Vendôme and frequented the community of the Temple.[45] Like their father, the Lully sons also had strong connections at the Temple, through the duc and his brother, and with the Dauphin. In 1687 and again in 1691 they were commissioned by the duc to compose elaborate divertissements at Anet in honor of the Dauphin.[46]

Zéphire et Flore, produced on the anniversary of Lully's death, opens with a dialogue between Vertumnus and Pales, the god of gardens and the goddess of shepherds, praising Louis XIV in the gardens of the palace of the Trianon. In the midst of the celebration, the shepherd Tircis declares that he is lacking the only thing that could please him, calling this the "secret" of his heart. Pales responds that "to praise him [Louis XIV] in a manner worthy of him [dignement] is not in my power."[47] Pales, who has praised the king earlier in the prologue, declares his inability to continue as a sign of Louis's greatness. Yet taken literally, *dignement* means "in a dignified manner." Tircis's secret and Pales inability to praise in a dignified manner also might

44. "Heroism Undone in the Erotic Ms. Parodies of Jean-Baptiste Lully's *Tragédies en Musique*," in *Music, Sensation, and Sensuality*, ed. Linda Austern (New York: Garland Press, 2001).

45. Roger Picard, *Les salons littéraires et la société française, 1610–1789* (Paris: Brentano's, 1943), 125; Pitou, *Paris Opéra*, 1: 181.

46. Jules Écorcheville, "Lully gentilhomme et sa descendance: les fils de Lully," *Bulletin de la Société internationale de musique* 7 (1911): 1–27. Neither of Lully's sons' operas found favor with Louis XIV, who received them coldly.

47. Pure, *Recueil général*, 1: 324: "Le loüer dignement, n'est pas en ma puissance."

reflect an unwillingness or reluctance on the part of the opera's creators to adhere to the prologue's required encomium. In Louis Lully's *Orphée*, an audience expecting to be entertained finds only an empty theater, through whose back portico may be seen the bleak signs of winter. Venus, coming to the aid of the disappointed audience, inveighs against "useless pomp" and the horrors of war. As in earlier opera prologues, the Games and Pleasures are summoned, and in typical fashion the prologue ends with the praise of the king. The effect is darkened, however, by Venus's diatribe and, as an introduction to the succeeding opera, her lament for her son Orpheus, which is joined by the Games and Pleasures, as well as Cupid and the Graces.

Zéphire et Flore embodies the negative aspects of aggression and tyranny in the character of Boreas. Cruel god of the north wind, this character does not figure in the original myth of Zephyrus and Flora, a happy story of gentle and free love, evoked by the mild breath of the roving west wind. Conflating this myth with that of Boreas's abduction of the nymph Orythia, the opera depicts the abduction of Flora, goddess of spring and traditional symbol of abundance, to the accompaniment of a furious "storm" symphony. Holding her in captivity, and along with her the symbolic qualities of beauty, abundance, and joy, Boreas tortures her by forcing her "to flatter." The conflation of the two myths brings together the libertines' belief in freedom of both a personal and a political nature. It may also be read as an elaborate reversal of the mystique of the Sun King, revealing the true character of Louis XIV as the winter wind, cause of deprivation, hardship, and woe. Although the Sun makes a brief appearance as a deus ex machina, the plot of *Zéphire et Flore* highlights the violence and loathsomeness of Boreas as absolutist villain.

If the Lully sons' operas are considered as a pair of sorts, then it follows that the barren landscape, deprived audience, and "odious presence" of winter in the prologue of Louis Lully's *Orphée*, like the north wind Boreas in *Zéphire et Flore*, would signify the bleakness of a France plagued by tyranny, war and famine in the late 1680s. In both instances, one may also read the victimization of the theaters of Paris and their audiences as a result of the policies of the king. The plot of *Orphée* is even more pointedly subversive than that of *Zéphire et Flore*. Pluto is cast as a militaristic, cruel tyrant opposing the musician-hero Orpheus. Frequent allusions to music and freedom support the underlying theme of the tyrant defied by the artist. Pluto's dwelling is a royal palace surrounded by exquisite gardens (perhaps the Trianon, in whose gardens the prologue of *Zéphire et Flore* is set), with the

Example 4.2. Louis Lully, *Orphée* (Paris: Ballard, 1690), Act 2, sc. 2, 124–25, mm. 1–4.

flames of Hades flickering in the distance. There are a number of allusions to the violence of Pluto's "cruel ministers," the torturers of Eurydice, while Orpheus, "the liberator," brings hope and freedom through his life-giving music. The contrast is expressed by opposing musical characterizations of Pluto and Orpheus. With trumpet-like fanfares outlining triadic harmonies, Pluto's bellicose call to arms mocks the military fanfares associated with the king (see ex. 4.2.). Orpheus's song, in contrast, draws on the sweet sound of harmonious strings.

Zéphire et Flore may be interpreted at a second level, as a reversal not only of the absolutist image of the sun but also of the sun imagery of the *Ballet de Flore*. The reversals in *Zéphire et Flore* had actually been set up in the *Ballet de Flore*, where Benserade had balanced the celebration of Louis XIV as the sun with a chorus of icicles celebrating the icy chill that Louis's militarism threw into the hearts of his enemies. Though ostensibly offered in praise of Louis, this depiction of the cold, forbidding side of the Sun King opened the way for expansion and manipulation in the Lully sons' *Zéphire et Flore*, with its main absolutist protagonist identified no longer with the life-giving sun but with the cold, villainous north wind.

There is also a possible connection between the eponymous protagonists of the opera and the Grand Dauphin and his wife, who had danced
the roles of Zephyrus and Flora in *Le triomphe de l'Amour*, the court ballet
celebrating their wedding in 1681.[48] The Dauphine, official patroness of the
Comédie-Italienne, shared her husband's love of the theater. To the faction
that supported the Dauphin, this couple would have represented the possibility of a future political and cultural era associated with the arts and theater of the public sphere.[49] This idealized future would have seemed even
brighter in contrast to the current reality of the War of the League of Augsburg (1688–97), in which France for the first time found itself without allies against an array of enemies, including England, the Dutch Netherlands,
Spain, the Holy Roman Empire, Sweden, Brandenburg-Prussia, Saxony,
Bavaria, and Savoy.

Orphée, like its sister work *Zéphire et Flore*, may also be interpreted on
a second level in the context of an earlier court ballet, the *Ballet des Muses*
of 1666. In that work, the role of Orpheus, danced by Lully in pantomime
with his violin, constituted a passionate expression of individual emotion as
against the imperialist program celebrated in other parts of the work. As discussed in chapter 2, the Orpheus myth had been used by Tristan L'Hermite,
in his long poem *Orphée*, as the symbol of artistic passion victimized by absolutist tyranny. In that sense, the lament of Orpheus/Lully in Louis Lully's
Orphée may perhaps be linked less directly to the *Ballet de Psyché* of 1657, in
which Louis XIV danced the role of Pluto, absolutist sovereign of the underworld. The violent ending of *Orphée*, in which Orpheus is torn limb from
limb by the bacchantes, might also have referred to that earlier court ballet,
where in addition to his role as Pluto, Louis XIV also appeared as one of the
bacchantes gleefully destroying the musician. In the earlier work the scene
was treated comically; in the later, it capped the unrelieved oppression of
the plot. Whether or not these connections were intentional, one could interpret the conflict between the tyrannical Pluto and Orpheus—a figure
closely associated with Lully as well as with the artist prototype—as the
conflict between Lully and the king. *Orphée* was not well received, probably
because of the awkwardness of the score as well as the unrelieved tension
and violence of the *livret*.

48. It is possible that the Dauphin himself fostered the association; his bedroom at Versailles was dominated by a painting by Poussin entitled *Le triomphe de Flore;* it is reproduced
in Nancy Mitford, *The Sun King* (London: Penguin Books, 1966), 108–9.

49. The Dauphine's well-documented struggles with the austere Mme de Maintenon are
hinted at in the opera in the relationship between Flore and the villainous Clétie.

Despite enthusiastic reviews indicating a favorable reception, *Zéphire et Flore* was withdrawn soon after its première.[50] Since the work was revived in 1715, immediately after the death of Louis XIV, its short run suggests the possibility of censorship. If that were the case, two airs attributed to Louis Lully in a collection of 1690 take on added significance. Labeled *additions* to *Zéphire et Flore*, these airs take their place among the earliest examples of the da capo form in France. Unlike later examples of the *ariette* (a French term for the setting of French texts in an Italianate idiom), both of these works yoke a da capo form to the florid French idiom of the *air sérieux,* and both represent florid pleas to Cupid. The first, "Amour vole," contains elaborate melismas representing a striking contrast to the simpler, more traditional French operatic style that characterizes the remainder of the opera. Set as a prayer to Cupid—a plea for help from the god of love—the air captures the emotional intensity of the opera. The text recalls Benserade's *vers* for Lully as Orpheus in the *Ballet des Muses,* similarly cast as an emotional plea to the god of love (see chap. 2); the elaborate violin obbligato recalls Lully's performance as a violinist in that scene. In the second *addition* to *Zéphire et Flore,* "Puissant fils de Vénus," the singer praises the reign of Cupid with elaborate melismas. Once again a florid style underlies a celebration of the cult of love in the Orphic terms described above. The use of transverse flutes reinforces an association, common by this period, of Cupid with that instrument. These cries to Cupid, linked to the sentiment of the *vers* for Lully as Orpheus in the *Ballet des Muses,* may be understood as the symbolic expression of a discourse linking Flora with political well-being and her abduction with Louis XIV's tyranny.

Given the nature of the imagery in these two operas, Louis Lully's *Orphée* may be seen as a subversive portrait of his father, destroyed by the ruthless absolutism of Louis XIV. In the larger quarrels over ancient and modern music, begun in the year of Lully's death, Lully was in turn praised as a "modern Orpheus" and criticized as a shameless imposter.[51] It is well

50. Théodore Lajarte, *Bibliothèque musicale du Théâtre de l'Opéra: Catalogue historique, chronologique, anecdotique* (Paris, 1878; Hildesheim: Georg Olms, 1969), 57.

51. On the negative side, two satires of Lully, by Bauderon de Sénecé and François de Callières, appeared in 1688. Both set in the underworld, they make unfavorable comparisons between Jean-Baptiste Lully and the "real" Orpheus, castigating Lully not only as a bad musician but also as a moneygrubber, moral reprobate, and petty tyrant. See Cowart, *Origins of Modern Musical Criticism,* 44–48. Lully had been associated with the ancient musician at least since 1661, when Loret had hailed the composer as "a true imitator of Orpheus" (J. P. Cassaro, introduction to Lully, *Ballet des saisons, Oeuvres complètes,* 1: xxvi).

known that propaganda campaigns swirled around Lully just as they did around Louis XIV. What emerges from a study of Louis Lully's *Orphée* and its models is a complex portrait of the musician as artist. As a part of the pamphlet war that arose after Jean-Baptiste Lully's death, the son's opera could have served as a defense of the father against the attacks of the Ancients and against the king who had dismissed this "modern Orpheus." If so, the execution of this idea should be attributed to a wider circle than just Louis Lully, who, said to have been unstable emotionally and at times violent, was institutionalized a number of times before and after the death of his father. Contemporary sources indicate that the composer Pierre Vignon and Marin Marais also may have collaborated on *Zéphire et Flore*, and that Marais may have later contributed to Jean-Louis Lully's *Alcide*. A letter from a contemporary indicates that Desmarets, who lived with the duc de Vendôme and the Grand Prieur, was charged with assisting the Lully sons on yet another occasion, and the additional confusion of the Lully sons' work with that of Collasse might indicate that Collasse, another member of this libertine circle, also served in this way. Campistron and Boulay, the librettists for *Acis, Zéphire et Flore*, and *Orphée*, both served as secretary to the duc de Vendôme, further implicating the libertine duc in the shaping of the subversive orientation of all three of these works.

Opera Parodies at the Comédie-Italienne

The system of satiric reversals at the Paris Opéra in the late seventeenth century, especially as found in the operas of Lully's sons, could have been inspired by a unique brand of satire that had developed at the Comédie-Italienne, now housed at the theater of the Hôtel de Bourgogne. Directed at customs, manners, and a wide assortment of professions, individuals, and literary genres, the Italians' humor often targeted the tragédie en musique during its heyday in the 1670s and 1680s. Parodied material could include anything from a couple of lines or a quote from the music or the text of an air to the systematic parody of an entire opera.[52]

Though the political content of the Comédie-Italienne has attracted little recognition or systematic study, perusal of the Italians' opera parodies reveals a clear deconstruction of the heroic image presented in the operas

52. The plays of the Comédie-Italienne, as they were performed at the turn of the eighteenth century, have been preserved in Everisto Gherardi, *Le théâtre italien de Gherardi* (Paris: Briasson, 1751), ed. Charles Mazouer (Paris: Société des textes française modernes/Klinksieck, 1994–).

of Lully and Quinault. Their writers consistently ridiculed figures such as Jupiter, Mars, Apollo, Pluto, Hercules, and Rinaldo, all of whom had stood as standard surrogates for Louis XIV in the pantheon of royal propaganda. Indeed, these gods and heroes, like the *vieillards* of the plots, are often bested and outwitted through the triumph of lovers and lower-class servant characters such as Arlequin and Scaramouche. These clowns or masks use their insider status to manipulate the situation to the advantage of the young lovers, who overturn the household order of the old men such as Pantalon, the doctor, and other *vieillard* types. Typically based on the machinations of wily servants in the aid of young lovers against tyrannical old guardians, these plots bear a resemblance to those of Molière, whose troupe had alternated performances with the Italians on the stage of the Palais-Royal in the 1660s. Along with the plot structures, characters, and musical divertissements, the Italians shared with Molière a propensity for satire, a general disrespect for authority, and strategies undermining official image making.

Pierrot, an important character of the Comédie-Italienne from the late 1660s, first appeared in Molière's *Dom Juan, ou le festin de Pierre* of 1665, and his character was imported into the Comédie-Italienne in its *Festin de Pierre* later in the same year. Basing his character on the French peasant, with his white ruff and coarse, baggy white suit, Molière invested him with a simultaneous innocence, pluckiness, and winsomeness. Like the valet types of Scaramouche and Arlequin, Pierrot (played by Giuseppe Giaratoni) became a favorite character of the Comédie-Italienne and a French antihero and everyman in the later *théâtre de la foire*.[53]

Though the Italians' plays were not recorded until the 1690s, anecdotes point to a mildly subversive, libertine attitude dating from the 1660s. An incident reported by Domenico Locatelli (Trivelin), for example, refers to a questionable passage in a scene from the 1665 performance of *Le festin de Pierre:* "In the last scene (it is suppressed) when the King comes on the stage I fall on my knees and I say to him, "Oh, King you should know that my master is with the devils where you other great lords will also go some day."[54] From the casual manner in which Locatelli mentions the suppression of the scene, we may gather that such was the end of other attempts at monarchical satire. Later evidence may be inferred from a report from Pierre Bayle, the freethinking editor of the *Nouvelles de la république des lettres:* "We hear from Paris that the troupe of the Hôtel de Bourgogne, which is that of

---

53. Scott, *Commedia dell'arte in Paris,* 119–20, 250–51, 332, 340–41, 190–91.
54. Ibid., 75.

the Italian actors, is performing a very diverting comedy which attracts an extraordinary crowd. It is a satire of the opera *Amadis,* according to our correspondent." Bayle adds, almost certainly tongue-in-cheek, that he doesn't believe the report, because "since it is known that the king himself gave the subject for the opera, who would dare parody it in public?"[55] Whereas the operatic satire discussed above seems to have targeted mainly the king and his ministers, the humor of the Italians often appealed to its bourgeois audience by targeting, like Molière, a wide variety of social groups including the nobility.

In the 1680s, when the court had moved to Versailles and the Italians had largely lost the interest of the king, they sought to appeal rather to an audience composed of Parisian bourgeois and nobles attending their theater in Paris. In this decade, with a lessening fascination with *italianisme,* their plays began to be written by French playwrights, with some scenes remaining in the form of synopsis, to be improvised in Italian. By this time the Italians had become more fluent in French, and a second generation included the native French speakers Isabelle (Françoise-Marie Apolline Biancolelli, daughter of Arlequin), who debuted as *amoureuse* in 1683, and Léandre (Charles-Virgile Romagnesi de Belmont), who debuted as *amoureux* in 1694.[56] With its increased emphasis on the French language and with the participation of some of France's finest playwrights, including Jean-François Regnard and Charles Rivière Dufresny, the Comédie-Italienne became a more stylized and verbally elite entertainment than its Italian counterpart. With the shift to the French language, its plays also began to portray situations of particular interest to a Parisian public. As with the French theater of the Comédie-Française, a taste for the satire of manners began to dominate subject matter, and audiences demanded situations that reflected their own experiences, both personal and political.

Regnard, a musician-composer who contributed a number of original songs, initiated an important shift toward an emphasis on musical spectacle in the 1690s. Lully's prohibitions against the use of more than two singers and six orchestral players in any theater other than his own began to be relaxed after his death in 1687, making it possible for the Comédie-Italienne to include, in addition to the traditional singing scene, large-scale musical divertissements including instrumental music, singing, dancing, elaborate

---

55. Ibid., 307. The comment dates from March 1684.

56. Claude and François Parfaict, *Histoire de l'ancien Théâtre-Italien, depuis son origine en France, jusqu'à sa suppression en l'année 1697* (1753; Paris: Roget, 1767), 3–127. The actors, who customarily played only one role, were known by their stage names.

stage sets, and machines.[57] These divertissements, usually at the end of an act, included situations indirectly related to the action, such as serenades, balls, or plays (and even comic operas) within plays. Simple airs and chansons accompany the French texts, while Italian arias may be used in the divertissements. The arias exhibit the high quality of contemporary Italian operas or cantatas, from which they may have been taken.[58] Regnard and Dufresny, both talented musicians, often composed original chansons and airs, leaving arrangements to a composer-in-residence, the most important of whom was Jean-Claude Gilliers.

These two playwright/musicians, both of whom also wrote plays for the Comédie-Française, found a congenial home among the Italians, most of whom had considerable musical ability. In 1693 they produced a play entitled *La baguette de Vulcain*, which hastened the end of improvised Italian scenes and created a model oriented more toward spectacle. In this type a simple theme threads its way (often in verse rather than prose) through spectacular songs, dances, choruses, tightrope acts, gymnastic tricks, and machine effects.[59] The *Baguette de Vulcain* was so popular that it inaugurated a new genre of theatrical entertainment in which the divertissement overruns its former boundaries to form the basis of the play. This work also set a precedent for the practice of "augmentation," the substitution or addition of new entries designed to appeal to a public hungry for novelty. The emphasis on music also spotlighted a new star of the Comédie-Italienne in the 1690s, Mezzetin (Angelo Constantini), another servant character with a good singing voice and particular skills as a guitarist/lutenist, who in this period became known as the principal leader of the divertissements of the troupe.

The Comédie-Italienne was not the only theater to incorporate this spirit of carnivalesque reversal, but the consistency with which it did so and the success of its productions earned both the adoration of the public and the ire of the king. Though for years the Italian troupe had enjoyed a certain impunity under the protection of the king's patronage, the pervasive indecencies

57. Donald J. Grout, "Music of the Italian Theatre at Paris, 1682–97," *Papers of the American Musicological Society* (1941): 161–70.

58. The primary source for the musical repertoire of the Comédie-Italienne was Gherardi's collection (see above, n. 52), whose fifty-five plays are furnished with valuable musical supplements containing French songs and Italian arias. This collection was first published in Paris in 1694, before the influx of Italian cantatas and sonatas, and undoubtedly served, along with the stage performances of the troupe, to introduce the new Italian style to France.

59. Attinger, *L'esprit de la commedia dell'arte*, 199–293, 234–35.

and doubles entendres that permeated their plays of the 1680s and 1690s brought them under royal surveillance. Especially in the 1690s, when Louis XIV's chief of police, Gabriel-Nicolas de La Reynie, was charged with a stricter scrutiny of all Parisian theaters, the flagrant *moeurs* of Scaramouche and his compatriots also made them suspect. A passage from the prologue to *Les Chinois* (1692) confirms that the Italians still chose to flaunt questionable language and double entendres, despite stern warnings of dismissal issued at least by 1690. Surrounded by his Muses, Apollo (played by Columbine) says to a little girl (played by Pierrot):

> I don't know what this language can be that so shocks your mother. As for me, I find nothing there but language full of savor, language which does, to tell the truth, contain a double meaning sometimes. But all the most beautiful ideas in the world have two faces. So much the worse for those who always see the bad side; it's a true mark of their corrupt and vicious character.[60]

In 1694 Constantini/Mezzetin published a biography of Scaramouche, a work full of exaggerations and libertine innuendo that conflated the actual biography of Tiberio Fiorelli with his larger-than-life stage persona. Simultaneously, a series of bold attacks by the Italians on Louis XIV's public and personal relationships continued to draw the unwelcome attention of the king and his secret police. Already in 1689 an actor from the company had been banished for expressing his disapproval of the king's politics. In 1695 a prominent officer of the law was depicted on the Italians' stage as a "forger and thief," and the company received an official reprimand. In 1697, a letter from the comte de Pontchartrain to the marquis d'Argenson, the new lieutenant-general of police, stated that the king had discharged the Italian comedians and ordered that their theater be closed. D'Argenson appeared in person the next day to place locks on all the doors, with a notice that the king would no longer permit the Italians to perform.[61]

The banishment was attributed to various motivations in different sources. The *Gazette d'Amsterdam* accused Louis XIV of having seized the opportunity to recoup the 15,000 *livres* of the Italians' annual pension. Others believed that the king was offended by a new comedy, *La fausse prude*, variously attributed to Anne Mauduit de Fatouville or Eustache Lenoble, in which Mme de Maintenon was satirized in a scurrilous manner. (The content

60. Scott, *Commedia dell'arte in Paris*, 322.

61. Thomas E. Crow, *Painters and Public Life in Eighteenth-Century Paris* (New Haven: Yale University Press, 1985), 48–49.

of the play, as well as a libelous pamphlet on which it may have been based, is thought to have been confiscated when the theater was closed.) Still others believed that the expulsion was related to the more general satirical tone of the Italians.[62]

Recent studies of the Comédie-Italienne are also divided on the expulsion. François Moureau sees it as the result of a gradual deterioration of the relationship between the king and the Italians, as well as between the king and the theaters of Paris during the last decade of the century.[63] Others attribute the banishment more specifically to the scurrilous humor and subversive satire of the comedians.[64] In general, however, the study of satire in the Comédie-Italienne has been largely restricted to the Italians' general use of social satire or their rare references to actual political figures or situations. To date no one has studied in depth how the opera parodies functioned as political satire, not only through targeting roles traditionally associated with the king, but more importantly through ridiculing the aura of sovereign power as it was displayed at the Opéra. Such a study would have the potential to reveal a more dangerous side of the Italians' humor, and if not a motivation for the banishment, at least an explanation for Louis's growing antipathy. A study of patterns of satire developed in the Comédie-Italienne and picked up in other theaters, as for example in the Lully sons' operas, might also help to explain the growing rift between Louis XIV and the theaters in general during the difficult years of his late reign.

The Muses' Discontent

Several influences caused Louis XIV and the Opéra to part ways after Lully's dismissal and death. The breach with Lully undoubtedly contributed to

62. Nicolas Boindin, *Lettres sur tous les spectacles de Paris* (Paris: P. Prault, 1719), 641, 654. In general, the most reliable recent accounts are given by Jan Clarke, "The Expulsion of the Italians from the Hôtel de Bourgogne in 1697," *Seventeenth-Century French Studies* 14 (1992): 97–117, and Virginia Scott, *The Commedia dell'Arte in Paris, 1644–1697* (Charlottesville: University of Virginia Press, 1990), 325–31. For an authoritative discussion and updating of those sources, as well as new evidence on *La fausse prude,* see William Brooks, "Louis XIV's Dismissal of the Italian Actors: The Episode of *La fausse prude,*" *Modern Language Review* 91 (1996): 840–47.

63. *De Gherardi à Watteau: Présence d'Arlequin sous Louis XIV* (Paris: Klinksieck, 1992), 30.

64. Julia Anne Plax, *Watteau and the Cultural Politics of Eighteenth-Century France* (Cambridge: Cambridge University Press, 2000), 12. See also Crow, *Painters and Public Life,* 48–49.

a lessening of the king's interest in opera. He never established relationships with other artists like the one he had enjoyed earlier with Lully and Quinault, and his love for Lully's music never extended to later works produced at the Opéra. Also, the religious piety that had overtaken the king in his late years caused him to abhor the moral laxity more than ever associated with the institution after the death of Lully. Seized by a retrospective guilt for his earlier indulgences, he began to tax the Académie one sixth of all its revenues to subsidize the Hôpital des pauvres.[65]

Louis's lack of interest in the Opéra, along with artists' disapproval of his neglect of the arts, exacerbated a mistrust that was clearly mutual. In the 1680s and 1690s, these artists' discontent is given voice through the mouthpiece of the Muses. We have seen earlier how the role of the Muses changed from absolutist encomium, promulgated in the *Ballet des Muses* and parodied in *Le bourgeois gentilhomme* and the prologue to *Les fêtes de l'Amour et de Bacchus*, to complaints, in *Isis*, of the noises of war threatening to drown out the Muses' harmony. In a series of works immediately following Lully's death in 1687, the nine sisters can be found haunting the public theater and lamenting its plight or restored to Parnassus, a haven of peace and plenty. Despite their differences, all of these prologues have in common the withdrawal of the Muses from royal flattery and a withdrawal of the arts to their home on Parnassus, separated by a wide gulf from Olympus, home of politics and war.

This series of works begins with *Achille et Polixène* , the opera begun by Lully before his death and completed by Collasse, with a *livret* by Campistron. Significantly, the overture—the component of the tragédie en musique most associated with the power of the king—is missing in this work.[66] In its prologue three Muses—Melpomene, Terpsichore, and Thalia—appear in a "setting appropriate for producing spectacles, and which can be used for tragedies and comedies"—obviously the Opéra itself. According to the stage directions, this venue, having lost its former magnificence, is approaching complete ruin. The Muses, alone without their suites, appear desolate. Melpomene complains that the "greatest of kings," intent on extending his conquests, has forgotten the Muses' "most superb fêtes," and Terpsichore expresses the Muses' shame and sadness that they cannot please him:

65. La Gorce, *Jean-Baptiste Lully*, 111.

66. The significance of this omission has been noted by Couvreur, *Jean-Baptiste Lully*, 402. Collasse did not choose to reinstate it.

Melpomene:	Don't you know that the greatest king
	Expands his conquests every day
	And distinguishing himself by his arms in new exploits,
	Has neglected our most superb fêtes?
Thalia:	Since this fatal moment,
	Our spectacles, having lost their magnificence,
	No longer are able to have the splendor and charms
	That they owed only to his presence.
Terpsichore:	Sadness reigns in these places,
	We are embarrassed not to be able to please him,
	Alas! Would we be incapable of doing anything
	Worthy of appearing before his eyes?[67]

Upon hearing the Muses' laments, Mercury appears and, at the behest of Jupiter, magically restores the theater to its former magnificence. A chorus of praise to Jupiter leads to a final chorus of praise to Louis XIV, but only after the Muses' call for the surrender of arms to Cupid and once again for the return of the Pleasures. In effect, the magical restoration of the theater represents a new phase in the royal panegyric, in which praise of the king is accorded not on the basis of his deeds but rather on the basis of a kind of fantasy answering the artistic community's unfulfilled desire for his political support. One cannot read the Muses' lines without thinking of Lully's own failure to please the king and undoubtedly his own sadness regarding the state of the arts in his late years.

The year that *Achille et Polixène* was produced at the Opéra marked the beginning of the War of the League of Augsburg. In the 1690s, as France's fortunes waned, we find a return to the Muses' complaints of war, beginning with *Coronis, pastorale heroïque*, composed by a M. Theobal (probably Theobaldi di Gatti, an Italian student of Lully) to a text by a M. Bauge (1691). Its prologue reveals Clio, Thalia, Euterpe, and the other Muses on Parnassus. Thalia and Euterpe, Muses of comedy and pastoral, invite the fortunate inhabitants of this sacred mountain to take part in their games. Clio speaks of their happiness, pointed up by contrast to the "frightful cruelty" of war.

---

67. Pure, *Recueil général*, 1: 309: "Melpomène: Ignorez-vous que le plus grand des Roys / Etendant chaque jour ses conquêtes / Et signalant son bras, par de nouveaux exploits, / A negligé nos plus superbes fêtes? Thalie: Depuis ce fatal moment, / Nos spectacles privez de leur magnificence, / Ne sçauroient plus avoir l'éclat & l'agrément / Qu'ils ne devoient qu'à sa presence. Terpsichore: La tristesse regne en ces lieux, / Nous rougissons de ne pouvoir luy plaire, / Helas! ne sçaurions-nous rien faire / Digne de paroître à ses yeux?"

Gradually Parnassus, with vines full of grapes, fields full of flowers, and fertile land, emerges as a peaceful haven. Praise that would ordinarily address the king in a prologue of this sort is now displaced onto one of the peripheral mythological figures of the pastoral that follows. Taken as a whole, the prologue may be interpreted in two ways. On one hand, the peaceful home of the arts may be taken as France itself, as opposed to its warlike enemies. At the same time, however, the suggestion emerges that it is now the Opéra, and, moreover, not the tragédie en musique but the comedy and pastoral, that provide a haven from the horrors of war. This is accomplished through a possible double entendre on the word *here:* "Despite the war and its cruel ravages, / A happy calm here fulfills our desires, / This beautiful dwelling fears no storms, / And we will come, under this charming shade, / To sing of love and its pleasures."[68] Significantly, it is the Muses of poetry, comedy, and pastoral who speak in this prologue, with the voice of the tragic Muse relegated to the general chorus.

In *Les saisons* of 1695, the Muses of tragedy, poetry, and pastoral (Melpomene, Clio, and Euterpe) appear, this time as actual victims of the somber sadness that has overtaken Parnassus. Lamenting their "frightful pain," the Muse of pastoral recounts the ways in which Glory, with whom they formerly collaborated, now has usurped their place. A personified Permessus,[69] sacred river of the Muses, hints that they encourage Louis XIV's glory by memorializing it without encouraging any other qualities in him. The Muses then resolve to make Louis loved as well as feared, and the prologue ends with the chorus of the Muses from the *Ballet des Muses*.[70] Finally, in the prologue to *Ariane et Bacchus* (1696), an opera by Marin Marais with text by a M. S. Jean, Terpsichore, as "Muse of spectacles," speaks for the other Muses. Hearing the noise of trumpets and drums, she sings: "What noise resounds in the air? / The drums and trumpets / Are resounding in our peaceful retreats. / Ah, I recognize Glory by these noisy concerts."[71] The

68. Pure, *Recueil général*, 1: 382: "Malgré la guerre & ses cruels ravages, / Un calme heureux comble icy nos desires, / Ce beau séjour ne craint point les orages, / Et nous viendrons, sous ces charmants ombrages, / Chanter encor l'amour & ses plaisirs."

69. An actual as well as mythological river in Boeotia where the Muses were thought to reside on the mountain of Parnassus (also known as Helicon); Permessus was also the name of a river god associated with that location.

70. This work will be discussed at greater length in chapter 5 below.

71. Pure, *Recueil général*, 1: 552: "Quel bruit se repand dans les airs: / Les timballes & les trompettes, / Font retentir nos paisibles retraites; / Ah, je connois la Gloire a ces bruyants concerts."

ensuing dialogue between Glory and a nymph presents a clear picture of Louis as uninterested in the arts, preferring his heroic exploits.

In considering all these works, it is important to review the process by which Louis's propaganda was shaped in operatic livrets. We know that the king was instrumental in the choice of subject matter and its working out, but this was a facet of the process that was rarely advertised. As Pellison had stated in 1670, speaking of the historian's project, "It would no doubt be hoped that His Majesty approve and accept this design, which can almost not be well executed without him. But he must not seem to have accepted, known about, or ordered it."[72]

Until the mid-1670s, Louis XIV seems to have vested Colbert with the authority to review works in progress. Colbert in turn consulted a select but informal group of intellectuals, known as the Petite Académie. This body, whose founding members included the writers Jean Chapelain and Charles Perrault, held the responsibility of monitoring royal image making in literature, fêtes, ballets, comedies, medals, etc., to ensure that the *gloire* of the king was appropriately upheld. Contemporaries were aware that the tragedies en musique were among those genres submitted to official review; Mme de Sévigné, for example, expressed surprise that a scene from *Proserpine* had escaped the eyes of the academicians. Members of the Petite Académie, consisting of writers and artists, were encouraged in their loyalty to the king by the mechanism by which they were recompensed; instead of pensions, they received annual allotments.[73]

By 1674, Quinault himself had become a member of the Petite Académie. His livrets, then, should be seen as representing not only Louis XIV's artists but the official position of the Petite Académie as well, both in their celebration of the heroism of Louis XIV and in their pleas for a peace without which his *gloire* was meaningless. In orations addressed to that body and to the Académie française, members consistently exhorted the king to control the excesses of his *gloire*. In 1675, for example, Quinault addressed the king after his crossing of the Rhine, "The impetuosity of your courage has only too often prevailed over the crown which ought to restrain you."[74] In 1677, af-

72. In *Project for the History of Louis XIV: To M. Colbert*, quoted in Louis Marin, *Portrait of the King*, 39–41. See chapter 2 above.

73. Couvreur, *Jean-Baptiste Lully*, 43–52, 407; Apostolidès, *Le Roi-machine*, 29–31.

74. "L'impetuosité de vostre courage n'a que trop souvent prévalu sur le poids de la Couronne qui vous doit retenir." *Harangue au roy sur ses heureuses conquêtes*, July 30, 1675, quoted in Couvreur, *Jean-Baptiste Lully*, 393.

ter another victory in the Dutch war, Quinault took the rostrum in another *harangue au roi:* "We hardly dare to paint brilliant portraits of the *gloire* that so often puts you in peril; it appears only too beautiful to you and carries you too far. . . . France no longer needs you to extend its borders; its true greatness is to have so great a master."[75] Quinault's successors in the Petite Académie, later the Académie royale des inscriptions et belles-lettres, included a number of librettists for the Opéra, including Fontenelle, Thomas Corneille, Jean-Baptiste Rousseau, and Antoine Danchet.[76]

The findings of this chapter indicate that the artists of the Opéra should not be thought of as mere mouthpieces, subordinating their genius to the exigencies of royal propaganda. Quinault's strongly worded pleas for a return to peace may still be seen as adhering to the proprieties of the official preface or the official oration, in which such pleas, while testing the limits of advocacy, were not considered out of place. With the late operas of Lully and Campistron, and with the operas of Lully's sons, however, a truly subversive tone began to enter the Académie royale de musique. This would appear to have been inspired by the satire of the Comédie-Italienne, which lampooned images of Louis XIV and his glory. This mode of operatic satire, surpassing even the Italians in its intensity, provided a model for later composers such as André Campra, who would pay allusive tribute to the Lully sons' *Orphée* and *Zéphire et Flore* in ballets he produced at the Paris Opéra in 1699 and 1710.[77] Reaching back to strategies of resistance in the court ballet and comédie-ballet, this satire worked through the process of representation in two ways. First, it undermined images of Louis XIV and the monarchy through the negative depiction of tyrannical figures such as Polyphemus, Boreas, and Pluto. Secondly, it allowed for an actual self-representation of Louis's image-makers. In this way, Lully as Orpheus and the artists of the Opéra as Muses could be vividly depicted at once as the upholders of truth and beauty, victims of absolutist aggression, and commentators on the state of the arts vis-à-vis sovereign power in the late years of the century.

---

75. *Harangue au roy*, June 2, 1677, quoted in Couvreur, *Jean-Baptiste Lully*, 393: "Nous n'osons Presque vous faire voir de brilliants portraits de la Gloire qui vous engage si souvent dans le peril; elle ne vous paroist que trop belle, & ne vous emporte que trop loin. . . . La France n'a plus besoin que vous estendiez ses limites; sa veritable grandeur est d'avoir un si grand Maistre."

76. Ibid., 396.

77. These will be discussed in chapter 6.

❋

Sappho, Cythera & the Triumph of Love

The Ballet at the Paris Opéra, 1700–1713

In 1694, François de Salignac de La Mothe Fénelon, archbishop of Cambrai and tutor to Louis XIV's grandson the duc de Bourgogne, wrote an anonymous letter to Louis XIV. This document remains one of the most scathing denunciations of sovereign authority throughout Louis's reign:

> Your people, whom You should love as Your children and who until now have been such passionate supporters of Your Cause, are dying of hunger. . . . You have destroyed half the real forces within Your State in order to carry out and to defend vain conquests outside it. The whole of France is nothing but one great hospital, without equipment or provisions. . . . While Your people lack bread, You do not wish to see the extremity to which You are reduced. . . . You fear to open Your eyes. You fear that others will open them for You. You fear being reduced to losing some part of Your glory. That glory that hardens Your heart is dearer to You than justice, than Your own repose, than the preservation of Your peoples who perish each day from sicknesses caused by famine, even than Your eternal salvation.[1]

Whether Louis XIV ever saw Fénelon's letter is unknown; in any case, he maintained his customary, regal silence. By the last, eighteenth-century phase of his long reign, he rarely emerged to participate in the stream of entertainments he produced for the courtiers at Versailles. Aging and ill, he

---

1. Quoted in Prince Michael of Greece, *Louis XIV: The Other Side of the Sun*, trans. by Alan Sheridan (New York: Harper & Row, 1983), 284.

had given up displays of glory in favor of pious seclusion, while his musical tastes had turned from opera to sacred music.

Between 1685 and Louis XIV's death, a series of devastating military defeats, an unprecedented deficit, crippling taxation, and the loss of over a million inhabitants to emigration and death by starvation had undermined the claims of royal propaganda. Also, in the half century since Louis XIV had danced the role of the Rising Sun in the *Ballet de la nuit*, new ideas and ideologies had transformed the way rulers were viewed by their subjects. Earlier conceptions of kingship had depended on a profound, quasi-mystical correspondence between the king and the power of the state, as represented by gods, heroes, and Roman emperors. By the end of the century, however, new ideological currents had begun to undermine the identification of ruler and state. For one thing, the rise of science and a mechanistic, pragmatic worldview helped to demythologize kingship and, as I have mentioned in chapter 2, to expose political representation as a type of propaganda rather than as a transcendent reality. In addition, the glorification and virtual worship of antiquity as a cultural model fell into decline, accompanied by a more general discrediting of the power earlier considered to be inherent in the iconography of kingship. Finally, what had begun in the seventeenth century as radical political ideals of equality and liberty were gaining acceptance in a century that would later move from Enlightenment to Revolution.

For all these reasons, continuing traditions of royal iconography began to lose their fascination. At the Opéra, although the tragédies en musique of Lully and Quinault continued to be performed and enjoyed, the amorous divertissements, rather than the adulatory prologues, seemed more in line with a changing public taste. A new generation of librettists, notably Antoine Houdar de La Motte and Antoine Danchet, further emphasized the element of galanterie, overshadowing the old heroic ideals. These changes catered to an upper-class elite, who, bored with the lackluster atmosphere at court and freed by Louis's lack of interest, had moved to fashionable new *hôtels* in Paris and joined with an increasingly wealthy upper bourgeoisie to form a "shadow court" at the Opéra. There, unhampered by the presence of the king, they could celebrate themselves as a new audience of distinction and privilege.[2]

In the years after the death of Lully, the Opéra had begun to overshadow the court as a noble gathering place and center of hedonism, not only in its

---

2. On Louis XIV's courtiers in Paris, see Jacques Levron, "Louis XIV's Courtiers," in *Louis XIV and Absolutism*, ed. Ragnhild Hatton (London: Macmillan, 1976), 130–53.

foyers, vestibules, and loges, but also in the depictions of festive celebration on its stage. It was not the tragédie en musique, with its gods and heroes, but rather a resurgence of the stage ballet that provided the perfect vehicle for this new audience, for it both entertained and showcased them as a social elite, just as the court ballet had done for the old nobility. Instead of Melpomene, Muse of tragedy, it was Thalia, Muse of comedy, and Euterpe, Muse of pastoral, who represented the interests of this new audience. In fact, even while Melpomene presided over the tragédie en musique, a series of fêtes produced in the last quarter of the seventeenth century prepared the way for the blossoming of the opéra-ballet at the turn of the century.

Forerunners of the Opéra-ballet, 1675–1697

A hodgepodge of different genres and styles, the first group of these light-hearted entertainments, all composed by Lully, had in common an emphasis on dance, an absence of heroism, and the continuation of the two elements that had largely been purged from the tragédie en musique: comedy and a satiric galanterie. Together they establish a tradition of nondramatic, dance-based spectacle growing out of the pastoral, court ballet, comédie-ballet, and ballet-mascarade. These works include *Psyché* (1671), a *tragédie-ballet* based on La Fontaine's *Les amours de Psyché et de Cupidon* (discussed in chap. 4); *Le Carnaval, mascarade* (1675), a pastiche from an earlier court ballet and several comédie-ballets; *L'Égloge de Versailles* (1685) a revival of a divertissement produced at court in 1668; and *Le temple de la paix* (1685), created for the Dauphin. In the same year the Dauphin also produced a concert version of Lully's *Idylle de Sceaux* in his apartments at Versailles. Splitting off from the opera and its glorification of Louis XIV's militant, heroic image, these works focus on the pleasures of peace rather than the glory of heroism and military victory. During the lifetime of Lully, these entertainments were overshadowed by the tragédie en musique, but they prepared the way for a veritable explosion of entertainments in a similar vein after his death in 1687.

A revival of interest in dancing, perhaps connected with the vogue of the public masquerade, contributed to a marked revival of interest in the ballet around the turn of the century.[3] This was intensified by the publication of

3. The vogue of dancing may be attributed in part to the duchesse de Bourgogne's love of the dance. Marie-Adélaïde of Savoy had married the duc de Bourgogne, Louis XIV's grandson, in 1697, and was the mother of Louis XV, who succeeded his father as heir to the throne upon his death in 1712.

Benserade's texts for the court ballet in 1698. Despite efforts by Louis XIV to provide entertainment for the courtiers, the court balls and masquerades, lacking the distinction of his presence, could not compete with the allure of the Paris Opéra. In the last decades of the seventeenth century, a second generation led by Collasse produced a series of immediate forerunners to the opéra-ballet. Collasse's *Les saisons* (1695) and *La naissance de Vénus* (1696) initiated a practice that would be imitated by later composers of the ballet, namely, the appropriation of titles from Louis XIV's court ballets of the 1660s. This practice may have been inspired by Lully's pastiche, *Le Carnaval, mascarade* (1675), which took its frame and title from the court ballet *Le Carnaval, mascarade royale* (1668). The new ballets, however, are not so much revivals as new conceptions, refashioning the ideology of these works to bring them into line with the expectations of a new public audience. In *Les saisons,* for example, the "frightful pain" of Melpomene, Euterpe, and Clio at the aggrandizement of Glory[4] stands in stark contrast to the political message of the *Ballet des saisons* of 1661, a bucolic paean to Louis XIV at his castle at Fontainebleau. Casting the king in the roles of Spring, Summer, and the goddess Ceres—source of fruition, well-being, and harvest—the court ballet had concluded with an entry featuring the nine Muses, danced by women of the court, enjoying the peace and prosperity conducive to their arts. In contrast, the complaints of the Muses in Collasse's *Les saisons* may be read as a call for a return to the bucolic pleasures forgotten by the king. The *livret* of *Les saisons,* by Jean Pic, only loosely follows the conceptual frame of Benserade; Collasse's score is almost completely newly composed.

La naissance de Vénus, produced by Collasse and Pic in the following year, also had connections to a court ballet of the same name. The later work was called an "opera," distinguishing it from the tragedies en musique and probably calling attention to the increased prominence of its danced portions. The music, mostly newly composed, also includes inserted excerpts of Lully's music from the court ballet. If the ideology of *Les saisons* rests on gentle complaints and polite efforts to restrain the excesses of Louis XIV's glory, *La naissance de Vénus* may be viewed as a more direct critique of his militarism. In the plot, a general happiness attending the birth of Venus is spoiled by Jupiter and his jealous wife Juno, who cruelly quell the "revolu-

4. See chapter 4 for a discussion of the prologue of this work. Several of the works discussed here have been mentioned in chapter 4; they are revisited here as they relate to the new genre of the ballet at the Paris Opéra.

tion" it creates. The *livret* transforms Jupiter into a tyrannical villain and the goddess of love into a victim of royal aggression. At the climax of the opera, Jupiter's lightning bolts fill the stage in a spectacular display of destructive power. The work may be read as an undermining of the imagery of the court ballet, with Jupiter and Juno as negative portraits of Louis and Mme de Maintenon. As such it reflects a pattern of contemporary underground literature satirizing the king and his hated wife, as his bellicose policies met with increasing criticism in the late years of his reign.[5] Cythera, with its delightful groves and meadows, continues to serve as a counterutopia to Louis XIV's court, and Venus, ruler over an "amorous empire," as a pacific counterpart to the monarch. The plot of *La naissance de Vénus* deliberately overturns the careful balance, found in the court ballet, between the images of Louis XIV as heroic conqueror and galant lover. This public ballet challenges the propaganda of the earlier work by portraying Louis, under the mask of Jupiter, as a vindictive warmonger and his court as the home of cruelty and terror. As its polar opposite, Cythera represents a matriarchal utopia, characterized by the fête galante and the peaceful joining together of nations in the festive worship of Venus.

Jean Pic also wrote the *livret* for a ballet entitled *Aricie* (1697, music by Louis de La Coste), another Cytherean prototype taking as its heroine the "princess of the unknown isle." Forming an optimistic complement to the tragedy of *La naissance de Vénus*, the ballet introduces the festive, utopian atmosphere that would characterize the future opéra-ballet. This bright setting is darkened only in the prologue, where Apollo is depicted as the perpetrator of injustice and cruelty for his refusal to allow Marsyas, a common mortal, to challenge the eulogies of his Muses. In this work not only the Muses but even Apollo reverts to the role of absolutist censor, chastising the arts of individual expression in order to ensure appropriate monarchical praise. Euterpe, Melpomene, and Polymnia, the Muse "presiding over the arts," interrupt the prelude, announcing the arrival of Apollo. Castigating Marsyas for his temerity, they chase him and his fellow satyrs, fauns, and wood nymphs from the banks of the Seine where the scene takes place. Apollo and the Muses then sing the praises of the "hero" in typical fashion, but framed by Marsyas's exile (along with that of the natural world as represented by the forest creatures) their praise is overshadowed by its cost—the

5. On satires of Louis XIV's relationship with Mme de Maintenon, see Burke, *Fabrication of Louis XIV*, 142–48.

suppression of mortal song. Once again the Muses are portrayed as villains, working under the aegis of the jealous Apollo/Louis to stamp out the arts that lie outside the frame of royal flattery. The prologue, then, may be seen as a protest of Louis XIV's failure to support the arts of the public sphere, more specifically of the Opéra, as they turned to subjects outside the frame of flattery. It should be further noted that the flaying of Marsyas was the theme of a ceiling painting commissioned by Louis XIV in 1666. According to André Félibien, a royal historiographer, the figure of Marsyas referred directly to Fouquet, whose fête of 1661 had aspired to heights too great.[6] Félibien's commentary, first published in 1666, was reprinted in 1696, only a year before the appearance of *Aricie*. Its availability to the creators of *Aricie* opens the possibility that they deliberately inserted this unusual passage as a way of implying a direct parallel between Louis XIV's treatment of Fouquet and his treatment of the arts in late seventeenth-century France.

The princess's magical island, drawing on the Cytherean setting of *La naissance de Vénus,* presents a libertine contrast to the court of Louis XIV and his arts of flattery. On the island is a temple dedicated to Cupid, where a group of lovers comes to pay homage to the god of love. Their songs, opposing the service of Cupid to the "destiny of kings," conclude with a declaration of the ultimate power of love over tyranny. Just as *La naissance de Vénus* revolved around the fête galante, this ballet revolves around the pleasures of the *fête champêtre,* its pseudorustic equivalent, featuring the musette as symbol of the pastoral life. In both works the beauty, simplicity, and naturalness of the fête are contrasted with the martial, totalitarian cruelty of Jupiter, Apollo, and the Muses.

The magical islands of both *La naissance de Vénus* and *Aricie* might have called to mind the earlier production of a highly publicized *grand divertissement* produced in 1664 at what was still a modest hunting lodge in the suburb of Versailles. Its week-long series of fêtes included an equestrian parade and tournament, a mythological procession, two comédie-ballets and a play, various collations and smaller divertissements, and a *ballet à l'entrées.* The combined entertainments of the first three days, centered on the defeat of the sorceress Alcina by Roger and his knights, were called *Les plaisirs de l'île enchantée.* Clearly capitalizing on the success of the destruction of Armida's

---

6. *Entretiens sur les vies et sur les ouvrages des plus excellens peintres anciens et modernes* (Paris, 1666, reprinted 1696), 2: 501, cited by Chae, "Music, Festival, and Power," 6. On Fouquet, see chapter 2 above.

palace in *Les amours déguisés* of the same year, the ballet represented the final defeat of Alcina and the destruction of her enchanted island in a similar fireworks conflagration.[7] Pic's *livrets*, like the earlier *grand divertissement*, present the ruler of the enchanted island as the "Other of sovereignty," but they reverse the symbolism of the earlier work by making both these feminine rulers sympathetic protagonists. In *La naissance de Vénus*, the goddess/heroine is threatened by a figure of absolutist authority, and in *Aricie*, the sovereignty of Cupid is substituted for that of the king/hero figure.

André Campra and the Opéra-ballet

These experiments with a new form of spectacle, reconfiguring the conventions of the old court ballet to reflect the identity of a new social elite, reached their fruition with the opéra-ballet of André Campra (1660–1744) and his contemporaries. This genre combined the sophistication of the tragédie en musique with the qualities of lightheartedness, brilliance, and galanterie that had characterized the court ballet of the 1650s.[8] It attests to a general celebration of hedonism as courtiers, enjoying their newfound freedom from an oppressive court, provided a social and aesthetic model for an emerging public sphere.

Perhaps because of their apparent frivolity, the ballets of Campra and his collaborators have never been examined as vehicles of social critique or political ideology. Yet a study of their libretti reveals a carefully encoded dialogue between the opéra-ballet as a modern fête galante embodying the ideals of love, equality, and freedom, and the court ballet of the 1660s as an archaic *fête monarchique* embodying the ideals of absolutism, patriarchy, and

---

7. The *grands divertissements* of Louis XIV, produced at Versailles between 1661 and 1674, are analyzed in detail in Chae, "Music, Festival, and Power."

8. In "The French Opéra-Ballet in the Early Eighteenth Century: Problems of Definition and Classification," *Journal of the American Musicological Society* 18 (1965): 197–206, James Anthony makes a persuasive case for defining the opéra-ballet by its lack of continuous dramatic action. As he acknowledges, however, the term was rarely used in the eighteenth century, when the term "ballet" was the standard designation for operatic works based on the dance, whether or not their action was continuous. As the works under discussion here differ in their use of continuous action, yet hold important similarities in other ways germane to the investigation, I will follow eighteenth-century practice in designating them simply by the term "ballet." I will reserve the term opéra-ballet for ballets produced at the Paris Opéra, as opposed to works produced at court.

sovereign praise. Their common language is the utopia of fête. The opéra-ballet, however—following the model of Molière in the "Ballet des nations"—substitutes the public theater, and particularly the stage ballet itself, for the old utopia of Louis's court. This modernist utopia, characterized like the court ballet by luxury, voluptuousness, and pleasure, embraces in addition an artistic freedom and social leveling that subtly confront the premises on which the court ballet, as well as all official propaganda, was founded. The public ballet of the Paris Opéra, under the guise of a *libertinage de moeurs*, a social libertinism that it shared with the court ballet of Louis's early reign, also espoused a *libertinage d'esprit*, a political outlook serving as a bridge between seventeenth-century libertinism and eighteenth-century Enlightenment thought.

The opéra-ballet, as it was developed around 1700, announced an aesthetic of modernism based on a radical freedom from the rules of literary classicism and traditional heroic themes, along with a celebration of the human body and its capacity for sensuous and virtuosic movement.[9] The open libertinism of the Opéra and other public theaters left them vulnerable to the attacks of the *dévots* and to the official surveillance and censorship of the king and his police. At the same time, the Opéra in particular served as an oasis for an audience, mostly noble but comprising other social classes as well, that tended to oppose the severe restrictions the monarchy had placed on the arts.

While Collasse's *Les saisons* (1695) and *La naissance de Vénus* (1696) served as important prototypes, Campra's *L'Europe galante* is generally considered the first fully developed exemplar of the genre. It returned, like Molière's *Bourgeois gentilhomme,* to the concept of the *ballet des nations,* depicting love in Italy, France, Spain, and Turkey. Again, however, as in Molière's comédie-ballet, Campra's librettist Antoine Houdar de La Motte abandoned the old ideal of French superiority or monarchical praise, treating instead the victory of Venus and a libertine galanterie throughout Europe. La Motte's *livret* reflected the vogue, at the turn of the century, of a harder-edged form of galanterie, associated with illicit behavior as well as a somewhat more cynical attitude. Undoubtedly influenced by the comedy of manners of Florent Carton Dancourt and others, which catalogued the

9. On this new aesthetic of modernism as it grew out of the quarrel over French and Italian styles in music and the arts, see Cowart, *The Origins of Modern Musical Criticism: French and Italian Music, 1600-1750* (Ann Arbor: UMI Research Press, 1981). On the body and politics, see Melzer and Norberg, *From the Royal to the Republican Body.*

scandals of a libertine society, *L'Europe galante* may have also contributed to this newer conception of galanterie.

As the genre developed over the first decade of the new century, it drew on many of the scenarios and mythological personages of the court ballet. Important departures included a propensity for a four-act structure with separate but loosely related plots and the omission or reversal of former absolutist scenarios and images. The music of the opéra-ballet, though reflecting developments in the tragédie en musique, eschewed heroic and martial elements for a lighthearted, dance-based style. Campra, originally from Aix-en-Provence near the Italian border, also incorporated elements of a late seventeenth-century Italian style; these will be explored in chapter 6. The choreography of these works, under the direction of Guillaume-Louis Pecour, matched the music of Campra in its spectacular brilliance. Pecour was also widely acclaimed as a dancer, as a letter from 1695 attests:

> Many people come to see the *Ballet des Saisons* and simply cannot wait to come again; yesterday, the situation was extreme, people doubling up in the first and second boxes, people suffocating in the pit . . . and all because Pecour danced a Spanish sarabande.[10]

Like the court ballet, the opéra-ballet also celebrated the world of the pastoral. Imported from Italy and Spain in the late sixteenth century, the pastoral had enjoyed a tremendous vogue in early seventeenth-century France. It was carried into the court ballet of the 1650s and 1660s, where its simple pleasures and sentiments seemed ideally suited to musical setting and dance. Pastoral settings, often situated in the French countryside and characterized by minuets, flutes, and oboes, typified the ideal of galanterie with which the court aristocracy was identified. For this noble elite, the quasi-human nymphs, satyrs, and fauns of the pastoral evoked a delicate, erotic world embodying the artful hedonism of the aristocratic ideal. The pastoral element,

---

10. Quoted by Jérôme de La Gorce, "Guillaume-Louis Pecour: A Biographical Essay" (trans. by Margaret McGowan), *Journal of the Society for Dance Research* 8 (Autumn, 1990): 3–26. Pecour had danced at the Opéra since the early 1670s, assuming sole responsibility for the choreography in 1689. Several of Pecour's choreographies, published by Feuillet during this period, have been preserved; see Anne L. Witherell, *Louis Pécour's 1700 "Recueil de dances"* (Ann Arbor, MI: UMI Research Press, 1983). For a more general inventory of early eighteenth-century choreographies and their sources, see Meredith Ellis Little and Carol G. Marsh, *La danse noble: An Inventory of Dances and Sources* (Williamstown, MA: Broude Brothers, 1992).

overshadowed by the heroism of the tragédie en musique, nonetheless continued to inhabit its divertissements. With Lully's *Acis et Galathée* and other pastoral settings by Collasse and others, the pastoral reasserted its authority at the Opéra in the late years of the century. Along with the renewed vogue of the pastoral, the popularity of the minuet continued, and a new dance, the musette, was introduced. A variant of the minuet using the pedal points of the small, elegant bagpipe for which it was named, this dance, like the instrument, alluded to the peasantry for the pleasure of an aristocratic elite.

The pastoral ideal blended with the social and aesthetic phenomenon of the fête galante to define the tone of festive celebration that would characterize the opéra-ballet. As the 1698 ballet *Les fêtes galantes* demonstrated, the ballet and the social fête underwent a continual reciprocal influence. The popularity of the stage ballet intensified a vogue for social dancing and for the staging of private entertainments in the homes of the nobility and bourgeoisie.[11] In turn, the ballet took as its most privileged subject matter the social fête galante, in the form of serenades, balls, garden parties, boating parties, and other excuses for divertissements combining song and dance in the service of love. Part of the appeal of the Opéra was its double status as a venue not only for elaborate theatrical events on stage but also for intimate private parties within the confines of its loges. These parties became veritable fêtes galantes from which the larger spectacle could be enjoyed. The fête galante as the icon of a utopia of pleasure had been advanced as early as 1653, by Madeleine de Scudéry in her *Story of Sapho,* and supported by La Fontaine's advocacy of the delicate *air sérieux* and the intimate settings of private salon concerts (see chaps. 2 and 4). The fête galante that the opéra-ballet took as its subject matter combined three qualities that made it an appropriate counterpart to the old tragédie en musique for a new public audience. First, it reflected a world of beauty and art unhampered by the constraints of royal image making; second, it embraced in its public audience a microcosm of the social diversity that would characterize the utopia it heralded; and third, it provided a means for masking political critique under the frivolous guise of song and dance.

The opéra-ballet perfectly epitomized the ideals of leisure and pleasure of an audience that embraced the actual aristocracy as well as newly wealthy members of the bourgeoisie (some also newly ennobled) seeking to join its "aristocracy of manners." Released from the restraint of praising the king, the genre reverted in tone (though not in structure or style) to the praise of

11. Hilton, *Dance of Court and Theater,* 17.

the noble audience and the paean to court life found in the earlier court ballet, newly adapted to a public audience. Therefore it was natural for artists of the ballet to exorcise the elements of absolutist overlay that had accrued in the 1660s and to refocus the celebratory element of the ballet on its upper-class audience. This aim was primary and undoubtedly sealed the opéra-ballet's success as a genre. Within the spaces of difference between the opéra-ballet and the court ballet, an esoteric form of satire, influenced by Molière and the Lully sons, also began to emerge. Like *Le bourgeois gentilhomme* and the early prototypes of *Les saisons* and *La naissance de Vénus,* these opéra-ballets subtly critiqued the king through allusion to the old court ballet. The connections with the earlier genre are subtle and sometimes difficult to define with certainty. With the exception of *La naissance de Vénus,* in which Collasse interleaved excerpts from the music of Lully's court ballet, almost all the content, both musical and textual, of these new works is newly conceived. What generally remain of the old court ballets are the titles, thematic allusions and general ideological reversals.

Though public audiences would not have had access to stage performances of the court ballets, their *livrets* circulated widely in manuscript throughout the late seventeenth century. Frequent allusions in the correspondence of Mme de Sévigné attest to a general familiarity with the genre among an educated class. Further, the *livrets* of the court ballets had been saved as souvenirs; these became especially prized in the 1680s and 1690s, and a number were bound as collectors' items in the eighteenth century. In 1698 they were published in a widely distributed new edition, allowing the reading public a ready access to the old genre. Even for those who did not know these *livrets,* however, the roles that Louis had danced in the court ballet had passed, through constant repetition in paintings, engravings, statuary, monuments, and literary panegyrics of all sorts, into a common vocabulary that was well known by the French people. The strategy of reversals found in the opéra-ballet plays on that vocabulary in a multivalent manner that often blurs one's ability to distinguish between deliberate satire, double entendre, and mere coincidence. At the same time, since the connection had to do more with image than with plot, the satire could be universally appreciated, or at least vaguely apprehended, in a way that could not be seized on as incriminating, especially in the frame of lavish spectacle bearing natural associations with the court fête.

Composers, though not the general public, would have had access to the scores of the ballet, newly copied toward the end of the century and housed with Mazarin's collection. (Campra, for example, knew the music of the court ballets, arranging a number of them for his 1702 pastiche *Les fragments de Lully*.) With this new familiarity, the process of allusion and reversal, already begun in 1695, intensified and accelerated. The utopian vision presented in these works may be understood in two ways. On the surface, these works celebrated the peace established by the Treaty of Ryswick in 1697. At another level, recognizing Louis's age and the natural succession of his heirs, they also paid tribute in some cases to the Dauphin and in others to Louis's grandson, the duc de Bourgogne. In doing so, they served as a blueprint for a future ruler who would be guided by the arts in establishing a more equitable and pacific society. In this future vision may be read an ideological program representing alternative visions of leadership and society that, challenging the premises of Louis XIV's kingship, embody the proto-Enlightenment views espoused by certain members of the nobility, intellectuals, and the artistic community.

Le triomphe des arts, *Les trois cousines*, and Pilgrimages at (and to) the Théâtre de la foire

In the late seventeenth and early eighteenth centuries, a controversy known as the "war of the theaters" (*guerre des théâtres*) embroiled the theaters of Paris and their patrons. The causes can be traced back to 1672, when Louis XIV granted Lully the Opéra *privilège* or monopoly, forbidding other theatrical establishments to produce opera or to use more than two singers and six instrumentalists in their own musical divertissements. The *guerre* may be more immediately attributed to the unification in 1680 of the Théâtre de Guénégaud and the Hôtel de Bourgogne to create the Comédie-Française, which thereafter began to produce machine plays imitating the spectacular effects formerly seen only at the Opéra. The increasing use of French in the Comédie-Italienne and the rise of the théâtre de la foire subsequent to the Italians' expulsion contributed further to an intense and at times ruthless competition among the Comédie-Française, Opéra, Comédie-Italienne, and théâtre de la foire. The result was their increasing tendency to borrow material, to criticize each other (both in their plays and in the media), and to parody each other's works.[12]

12. Guy Spielmann, *Le jeu de l'ordre et du chaos: Comédie et pouvoirs à la fin de règne, 1673–1715* (Paris: Champion, 2002), 157–67.

The practice of opera parody, often assumed to have originated with the Comédie-Italienne, actually may have been initiated by French playwrights, most notably Florent Carton Dancourt, whose parodies of Quinault's *livrets* established the genre as early as 1674. While Dancourt's opera parodies have been acknowledged, his relationship to the opéra-ballet has attracted almost no scholarly attention.[13] In fact, his play *Les trois cousines*, well known as a model for Antoine Watteau's *Pilgrimage to Cythera,* may be recognized as a parody of one of the earliest examples of the opéra-ballet, *Le triomphe des arts,* created by the writer Houdar de La Motte in collaboration with the composer Michel de La Barre in 1700. This opéra-ballet is also connected with a number of parodies at the théâtre de la foire.

As with the later stage works discussed in this chapter and chapter 6, the nexus linking these three companies and their related works may be found within the charged atmosphere of the *guerre des théâtres.* Yet it is not antagonism, but rather a sense of commonality that emerges from a closer study. Although probably motivated by the intense rivalry among the three theaters, these pieces all comment on the current state of the arts from a similar ideological position. Further, like the "Ballet des nations" in *Le bourgeois gentilhomme* (discussed in chap. 3), they also present a utopia of spectacle and its united arts as the blueprint for a new society. Table 5.1 shows the titular relationships of the opéra-ballets in this group of works with the main court ballets produced in the 1660s. These had a precedent in the connection between *Le Carnaval, mascarade* of 1675 with the earlier *Le Carnaval, mascarade royale* of 1668. The later opéra-ballets do not use pastiche or direct quotation, but instead reshape or in some cases reverse the ideology of those older works. Of the opéra-ballets listed here, those related to the topos of Cythera will be discussed in this chapter, while those related to the topos of Venetian carnival will be discussed in chapter 6.

13. Dancourt's opera parodies are discussed in Perry Gethner, "Le divertissement dans la comédie de Dancourt," *Littératures classiques* 21 (1994): 103–12, and John S. Powell, "The Opera Parodies of Florent Carton Dancourt," *Cambridge Opera Journal* 13, no. 1 (2001): 87–114. See also Delia Gambelli and Letizia Norci Cagiano, eds., *Le théâtre et son double (1600–1762): Actes du colloque "L'Académie de musique, Lully, l'opéra et la parodie de l'opéra"* (Paris: Champion, 2005). Dancourt's relationship to the opéra-ballet was first discussed by Georgia Cowart, in "Watteau's *Pilgrimage to Cythera* and the Subversive Utopia of the Opera-Ballet," *Art Bulletin* 83 (2001): 460–78. Portions of this chapter, as well as chapter 7, are reproduced from that article.

TABLE 5.1. Ballets Produced at the Paris Opéra, 1675–1713, with Title or Content Connections to Earlier Court Ballets

Ballet/Opéra	Date	Composer/Librettist	Court Ballet (Lully)	Date
Le Carnaval, mascarade (pastiche)	1675	Lully/Quinault/ Molière	*Le Carnaval, mascarade royale*	1668
Les saisons	1695	Collasse/Pic	*Ballet des saisons*	1661
La naissance de Vénus	1696	Collasse/Pic	*Ballet de la naissance de Vénus*	1665
Le carnaval de Venise	1699	Campra/La Motte	*Le Carnaval, mascarade royale*	1668
Le triomphe des arts	1700	La Barre/La Motte	*Ballet des arts*	1663
Les Muses	1703	Campra/Danchet	*Ballet des Muses*	1666
Les fêtes vénitiennes	1710	Campra/Danchet	*Le Carnaval, mascarade royale*	1668
Les amours déguisés	1713	Bourgeois/Fuselier	*Ballet des amours déguisés*	1664

Le triomphe des arts represents one of the most complete expressions of an alternative program for the arts, presenting an indirect challenge to the ideology of Louis XIV's *Ballet des arts* of 1663. This court ballet had presented the arts as celebrating a peace dependent on military victory. An exhibition of the liberal and mechanical arts (agriculture, navigation, metallurgy, painting, the chase, medicine, and war) in the service of Athena, it had ended with a *grand ballet* depicting war, in which Henriette d'Angleterre, descending on a cloud machine, had danced the role of the goddess of war. *Le triomphe des arts* updates the symbolism of the court ballet by presenting the arts as leading the way to a new, peaceful society under the direct inspiration of Venus. In the first entry of *Le triomphe des arts*, entitled "L'architecture," the goddess challenges the monarchical figure Apollo by successfully dedicating a rival temple to her son Cupid. As she does so, the statues decorating this new temple come to life as cupids holding the emblems of the arts. Apollo, in a spirit true to the utopian nature of the ballet—and quite out of keeping with the usual strategies of royal propaganda—graciously awards the new temple a status equal to that of his own. In succeeding entries, Venus serves as patron goddess to a series of artists who use their art to establish the values of love and beauty in the service of humanity. Alexander the Conqueror cedes to the artist Apelles, painter of Venus ("La peinture"), and in "La musique," the musician Amphion takes the city of Thebes by music rather than by war.

The second entry,[14] "La poésie," dedicated to the poet Sappho and set before a temple of Venus overlooking the ocean, may be seen as a tribute to the other "Sapho," Madeleine de Scudéry. By 1700 Scudéry, who would die the following year, had come to stand (like the ancient poet) for a literature of galant passion which, though scorned by Boileau and the classicists, continued to enjoy the fervent approbation of a reading public. In "La poésie," the ancient Sappho is depicted in her historical role as leader of a cult of Venus on an island sacred to the goddess—presumably Lesbos, which La Motte conflates here with the utopia of Cythera set out in *La naissance de Vénus*. Sappho's surviving hymn to the goddess, loosely paraphrased by La Motte, serves as the sung text underlying the sacred ritual of the fête galante. As they sing and dance a minuet, a group of lovers, offering as sacrifices the attributes of the other gods, dedicate a trophy to Venus. A priestess of Venus, transported by a vision of the future, foresees happiness for Sappho and for the world. The suicide of Sappho, betrayed in love, and her subsequent apotheosis as the "tenth Muse" may be read, along with the coming to life of the Temple de l'Amour, as the transformation of an artistic vision of love and beauty into a living, societal reality.[15]

Another transformation of love and art may be seen in the final entry, "La sculpture," a depiction of the Pygmalion story. In this entry Venus herself makes an ex machina appearance, paralleling that of Athena in the *Ballet des arts*. In this version, Venus effects the transformation of Pygmalion's statue by summoning a cupid, who animates the statue by flying before it with his torch. The conclusion to this entry, and to the ballet as a whole, features a chorus representing Dance and a soloist representing Music, celebrating the victory of Pygmalion, love, and the arts. Two other soloists from the chorus, costumed as a peasant representing agriculture (replacing

14. The term was retained for the opéra-ballet, though its entries were—like the acts of opera or the spoken theater—longer and fewer.

15. This entry is probably related to *Le Triomphe de Madame Deshoulières*, written in 1695 by Mlle L'Héritier as an *éloge* to the famous galant poet Mme Deshoulières, and dedicated to Scudéry. In it, Mme Deshoulières is welcomed to Parnassus by the Muses, and accorded the privilege of becoming the "tenth Muse." In 1701, the year after *Le triomphe des arts*, Mlle L'Héritier would write another *éloge* on the death of Scudéry. It is possible that all these works are connected; if so, those connections would be typical of galant coteries of writers who tended to employ a playful intertextuality. See Delphine Denis, *Le Parnasse galant: Institution d'une catégorie littéraire au XVIIe siècle* (Paris: Champion, 2001), 75–77.

Louis XIV as shepherd/hero in the *Ballet des arts*) and a sailor representing navigation (replacing a group of pirates in the earlier work), communicate directly to the audience in airs that praise the peaceful pleasures of land and sea. The peasant sings of the beauty of the woods and the pleasures of love, and the sailor invites the audience to embark on the seas of love: "Embark, too timid youth, / Benefit from a happy leisure; / Give yourselves to love, Cupid is the only guide / Who leads hearts to pleasure."[16]

In the same way that several of the entries of *Le triomphe des arts* end in apotheoses of their own, this final chorus represents not only dance but also a grand apotheosis of the ballet as a whole. Its text confirms that the living sculpture of Pygmalion's statue (like the cupids coming to life on the Temple de l'Amour) can be understood as the dance itself, literally bringing to life the utopian qualities suggested in the ballet. Further, the dialogue of Music and Dance, complementing the succession of entries that have gone before, points to the larger genre of the ballet as the site of the confluence of the arts of peace. As a whole, the entries of *Le triomphe des arts* may be read as the successive awakening of this new genre, and the final scene—paralleling the *grand ballet* devoted to war in the court ballet—as a direct appeal to its audience to join in its cult of peace and freedom.

Le triomphe des arts may also be read as a defense of the libertinism of the Paris Opéra against the criticism of the *parti des dévôts*. The *querelle des théâtres* of the 1690s, related to the larger quarrels of the Ancients and the Moderns as well as earlier attacks on the theater in the time of Molière, had reflected the wrath of the *dévôts* against the public theater, especially the Opéra and its *chanteuses* and *danseuses* (collectively known as *les filles de l'Opéra*), whom they chastised as immoral, corrupt, and scandalous.[17] After the death of Lully, the Opéra had become a public scandal. Police records from the eighteenth century confirm that the Opéra chorus or ballet troupe provided the ideal front for Parisian courtesans placed there by powerful and influential lovers, since performers in royal theaters obtained automatic immunity from prosecution for immoral conduct. Attacks on the theater came primarily from clergymen associated with Port Royal, the Jansenist stronghold, and with a circle associated with Mme de Maintenon. The powerful cleric Bossuet, a friend of Maintenon, was a participant in this quarrel.

---

16. Pure, *Recueil général*, 2: 19: "Embarquez-vous, jeunesse trop timide, / Profitez d'un heureux loisir; / Aimez, aimez, l'Amour est le seul guide / Qui mene les coeurs au plaisir."

17. The *querelle*, between the theater and its critics, should not be confused with the *guerre* among the theaters themselves.

In 1694, the Sorbonne itself issued a formal statement declaring opera even more dangerous than comedies.[18]

The libertine utopia advanced in *Le triomphe des arts* therefore depicts not only a society led by the arts but also the ballet as a model for that society. Any audience assembled there in 1700 would have understood the temples of Cupid and Venus, depicted in the first and second entries respectively, as the Opéra itself, known as "Temple de l'Amour" or "Temple de la Volupté," and the temple of the gracious Apollo as that of a benevolent ruler willing to be guided by the arts rather than to exploit them. Through the omission of the art of war and the showcasing of the arts of architecture, poetry, painting, music, and dance, *Le triomphe des arts* presents the united arts of the stage ballet as a utopian alternative to Louis XIV's arts of war and flattery. The work as a whole may also be seen as a dedication of the new genre, created by La Motte only three years earlier, to the public audience as a new collective patron and the metonym for a new society.

All the premises on which *Le triomphe des arts* are based represent an inversion of the traditional modes of absolutist encomium. The ballet as a whole inverts the premise of Louis XIV's *Ballet des arts*, the presentation of the liberal arts flourishing under the glorious patronage of the king. It also inverts the monarchical flattery common to the opera prologue. Finally, it inverts the idea of "triumph" as the triumphal procession by which the monarch made his "entry" into a city or arena of praise. Thus each entry of this ballet represents the triumph not of the monarch but of an artist in the service of a new society. In contrast to official panegyrics demanding homage to the king, La Motte's "Hymn to Venus" demands only pleasures ("Your pleasures are the only homage / That Venus expects from you").[19] This encomium of the goddess posits her selfless "empire of love," the fruits of which are shared with all her followers, as a direct antithesis to the greedy imperialism of Louis XIV. In that sense these words of the "Hymn to

---

18. Jerôme de la Gorce, ed., *Description de la vie et moeurs de l'exercice et l'estat des filles de l'Opéra* (Paris, 1993). La Gorce's introduction, and Spielmann, *Le jeu de l'ordre et du chaos,* 167–73, present helpful information on the *querelle des théâtres.* On the role of women in the *querelle,* see Kathryn Norberg, "Prostitutes," in *A History of Women in the West,* vol. 3, *Renaissance and Enlightenment Paradoxes,* ed. Natalie Zemon Davis and Arlette Farge (Cambridge: Belknap Press of Harvard University Press, 1993), 469, and Georgia Cowart, "Of Women, Sex, and Folly: Opera under the Old Regime," *Cambridge Opera Journal* 6 (1994): 205–20.

19. Pure, *Recueil général,* 2: 12: "Vos Plaisirs sont les hommages / Que Venus attend de vous."

Venus" summarize the message of the ballet: "Rule over the world in a supreme empire, / Make your charming languor be felt everywhere, / An extreme sweetness is enjoyed under your laws, / And you share with these hearts / All the pleasures that you enjoy yourself."[20]

Sappho's poetry, identified with a discourse of passion,[21] stood out in high relief against official propaganda, which drew much of its imagery from the Homeric tradition. La Motte obviously chose the character of Sappho as poet of Venus in order to highlight the new union of passion and art over which she was to preside as the tenth Muse. Her sacred island also embraced a wider symbolism linking the imagery of the Renaissance isle of love with Enlightenment ideals. In 1700, then, the ballet served as a useful symbol for an artistic modernism, based on the pleasurable arts of song and dance, that marked a radical break from traditional image making. The fête galante, rather than a trivial, nonconsequential pastime, became the emblem of the sacred ritual of love by which Venus and her son Cupid were virtually worshiped as the embodiment of a pagan, libertine ideal.[22] Finally, the ballet, site of the confluence of the arts depicted in *Le triomphe des arts,* stood as a symbol of art itself, the vehicle transporting its audience to the new utopia. In her metamorphosis as tenth Muse, La Motte's Sappho represents the artist who mediates between the prosaic human and the poetic divine.

Le triomphe des arts affords the most complete explanation of the cult of Venus as it had emerged in the work of Marino, La Fontaine, and Scudéry and in *La naissance de Vénus.* Beginning with Venus's extraordinary dedication of a temple to her son L'Amour as a rival of Apollo, the entire work builds an alternate program to Louis XIV's militaristic imperialism and self-serving propaganda. This program sets out a new society under the matriarchy of the goddess of love and under the temporal rule of a beneficent ruler (signified by the gracious figures of Apollo and Alexander) who is willing to be led by the arts of love and beauty.[23] Through an embracing metaphor

---

20. Ibid.: "Exercez dans le monde un empire suprême, / Faites sentir par tout vos charmantes langueurs, / On joüit sous vos loix d'une douceur extrême, / Et vous répandez dans les coeurs / Tous les Plaisirs que vous goûtez vous-même."

21. Joan DeJean, *Fictions of Sappho, 1546–1937* (Chicago: University of Chicago Press, 1989), 115.

22. On the relationship of paganism and *libertinage* in the seventeenth century, see Pintard, *Le libertinage érudit,* 186–87, 285–88, 508–10, 520–22.

23. There is probably a connection here also with Louis XIV's *Ballet de la naissance de Vénus,* in which Louis XIV as Alexander paid obeisance to a statue of Venus representing her temple. La Motte's work may be considered a call for a return to this obeisance.

of transformation, La Motte posits the ballet itself as the Epicurean shrine to Venus and L'Amour, and its audience as worshipers embarking upon the regenerative seas of art and love. The transformations portrayed within each act of the ballet, beginning with the awakening of the cupids on the Temple de L'Amour and continuing with the series of triumphs of artists over absolutism and the metamorphoses creating a new artistic and social order, stand for the triumph of the united arts of the ballet as they depict a new society awakened by love. Thus, following Scudéry (and underlining the importance of his allusion to Sappho), La Motte initiates a shift from a tragic lament for the lost art and beauty of Cythera to a victorious celebration of the arts of the ballet as they revivify the ideals of Venus's island shrine.

It is possible that after a series of treaties with France's European neighbors regarding the Spanish succession, in 1698, 1699, and 1700, the temporary peace allowed a more immediate contemplation of a society led by the arts under Louis XIV. More probably, given the dedication, La Motte's vision embraced a future utopia led by the duc de Bourgogne, who would become Dauphin on the death of his father in 1711, and who himself would precede Louis XIV in death in 1712. The dedication of the ballet, addressed to the duc, praises this future ruler for his willingness to be led by the arts, while denouncing those who restrict the arts to the servile role of monarchical flattery.

From the late seventeenth century, a faction had arisen around the duc de Bourgogne. Its spokesperson was Archbishop Fénelon, tutor to the young duc, who had merged the mystical doctrine of "pure love," advanced by a sect known as the Quietists, with a program of radical political reform laced with elements of pacifism. Even if Louis XIV was not aware of Fénelon's authorship of the incendiary letter of 1694 quoted at the beginning of this chapter, two developments at the end of the 1690s turned his wrath on the archbishop. The first was the censorship of Fénelon's *Explication des maximes des saints sur la vie intérieure*, which brought the Quietist affair to Louis XIV's attention and caused him to banish Fénelon to his bishopric in Cambrai. The second was the anonymous publication, in 1699, of Fénelon's *Télémaque*. This treatise, originally written for the instruction of the young duc de Bourgogne, was judged by many to be a satire on Louis XIV and his regime. When Fénelon was discovered to be its author, the king had the work confiscated and forbade the archbishop ever to return to Versailles or Paris or to communicate with any member of the royal family.[24]

24. James Herbert Davis Jr., *Fénelon* (Boston: Twayne, 1979), 15–29. Our knowledge of factions, or cabals, stems mostly from the *Mémoires* of the duc de Saint-Simon. At the

The faction around the young duc de Bourgogne, unlike the one surrounding the Dauphin, his father, followed a moral high path that precluded
a natural sympathy with the mystique of the Opéra. In general it included
some of the most progressive thinkers and reformists of the period, including a number of aristocrats concerned with the plight of the lower classes.
It is likely, then, that La Motte, a close friend of Fénelon and leader of the
Moderns in the quarrel between the Ancients and the Moderns, sought to
use the platform of *Le triomphe des arts* to offer praise to the duc de Bourgogne (and indirectly to the disgraced Fénelon), and to persuade the duc, his
followers, and the audience at the Opéra that the arts could lead the way to
the new society envisioned by archbishop.[25] Despite its lofty utopianism, *Le
triomphe des arts* was not a success, perhaps because of inherent weaknesses
in the *livret* and the musical score, and also because the Opéra was not a natural home to the cabal of the duc de Bourgogne, as it was to the cabal of his
father the Dauphin.

Later in the same year, Florent Carton Dancourt produced a play for
the Comédie-Française entitled *Les trois cousines*, the final divertissement
of which represents a burlesque version of *Le triomphe des arts*.[26] Although
the mode of parody provides a framework, this "dialogue" between the two
theaters also reflects an increasing fascination with the interplay between
high and low styles as they define the parallel cultures of the public sphere.
In Dancourt's divertissement Venus's sacred island has become a libertine
suburb of Paris, and the worshipers of Venus have become "pilgrims," a
euphemism for the village boys and girls who journey there in search of a
mate.[27] In their freedom to do so, and in the joyous atmosphere of fête, one
observes an emulation of the utopian ideology of the ballet and a transfer of
that ideology to the libertine suburbs of Paris. Dancourt's addition of the
notion of pilgrimage adds a valuable element to the eighteenth-century mythology of love, as does the egalitarianism with which he treats the theme:

---

end of Louis XIV's reign, there were three primary factions: those of the king and Mme de
Maintenon, the Dauphin, and the duc de Bourgogne. The phenomenon was complex, with
members of one faction often also serving, or paying lip service to, another. It is treated in
Le Roy Ladurie, *Saint-Simon and the Court of Louis XIV,* 121–60.

25. On La Motte and Fénelon, see Finch, *Sixth Sense,* 56.

26. *Oeuvres de théâtre,* 3 vols. (1760; Geneva: Slatkine, 1968), 2: 310–42.

27. Dancourt was not the first to depict this theme; already at the court of Henri IV
a *Ballet des pélerins d'amour* had been performed (Bibliothèque nationale MS 24356, fol.
262r); see Robert Tomlinson, *La Fête galante: Watteau et Marivaux* (Geneva: Droz, 1981),
110–11.

"Everyone makes a pilgrimage to the temple of the son of Venus; the court, the town, the village are equally received there."[28] Dancourt's play, extending the utopia of the ballet to the comedy of manners, also extends its society to the lower class ("the village").

Disguised Cupids at the Opéra and the *Foire*

In the second decade of the eighteenth century, the topos of love was most thoroughly developed in the ballet *Les amours déguisés* of 1713 (*livret* by Louis Fuselier; music by Thomas Bourgeois),[29] which took its title from the *Ballet des amours déguisés* of 1664. In the earlier work, discussed in chapter 2, Venus had fared better than in most of the court ballets, as she engaged in fiery debate with the goddess of war and scored some victories over Athena by disguising her cupids as they came to the aid of famous lovers of antiquity. Ultimately she was overthrown by the greater power of Athena, favored by the king. To climax the final defeat of Venus, the librettist depicted a mutiny, in which the cupids, supposed to be helping Helen, Paris, and Venus, defected to the side of Menelaus, Athena, and the Greeks, once again underscoring the potency of patriarchy and the futility of resistance.

Fuselier's *livret* of 1713 overturns this absolutist ending. In his prologue, the setting represents a port, where a fleet manned by cupids is preparing to set sail for the isle of Cythera. Venus, accompanied by her Games and Pleasures disguised as sailors, invites mortals to accompany them, and in fact has her cupids enchain the lovers with garlands of flowers. The troops of Athena (now under her Roman name of Minerva) storm the scene and attempt to break these garland chains, whereupon a host of cupids, flying out of the clouds shooting arrows of love, engage and immediately subdue them. Minerva, humiliated, leaves her followers, new members of an "amorous empire," to join with Venus, the lovers, and Pleasures in an embarkation for Cythera. The remainder of the ballet is devoted to three entries depicting love disguised as hate, esteem, and friendship. Like *Le triomphe des arts*, it positions young lovers and artists devoted to love, most notably the poet Ovid, against tyrannical figures. Its negative depiction of Augustus Caesar, more usually presented as a royal surrogate, may return to the similar treatment of the novelist La Calprenède in his *Cléopatre*. Paeans to peace abound,

---

28. Dancourt, *Oeuvres de théâtre*, 2: 341: "Au temple du fils de Vénus / Chacun fait son pèlerinage; / La cour, la ville, le village, / Y sont egalement reçus."

29. Libretto in Pure, *Recueil général*, 2: 510–22.

especially in the entry devoted to prisoners threatened by the cruel hench-men of the cult of "the sun," a blatant allusion to the Sun King and his minis-ters. The work ends with citizens of "many nations" joining together to wit-ness a fête in honor of Cupid who has triumphed over Mars. The audience includes even the bellicose Scythians, who have turned from the service of Mars to that of Cupid.[30]

Like *Le triomphe des arts* to which its message and imagery allude, *Les amours déguisés* was produced at a moment of relative peace in Europe, as the Treaty of Utrecht was being forged in 1713–14. Much had changed, however; the Dauphin had died in 1711, and the duc de Bourgogne, who succeeded him as Dauphin, had also succumbed in 1712. In 1713 the new Dauphin, Louis XIV's great-grandson, was only five years old, and the duc d'Orléans, the son of Louis's brother and the future regent, stood next in line to the kingship.

Both of these ballets overturn the court ballet's glorification of war through a new celebration of Venus and Cupid over Athena. Both celebrate Venus's island shrine as a haven of peace and love. While La Motte followed Ovid's story of the metamorphosis of Sappho as the tenth Muse, Fuselier takes Ovid himself, "favored at the court of Cythera,"[31] as a symbol of the passionate ideal that lay at the heart of this artistic countermovement. In both these opéra-ballets, love may be seen not only as an ideal in itself but also as a symbol for a wider advocacy of political freedom. This symbolism is spelled out in Fuselier's *Les amours déguisés,* in which the daughter of Caesar Augustus, forsaking her father's throne for the love of the poet Ovid, evokes the Roman republic, where "liberty, resembling tender love, / Made equal in this happy realm / All mortals who submitted to its dominion."[32] Like Sappho's ritual fête galante in *Le triomphe des arts,* the fête galante that ends Fuselier's *Les amours déguisés* includes people of "all nationalities," now as a symbolic audience representing the universality of fête.

The musical scores of *Le triomphe des arts* and *Les amours déguisés*[33] exhibit a style which, growing out of the dances of the court ballet and the pastoral

30. For a discussion of La Calprenède, see above, chapter 2. Louis Fuselier was later to write the *livret* for Jean-Philippe Rameau's *Les Indes galantes* (1735), which would carry sim-ilar thematic elements, including a cruel "ruler of the Sun," into the period of Rameau.

31. Pure, *Recueil général,* 2: 520.

32. Ibid.: "La liberté semblable au tendre amour / Egaloit autrefois dans cet heureux séjour / Tous les mortels soumis à son empire."

33. *Le triomphe des arts* (Paris: Ballard, 1700) and *Les amours déguisés* (Paris: Ballard, 1713).

divertissements of the tragédie en musique, contributes to a growing taste for the light and pleasurable in music, as well as the other arts, in the early eighteenth century. Michel de La Barre, the composer of *Le triomphe des arts* and flutist in the orchestra of the Opéra, introduces the pastoral sounds of woodwinds in chains of "sweet" thirds and sixths above slow harmonic rhythms in the bass. The effect is exaggerated in example 5.1, the apotheosis of the work in which Sappho rises from the sea as the tenth Muse. A long pedal point, as in a musette, highlights this pastoral orientation as the trademark of the new art represented by Sappho as the Muse of an eighteenth-century modernism. La Barre also celebrates the minuet, of all dances the one that by the late seventeenth century most clearly captured the blend of pastoral elegance and amorous desire that became synonymous with the ballet itself. Thomas Bourgeois, the composer of *Les amours déguisés*, also spotlights the minuet and includes the slow harmonic rhythms and delicate timbres of the musette, which, like the minuet, links the pastoral simplicity and bucolic pleasures of the countryside with the goddess of love. Against this style, Athena's recitative and call to arms recall the more dramatic musical style of the tragédie en musique. Similar distinctions characterize the entire ballet, underscoring a subtle web of musical allusion to the contrast between war and peace. In the entry "L'amitié," soprano recorders, engaging in intricate roulades to imitate the song of the nightingale, form a striking musical image of an idealized pastoral existence claimed to have existed before the ravages of the Trojan War (ex. 5.2). Again, the trilling of the recorders in thirds above a slow-moving bass serves to capture an effect—in this case, of birdsong—but it also captures a pastoral mood that typifies an eighteenth-century modernism.

Finally, just as Dancourt parodied *Le triomphe des arts* in his libertine Parisian pilgrimage, Fuselier created a burlesque version of his own ballet, entitled *Les pélerins de Cythère*. Unlike previous writers for the ballet, Fuselier was more closely associated with the popular theaters of the *foire* than with the Opéra. Thus, reversing the standard chronology of parody, the première of *Les pélerins de Cythère* at the Foire Saint-Laurent in 1713 actually preceded the opening of the opéra-ballet. It was still playing when *Les amours déguisés* made its operatic debut in August; the future regent was said to have attended both these performances in the same evening.[34] Unlike Dancourt's pilgrimage on foot, *Les pélerins de Cythère* depicts a Parisian "maritime" scene, a trip on a pleasure boat rowed by cupids down the Seine

---

34. Tomlinson, *La Fête galante*, 114.

Example 5.1. Michel de La Barre, *Le triomphe des arts*. Entrée 2, apotheosis of Sappho.
Paris: Ballard, 1700, 89.

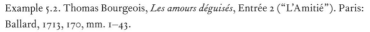

Example 5.2. Thomas Bourgeois, *Les amours déguisés*, Entrée 2 ("L'Amitié"). Paris: Ballard, 1713, 170, mm. 1–43.

Example 5.2. (*continued*)

airs, par leurs ai - ma - bles chants, pré - vien - nent nos con-certs.

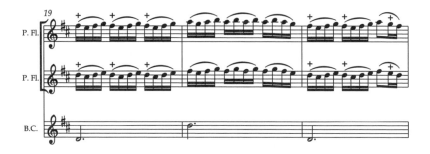

Example 5.2. (*continued*)

to the fashionable libertine suburb of Saint-Cloud. The piece, amounting to an early form of comic opera, revolves around a series of characters taking various disguises in order not to be recognized by their spouses. The close proximity in time and subject matter of Fuselier's two works confirms their connection. Most important, Fuselier's treatment of Cythera-related topics in both a "high," operatic style and a "low," burlesque style indicates a motivation to address, and depict, audiences of all social classes. Fuselier's *Les pélerins de Cythère*, in fact, represents the first of a series of plays, all on the subject of Cythera, inviting their audience to come as "good pilgrims" to the theater. These invitations point to an interpretation of the theater itself as Cythera, libertine mecca of love and pleasure. As in Molière's time, the theater continued to serve as one of the few venues inclusive of all social classes in the early decades of the eighteenth century, and thus a worthy destination for "pilgrims" in search of a new society. The notion of pilgrimage, moreover, plays directly off the conventional image of Christian pilgrimages, creating an idea of the theater as a rival shrine not only to the monarchy, but also to the church and to the *parti des dévôts*. Created by the same author, the operatic work and its parody serve not so much as typical salvos in the *guerre des théâtres* as two different faces of a libertine utopia.

Les pélerins de Cythère launched a series of comedies on the theme of Cythera at the *foire* and at the new Comédie-Italienne. These treatments reinforce the symbolism and meaning of the ballets. Robert Tomlinson has explored the erotic imagery of the pilgrim's staff and Venus's shell in the explicit sexual allusions of these plays.[35] Commentators, however, have failed to note the transfer, in Fuselier's self-parody and in the plethora of works (largely under his authorship) following in its wake,[36] of some themes as-

35. Ibid., 122.

36. The theme of Cythera was inaugurated by this piece at the Foire Saint-Laurent and continued in *Les pélerins de Cythère* of Letellier in 1714; *Les avantures de Cythère* of Charpentier in 1715; *L'école des amants* of Lesage and Fuselier in 1716; *Les arrêtes de l'Amour* of Lesage and d'Orneval in 1716; *Le rémouleur d'Amour* of Lesage, Fuselier, and d'Orneval of 1722; *La folle raisonnable* of Dominique in 1725; *Les pélerins de Mecque* of Lesage, Fuselier, and d'Orneval in 1726; *La Pénélope moderne* of Lesage, Fuselier, and d'Orneval in 1728; and *L'Amour marin* of Lesage, Fuselier, and d'Orneval in 1730. Tomlinson (*La fête galante*, 174–75) includes a listing of plays treating Cythera at the Opéra, the *foire*, and the Comédie-Italienne but fails to note a play actually entitled *Les amours déguisez* performed at the *foire* in 1722. Whereas Fuselier's *Pélerins* parodied the prologue to the ballet *Les amours déguisez*, the eponymous play, in which a series of comic characters discover love masquerading as other qualities, parodied the following three acts.

sociated with Cythera from the ballet to the *foire*. One is the equation of love and freedom, of a *libertinage de moeurs* with a *libertinage d'esprit*. Another is the equation of the theater itself with Cythera, a motif that is picked up in later plays inviting the public to participate in the games of Venus.[37] Of all Parisian audiences, those of the *foire* represented the clearest cross-section of all classes of society. In this period it was considered inappropriate to depict contemporary life in France on the stage of the Opéra. Therefore the entertainments of the *foire* subtly reveal elements in these opéra-ballets pointing to a libertine underground resistance. This process, moreover, positions the public theater itself, in its various manifestations the symbol of all classes of society, in opposition to Louis XIV. The ballet, as a galant form of theater, represents a meeting ground between the high style of tragedy and the low style of the *foire*.[38] Further, in its combination of many art forms, it becomes a representation of art itself, the point of embarkation for Cythera. The expansion of this artistic resistance to other forms of theater serves to intensify its symbolism, widening its scope to represent various arts and classes of society in opposition to a regime that, after seventy-two years, had outlasted its time.

Unlike the opera parodies of the Comédie-Italienne and the later parodies of the théâtre de la foire, which followed their models almost immediately, the opéra-ballets take aim at works preceding them by years and even decades. Also, whereas the Italians' parodies clearly announced their parodic intents and objects, the political innuendo of the opéra-ballet operates in a more covert fashion. An obvious reason for these differences is that more conventional parodies, though often practicing a similar brand of political satire, usually took as their targets only the most generalized monarchical surrogates of the tragedy and tragédie en musique. The librettists of the opéra-ballet follow the pattern established in the Lully sons' *Zéphire et Flore* and *Orphée* in implying a different type of satire, seemingly unique to the Opéra itself, more directly targeting the icons of royal propaganda through specific reference to the ideological content, and occasionally to specific roles, of the court ballet. These works not only satirize genres and roles associated with the king and the court but also pay tribute to an interconnected group of arts and artists. They do not seem to make use of actual

---

37. Alain René Le Sage and Jacques-Philippe d'Orneval, *Le Théâtre de la Foire ou l'Opéra comique, contenant les meilleures pièces qui ont été représentées aux foires de Saint-Germain et de Saint-Laurent* (1737; Geneva: Slatkine, 1968), 2: 173 and 66.

38. On the *galant* as a "middle style," see Cowart, "Lully *enjoué*."

musical quotation,[39] probably because the general public, while having access to the published texts of Benserade's *livrets* and other works to which the opéra-ballets allude, would have had no familiarity with the music of the court ballets and the earlier operas.

As I have mentioned above, opera parodies produced at the *foire* generally attacked the Opéra itself as a rival, official theater. The process is complicated here, however, by the fact that it was in *Le triomphe des arts* and *Les amours déguisés,* works produced at the Opéra itself, that a subtle process akin to parody of the court ballet originated, before the opéra-ballets themselves were parodied by Dancourt at the Comédie-Française and Fuzelier at the *foire.* In a way, then, Dancourt's *Les trois cousines* and Fuzelier's *Les pèlerins de Cythère* echo the general ideological message of their operatic models, though in different modalities. That message includes both a subtle critique of Louis XIV's propaganda and a glorification of public entertainment and its audiences, now aligning to reflect the transfer of privilege from the king to a new society comprising all social classes.

39. Collasse's *Naissance de Vénus,* which incorporates sections of Lully's music for the earlier court ballet, is an obvious exception, though the process there might be considered more incorporation than quotation.

CHAPTER SIX

Carnival, Commedia dell'arte & the Triumph of Folly

The Ballet at the Paris Opéra, 1699–1718

The new place of the arts in the changing operatic landscape at the turn of the century is made tangible through a transformed image of the Muses, liberated from the service of Louis XIV and now in the service of a new group of deities and allegorical characters representing the public sphere. The most important of these, Folly (La Folie, the female fool), represents a bold spirit of carnivalesque satire, traceable to Erasmus, Molière, and the commedia dell'arte. She is joined by Momus, ancient Greek god of satire and jester of the gods; Bacchus, god of wine; Ceres and Flora, goddesses of abundance; and Plutus, god of commerce and symbol of a new commercial theater. This new pantheon rules over a group of opéra-ballets and plays at the théâtre de la foire, in which an enactment of public pleasure continues to supplant the old enactment of sovereign power. Paralleling the cult of love discussed in chapter 5, the themes of carnival, commedia dell'arte, and comic madness constitute a cult of folly that directly challenges the rational order and humorless control characterizing the final phase of Louis XIV's long reign.[1]

The Muses of Folly

Campra's ballet *Les Muses* of 1703 presents an alternative to Louis XIV's artistic program as set out in the *Ballet des Muses* of 1666, glorifying instead

1. Portions of this chapter, as well as some related paragraphs in chapter 4, are reprinted from Cowart, "Carnival in Venice or Protest in Paris: Louis XIV and the Politics of Subversion at the Paris Opéra," *Journal of the American Musicological Society* 54 (2001): 265–302.

the arts and entertainments of the public sphere. Clearly following the parody by Molière and Lully of the *Ballet des Muses* in *Le bourgeois gentilhomme*, Campra and his librettist Antoine Danchet also target the same court ballet as a way of pointing up the social, ideological, and aesthetic shifts resulting from the ballet's move, in this case, to the Paris Opéra. In the prologue, Momus declares that the Muses now serve the powerful Plutus (the commercial theater) and spend their time with Cupid (patron god of the Opéra). The Muses return and begin to sing of the gods and heroes, but their song is interrupted by Bacchus and Ceres, celebrating pleasure, abundance, and love as the wellspring of the arts. They also celebrate the "river of forgetfulness" created by Bacchus's wine—a reversal of the ideology of royal memorial presented by Mnemosine, the mother of the Muses and master of ceremonies in the opening of the *Ballet des Muses*. The music of the prologue, drawing on burlesque techniques of interruption and fragmentation, shifts between a rollicking compound meter, depicting the pleasures of Bacchus and Ceres, and a slower duple meter, marked *gravement*, mocking the pompousness of traditional praise. The climax of the prologue is a chorus comprising the suites of Bacchus and Ceres, singing praise to Bacchus's reign of pleasure.

Momus agrees with Apollo to judge the entries of the ballet representing different forms of theater: pastoral, satire, tragedy, and comedy. Like the prologue, these signal a new aesthetic and politics of the arts. The first entry, "La pastorale," develops the concept of Arcadia as an alternate utopian empire, privileging an honest and tranquil countryside over the noise of war and the fate of kings. In its fête champêtre, recalling the central fête galante of *Le triomphe des arts* and the central fête champêtre of *Aricie* (discussed in chap. 5), shepherds and shepherdesses gather before a rural altar to renounce grandeur and to pledge their faith to Venus, Cupid, and Flora.[2] "La satire," alluding to the singing role of a satyr in the *Ballet des Muses*, pays tribute to the genre of satire. Set before an ancient "Temple of Satire," it presents the Cynic philosopher Diogenes, denouncing the courtly art of flattery that masks the truth. Its final scene depicts the festival of the Saturnalia and the coming together of the people at the Temple of Raillery, and the entry ends with a celebration of the satirical arts. The third entry, "La tragédie," presents the story of Meleager, the victim of cruel poisoning by the queen, his aunt. Its brief six scenes, depicting the breathless successive deaths of all the principal characters except one, might be seen as a satire on tragedy itself.

---

2. This entry was later replaced by another entry of a pastoral nature, which differed from "La pastorale" in plot but retained the fête champêtre unchanged.

In bright contrast to this somber tragedy, *Les Muses* ends with an entry entitled "La comédie," in which the female protagonist takes on the disguise of a physician in order to cure her lover, the son of a *vieillard* who opposes their marriage. Healing the son through love, she wins the approval of the father, and the work ends on a comic note of celebration and regeneration.

Momus appears in a brief epilogue, refusing to award the prize to one of these works over another, but it is clear that satire, along with its related genres of pastoral and comedy, has established itself at the Opéra. The tragic Muse Melpomene must accommodate Thalia and Euterpe, who preside over the genres of comedy and pastoral, as well as the new genre of satire, presided over by the fool. Campra's *Les Muses* not only parodies the general conceptual framework of the *Ballet des Muses* but also pays tribute to the satire of the inserted portions of that work (discussed in chap. 3). The Temple of Raillery that provides its setting is embellished with statues representing, among other ancient satirists, Democritus, Heraclitus, and two Cynic philosophers—the same characters who appeared in the spoof performed by French and Italian players in the *Ballet des Muses*. Like the Hôtel de Bourgogne's inserted comedy *Les poètes,* which commented self-reflexively on the arts at court, Campra's *Les Muses* comments self-reflexively on the Opéra and the various genres performed there. Of the four genres parodied in *Les Muses,* tragedy, comedy, and pastoral represent the main fare of the Académie royale de musique, and, as Danchet's libretto implies, the genre of satire now takes its place among them.

The music of *Les Muses* represents an exhibition of the styles appropriate to each genre. The pastoral features the musette as the auditory emblem of the bucolic ideal, while the tragedy predictably incorporates more recitative, with longer lines. The comedy incorporates shorter lines to create a sense of quick repartee, a larger number of dances (especially the minuet), and an emphasis on the *air galant.* It ends with an Italian buffa chorus. Campra's illustrations of the pastoral, the tragedy, and the comedy represent textbook examples of their respective musical styles. Although they do not draw on the musical content of the *Ballet des Muses,* they clearly represent a similar kind of theatrical compendium.[3]

The satire in this work—obviously a work about satire—is more aggressive than that of the Cytherean ballets discussed in chapter 5. Whereas

3. The music of Campra's *Les Muses* is discussed in Georgie Durosoir, "*Les Muses* de Danchet et Campra (1703) ou la diversité des tons au théâtre lyrique," *XVIIe siècle* 198 (1998): 51–61.

those drew on a neo-*précieux* aesthetic under the auspices of the goddess of love, in *Les Muses* Campra and Danchet articulate an aesthetic of burlesque mockery under the auspices of the fool. The character of Momus figured prominently in, and was actually a symbol of, ancient Greek satire. He served in the plays of Lucian in the same capacity as a fool would serve at court: to speak the truth under the guise of humor and mockery. As such he also figured as an occasional character in the commedia dell'arte and from there passed into the Opéra with *Les amours de Momus* (1695), a ballet with music by Desmarets and *livret* by Campistron.

The character of Folly was introduced at the Opéra in 1704, the year following the production of Campra's *Les Muses,* in a ballet entitled *Le Carnaval et la Folie.* It was composed by André Cardinal Destouches, Campra's student and friend, with a *livret* by Antoine Houdar de La Motte, the librettist for *Le triomphe des arts* four years earlier. Though the genre of the comédie-ballet had disappeared with the death of Molière in 1673, La Motte revived that term on his title page, probably as a tribute to Molière and a sign of his influence, as well as to call attention to the comic nature of the work. Another influence and the source of the character Folly was Erasmus, whom La Motte credits in the preface with furnishing "the scene and almost all the characters of my play."[4] The plot is simple, resembling the plays of the théâtre de la foire as they were taking shape after the ouster of the Comédie-Italienne: Folly decides against her imminent marriage to Carnival (Le Carnaval) because her parents approve. After some intrigue, Folly's parents decide they disapprove, whereupon she agrees to marry Carnival. In the prologue, Carnival declares, "In vain Glory complains; love is a more worthy object,"[5] and later declares, as he drowns his sorrows, "Love brings me pleasures, / And Bacchus brings me glory / Bacchus, let me sigh / Love, let me drink."[6] Wine, then, and the forgetful blissfulness it bestows, join with singing and dancing to replace the old ideals of glory and absolutist memorializing with the new ideals of carpe diem, forgetfulness, and sensual pleasure. Throughout this work, Folly's signature rhythm is that of the gigue, a dance associated from earlier times with madness and otherness, and almost all her music involves Italianate features: melismatic passagework, chromaticism, self-contained forms, strong rhythms, and a

---

4. Pure, *Recueil général,* 2: 172.

5. Ibid., 174: "En vain la Gloire gronde, / L'Amour est un plus digne objet."

6. Ibid., 175: "L'Amour fait mes plaisirs, / & Bachus fait ma gloire. / Bachus, laisse-moy soupirer, / Amour, laisse-moy boire."

general extroverted character. The work ends with a chorus on an Italian text, "Viva, viva sempre viva il Dio de l'allegria."

The supremacy of the fool, reaching its climax in the figure of Folly, may have connections with an early eighteenth-century society known as the Régiment de la Calotte, with which La Motte had an association. Founded in 1702, this brotherhood included among its aims the satire of contemporary manners, opposition to the abuse of power in all forms, and an extravagance in discourse and action, apparently in reaction to the simplicity and purity of the Académie française. The group was associated with a lighthearted libertinism and license, and with freethinking and a spirit of equality. It included a number of prominent figures among its members over the years, of which the most famous was probably Voltaire. The artist Charles Coypel, an associate of the group, created its *devise:* a lead skullcap holding a fool's cap and bells, surrounded by butterflies, symbol of change. The device includes the motto, "Luna influit, favet Momus" (Influenced by the moon, favored by Momus). Coypel's design for a flag is also preserved, which depicts Folly on a throne supporting this device.[7]

The society's bylaws included the aims of defending the common interest (*res publica*); laughing at everything; and attacking injustice, whether of persons or acts of authority, with ridicule. It operated through serving brevets in extravagant language on targets of its criticism, usually figures in society and in government administration, all in a lighthearted spirit avoiding official censure. Louis XIV, who knew of the Régiment, did not restrict its activities. The society officially ceased operations during the period of Mme de Pompadour, mistress of Louis XV, who feared its ridicule and demanded its end. Somewhat like the Freemasons, however, the Régiment went underground and was still alive at least into the late nineteenth century.[8]

The theme of the Muses, as they represent the arts of the public sphere in the subversive company of the fool and the gods of pleasure, may also be

7. Léon Hennet, *Le Régiment de La Calotte* (Paris: Librairie des bibliophiles, 1886), iv–v, 1–35, 229; Antoine De Baecque, *Les éclats du rire: La culture des rieurs au XVIIIe siècle* (Paris: Calmann-Lévy, 2000). Henri Duranton, in "La très joyeuse et très véridique histoire du Régiment de la Calotte," *Dix-huitième siècle* 33 (2001): 399–417, criticizes both Hennet and De Baecque for errors of scholarship. Duranton mentions the copious references to Jansenism in the Callotine literature and charges the earlier authors with failing to look beyond the official Callotine scholarship, which suppressed these controversial references; unfortunately, Duranton's short article, while calling for further research on the topic, does not redress the lacunae that still exist.

8. Hennet, *Le Régiment de La Calotte*, 38–101, 245.

traced in a series of ballets on the subjects of Venice and carnival. The two most important of these are Campra's *Le carnaval de Venise* (1699) and *Les fêtes vénitiennes* (1710). Training a keen satirical wit on the arts of absolutism and substituting the arts of a new public society, these works use the *loci amoeni* of Venetian carnival and commedia dell'arte to mask a celebration of the public arts of Paris. In further spinoffs at the Comédie-Française and the *foire*, the theaters of Paris metaphorically join hands to celebrate the triumph of Folly and her madcap Muses and the demise of the outdated arts of monarchical glory.

Carnival in Venice or Satire in Paris?

The exile of the Comédie-Italienne in 1697, far from quelling its satire, served only to intensify the French infatuation with its plots, characters, and satirical orientation. The figures of Arlequin, Scaramouche, Polichinelle, Pierrot, Isabelle, Léandre, and Columbine were embraced by French players of the théâtre de la foire and by the acrobats, tightrope walkers, and charlatans who entertained pedestrians on the sidewalks of the Pont-Neuf and in other public venues. The théâtre de la foire had begun as farce interspersed with tightrope or acrobatic acts at the fairs of Paris, most notably the Foire Saint-Laurent and the Foire Saint-Germain. After the expulsion of the Comédie-Italienne in 1697, the French players of the théâtre de la foire took over their repertoire. The songs and opera parodies inherited from the Italians' repertoire were to become the basis of the later *opéra-comique*, first designated as such in 1715. They were also appropriated by members of an upper-class elite, who not only attended these popular performances but also staged their own costume balls and amateur plays *à l'italienne*. It has been suggested that this process served as a means of indirect protest, allowing members of the upper class to distance themselves from the policies of the crown by means of their identification with the banned *commedia*.[9] As we have seen in chapter 5, the Paris Opéra represented not only an elite venue for public entertainment but also an aristocratic countercourt and haven for the aesthetic and ideological identity of an upper-class elite. Therefore it was only natural that the themes of carnival, commedia dell'arte, and foolery should come together in several ballets presented on its stage in the years following the banishment of the troupe.

9. Robert Isherwood, *Farce and Fantasy: Popular Entertainment in Eighteenth-Century Paris* (New York: Oxford University Press, 1986), 3–21; Crow, *Painters and Public Life*, 49–55; and Plax, *Watteau and the Cultural Politics of Eighteenth-Century France*, 40–52.

Figure 6.1. Monsieur Debreil, a dancer of the Paris Opéra, costumed as
Scaramouche. Musée Méjanes, Aix-en-Provence.

In 1697, following the expulsion, the *cantarina* of the Comédie-Italienne,
Elisabeth Danneret, entered the Opéra as a singer. In 1699, Campra chose
Jean-François Regnard, the principal playwright for the exiled Italians,
as the librettist for *Le carnaval de Venise*. With this ballet, the commedia
dell'arte entered the Opéra, bringing along its characteristic plots, characters, and satire. In 1702, Campra and Danchet produced a pastiche based
on excerpts from Lully's ballets and comédie-ballets, entitled *Les fragments
de M. Lully*. This work contained a newly composed entry by Campra and
Danchet, *La sérénade vénitienne*, in which four dancers, costumed as Scaramouche, rescue a young heroine from a tyrannical old guardian. (See fig. 6.1

for an image of one of these dancers costumed as Scaramouche.) This presentation of figures from the commedia dell'arte as a new breed of hero is continued in *La Vénitienne*, a ballet (like *Le Carnaval et la Folie*, dubbed *comédie-ballet*) by La Motte and Michel de La Barre. The prologue of this work presents a tableau of the familiar masks of the Italian troupe as statues brought to life by Momus (fig. 6.2)—a metaphor for the revivification of the commedia dell'arte in the ballet and at the *foire*.

Campra's *Les fêtes vénitiennes* (1710), which held the French operatic stage to wide acclaim for almost half a century, climaxed the series of ballets on Venice and carnival. As in *Le carnaval de Venise* and *La sérénade vénitienne*, the Venetian topos allowed a concentration of Italian conventions never before seen on the French operatic stage. The well-known lovers of the Comédie-Italienne serve as protagonists in these works, while the burlesque characters Arlequin, Pantalon, the doctor, Scaramouche, Polichinelle, and Pierrot appear in dancing roles. The plots, like those of the Comédie-Italienne, revolve around pairs of sighing lovers, love triangles, masks, disguises, clever escapes from aged guardians and tutors, and *divertissements à l'italienne*.

The music of these works, incorporating Italianate features clearly alluding to the *italianisme* of the Comédie-Italienne, may be seen as the debut of a new musical style and the primary entry point of the da capo aria into French opera.[10] Campra tends to follow the plays of the Comédie-Italienne, as well as the musical style of its da capo arias, in using an Italianate style for lovers' declarations and serenades. The Italian style is also associated with exoticism, especially in female roles, derived from the *cantarina* of the Comédie-Italienne. The complexity of the Italianate divertissements in *Les fêtes vénitiennes* reflects the flowering of the Italian style through the first decade of the century in France, when Italian sonatas and cantatas became fashionable. In fact, the male lover Léandre, the gypsy, and Cupid sing not only Italianate arias but fully developed cantatas, complete with recitatives, ariettes, and interpolated dances.

Campra's *Le carnaval de Venise* and *Les fêtes vénitiennes*, the most extended of the Venetian works at the Opéra, echo the bilingual structure of the Comédie-Italienne in confining Italianate elements to the elaborate divertissements.[11] As in the plays of Regnard, these divertissements spill over their boundaries to form the very structure of the ballet. Their arias (usually

10. For a discussion of the music and dance of these ballets, see Rebecca Harris-Warrick, "Staging Venice," *Cambridge Opera Journal* 15 (2003): 297–316.

11. Even there, as Harris-Warrick points out (p. 312), the manner of constructing the divertissement remains basically French. As she puts it, Campra "appears to be having his

Figure. 6.2. Jean Berain, frontispiece, Michel de La Barre, *La vénitienne*. Bibliothèque nationale de France.

marked *air italien* or *ariette,* sometimes simply *vivement* or *gai*) stand in vivid contrast to the French *récits,* binary airs, and maxims by virtue of their da capo form, bolder harmonic progressions, accented meters, florid melodic lines, and motto openings. "Orfeo nell'inferi," a miniature Italian opera representing one of the carnival festivities of *Le carnaval de Venise,* contains a series of Italian recitatives and arias, and the inserted cantatas of *Les fêtes vénitiennes,* while set to French texts, follow the lines of late seventeenth-century Italian models. Among these models are the operatic works of Alessandro Scarlatti and Giovanni Bononcini, as well as Italian comic opera with its bass arias, dance-like meters, and homophonic textures. All of these traits contributed to an idiom later known as the *style galant.*[12] The 6/4 meter and lively rhythms of Campra's forlanes, based on the music of the traditional Venetian gondoliers' dance accompanied by tambourines, permeate the two ballets.[13] Like the Italianate vocal music, the instrumental music is characterized by gaiety, verve, and extroversion. Although the musical influence of the Comédie-Italienne awaits further study, these ballets suggest that the blossoming of a spectacular *italianisme* in Campra's works owes much to the music of the Italian theater. Aspects of that influence include a bilingual stylistic idiom, an emphasis on the songs and dances of the divertissement, and the practice of "augmentation," the addition of new entries with new productions.

A satiric, carnivalesque spirit, directly related to that of the Comédie-Italienne, is developed most fully in Campra's two full-length Venetian

---

cake and eating it too" by dropping Italianate numbers into a French structure, a practice that promoted sufficient audience familiarity to ensure the work's popularity.

12. The term *galant* as a descriptor of musical style derives from mid-eighteenth-century German critics, whose usage referred generally to an early eighteenth-century, international style absorbing features of Italian as well as French composers. On the Italian side, Johann Mattheson lists Giovanni Bononcini, Antonio Caldara, Giovanni Maria Capelli, Francesco Gasparini, Antonio Lotti, Benedetto Marcello, Alessandro Scarlatti, and Antonio Vivaldi as "the most famous and galant composers in Europe" (quoted in Daniel Heartz, *Music in European Capitals: The Galant Style, 1720–1780* [New York: Norton, 16–23]).

13. On the forlana, see Paul Nettl, "Notes sur la forlane," *La revue musicale* 14 (1933): 191–95, and James Anthony, "Some Uses of the Dance in the French Opéra-Ballet," *Recherches sur la musique française classique* 9 (1969): 75–90. In 1683, in a special report on Venice, the *Mercure galante* called the forlana the "prettiest" of the Venetian dances; in other sources it is associated with exoticism, paganism, and orgy. As Carol Marsh has shown (paper delivered at the Society for Seventeenth-Century Music at Princeton University, 2002), Pecour's choreography for the forlane probably had little relation with the dance as it was performed in Venice.

ballets. Like the plays of the Italians and the later théâtre de la foire, these operate on the basis of a sophisticated blend of satire, allusion, and parody. Whereas the Comédie-Italienne most often targeted contemporary operas and tragedies, the ballets of Campra, following the pattern set by the Lully sons; and paralleling La Barre's *Le Triomphe des arts* and Bourgeois's *Les amours déguisés*, hint at images more concretely associated with Louis XIV from the beginning of his reign—especially those connected to roles he danced in the early court ballet.

Le carnaval de Venise (1699)

Campra, who came to Paris as *maître de chapelle* at the cathedral of Nôtre Dame in 1694, soon began a second career as the composer of secular works for a group of aristocratic patrons with libertine connections. These included the duc de Vendôme, the libertine benefactor of Jean-Baptiste Lully and his sons, the duc de Chartres, the future regent; the libertine duc de Sully, who had commissioned *L'Europe galante*, Campra's first opéra-ballet, in 1697; and the Dauphin, to whom *Le carnaval de Venise* is dedicated.[14] The composer, who never found favor with Louis XIV, was to become a protégé of the Dauphin, for whom he composed a divertissement, entitled *Vénus, feste galante*, in honor of the Dauphin and his sister-in-law, the princesse de Conti, at the home of the duchesse de la Ferté in 1698. Fearful of losing the security of his position at Nôtre Dame, Campra published *L'Europe galante* anonymously and *Le carnaval de Venise* under the name of his brother Joseph, a performer in the orchestra of the Opéra. Regnard, the librettist for *Le carnaval de Venise*, had associations not only with the banned Comédie-Italienne but also with the libertine nobility in the late years of Louis XIV's reign.[15]

The prototype for *Le carnaval de Venise* was undoubtedly a play by the same name, written for the Comédie-Française by Florent Carton Dancourt,

14. Maurice Barthélemy, *André Campra: Sa vie et son oeuvre (1660–1744)* (Paris: Picard, 1957), 44–46.

15. James Anthony, introduction to André Campra, *Le carnaval de Venise, French Opera in the Seventeenth and Eighteenth Centuries*, vol. 17 (Stuyvesant, NY: Pendragon Press, 1989), viii. Neither of Campra's ruses seems to have fooled anyone. A contemporary chanson, punning on the composer's name, quipped, "Quand notre Archevesque sçaura / L'Auteur du nouvel opéra, / De sa Cathédrale Campra / Décampera" (When our archbishop knows the author of this new opera, Campra will decamp from his cathedral). On Regnard, see Gifford P. Orwen, *Jean-François Regnard* (Boston: Twayne, 1923), 15–28; also Alexandre Calame, *Regnard, sa vie et son oeuvre* (Paris: Presses universitaires de France, 1960).

produced in 1690. No longer extant, Dancourt's play is known to have had its divertissements withdrawn because of censorship.[16] Regnard's libretto for *Le carnaval de Venise* of 1699, probably linked to these divertissements, depicts a pair of lovers overcoming a series of obstacles presented by jealous suitors. Besides its connections with Dancourt's play, *Le carnaval de Venise* also contains allusions to Louis Lully's *Orphée*, produced at the Opéra in 1690. In addition, it may be seen as a more subtle satire of Louis XIV's roles in the early court ballet entitled *Le carnaval, mascarade royale* of 1668, and as a reversal of the meaning and uses of carnival in that work.

Louis XIV's role as a Pleasure in *Le carnaval, mascarade royale* connected the pleasures of carnival—as represented in entries devoted to gambling, feasting, dancing, and singing—with the patronage of the king. The insouciant nature of the ballet's carnival celebration is balanced by the praise of the king contained in its frame, as well as by an underlying subtext provided by Benserade's *vers de personnage* for Louis in this role. These *vers* paint a portrait more fierce than benevolent, a "terrible Pleasure" who has shown his enemies how greatly he is to be feared. In the same vein, the tragic mask he wears in the final entry is said to hide the even more frightening visage of the fearsome warrior underneath. The propaganda of this work, then, like that of most court ballets, walks a tightrope between pleasure and power, seeking to balance images of peacetime diversion with those of warlike heroism.

Regnard's *livret* for *Le carnaval de Venise*, set in the republic of Venice, suggests a utopia with distinct political overtones in its references and reversals.[17] For example, the gamblers in one of its entries celebrate the vicissitudes of the allegorical heroine Fortune, who is able to destroy "the most glorious of thrones."[18] The most extended allusion in *Le carnaval de Venise*, however, may be found in the internal "Venetian" opera "Orfeo nell'inferi"

16. Mélèse, *Le théâtre et le public*, 77.

17. Recent scholarship has identified a "myth of Venice," a carefully orchestrated campaign through which the Venetians themselves consciously presented their republic as a haven of justice and the center of ongoing celebrations of freedom, both political and artistic. Venetian carnival, famous throughout Europe, served as the political means of drawing travelers on a secular pilgrimage to the city of Venus, as Venice was called. In the second half of the seventeenth century, the "myth of Venice" was kept alive in France by travelers' reports and journal articles. See Ellen Rosand, *Opera in Seventeenth-Century Venice: The Creation of a Genre* (Berkeley: University of California Press, 1991), 44–45 and 113–19, and "Music in the Myth of Venice," *Renaissance Quarterly* 30 (1977): 511–37.

18. Pure, *Recueil général*, 2: 677.

set into the larger finale of the work. The only complete scene of the work cast entirely in Italian, this interpolated divertissement is modeled on the confrontation between Pluto and Orpheus in Louis Lully's *Orphée*. Like the scene in *Orphée*, the one in *Le carnaval de Venise* positions Orpheus's bucolic lyricism against the militarism of Pluto's call to arms in an allegorical treatment of the plight of the artist vis-à-vis the king. In both works, Pluto, sitting on a throne surrounded by his ministers,[19] greets the strains of Orpheus's lyre with outraged chagrin. Regnard's Italian text is closely related to the equivalent French passage in *Orphée:*

ORPHÉE

Qu'entends-je? Il est donc	(What do I hear?
vray que jusques	So it is true that even
Dans ces lieux	In this place
Un mortel insolent s'avance? . . .	An insolent mortal advances? . . .
Armons-nous, armons-nous	To arms! To arms!
Mais, quels sons éloignez	But what far-off
surprennent mes oreilles?	sounds surprise my ears?
Qu'ils sont nouveaux!	How new they are!
qu'ils ont de quoy toucher![20]	How they have the power to move!)

LE CARNAVAL DE VENISE

Un Mortal insolent,	(An insolent mortal
Al dispetto della sorte,	In defiance of destiny
Passa vivo nel regno	Passes while still living into the
della morte,	realm of death?
All'armi, all'armi . . .	To arms! To arms! . . .
Ma qual nuova Armonia?	But what new harmonies?
Qual soave Zinfonia?	What sweet symphony?
D'al cor di Plutone,	From the heart of Pluto,
L'ira depone.[21]	Fury departs.)

Besides the close correspondence of these texts, a satirical emphasis on Louis XIV's militarism links these two examples. Though Campra masks Pluto's call to arms in an Italian musical style, both passages contain an inordinate number of repetitions of the words "To arms!" (in *Orphée*, eight

19. A reproduction of Jean Berain's stage design is included in Campra, *Le carnaval de Venise*, ed. Anthony, xxv.

20. Pure, *Recueil général*, 1: 359.

21. Ibid., 1: 683.

repetitions in the space of sixteen measures, and in "Orfeo," nineteen repetitions in the space of forty measures). Reversing the tragic ending of Lully's opera, however, Regnard transforms Pluto into a ridiculous buffoon. Campra sets the final bass aria for Pluto and chorus in the style of contemporary comic opera in Italy, with its bass voice, dancelike 3/4 meter, simple triadic harmonies, slow harmonic rhythm, and light texture (ex. 6.1). Clearly, the enclosed opera represents a tribute to Louis Lully's *Orphée* as a subversive moment in the history of public entertainment.

The allusions to previous works are reinforced at the beginning of "Orfeo nell'inferi," when a stage-within-a-stage descends, complete with loges on either side, filled with stage spectators viewing the performance in its entirety. Like a deus ex machina, the performance of this inserted "opera," along with its audience and the confusion surrounding its production, provides a means of escape for Isabelle and Léandre, the protagonists of the larger play. Of even greater symbolic value is the spotlight that this scene throws on Louis Lully's *Orphée* and its audience[22] and on the Opéra itself, to which the scene clearly alludes. By ending the work with a triumphant escape provided by the inserted opera, along with its stage audience composed of satisfied spectators, Regnard effectively reverses the motif of the deprived audience and deserted theater in the prologue to *Orphée*. The theme of theatrical renewal, moreover, is set up in the prologue to *Le carnaval de Venise*, in which a new theater is being constructed under the guidance of the "divinities who preside over the arts [of] music, dance, painting, and architecture" (i.e., the arts of the ballet). This new theater, like the work itself, is dedicated to the Dauphin. *Le carnaval de Venise* itself may be considered a new form of theater, dedicated to the Dauphin by the artists of this operatic countercourt. Obviously flattered by this tribute, the Dauphin showed his favor by attending five performances of *Le carnaval de Venise* during the carnival season of 1699.[23]

During the period that the ballet held the boards at the Opéra, the Dauphin—possibly under its inspiration—interceded for the Italians when they petitioned Louis XIV to be allowed to return to Paris, but the king refused.[24] *Le carnaval de Venise* ran until the end of March and was revived in April. As the Dauphin's intercession for the Italians took place some time in March, had the king acceded and the company returned to Paris, it would

22. On *Orphée*, see chapter 4 above.

23. Anthony, in Campra, *Le carnaval de Venise*, xxii–xxiii.

24. Brooks, "Louis XIV's Dismissal of the Italian Actors," 843.

Example 6.1. André Campra, *Le carnaval de Venise*, Act 3, sc. 8 ("Orfeo nell'inferi," Pluto's aria). Bibliothèque nationale de France, Pn Rés. F 1668, 139–40.

Example 6.1. (*continued*)

have given new meaning to the prologue in which statues of the players are depicted coming to life. In any case, like Fuselier's dual *livrets* for the Opéra and the foire discussed in chapter 5, Regnard's spoken version of *Le carnaval de Venise* for the Comédie-Française and the ballet for the Opéra make use of parody, not merely for the purpose of competition more typical of the *guerre des théâtres*, but to pay tribute to the disgraced company. In addition, the revival of *Le carnaval de Venise* as a ballet at the Opéra in 1699 might have had a further purpose—at least on the part of Regnard, who was identified with the company—to enlist the Dauphin as an ally in the Italians' attempt to return to Paris.

The final scene of *Le carnaval de Venise*, immediately following "Orfeo nell'inferi," depicts a public masquerade, a masked ball typical of those held during carnival season in both Venice and Paris. Alluding to the final entry of *Le carnaval, mascarade royale*, it plays on the king's role as a tragic mask in that work. There, the *vers* for Louis XIV set up the ultimate superiority of his militarism to the comic trivialities of carnival. In contrast, the final masquerade of *Le carnaval de Venise* presents a magnificent carnival float, covered with comic masks and filled with comic maskers, overturning a *bal sérieux* as they sing of carpe diem and public pleasure. As part of this finale, a soprano disguised as a comic mask sings a full-blown da capo aria, unusu-

Example 6.2. André Campra, *Le carnaval de Venise*, Act 3, sc. 2 ("Le bal, dernier divertissement"). Bibliothèque nationale de France, Pn Rés. F 1668, 156ᵛ-57, mm. 1–15.

ally ornate for the period. Her invocation of the cupids, "Amori volati," ends the work in the most exuberant Italian manner (ex. 6.2).

Les fêtes vénitiennes (1710)

With a libretto by Campra's longtime collaborator Antoine Danchet, *Les fêtes vénitiennes* parallels *Le carnaval de Venise* not only in subject matter but also in almost every aspect of its intertextual structure. Like the earlier work, *Les fêtes vénitiennes* alludes to specific entertainments of the Parisian public sphere, among them Molière's *Bourgeois gentilhomme*, the Lully sons' *Zéphire et Flore*, and Campra's own *Muses* and *Carnaval de Venise*. Broader in scope than Campra's two earlier works, *Les fêtes vénitiennes* combines the satiric methods found in both. Like *Les Muses*, it takes the general structure and aesthetic program of Louis XIV's *Ballet des Muses* as its starting point, and like *Le carnaval de Venise*, it depicts an opera by Lully *fils* and reverses a role danced by Louis XIV in *Le carnaval, mascarade royale*. In contrast to the *Ballet des Muses* and other entertainments at court, these later works pay tribute not to the royal patron but to the artists and audiences of the Parisian public sphere.

Like Campra's earlier *Les Muses*, *Les fêtes vénitiennes* maps the entertainments of Paris as they move from the court to public Paris. Campra takes his characters of the music and dance masters directly from *Le bourgeois gentilhomme*, and indirectly from the directors of the fête from *Les poètes*, the inserted comedy in the *Ballet des Muses*. In those two works, these artist prototypes commented on the state of the arts in the service of the royal and the bourgeois patron, respectively. In *Les fêtes vénitiennes*, they appear in an entry entitled "Le bal," as servants to an enlightened prince from Poland (an elective monarchy). In a metaphorical game of masks, they make reference to the achievements of "Venetian" public entertainment, as actually found at the Paris Opéra. The music master, boasting of his compositional skills (and belying the work's Venetian setting), quotes passages that can be identified as excerpts from three operas premiered or reprised at the Académie royale de musique in the years immediately preceding *Les fêtes vénitienne*s: Marin Marais's *Alcyone* (1706), Jean-Baptiste Lully's *Atys* (1708), and Destouches's *Issé* (1708). In addition to paying tribute to the power of music, these excerpts also pay tribute to the Opéra and its composers in the first decade of the century.

Using the *maître de musique* as his own mouthpiece, Campra subtly places himself in this illustrious company, yet sets himself apart by means of an elaborate Italian style. Demonstrating a florid passage to the text "Amori, volate" (ex. 6.3), he subtly alludes to his own Italian aria invoking the cupids, set to the text "Amori, volate" for the comic mask in *Le carnaval de Venise* (see ex. 6.2 above). In each case, a melismatic style extends the short melisma, typically associated in French opera with the word *voler* (to fly), to an extreme unprecedented in France. In *Les fêtes vénitiennes*, Campra intensifies the process, setting its opening as an even more ornate, cadenza-like dialogue between the soprano and solo violin. This text climaxes an accumulation of florid references to the advent of Cupid, beginning with Benserade's *vers* for Lully as Orpheus in the *Ballet des Muses* ("I do not pretend that Cupid through my voice / Will come to constrain nature and its laws") and continuing with Louis Lully's *addition* to *Zéphire et Flore*, "Amour, vole"

Example 6.3. André Campra, *Les fêtes vénitiennes*, Act 3, sc. 2 ("Le bal"). Ed. Max Lütolf (Paris: Heuget, 1970), 377–78, mm. 19–25.

(also set for voice and solo violin), a plea for Cupid's aid in time of need.[25] Campra's settings of the text "Amori, volate" in *Le carnaval de Venise* and in *Les fêtes vénitiennes* signify his own participation in a line of allusions to the god of love and patron deity of the Paris Opéra.

An extended reference to Louis and Jean-Louis Lully's *Zéphire et Flore* is cleverly crafted as an opéra-ballet-within-an-opéra-ballet entitled "Ballet de Flore," set within the framing entry "L'Opéra." The setting, ostensibly the famous opera house of the Teatro Grimani ("le Palais Grimani") in Venice, may be read as the backstage to the Paris Opéra, where Léontine, a famous *chanteuse*, is preparing to sing the role of Flora. Through a clever play on plots and titles, the encapsulated "Ballet de Flore" both alludes to the Lully sons' *Zéphire et Flore* and like that work may be seen as an allusion to Louis XIV's *Ballet de Flore* of 1669. The pastoral idyll of Campra's "Ballet de Flore" includes an air of great floridity in the style of the French *double* (now extremely rare in stage works), sung by Flora as an invitation to her "brilliant court" and by implication to the brilliant countercourt of the Paris Opéra. Like the abduction scene from *Zéphire et Flore* to which it alludes, it is rudely interrupted by a "storm" symphony. In this version, however, instead of being abducted by the north wind, Léontine is abducted by her lover Damire, a passionate fan of her singing and of the Opéra itself, who has disguised himself as Boreas in order to escape with her. In a reversal of the plot of the tragédie en musique, Damire states his intention to make "Flore" (and the art she represents) his "sovereign" rather than his captive. Ultimately, then, both Pluto and Boreas, the villains of the Lully sons' tragédies en musique, are transformed into harmless or even benevolent instruments of omnipotent and changeable Fortune through the intervention of song and dance, and the artist is glorified as the king was earlier. Both of these reversals use carnival masking to transform the grim realities of France in 1710 into an idealized utopia of public festivity. They also point up the similarity between spectacle and Fortune, both of which, through their capacity for sudden change, can inspire the hope for a new social order.

Layers of intertextuality reach a pinnacle of complexity in this entry. Léontine, the soprano enacting the role of Flora, is also famous for the title role of Lully's *Armide* (enthusiastically described by Damire), allowing the librettist a reference not only to Lully's opera but also perhaps to the *Ballet des amours déguisés* of 1664, in which Louis XIV danced the role of the hero Rinaldo. In both those works, Rinaldo resisted and overcame the

25. These are discussed in chapters 2 and 4, respectively.

enchantment of Armida, confirming the superiority of glory over love. In an important reversal, Damire (likened in Danchet's libretto to Rinaldo) now chooses the enchantment of the soprano, and of the Opéra itself, over duty and glory. In another significant twist, a Mlle Journet, the soprano who sang the role of Léontine/Flora in the première of *Les fêtes vénitiennes* in 1710, had actually made her début in the role of Armida in a revival of Lully's opera in 1703.[26] This opens the possibility that the piece may be a tribute to her personally, as well as to the Opéra and its *chanteuses* in general.

Like *Le carnaval de Venise*, *Les fêtes vénitiennes* not only acknowledges the entertainments of a French public sphere but also may make more indirect reference to *Le carnaval, masquerade royale* of 1668. As in the court ballet, the prologue to *Les fêtes vénitiennes* is introduced by Carnival, but rather than flattering the king, this Carnival again invokes the cupids as symbols of love and public pleasure. His words, "Volez amours," the final culmination of the long line of invocations to Cupid, weave through the large choral framework substituted for the choruses of monarchical praise in the standard operatic prologue. As if in answer to all these invocations, Cupid appears, in a later entry entitled "L' Amour saltimbanque" (Cupid as charlatan). At least since the Renaissance, the charlatan had served as a symbol of marketplace culture and of public entertainment as well, and the shows produced by charlatans as advertisements for their wares constituted a primary site for public diversion among all classes.[27]

Les fêtes vénitiennes may also be read as satirizing Louis XIV's role as a Pleasure in *Le carnaval, mascarade royale*. In this version, the Pleasures are doubly disguised as Cupid's assistants and commedia dell'arte characters, dispensing the charlatan's "remedy" to the members of a stage audience. The scene uses Saint Mark's Square ("la Place Saint Marc"), where it is ostensibly set, as a mask for the Parisian Pont-Neuf, the hub of Paris's popular festive life, where satirical chansons and subversive pamphlets were traded with relatively little censorship. Here charlatans came to peddle their wares, while their assistants, drawing audiences by their acrobatic acts, dispensed "remedies" and collected payment.[28] The scene is introduced by a chorus of charlatans, inviting spectators to "step right up" to their show. The remainder of the

26. Pitou, *Paris Opéra*, 1: 246.

27. The term *saltimbanque* was used interchangeably with *charlatan* to mean mountebank, showman, buffoon, or, in some cases, quack.

28. Isherwood, *Farce and Fantasy*, 3–21. On the Pont-Neuf, built in 1603, poets sold ballads relating the news of the day. So important was the Pont-Neuf as the pulse of public Paris that the vaudeville, or popular song, was often referred to as a *pont-neuf* and the news of the

entry is structured as a brilliant Italianate cantata, sung by Cupid and punctuated with dances by his comic entourage. Like the chorus, Cupid hustles the crowd, urging his audience to make their purchases. The dances of the comic characters include instrumental airs for the Arlequins and Polichinelles and a chaconne for the entire assembly of comic masks, including these characters as well as male and female Scaramouches and Pantalons. The ideological message of this scene resides in the substitution of the humble public figures of the commedia dell'arte (now a symbol not so much of Italy as of the Parisian public sphere) for the king's image as supreme dispenser of pleasure.

The role of master of ceremonies in *Les fêtes vénitiennes* is shared by Cupid, Carnival, and Folly. At the hands of Campra and Danchet, Folly becomes the omnipotent queen of carnival madness,[29] and in a substitution for Louis XIV, the object of universal homage. As the king presides over the entertainments of his court, she presides over the high and low entertainments of the public sphere; as he enters captured cities in triumph, so does she, in a prologue entitled "Le triomphe de la Folie," celebrate her victory over the known world.[30] In this prologue she follows Carnival's invocation of the cupids by claiming for herself alone the power to inspire the Pleasures, and for herself and her cohort Cupid a new empire of love and folly, from which "cruel reason" is banished. Like Cupid and the Pleasures in this work, she also takes on the role of charlatan. Her ariette "Accourez, hâtez-vous," like Cupid's "Venez tous, hâtez-vous" and the charlatans' chorus "Accourez, venez-vous, volez," connects the strong rhythms and harmonies of the Italian da capo style with the theme of marketplace entertainment. In opposition to a patriarchy of order and "severe Reason," Folly

---

day was referred to by the expression, "On chante sur le Pont-Neuf." These songs often contained subversive material. See also Clifford Barnes, "The *Théâtre de la foire* (Paris, 1697–1762), Its Music and Composers" (Ph.D. diss., University of Southern California, 1965), 136.

29. For a discussion of Folly in the context of seventeenth-century feminist thought and opera criticism, see Cowart, "Of Women, Sex, and Folly." The laughing madwoman was a prominent figure of carnival; Dijon, particularly, was known for its carnival celebration of *la mère folle*. See Fabre, *Carnaval ou la fête à l'envers*, 66–70.

30. The work was first performed on June 17, 1710. Beginning with the twenty-third performance on August 8, 1710, the original prologue, "Le triomphe de la Folie sur la Raison dans le temps du carnaval," was suppressed. With the fifty-first performance, it reappeared in a cut and revised version, entitled "Le carnaval dans Venise." In December of 1710 or spring of 1711, a new prologue was added, entitled "Le triomphe de la Folie, comédie." Despite the title, there is no connection between the two prologues except for the title character. The substitute prologue, however, continues the displacement of the king, more usual subject of triumphal entries, by Folly.

represents a matriarchy of comic madness and public pleasure. Her domain ultimately represents the chaotic, irrepressible public spirit, released from official control. Implicit within the celebration of Folly, then, lies an unmistakable allusion, in the carnivalesque reversal of king and fool, to a more general reversal (as in Erasmus) of the established social order.[31]

There is a relationship, though not exact, between the entries of *Les fêtes vénitiennes*, in its various incarnations and additions, and the structure of the *Ballet des Muses* and *Le bourgeois gentilhomme*. A comparison of the three works yields the correlations found in table 6.1. This comparison reveals the possibility that Danchet and Campra drew on the mechanisms found in *Le bourgeois gentilhomme* to satirize Louis XIV through his *Ballet des Muses*. Like *Le bourgeois gentilhomme* and *Les Muses*, *Les fêtes vénitiennes* represents a commentary on the arts in the late years of Louis XIV's reign. It may be seen as the culmination of a process, begun in *Le bourgeois gentilhomme*, in which the festive celebration of the monarch and his court is transformed into a festive celebration of the public sphere and its audiences.

Le carnaval de Venise and *Les fêtes vénitiennes*, then, like the earlier operas of the Lully sons, may be considered a tribute to earlier pieces of Parisian theater. Campra's two works together make specific allusion to Dancourt's *Carnaval de Venise*, Louis and Jean-Louis Lully's *Zéphire et Flore* and *Orphée*, Molière and Lully's *Le bourgeois gentilhomme*, Lully's *Carnaval, mascarade*, and Campra's own *Carnaval de Venise* and *Les Muses*, with perhaps more indirect or subtle reference to several earlier court ballets, including *Le carnaval, mascarade royale*, the *Ballet de Flore*, and the *Ballet des Muses*. The use of a complex intertextuality seems to have presented an effective method of avoiding censorship, for unless the authorities knew the works alluded to, the questionable intent would have passed unnoticed. Other safeguards may be seen in the use of the mask of spectacle, shielding these allusions behind seemingly innocent song and dance in an exotic, Venetian setting.

31. See Mikhail Bakhtin, *Rabelais and His World*, trans. by Hélène Iswolsky (1968; Bloomington: Indiana University Press, 1984), 196–277 ("Popular Festive Forms and Images in Rabelais"), for a discussion of Rabelais's treatment of the fool, folly, charlatans, games, and the commedia dell'arte. Bakhtin's concept of the "carnivalesque," which celebrates carnival as a temporary ascendancy of popular culture over absolutist hegemony, has been used as a model for literature and culture far beyond the time of Rabelais. See particularly Peter Stallybrass and Allon White, *The Politics and Poetics of Transgression* (New York: Cornell University Press, 1986). Bakhtin, however, viewed the seventeenth century as a time when the regenerative power of popular culture, represented by carnival, was disastrously severed from serious literature.

TABLE 6.1. Comparison of the *Ballet des Muses*, *Le bourgeois gentilhomme*, and *Les fêtes vénitiennes*

Muse	ENTRY (*Ballet des muses*)	ENTRY (*Bourgeois gentilhomme*)	ENTRY (*Fêtes vénitiennes*)
[Prologue]	Mnemosine, mother of Muses, sings *récit* in praise of Louis XIV	Imposing *récit* of court ballet parodied by music student's bungled air	Folly as charlatan invites audience to public entertainment; praise of public entertainment substituted for praise of king
Urania (astronomy)	Noble dancers' costume parade (reflects brilliance of stars)	Act 2, tailor scene: M. Jourdain parades in his new costume	Instead of noble dancers, acrobats dressed in commedia dell'arte costume
Melpomene (tragedy)	Pantomime of tragic myth of Pyramus and Thisbe	Frame plot of star-crossed lovers but with happy ending	Opera ("L'Opéra ou le maître à chanter") represents a mock tragedy
Thalia (comedy)	Inserted comédie-ballet by Molière and Lully: *Mélicerte* (later replaced by *Pastorale comique*)	Celebrates comedic universe	Entire work celebrates comedy, establishes comedy in operatic repertoire
Euterpe (pastoral, music)	Pastoral danced by king and courtiers as shepherds and shepherdesses	Act 1: pastoral dialogue in music	Pastoral scene ("Ballet de Flore") presented as ballet within opera ("L'Opéra ou le maître à chanter")
Clio (history)	Pantomime of Alexander's battle with Porrus	Act 2: scene of master of arms as spoof on militarism	"Fêtes des barquerolles," contest of gondoliers portrayed as "innocent face of war"
Calliope (poetry)	Inserted comedy *Les poètes*; self-reflexive depiction of creators of the comedy and the ballet as spokespersons for the arts	Act 1: music master and dance master as spokespersons for the arts	Music master and dance master reappear as spokespersons for the arts, in "L'Opéra ou le maître à chanter," "Le bal ou le maître à danser"
Erato (love poetry)	King and nobles appear as heroes of chivalric novels	Act 3: M. Jourdain's ridiculous infatuation with Dorimène (banquet scene)	Cupid mocks chivalric heroes in "L'amour saltimbanque"

TABLE 6.1. (*continued*)

Muse	ENTRY (*Ballet des muses*)	ENTRY (*Bourgeois gentilhomme*)	ENTRY (*Fêtes vénitiennes*)
Polymnia (rhetoric)	Comic actors from Comédie-Italienne and Hôtel de Bourgogne, spoof on ancient Greek philosophers Democritus and Heraclitus, and Latin orators	Act 2: master of philosophy; lesson on consonants and vowels	Spoof on ancient philosophers Democritus and Heraclitus
Terpsichore (dance)	Dance of fauns and Amazons	Act 1: dancing master produces exhibition of "the most beautiful noble dance"	"Le bal ou le maître à danser"; dance demonstration. Dialogue and contest of dance and music masters directly derived from *Bourgeois gentilhomme*

To what extent the political nature of these works would have been grasped by Campra's audience is impossible to know. Since a clear pattern of subversion emerged in the cabal around the Dauphin, it is possible that members of that group would have regarded its language as a private code, operating something like a roman à clef. Campra's carnival ballets have direct links to the Lully sons, the duc de Vendôme, and the Dauphin. They were well received at the Opéra, perhaps not only because of their high artistic quality but also because of the popularity of the Dauphin among the audience. The mood at the Opéra was generally opposed to the monarchy of Louis XIV in his last years. In 1712, during a performance of the prologue of Campra's *Les amours de Mars et de Vénus*, the libertine Abbé Servien interrupted the prologue's praise of the king by loudly singing words to the exact opposite effect, whereupon the laughter and applause of the audience brought the performance to a halt. The abbé was served with a lettre de cachet, and when a similar incident occurred again in 1714 (again applauded and this time taken up by the crowd), he was sent to prison, where he remained until the death of Louis XIV the following year.[32]

32. Both incidents are recounted by Saint-Simon, quoted in La Gorce, *L'Opéra à Paris*, 155 and 194 n. 51.

Figure 6.3. J. B. Scotin, frontispiece, André Campra, *Les fêtes vénitiennes*.
Bibliothèque nationale de France.

The frontispiece of *Les fêtes vénitiennes* reinforces its theme of carnivalesque reversal. It represents an image of the Piazzetta of Saint Mark's Square, the area between the Doge's Palace and the Biblioteca Marciana. The entire orientation of the scene, however, is reversed (fig. 6.3).[33] Moreover, instead of the lion of Saint Mark and the statue of Teodoro of Amasea that sit atop the two columns at the edge of the water, two comic figures are seen, one gesturing theatrically, the other sitting cross-legged. Two satyrs, symbol of satire, hold the banner containing the title of the work at the top of the page.[34] Many years later, in 1750, the young Giovanni Casanova is reported to have burst out laughing when he saw the stage design with the same reversed images,[35] an indication that a similar reversal still characterized the scenic design forty years year.

Parodies of *Les fêtes vénitiennes* at the Comédie-Française and the *Foire*

A few months after the première of *Les fêtes vénitiennes*, Dancourt produced a play for the Comédie-Française entitled *La comédie des comédiens*.[36] The play-within-a-play that stands as its climax, "L' Amour charlatan," represents a parody of the entry "L' Amour saltimbanque" from Campra's *Les fêtes vénitiennes*. The frame plot depicts four well-known comedians from the French troupe, playing themselves, donning the costumes of the commedia dell'arte characters Pierrot, Léandre, Mezzetin, and Scaramouche in order to produce the internal play. Like Campra's "L' Amour saltimbanque" and the inserted divertissements of *Le carnaval de Venise* and *Les fêtes vénitiennes*, "L' Amour charlatan" provides the young lovers a means of victory and a resolution to the complications of the larger play. Cupid, "a little libertine," is disguised as a charlatan in order to escape the wrath of an avenging Jupiter, now a pathetic figure whose power has been severely diminished by the success of Plutus, god of commerce. As in "L'Amour saltimbanque," Cupid

---

33. This backward depiction was noted by Rebecca Harris-Warrick, in a paper delivered at the Society for Seventeenth-Century Music (Princeton, 2002).

34. The two words are not related linguistically, but writers of the time thought that they were (private conversation, Orest Ranum).

35. Harris-Warrick, "Staging Venice," 297. Casanova assumed that the scene painter had copied an engraving that had been printed in reverse.

36. In Dancourt, *Oeuvres de théâtre*, 3: 167–99. An appendix (232–40) contains the musical numbers of the divertissement.

uses the charlatan's platform to hawk his libertine "remedy" of love, and in a denouement with clear political overtones, he subverts the power of the king of the gods. Dancourt's play, again alluding to *Les fêtes vénitiennes*, also contains a "Venetian" divertissement, performed by members of M. Grichardin's household, costumed as two Venetian women and a Pantalon.

Both "L' Amour saltimbanque" from Campra's *Les fêtes vénitiennes* and "L' Amour charlatan" from Dancourt's *La comédie des comédiens* use the characters and characteristic plots and music of the commedia dell'arte to allude to the théâtre de la foire. The reverse process takes place in an actual play from the *foire*, produced at the Foire Saint-Germain in 1712, entitled *Les fêtes parisiennes*. All that remains from the play are stage directions and the anonymous words of its *écritaux* or placards displaying substitute texts to be sung to the tunes of *Les fêtes vénitiennes*.[37] These texts shift the scene from Venice to popular haunts of lowbrow Paris, finally unmasking the Venetian ploy of Campra's ballets. In a manner typical of the théâtre de la foire, French players wearing the masks of the commedia dell'arte—Arlequin, Pierrot, Polichinelle, and Scaramouche—portray the lower classes enjoying the festivities of carnival. Closely following *Les fêtes vénitiennes* through the parodies of its arias, *Les fêtes parisiennes* also follows, even more closely than the opéra-ballet, the sequence of entries in Louis XIV's *Le carnaval, mascarade royale*. Introduced, like *Le carnaval, masquerade royale* and *Les fêtes vénitiennes*, by a personification of Carnival, its prologue ("Premiere feste: Le carnaval") is set, rather than in the royal court of Versailles or on the shores of Venice, on the shores of the Seine at the Porte Saint-Antoine. Instead of descending a throne to flatter Louis XIV, as in the court ballet, Le Carnaval descends from a giant casserole, from which the cupids and the Pleasures are eating; and instead of a procession in honor of Louis XIV, there is a procession in honor of the fatted ox of Mardi Gras. The second fête is designated by a double title, "L' Amour saltimbanque/L' Amour charlatan," literally naming the plays set within Campra's *Les fêtes vénitiennes* and Dancourt's *La comédie des comédiens*. This scene is set on the Parisian Pont-Neuf, revealing the true identity of the "Place Saint Marc" in Campra's ballet.

A New Society of Pleasures

In his early reign Louis XIV offered the commedia dell'arte as a source of pleasure to his court. Members of the Italian company improvised skits

37. *Ecritaux des festes parisiennes dansées au public par la troupe des danseurs de corde des Jeu de Paume d'Orléans à la foire St. Germain au mois de février 1712* (Paris: S. I., 1712).

within certain court ballets, most notably the *Ballet des plaisirs* and the *Ballet des Muses*. In others, French dancers performed under Italian masks. Almost from the beginning, however, these Italian interludes were used to depict otherness, as a foil for an official French identity. Italianate portions of the ballets were strictly contained and, once Louis XIV was firmly established in the late 1660s and early 1670s, eventually suppressed. By the time of *Le carnaval, masquerade royale* in 1668, Louis's reins on pleasure had tightened, and he no longer needed the foil of this Italian presence.

Campra's ballets on Venetian carnival reinstate an overt Italian style, now to be read not only as a tribute to an evolving public taste but also as signifier of a public resistance to the crown. This style could take several forms, from the da capo form and floridity of the Italian operatic aria, to the more complex combination of arias and recitatives in the cantata, to more popular, metrical tunes of Italian popular music and dance. Conservative theorists perceived Italian music as exotic, feminine, excessive, and contradictory to the ideals of purity, patriarchy, and classical simplicity espoused by Louis XIV. Its popularity sparked a controversy over French and Italian music that, beginning in 1702, lasted over half a century and, resonating with political overtones, reflected the general challenge of the Italian style to a French hegemonic discourse.[38] In fact, the influx of Italian cantatas and sonatas into France, beginning in the last years of the seventeenth century, exactly coincided with the ouster of the Comédie-Italienne and was probably stimulated by a desire to retain the Italians' music, like their costumes and masks, not only because of their genuine popular appeal but also as a sign of antimonarchical taste.

In *Le carnaval de Venise* and *Les fêtes vénitiennes,* an Italianate music tends to characterize the divertissements, whereas a French style tends to characterize the scenes of more straightforward action. Almost invariably, the political allusions of the ballets are found within the Italianate spectacle of their divertissements. The interplay of two stratified discourses within one work, particularly in the positioning of a politically correct "rational" style against an oppositional, "irrational" one, constitutes a defining characteristic of the ancient genre known as Menippean satire.[39] This genre was trans-

---

38. This phenomenon is discussed in Cowart, *Origins of Modern Musical Criticism*, 49–85. The French style itself, of course, was based on layers of absorption of Italian elements.

39. On the use of Menippean satire in ancient and Renaissance literature, see Frederick Joseph Benda, "The Tradition of Menippean Satire in Varro, Lucian, Seneca, and Erasmus" (Ph.D. diss., University of Texas at Austin, 1979).

mitted through the late Greek writer Lucian and through his Renaissance translators Thomas More and Erasmus; in fact, the eponymous heroine of Erasmus's *Praise of Folly* at times speaks in the voice of Menippean satire.[40] The genre was embraced by the sixteenth-century French writer François Rabelais and by a wide circle of libertine writers in seventeenth-century France. It was also absorbed by the Italian commedia dell'arte and particularly the Parisian Comédie-Italienne. Imbued with the ancient philosophy of Cynicism, Menippean satire took as its starting point a mockery of traditional value systems based on religion, wealth, and power, along with a celebration of the reversals brought about by fortune or chance. Proceeding through a series of regressive stages containing genres within genres and allusion within allusion, this satire sought to undermine systems of established political control by showing that the world is never what one expects, but rather a "topsy-turvy place" (Thomas More's term) in which those who are kings today may be cobblers tomorrow. Despite the many metamorphoses of Menippean satire through the centuries, a single stylistic feature remained more or less constant: its prosimetric or "dialogic" form, consisting of a "counterpoint" of styles (originally prose and verse), pointing up through their juxtaposition the "topsy-turvy" nature of existence.[41]

Such a stratification of styles typifies Campra's *Le carnaval de Venise* and *Les fêtes vénitiennes,* which exhibit a marked contrast between a more metrical (and at times florid) style of their Italianate numbers and the proselike passages of the action. As I have shown earlier, a florid, extravagant literary style also characterized the works of libertine writers. In the early eighteenth century, a related comic extravagance was developed in the brevets of the Société de la Calotte. In similar fashion, Campra's use of a florid *italianisme,* often associated with the god of love and libertinism, reverses the official ideals of purity, subtlety, and simplicity of language mandated by the Académie française. Echoing an eastern exoticism, it signals a transgression of the boundaries placed by monarchical taste and academic rules around a carefully controlled and regulated French identity, and therefore an exoti-

40. Ibid., 210–27. See also Martin Fleisher, *Radical Reform and Political Persuasion in the Life and Writings of Thomas More* (Geneva: Droz, 1973); Geraldine Thompson, *Under Pretext of Praise: Satiric Mode in Erasmus's Fiction* (Toronto: University of Toronto Press, 1973); and James Tracy, *The Politics of Erasmus: A Pacifist Intellectual and His Political Milieu* (Toronto: University of Toronto Press, 1978).

41. On the prosimetric or dialogic style, see Bakhtin's essay "Discourse and the Novel," in *The Dialogic Imagination: Four Essays by M. M. Bakhtin,* ed. Michael Holquist (Austin: University of Texas Press, 1981), 259–422.

cism associated not only with Italy, but also with a public, libertine France.[42] Interestingly, in *Le carnaval de Venise* and *Les fêtes vénitiennes*, the Italian style is associated with forms of invitation, in florid invocations to Cupid as symbolic ruler of an alternative, idealized society and in simpler charlatans' calls to public audiences as the metonymic representatives of that society. The act of invitation itself, in fact, sets up a principle of inclusion representing the antithesis of the exclusivity proclaimed by royal entertainment.

The Triumph of Folly over the Ages

Campra's *Les ages*, an opéra-ballet composed in 1718,[43] represents the stages of life and love, from youth (*l'amour ingenu*) to adulthood (*l'amour coquet*) and old age (*l'amour joué*). Folly appears in the last entry, where her triumph over all the ages is hailed in a grand finale of chorus, dance, and song. In the first air Folly and Cupid are proclaimed as equals, but by the third air Cupid has become Folly's "most faithful servant," and in the final chorus, altars are erected to Folly to the exclusion of all the other gods. The airs are mostly brilliant Italianate ariette types; one, an *air italien*, addresses Folly as "Cara follia, follia cara." The curtain closes on a triumphant Folly, enthroned and guarded by Arlequin, Polichinelle, acrobats, and clowns.

By 1718, of course, the political landscape had changed substantially. Louis XIV had died in 1715, his son the Dauphin in 1711, and his grandson the duc de Bourgogne in 1712. Philippe d'Orléans, his nephew, had become regent for his great-grandson, Louis XV. The period of the Regency represented a return to the hedonist ideals that had held sway at the Académie royale de musique, but it was more a *libertinage de moeurs* than a progressive *libertinage d'esprit*. The death of Louis XIV did finalize a shift that had begun to take place in his late years, in which the tone of entertainment began to be set by the Opéra and other public theaters. Throughout the seventeenth century, under the reign of Louis XIII and Louis XIV, royal entertainment had placed its stamp on public taste. After Louis XIV, the public taste formed and reflected in the theaters of Paris would set a fashion that could only be imported or imitated at the royal court.

42. While most of the Italian musical styles and genres were authentic, some—such as the gigue—were only associations in the minds of the French, forged from the days of the court ballet, when the gigue served as all-purpose "exotic" music. Just as none of the exotic music of the ballets was anthropologically sound, much of the "Italian" music, such as the ubiquitous gigue, did not actually derive from Italy.

43. Bibliothèque nationale, MS Vm1 267.

CHAPTER SEVEN

❊

Watteau's Cythera, the Opéra-Ballet & the Staging of Pleasure

The painter Antoine Watteau is believed to have worked at the Opéra, probably as a set painter, for a certain period after his arrival in Paris in 1702.[1] The years of his Paris career (1702–21) coincide with the success of the opéra-ballet in its first two decades. With an avid interest in both the theater and reading, he would likely have attended the ballet and read its popular *livrets*, published in a widely circulating edition in 1703.[2] Later in his career, he would have been kept abreast of developments at the Opéra through close personal friends, such as the writer Antoine de La Roque (later owner and director, with Fuselier, of the *Mercure galant*), who had close connections there. Not only certain themes but also the general festive atmosphere of the ballet permeates Watteau's oeuvre. Like the opéra-ballet, his paintings celebrate the fête galante and the Parisian theater, especially the Comédie-Italienne, the théâtre de la foire, and, as I will suggest in this chapter, the Opéra itself.

Watteau was described by his friend, the art dealer Edme Gersaint, as "un libertin d'esprit, mais sage de moeurs" (a freethinker, though circumspect in behavior).[3] These words link Watteau with the earlier, seventeenth-

---

1. Jérôme de La Gorce, "Watteau à l'Opéra (1702)?" in *Watteau (1684–1721): Le peintre, son temps et sa légende*, ed. François Moureau and Margaret Morgan Grasselli (Paris: Champion; Geneva: Slatkine, 1987), 11–16. Three contemporaries specifically mention Watteau at the Opéra in 1702. He was said to have been brought to Paris by an unidentified artist working at the Opéra at that time.

2. Available in facsimile in Pure, *Recueil général,*, vols. 1–2.

3. Cited by Moureau, "Watteau libertin?" in Moureau and Grasselli, *Antoine Watteau,* 17–22.

century meaning of the term *libertin*, as well as with the ideology of the opéra-ballet in the early eighteenth century. Recent scholarship has begun to explore the painter's oeuvre in light of the cultural politics of early eighteenth-century France. Thomas Crow, in his *Painters and Public Life in Eighteenth-Century Paris*,[4] was probably the first to connect Watteau's paintings with the fashionable custom of costuming à la Comédie-Italienne as an expression of resistance to the crown. Julie Anne Plax has extended Crow's more general political reading to a number of specific paintings; her interpretation of *The Departure of the Italian Comedians* makes a strong case for the painter's affinity with the Italians' subversive politics.[5] Mary Vidal and Sarah Cohen, studying conversation and gesture, respectively, help to identify his canvases as reflections of a turn from the hierarchical structure of earlier academic painting and portraiture to the more egalitarian orientation of an informal group dynamic.[6]

Hal Opperman argues that a spirit of antimilitarism informs Watteau's war paintings.[7] As Opperman points out, Watteau grew up in Valenciennes, a town in Hainaut that was ruthlessly conquered by Louis XIV in 1677, seven years before the painter's birth. Subsequently treated by Louis as an occupied territory, it was used as a staging point for his maneuvers on the northern front during the War of the Spanish Succession. Traveling to Valenciennes in 1709, Watteau would have seen firsthand the horrors of war during the coldest winter on record, when famine was rampant and the armies demoralized and disillusioned. His friend La Roque lost a leg at Malplaquet, one of the war's worst battles. Opperman, challenging critics who have appreciated only the *pittoresque* in Watteau's war paintings, interprets the broken lines and chaotic representations of his military subjects as a negative commentary on Louis XIV's militarism.[8] Similarly, Plax reads the war paintings as an ironic commentary on the distance between outmoded military ideals and the contemporary experience of military reality.[9]

I suggest that the ideology of Watteau's fêtes galantes and *fêtes publiques*, depicting the private and public faces of an idealized society, may be under-

---

4. Crow, *Painters and Public Life*, 45–74.

5. *Watteau and the Cultural Politics of Eighteenth-Century France*, 7–52.

6. Mary Vidal, *Watteau's Painted Conversations* (New Haven: Yale University Press, 1992); Sarah Cohen, *Art, Dance, and the Body in French Culture* (Cambridge: Cambridge University Press, 2000).

7. "The theme of peace in Watteau," in Moureau and Grasselli, *Antoine Watteau*, 23–28.

8. Ibid., 24.

9. Plax, *Watteau and the Cultural Politics of Eighteenth-Century France*, 53–107.

stood as the opposite side of the same coin. Like the utopian novels discussed in chapter 3 and the opéra-ballets of Campra and his contemporaries, these paintings stage pleasure as a subtle but insistent alternative to the staging of Louis XIV's power, particularly as seen in history painting and royal portraiture. In addition, because of their theatricalism, they could be said to bring painting into the dialogue of theaters, discussed in chapters 5 and 6, that had embraced the Opéra, Comédie-Italienne, Comédie-Française, and the *théâtre de la foire*. That process operates most clearly in Watteau's well-known *Pilgrimage to Cythera*, which translates the utopia of the opéra-ballet, along with its aesthetic and ideology of galanterie, to the world of painting. More specifically, almost all the details of this work can be explained with reference to a series of works produced in Parisian theaters, most notably the Opéra, between the years 1700–1713.

The Pilgrimage *and Its Reception*

The *Pilgrimage* served as Watteau's reception piece at the Académie royale de peinture et de sculpture, to which he had been accepted as a candidate in 1712. Upon its acceptance in 1717, the records of the Académie show the deletion of its original title, *Le pélerinage à Cythère*, and the substitution of the words *une feste galante*. Within the next two or three years, Watteau completed a second version of the painting, more embellished and brighter in color, which now hangs in the Charlottenburg Palace in Berlin.[10] The Louvre painting (plate 4) comprises a Venus term, on the right, festooned with roses and a quiver of arrows. It is connected by amorous couples winding down a hill to a ship rowed by two oarsmen and crowned by a flock of cupids. In the Berlin version (plate 5), Watteau has omitted the oarsmen, multiplied the cupids fourfold, enlarged and defined the ship (plate 6), and substituted for the Venus term a statue (the same as in his *Plaisirs d'amour*) of Venus confiscating Cupid's arrows. Beneath the statue lies a coat of armor, in front of which there is a shield and the hilt of a sword that has been struck into the ground. Beside the armor, half hidden in the shadows, lie a wineskin, a lyre,

---

10. This version is sometimes known as *The Embarkation for Cythera*, a title given to an engraving of the work made in 1733, which has also been used, by extension, to refer to the original. Because scholars generally see this version, though not a copy, as an embellished "repetition," I prefer to follow the usage of American scholars who generally refer to both paintings as *The Pilgrimage to Cythera* and distinguish between the two by reference to their locations.

books, and a mask. A couple of rosy cupids seem to have emerged from the gray stone of the statue. One of them pulls a laurel wreath up from a coat of armor, hung over a club, that lies beneath the statue to the feet of Venus. In both paintings, the costumes of the lovers include various styles of aristocratic and peasant dress.[11] A number of these costumes include stylized versions of the capes and staffs (and in the Louvre version, the water gourds) used by pilgrims traveling to the various shrines of Europe and the Near East. In the Berlin version, garlands of roses bedeck the dress of the central female figure and entwine the lovers at the lower right of the painting. On the prow of the boat in the Louvre *Pilgrimage* appears a golden winged victory with a shell as a headdress, and on the stern in the Berlin version, a golden figure of a woman resembling a sphinx, supported by a decorative shell.

Since 1795 the original *Pilgrimage* has hung in the Musée du Louvre, where, as Watteau's quintessential fête galante, its reception has reflected changing critical opinion. In the aftermath of the French Revolution, it sparked the outrage of an audience that read it as a reactionary touchstone of aristocratic privilege. So incendiary was its effect that in the early nineteenth century, the curator of the Louvre was forced to place the painting in storage for a time in order to protect it from the defamation of angry protestors.[12] Later in the century, as revolutionary fervor turned to romantic nostalgia, the reception of the *Pilgrimage* took on a wistful longing for a bygone era. This sentiment may be seen in the writings of Gérard de Nerval and Théodore de Banville, who spoke of "sorrowful Cythera" and "Watteau's infinite sadness" and "bitterness of life."[13] Even as late as 1951, the painting was described as "a symphony of nostalgia" and, in 1977, a "dance of death."[14] Although Michael Levey claimed in 1961 to have discovered the "real theme" of Watteau's Cythera, his iconoclastic theory that the painting represented a departure from, rather than for, Cythera has served to reinforce and

11. Peasant status is indicated by the more disheveled, simpler costumes of the men and the peasant blouses with pushed-up sleeves of the women, along with less elaborate hairstyles, straw hats, and a peasant weskit. These costumes characterize several of the figures in the boat and at the foot of the hillock.

12. Pierre Rosenberg, "Le pèlerinage à l'isle de Cithère," in *Watteau: 1684–1721*, ed. Margaret Morgan Grasselli, François Moureau, Pierre Rosenberg, et al. (Paris: Éditions de la Réunion des musées nationaux, 1984), 396–98.

13. Gérard de Nerval and Théodore de Banville, quoted in Donald Posner, *Antoine Watteau* (Ithaca: Cornell University Press, 1984), 182.

14. R. Huyghe, "Vers une psychologie de l'art," and J. K. Ostrowski, "Pellegrinaggio a Citera, 'fête galante' o 'danse macabre,'" both quoted in Posner, *Antoine Watteau*, 184.

perpetuate this older, romantic notion of a lost idyllic past. Julie Anne Plax's interpretation of the *Pilgrimage* falls into this category as well.[15]

In the 1980s, a series of studies investigated sources for the painting in the early eighteenth-century theater. These studies renewed and elaborated an earlier hypothesis[16] that the *Pilgrimage,* or at least its precursor, *L'isle de Cythère,* represented a scene from Florent Carton Dancourt's comedy *Les trois cousines* of 1700. Robert Tomlinson first extended this hypothesis to include a list of works performed at the Comédie-Française, the Opéra and the théâtre de la foire, all of which contain references to Cythera, voyaging, or pilgrimage.[17] Following Tomlinson's lead, others have added titles to the list of possible models for the *Pilgrimage.*[18] To date this list comprises two main groups of works: (1) operatic pieces, most of which contain only passing mention of Cythera or metaphorical embarkations on the seas of love, and (2) comedies at the Comédie-Française or the *foire,* either based on or referring to Cythera as a cynical metaphor for the libertine suburbs of Paris, whose brothels provided a destination for city dwellers seeking anonymous pleasure. Directly contradicting the romantic, "nostalgic" school of thought, these findings, while serving to ground the myth of Cythera in its early eighteenth-century context, still do not thoroughly address the actual iconographic content of the *Pilgrimage* or the discrepancy between its refined tone and the low-culture humor of the comedies in question.

A fuller explanation of Watteau's *Pilgrimage,* as well as its pictorial forerunners, may be found in two opéra-ballets, *Le triomphe des arts* (music, La Barre; *livret,* La Motte) and *Les amours déguisés* (music, Bourgeois; *livret,* Fuselier) along with their parodies at the Comédie-Française and the théâtre de la foire (all discussed in chap. 5). Like those works, it embodies a utopian ideal that transforms the ideology of the old court ballet into a

15. Michael Levey, "The Real Theme of Watteau's *Embarkation for Cythera,*" *Burlington Magazine* 103 (1961): 180–85; Plax, *Watteau and the Cultural Politics of Eighteenth-Century France,* 142–53.

16. Louis de Fourcaud, "Scènes et figures théâtrales," *Revue de l'art ancien et moderne* 15, no. 83 (1904): 135–50, and no. 84 (1904): 193–213.

17. *La fête galante,* 110–26.

18. These findings are largely contained in Grasselli et al., *Watteau: 1684–1721;* and Moureau and Grasselli, *Antoine Watteau.* In the first collection, see particularly Moureau, "The Roads to Cythera," 493–501; in the second, Giovanni Macchia, "Le mythe théâtral de Watteau," 187–196; André Blanc, "Watteau et le théâtre français," 197–202; and Philippe Hourcade, "Watteau et l'opéra de son temps: problématique d'un parallèle," 213–18. Another useful source is Mary Louise Ennis's "The Voyage to Cythera: From Courtly Allegory to Erotic Utopia in French Literature, 1700–1750" (Ph.D. diss., Yale University, 1989).

celebration of the arts and artists of the public sphere. Moving in modernist circles, Watteau would have almost certainly encountered La Motte, the ubiquitous and well-known leader of the Moderns. He probably also knew Fuselier, the author of both *Les amours déguisés* and its parody, *Les pélerins de Cythère,* through their mutual friend (and Fuselier's later business associate) La Roque. It is possible that the fashionable performances of Fuselier's dual treatments of Cythera in 1713, just after Watteau's entry into the Académie in 1712, might have stimulated the painter's interest in the subject and brought him back to earlier theatrical treatments and pictorial predecessors. Based on Watteau's and many of those earlier artists' connections with Parisian theatrical life around the turn of the century, however, it is probably more likely that the theme originated in the theater, most especially the Opéra.

Forerunners

The myth of Cythera probably entered the visual arts around the turn of the century, at precisely the historical moment of La Barre's *Le Triomphe des arts* and Dancourt's parody *Les trois cousines.* Of the visual representations predating Watteau's *Pilgrimage,* four depict groups of amorous couples and a boat, directly foreshadowing the *Pilgrimage.*[19] Two of these, a sketch by Claude Gillot entitled *L'embarquement pour l'île de Cythère* (fig. 7.1) and an anonymous painting entitled *L'embarquement pour Cythère,* refer specifically to embarkations. The other two are both entitled *L'isle de Cythère.* Of these, the first is an engraving bearing the names of Claude Duflos and Jean Berain, and in a later version from which the signature of Berain has disappeared, those of Duflos and Bernard Picart (fig. 7.2).[20] The second is

19. Two seventeenth-century works, Peter Paul Rubens's *Garden of Love* and Jacob Jordaens's *The Boating Party,* have been seen as forerunners to Watteau's Cythera paintings; neither, however, contains explicit reference to Cythera. Two other pictorial treatments, one by Bernard Picart (dated 1708) and the other by an anonymous artist, are entitled *Les pélerins de Cythère.* Depictions of single couples rather than groups of lovers, these exhibit a different tone, quite in line with the comic portrayal in the play of the same name by Fuselier. At least one of these portrayals antedates that play, however, opening the possibility that the "pilgrim of Cythera" had already become established as a trope by 1708. Both depict cartoonlike pilgrim couples. In Picart's work, the male pilgrim pours water into the female pilgrim's shell, a sexual innuendo that would reappear at the théâtre de la foire, in Charpentier's *Les amours de Cythère* of 1715 (Tomlinson, *La fête galante,* 122).

20. Émile Dacier, "Autour de Watteau: *L'île de Cythère* avant *L'embarquement,*" *Revue de l'art ancien et moderne* 71 (1937): 257–58.

Figure 7.1. Claude Gillot, *L'embarquement pour l'île de Cythère*. Fogg Art Museum, Harvard University, Cambridge, Massachusetts, gift of an anonymous donor in honor of Agnes Mongan, 5.1992.

Figure 7.2. Bernard Picart, *L'isle de Cythère*. Bibliothèque nationale de France, Cabinet des Estampes.

Watteau's own earlier treatment of the theme (plate 8). Except for the Watteau, which has been dated around 1709–10 or 1712–13, most of these precursors to the *Pilgrimage* have been dated around 1700 or 1709, partially on internal evidence[21] but also based on the premiere of Dancourt's *Les trois cousines* in 1700 and its reprise in 1709. The content of Dancourt's play, however, provides less basis for the imagery of the *Pilgrimage* than the "city cousin" of his country play, La Barre's *Le triomphe des arts*. That work more than any other sets out a politicized mythology of Venus and Cupid and allegory of the arts, including a ritual of praise before Venus's temple as well as one of the earliest references to embarkation.

At least from 1711, Gillot had connections with the Opéra, for which he produced scenery and costume designs. Watteau studied with him sometime between the years 1702 and 1709, and Gillot's *Embarquement pour Cythère* (fig. 7.1) has recently come to light as a direct model for the *Pilgrimage*.[22] Though Gillot's treatment contains references to Dancourt's play, it may also be seen as an elaboration on the operatic theme of embarkation as adumbrated by La Motte. Judging from its angle, Gillot's *Embarquement* appears to have been sketched from the perspective of a theater box. A "village" treatment of the theme, it harks back to the peasant village of *Les trois cousines,* but unlike Dancourt's play, it also includes a boat, a shoreline, and a clear presentation of a nautical embarkation.[23] More important, Gillot's drawing clearly points up the connection between Cythera, the theater, and the arts, as it includes several groups of musicians and dancers, a painter working on a canvas, and what looks like an acrobatic or juggling show on a makeshift stage. As in the opéra-ballet *Le triomphe des arts,* these elements convey an unmistakable sense of a utopia of theater, based on a celebration of the arts of music, dance, theater, and painting. If Gillot, following the ballet, did mean the work as a "triumph of the arts," the arch at the

21. The Gillot and the anonymous *Embarquement* have been dated c. 1700–1702 on the basis of stylistic evidence and costumes. The version of the engraving bearing the names of Duflos and Berain has been dated between 1694 and 1714 on the basis of hairstyles, and the one bearing the name of Picart, after 1714.

22. Discussed by Dewey F. Mosley, "Claude Gillot's *Embarkation for the Isle of Cythera* and Its Relationship to Watteau," *Master Drawings* 12 (Spring 1974): 49–56; and Ennis, "Voyage to Cythera"; and earlier by Mussia Eisenstadt, *Watteaus Fêtes galantes und ihre Ursprüngen* (Berlin: Bruno Cassirer, 1930); and Dacier, "Autour de Watteau," 247–250.

23. Again, there is some ambiguity, in that the boat looks as if it could as easily be arriving as departing.

right of the painting might be compared with those created for the triumphal entries of Louis XIV, from the heights of which musicians often played
fanfares and festive music. Yet, though Gillot's arch supports such a festive symphony, on one side it depicts a humble village and on the other the
festive arts of a public sphere, with the implicit suggestion that it is these,
rather than the king, that are being celebrated. In depicting village festivities similar in tone to those of Dancourt's *Trois cousines*, along with an embarkation and a celebration of the arts reminiscent of *Le triomphe des arts*,
Gillot's sketch draws together the interconnected imagery of those two related works and like them transforms the tragic tone associated with previous representations of Cythera into a triumphant celebration of an artistic
utopia. As the perspective of Gillot's *Embarquement* embraces the viewer as
a member of its audience, his boat, transgressing the lower boundary of the
painting, pulls this audience into the festive celebration, denoting the spectacle itself as the point of intersection between its audience and the transformative experience of art.

Watteau's own *Isle de Cythère* (plate 8) conflates the island-of-Cythera
motif with an embarkation, continuing the ambiguity in Gillot and the later
Pilgrimage as to whether the action takes place on Cythera or represents an
embarkation for the island. In its stage-like figures and backdrop, Watteau's
painting seems to bear witness to a theatrical presentation. It is usually dated
c. 1709–10 and has been linked, more directly than the later *Pilgrimage*, with
the revival of Dancourt's *Les trois cousines*.[24] As a number of commentators
have noted, however, the work also incorporates a literal quotation of the
balustrade of Saint-Cloud, the libertine pleasure garden specifically mentioned in relation to Cythera in Fuselier's *Les pélerins de Cythère* of 1713.[25] It
also includes the image of cupids-as-oarsmen contained in the prologue of
that work. This evidence would support the alternate dating of 1712–13,[26]

24. Although earlier attempts, following Fourcaud, to read the painting as a literal reproduction of Dancourt's play are open to debate, there may be an actual quotation of the
play in the figure of Charlotte Desmarets, who had played one of its *pélerines*. In a separate
sketch, engraved by Desplaces after Watteau, the figure is entitled "Mlle Desmarets joüant
le role de Pelerine."

25. Margaret Stuffman, *Jean-Antoine Watteau: Einschiffung nach Cythera (L'Isle de
Cythère)* (Frankfurt: Städelisches Kunstinstitut and Städtische Galerie, 1982), 75. See also
Émile Magne, *Le château de Saint-Cloud* (Paris: Calmann-Lévy, 1932), 170; Tomlinson, *La
fête galante*, 117; and Ennis, "Voyage to Cythera," 125.

26. Pierre Rosenberg, "Les tableaux de Watteau," in Grasselli et al., *Watteau: 1684–
1721*, 261.

indicating that Watteau probably treated the theme for the first time *after* his nomination to the Académie in 1712. In either case, this painting, while setting up the general theme and a number of details found in the *Pilgrimage,* seems to respond more to the allusions of the Comédie-Française and the *foire* than to the lofty utopianism of the later work.

The engraving of Duflos and Picart (fig. 7.2) provides the most compelling link between an operatic and a pictorial Cythera. Its earlier version displays the name of Jean Berain, chief of scenic design for the Opéra from the early days of that institution until his death in 1711. The only work unquestionably set on the island of Cythera, the engraving depicts a group of elegant couples before a temple. Behind the couples, a cupid brings new arrivals, while under the trees to the right other couples sing to the accompaniment of a recorder or oboe. Of all the early representations of Cythera, this engraving most closely matches the island setting depicted in the entry "La poësie" from La Motte's *Triomphe des arts,* with its amorous couples performing a ritual of love at Venus's sacred temple beside the sea. A poem serving as caption to the engraving confirms this ritualistic connection; it reads:

Chacun pour son office	(Each one for his Office
Y chante ses plaisirs	Sings of pleasures there
Et pour tout sacrifice	And for his whole sacrifice
Vient offrir ses soupirs.	Comes to offer sighs.
On passe en ces Retraites	In these retreats,
Des jours delicieux	Delicious days are passed
Et bien des nuicts secretes	And also secret nights
Qui valent encore mieux.	Which are worth even more.)

Further connecting the engraving with *Le triomphe des arts* is a barely discernable cupid standing at the apex of the temple, perhaps a reference to the cupids coming alive on the temple in the first entry of the opéra-ballet. Finally, the temple of Duflos's engraving presents an almost exact replica of the temple depicted in a stage design by Berain, for an opera of the previous year, *Marthésie, reine des Amazons* (see fig. 7.3).[27] Other quite similar

27. Paris, Archives nationales, reproduced in La Gorce, *Féeries d'opéra: Décors, machines et costumes en France, 1645–1765* (Paris: Caisse nationale des monuments historiques et des sites/Éditions du patrimoine, 1997), 58. A similar but larger example of the same temple may be seen in the stage design for Lully's *Achille et Polixène* (1687), reproduced in La Gorce, *Berain dessinateur du Roi Soleil* (Paris: Herscher, 1986), 90.

Figure 7.3. Jean Berain, stage design for *Marthésie, reine des Amazons*.

versions of this design may be found in a number of frontispieces, some also by Berain. Since the earlier version of the engraving bears Berain's name, it is possible that Berain himself was responsible for the original conception. Although there are no known extant stage designs for *Le triomphe des arts*, elements of the stage settings described in the *livret* for the first and second entries may be seen as the source of almost all the iconography of *L'isle de Cythère*. That, along with its operatic temple and the authorship of Berain, would confirm the link between *L'isle de Cythère* and the Opéra. Given Watteau's own connection with the Opéra in 1702, probably working under Berain, he could therefore have known the operatic myth of Cythera firsthand from Berain, his stage designs, and his *Isle de Cythère*.

From another angle, the signature of Bernard Picart (1673–1733) attests to an enlightened libertinism. Picart, one of the finest engravers of his generation, moved briefly from France to Antwerp in 1696, returning to Paris from 1698 to 1708, therefore at the time of *Le triomphe des arts* in 1700. From at least 1700 he had a business on the rue St. Jacques in the Latin Quarter, probably "Chez Martel, rue S. Jacques, a S. Pierre," denoted in the lower right-hand corner of the version of *L'Isle de Cythère* that bears his name. In

1708 he left France to live in the Netherlands, where he was associated with a group of Protestants, Freemasons, freethinkers, and pantheists. Mostly associated with the book trade, they disseminated a doctrine of heterodoxy, the new science, and republicanism through the print media. As an artist, Picart's general style was informed by a pagan symbolism tied to his liberal philosophical ideals.[28] He is one of the few names associated with Voltaire's 1722 visit to The Hague, where he was asked to provide engravings for the volume later known as *La Henriade*. Probably more than any other figure, Picart links Watteau and his *Pilgrimage* to what has been called "the radical Enlightenment."[29]

The Pilgrimage and Le triomphe des arts

Besides studying with Gillot, Watteau is believed to have been personally acquainted with both Duflos and Picart.[30] The *Pilgrimage* shares visual elements with almost all its forerunners, both pictorial and theatrical. Many of these elements belong either to a generic Venus mythology (the rose and shell as attributes of Venus, the arrows, quiver, and torch as attributes of Cupid)[31] or to overlapping and often indistinguishable layers of motifs present in the various pictorial and theatrical models (embarkation, pilgrims, cupids, different social classes). At the same time, however, the aristocratic, utopian tone of the *Pilgrimage,* as well as specific iconographic information (especially in the Berlin version),[32] links the painting directly with the general ideology as well as specific visual images of the opéra-ballet. Several details are reminiscent of Fuselier's *Les amours déguisés,* including the flock of cupids and the lovers enchained with garlands of roses. Of even more sig-

---

28. Later in the century, with Jean Frédéric Berhard, an associate of Pierre Bayle, Picart began a massive survey of the world's religions, entitled *Cérémonies et coutumes religieuses de tous les peuples du monde* (Amsterdam, 1721–43). The book, whose cover later displayed the first documented representation of Freemasonry, evidenced a religious tolerance and at the same time a critique of many aspects of religious practice.

29. Margaret C. Jacob, *The Radical Enlightenment: Pantheists, Freemasons, and Republicans* (London: George Allen, 1981), 162–66, 245–46, and passim.

30. Dacier, "Autour de Watteau," 248.

31. A.-P. de Mirimonde, "Statues et emblèmes dans l'oeuvre d'Antoine Watteau," *Revue du Louvre et des musées de France* 1 (1962): 11–20. Mirimonde calls the two versions of the *Pilgrimage* "glorifications of the rose."

32. My comments refer to this version unless otherwise noted.

nificance, however, is the web of signification connecting the painting to La Barre's *Triomphe des arts.*

Le triomphe des arts praises the arts of political and societal regeneration and the ballet as the modern synthesis of the arts; it consists of a succession of entries commemorating the individual arts of the ballet (poetry, music, painting, and the dance as living sculpture) as they contribute to a new genre dedicated to Venus. In the painting, the awakening statue alludes to this living sculpture of the dance, as set out in the entries "La sculpture" and "La poësie" of *Le triomphe des arts.* (See plate 7.) A lyre, books, and mask— attributes of music, poetry, and theater, the other arts of the ballet—have been placed at the foot of the statue, indicating the dedication of the arts to Venus. In the ritual of love beside the sea in the second entry of the ballet, "La poësie," the lovers dedicate to Venus a trophy fashioned of attributes of the other gods. This scene may explain the wineskin, attribute of Bacchus, traditional rival of Cupid,[33] and the coat of armor, attribute of Minerva, traditional rival of Venus, also lying beneath the statue. The sword struck into the ground in front of the armor might refer to the "barbaric" practice in Scudéry's *Sapho,* in which followers of Mars plant a sword in a heap of ashes. If so, it too represents another offering to the goddess of peace. In the same vein, one of the enlivened cupids of the statue pulls a laurel wreath up from the armor of Minerva to the feet of Venus, symbolizing the victory of the goddess of love over the goddess of war. Another cupid, still encased in the gray stone of a less enlightened era, reaches for the weapons that Venus holds out of his reach. It is also significant that in the Louvre version of the *Pilgrimage,* one of the peasants wears a laurel wreath, indicating the victory of even the lowest classes in this utopian society.[34]

The movement of the lovers to the left of the painting then may represent their response to the invitation to embark, extended in the closing chorus of *Le triomphe des arts.* The peasant personifying agriculture in this chorus (counterpart to Louis XIV as shepherd/hero in the *Ballet des arts*)

33. A common trope in opera, at least since Lully's *Les fêtes de L'Amour et de Bacchus* in 1674.

34. See plate 6. The imagery of the laurel wreath, signifying victory, was frequently associated with monarchical encomium. According to Peter Burke, in *The Fabrication of Louis XIV,* 145, critics reversed this imagery as a form of satire: "Even the laurel wreath was used against Louis. A poem jokes about the hesitation of Victory in the act of crowning the king, while a parody-medal . . . shows Victory removing the laurel, a nicely literal example of what the Russian critic Bakhtin calls 'uncrowning.' "

is represented in the groupings of peasants at the bottom of the hill and in the boat. The singer costumed as a sailor, personifying navigation, is represented by the oarsmen of the Louvre version. The sailor-cupids guiding the boat in the Berlin version underscore the text accompanying his "navigation" air, exhorting the world to love and culminating in the line "Cupid is the only guide who leads hearts to pleasure."[35]

Since the Renaissance at least, nautical images had been associated with France and with a politicized ship of state;[36] an image of a ship also served as the central image of the coat of arms of Paris. The boat of the *Pilgrimage* may then be seen as a new state, guided by love as a signifier not only of social harmony, but also probably a libertine political outlook. On the boats of both the Louvre and Berlin versions of the *Pilgrimage,* golden figures of a woman (a winged victory and sphinx figure, respectively) merge into a golden shell, recalling the regeneration of love signified by Venus's birth from the sea. Perhaps related to the resurrection of Sappho, poet of Venus, from the sea as a tenth Muse, these golden figures announce both the victory of the arts in the service of Venus and the riddle in which that message is cast. Finally, in *Le triomphe des arts,* from the animation of the cupids in the prologue to the animation of Pygmalion's statue at the end, love serves as the instrument of transfiguration. This spirit also animates the painting, with cupids guiding (and occasionally, as in the case of a reluctant lover on the hill, urging) the lovers toward the embarkation.[37]

The connection of the *Pilgrimage* with the opéra-ballet is strengthened by Sarah Cohen's theory that the gestures of the figures in the *Pilgrimage* represent those of the minuet, one of the most amorous dances of the ballet. According to Cohen, their line of movement imitates the minuet's floor pattern of an S or a Z, while the gestures of Watteau's central couple, one turning out and the other in, with right shoulders contiguous, could be inter-

---

35. Pure, *Recueil général,* 2: 1.

36. The ship as a symbol of France is discussed in Frances Yates's *Astraea: The Imperial Theme in the Sixteenth Century* (London: Routledge & Kegan Paul, 1975). It was part of the usual language of royal propaganda; Rubens's painting of Marie de Medici as regent at the helm of a ship, for example, draws on this language to signify her guidance of the ship of state. In the frontispiece to *Les amours déguisés* a cupid is holding the tiller.

37. Though the torch-bearing cupid is a familiar trope, nonetheless the torch-bearing cupid over the ship in the *Pilgrimage* recalls a similar figure as the instrument of transformation in the entry of the ballet devoted to Pygmalion, and thus points up the transformation inherent in the embarkation itself.

preted as the passing of two dancers through the central axis of this pattern. The energy of their movement radiates out to the harmonious pattern of the ensemble, whose members seem to participate in the alternate "bending" and "rising" steps of the minuet in a generalized manner even when seated or engaged in other activity.[38]

Cohen does not discuss the minuet in light of the ballet, but her findings strengthen the connection suggested here between the *Pilgrimage* and the ballet, and especially *Le triomphe des arts*, in which a minuet accompanies the central sacred ritual of praise to Venus. Another facet of the minuet not mentioned by Cohen is that when danced at a court ball, it was preceded by a "reverence," or bow and curtsy, to the king and queen who sat on a dais at the end of the oblong room. The S pattern then encompassed the length of the room in repeated arrivals and departures from the royal couple. The Venus term and statue of Venus and Cupid on their pedestals, then, might be seen as a substitution for the king and queen on their dais, and the figures at the right of the painting, several of whom kneel in various positions, as "courtiers of Venus" making the reverence to each other, before the image of Venus and Cupid.

Watteau's *Pilgrimage*, then, may be traced to specific catalysts that explain the painting as well as the eighteenth-century myth itself. The most important of these, and the only source providing a full explanation of the ideology represented by Cythera, is La Motte's ballet *Le triomphe des arts* of 1700, which is further elaborated by related theatrical and pictorial treatments of the same period including Dancourt's *Les trois cousines*, *L'isle de Cythère* of Berain, Duflos, and Picart, and Gillot's *Embarkation for Cythera*. Related elements include the central ritual of praise on Venus's sacred island in *Le triomphe des arts*, along with a series of scenes providing a panorama of a Cytherean utopia of the arts directly opposing Louis XIV's artistic program, and finally an invitation to a symbolic embarkation extended to the audience of a new artistic order represented by the ballet. This modern myth of Cythera, however, does not seem to have become common currency until its revival in Fuselier's *Les amours déguisés* of 1713. It is therefore possible that this work and its related parodies led Watteau and others back to the ideological

---

38. Cohen, *Art, Dance, and the Body*, 232–41. Cohen compares this group movement with the *geranos*, "a line dance thought to have been performed at night around a garlanded statue of Venus" (242). Further evidence that the gestures of the *Pilgrimage* represents the dance of the ballet may be found in the dancing figures of Métayer's *Embarquement pour Cythère* (discussed in Ennis, "Voyage to Cythera," 113, and reproduced on 267).

source in La Motte's *Le triomphe des arts* at just the time of the conception of the *Pilgrimage*, after his acceptance to the Académie in 1712. An alternate, more probable scenario is that Watteau, through his own association with the Opéra in 1702, would have been privy to the operatic origins of the politicized myth even before it gained widespread currency. Whatever the path of assimilation and influence, it is clear that the *Pilgrimage* represents the most complete visual representation of the ideology and imagery set out in La Motte's ballet of 1700.

In response to the question of arrival or departure, these findings do not support Levey's theory of an embarkation *from* Cythera, with its attendant "air of transience and sadness."[39] They return instead to his comment that the title may be translated as a pilgrimage either *to* or *on* Cythera, and point to an interpretation of Cythera as a broader symbol for the transformative experience of art and beauty, inspired by love. If the utopia of Cythera is equated with the ballet and the Opéra itself, then the ritual may also be seen as one of dedication of the new arts of the public sphere, as represented by the opéra-ballet, to the goddess of love and her son Cupid as the patron deities of the Paris Opéra. Likewise, the invitation to embarkation may be understood as an invitation extended to the audience of the ballet, the denizens of a Cytherean utopia of spectacle, to set sail on regenerative seas of desire and fulfillment. By extension, the new arts dedicated to Venus, whether the ballet, the spoken theater, or painting, represent the point of embarkation for a voyage of transformation, at once personal, political, and societal, that both leads to and *is* Cythera.

Frontispieces as New Sources for the *Pilgrimage*

A series of frontispieces offers explanations of some remaining details, as well as the more general conception, of the *Pilgrimage*. Two of these are from different editions of *Le triomphe des arts*, one from a Jesuit panegyric in praise of Louis XIV, and a fourth from *Les amours déguisés*. The first of these, the original frontispiece to *Le triomphe des arts* (fig. 7.4), depicts a group of putti representing the cupids in the first entry of the ballet ("L'architecture"). As in that entry, they hold emblems of the arts, more specifically, the arts of the ballet itself: painting, music, architecture (stage design), and sculpture (dance, or living sculpture). A statue of Apollo represents the "new

---

39. Levey, "Real Theme," 185.

Figure 7.4. Franz Ertinger, frontispiece, Michel de La Barre, *Le triomphe des arts*. Bibliothèque nationale de France.

Apollo" hailed in the ballet's first entry, the ruler of a future utopia who is willing to be led by the arts. He holds a lyre in one hand and a laurel wreath in the other, signifying in combination the victory of the arts. On the right, the bust of a figure representing music (perhaps the muse Euterpe) forms the upper portion of a trophy made of musical instruments; she also holds a crown which she would seem to offer to the arts below. The figure of her counterpart Fame, holding a trumpet to the left, stands beside a trophy from which emerges a palette and brushes, signifying painting. The arch that frames the statue, in the fashion of an *arc de triomphe*, supports the title of the work, *Le triomphe des arts*. Together, the figure of Apollo and those of the cupids, along with the trophies and emblems of the arts, may be seen to represent the joining of the temples of Apollo and Cupid in the first entry of the ballet, and the praise of a future ruler who would be led by the arts.

Just as La Motte's praise of Venus in *Le triomphe des arts* reverses the monarchical encomium of the official opera prologue,[40] the frontispiece of the *livret* may be seen as reversing the official iconography of the arts in the service of royal propaganda, as depicted in the *Ballet des arts* (discussed in chap. 5). This official iconography may also be seen in the frontispiece of a panegyric by Jacques de La Beaune, printed in 1684 (fig. 7.5). The genre of the panegyric was derived from the ancient oration of praise. In the late seventeenth century, regular contests were held to reward the best panegyric on Louis XIV in French, while others were composed by the Jesuits in Latin; La Beaune's work is of the latter type.[41] Dedicated to "the most munificent Louis the Great, father and patron of the liberal arts," its frontispiece depicts a bust of Louis XIV looking down from a pedestal, while figures representing the liberal and mechanical Arts hover around, creating a monument that combines their attributes with the imagery of kingship. These include a medal to Louis XIV (metallurgy), a compass (architecture or sculpture), a caduceus (medicine), palette and brushes (painting), and a shield and military drum (war). The winged personification of war, inscribing the dedica-

---

40. This is probably why La Motte chose to make "L'architecture," similar to a prologue in most respects, the first entry of the work instead. Operatic prologues were associated with the praise of the king. The overshadowing of Apollo by Venus, in that entry as well as throughout the work, might have seemed even more suspect in a prologue. To judge from La Motte's defense of *Le triomphe des arts* against the attack of a "Monsieur le Noble," it seems that this aspect of the work, along with others, came under rather heated attack. See La Motte, "Réponse a la critique du Ballet des Arts," *Oeuvres complètes* (Geneva: Slatkine, 1970), 2: 182–91.

41. Burke, *Fabrication of Louis XIV*, 22–23.

Figure 7.5. Frontispiece to Jacques de La Beaune, *Panegyricus*.
Bibliothèque nationale de France.

tion on a banner, forms a central focus of the composition, secondary only to the king. Additional emblems of music (a wind instrument and musical score) and theater (tragic and comic masks) appear in the lower left-hand corner, under the figure of Orpheus playing his lyre. In the upper left-hand corner, a personification of Fame holds a trumpet from which falls a banner with the words, "Nec pluribus impar" (no unequal match for many), the motto assumed by Louis when he planned his subjugation of all of Europe; with the other hand she crowns the king with a laurel wreath. In the background, a statue of a warrior, signifying Louis's military achievements, stands high atop an obelisk supporting an orb adorned with fleur-de-lis, echoing those crowning the dedication. The focus of the imagery is directed toward Louis as signified by the bust, the statue, the fleur-de-lis, and the words of the dedication, with which the figure representing war illustrates the central banner.

The frontispiece to the original *livret* of *Le triomphe des arts* may be seen, then, as a summary of the visual imagery of the ballet, especially in contrast to royal depictions of the arts as summarized in the frontispiece to Le Beaune's *Panegyricus* of 1684. Elements common to the ballet *livret* and the *Pilgrimage* would suggest Watteau's familiarity at least with the frontispiece of the ballet, and perhaps with the *Panegyricus* as well. From the former, he has incorporated both the cupids and the attributes of the arts, arranged at the feet of Venus in the Berlin *Pilgrimage*. In both versions of the painting, the statue of Venus may be seen as the equivalent of the statue of Apollo in the frontispiece, both deities representing enlightened qualities that had failed to be realized under Louis's reign. A more important connection than these isolated images is Watteau's conception of the painting itself, like the frontispiece to *Le triomphe des arts*, as a counterpanegyric, reversing the ideology of the arts vis-à-vis the recently deceased Louis XIV. In that sense, the two versions of the *Pilgrimage* present the Venus term and the statue of Venus, respectively, as objects of praise analogous to those of the *Panegyricus*, with the rose of Venus substituted for the royal fleur-de-lis. Rather than a central focus, however, they represent an outward boundary of the *Pilgrimage*. As if allowing the image of Venus to share the space of praise with the denizens of a new landscape, they illustrate the lines from La Motte's "Hymn to Venus": "And you share with these hearts / All the pleasures that you enjoy yourself."

The 1703 edition of the *livret* to *Le triomphe des arts* supplied a new frontispiece by Franz Ertinger (fig. 7.6)[42] based on the entry "La sculpture." It

42. Pure, *Recueil général*, 2: 7.

Figure 7.6. Frontispiece, La Barre, *Le triomphe des arts* (1703).

depicts the moment when Pygmalion's statue awakens. Venus watches from
a cloud, restraining a cupid with his bow. At the foot of the statue are symbols of the art of sculpture: the measuring stick, compass, chisel, and mallet.
This frontispiece could have inspired the use of the statue of Venus restraining Cupid, in the Berlin *Pilgrimage*. Equally significant for the imagery of
the *Pilgrimage* is the awakening statue of Pygmalion, an obvious model for
the cupids awakening out of the statue in the *Pilgrimage*.[43] The final frontispiece of this series of models, to *Les amours déguisés* (by J. B. Scotin; fig. 7.7),
depicts a ship similar to that of the Berlin *Pilgrimage* (Plate 6), with the main

43. Awakening statues occur with some frequency in the ballet. To my knowledge, the
ballet has not been adequately studied as a source for similar images in Watteau, and in a
slightly later period for Gabriel de Saint-Aubin.

Figure 7.7. Frontispiece, Thomas Bourgeois, *Les amours déguisés*.

difference that its cupids are more carefully attending their mariners' duties. Watteau's transformation of these cartoon-like, two-dimensional frontispieces suggests that the artist, like Pygmalion, breathes life into the ballet, thus actually depicting the coming to life of a new society out of the matrix of its united arts.

The frontispieces for the two ballets, taken together, could then be seen as inspiration for the two parts of the Berlin *Pilgrimage,* with the 1700 frontispiece to *Le triomphe des arts* as the basis for the attributes of the arts at the feet of the statue; the 1703 frontispiece to that work, for the enlivening of the cupids on the statue itself; and the frontispiece to *Les amours déguisés,* for the cupids as mariners and the ship on the left. The unhoisted sail of the ship, resembling the curtain above the Opéra proscenium, might also allude to the Opéra stage, the point of artistic embarkation. The figures in aristocratic dress, high on the hill, would then signify the aristocratic members of the audience at the Opéra, seated in the higher boxes, who join with the lower-class members occupying a physically lower space in the parterre, all boarding the ship at the point at which the veil/curtain parts. If, as Opperman has shown, Watteau uses the dissonance of the broken line in his war paintings to symbolize discord, the spatial pattern of the *Pilgrimage* represents not only the S shape of the minuet but beyond that—as theorists of the dance had consistently maintained since the Renaissance—the ballet itself as a symbol of universal harmony.[44] Indeed, according to the *livrets* of the ballets, the myth of Cythera stands not for a one-time journey but for a continual process. The ship represents the embarkation of a new society under the sign of Venus, with Cythera the destination and love the means. Like La Motte's *Triomphe des arts* and Gillot's *Embarquement,* Watteau's *Pilgrimage* invites its audience into the transformative experience of art. Entering on the lower right of the painting, the viewer is swept into the S pattern that rises in a flourish to a triumphal arch of cupids framing the embarkation. Finally, then, the *Pilgrimage* celebrates a triumphal entry of a new public audience into an art of societal regeneration. Just as La Motte had, in "La poësie," inscribed the poet in the iconoclastic *livret* of *Le triomphe des arts,* and La Barre had inscribed the musician ("La musique"), Watteau must surely have been aware of inscribing himself as artist of the *Pilgrimage*—

---

44. The Neoplatonic theory underlying the ballet is discussed in Isherwood, *Music in the Service of the King,* 104, and, following Père Menestrier, by Néraudau, *L'Olympe du roi-soleil,* 126.

like Apelles, creating an image of Venus to be revered by future generations ("La peinture"), and like Pygmalion, bringing into the world a lifelike vision of love and beauty ("La sculpture").

The Fête galante, the Academy, and the Quarrels of the Ancients and the Moderns

Both the new genre of the opéra-ballet at the Académie royale de musique and the new genre of the fête galante at the Académie royale de peinture et de sculpture represent a rupture with the traditional styles of music and art associated respectively with those institutions. In fact, Watteau and the creators of the opéra-ballet faced similar situations vis-à-vis their respective academies in that all of these artists, working within the bastions of officialdom, were constrained by tradition and official censorship. At the same time, they were working within institutions whose authority had been considerably weakened by the death of Colbert in 1683, the deaths of Lully in 1687 and Le Brun in 1690, and by the lack of state support as well as a lack of interest, or actual antagonism, on the part of Louis XIV at the end of his reign. They were also working within institutions that, albeit official, were composed of members whose individual persuasions did not automatically coincide with official policy and image making. As discussed in chapter 4, Quinault, a member of the Petite Académie and a speaker before the Académie française, had admonished Louis XIV for his aggressive militarism. His successors in the Petite Académie included Antoine Danchet, Campra's librettist, and other writers such as Jean-Baptiste Rousseau, also an opera librettist and habitué of the Temple, and Fontenelle—individuals who could hardly be considered hard-line royalists.

I have mentioned earlier that the original title of the painting Watteau submitted to the Académie in 1717, *Le pélerinage à Cythère,* was struck out and replaced by the words *une feste galante.* Donald Posner suggests that the purpose of the title change was to deny Watteau the greater status accorded to paintings on the subjects of history and mythology, which the former title would have indicated.[45] Paul Duro maintains that it allowed the Académie a face-saving avoidance of conflict between genre and history painting.[46]

45. Posner, *Antoine Watteau,* 193–94.

46. Paul Duro, *The Academy and the Limits of Painting in Seventeenth-Century France* (Cambridge: Cambridge University Press, 1997), 232–33.

Whatever its origin, the title of *fête galante* gave academic status to Watteau's "modern" genre which, though drawing on the iconography of ancient mythology, used those images in an iconoclastic manner, as symbols of a new social order. In fact, the cult of galanterie had practically from the beginning been associated with a neo-*précieux* modernism and championed by writers such as Charles Perrault, whose *Parallèle des anciens et des modernes* of 1688 had inaugurated the debate between the Ancients and the Moderns in the Académie française. In his praise of galant poetry for its finesse, ingenuity, delicacy, freedom, agreeableness, and lightness of effect, Perrault accurately described the qualities that would characterize the fête galante of the ballet and of Watteau's canvases.[47]

Traditional academic painting, drawing on the heroic themes of ancient history, Greek mythology, and the Homeric epic, was associated with official propaganda and was regulated by the Académie. During the second decade of the eighteenth century, the period of the creation of the *Pilgrimage*, all of these academic values were being called into question. The final phase of the debate between the Ancients and the Moderns came to a climax with La Motte's critique of Homer's *Iliad* in 1713. La Motte's cause, hailed as the "liberation of the human spirit,"[48] had an immediate effect on public opinion, and it was not long before polite society had joined the literary Moderns in denouncing and even ridiculing Homer. Similarly, the triumph of Venus over Pallas Athena in Fuselier's *Les amours déguisés* may be seen as a triumph of the "modern" goddess of peace and love over the "ancient" goddess of war and patriarchy. Indeed, Venus's triumph in *Les amours déguisés* represents a literal reversal of both the *Iliad* and Louis XIV's *Ballet des amours déguisés,* both of which depicted the defeat of Venus and her favored Trojans. (It also reminds one of how, in Greek and Roman mythology, Aphrodite/Venus often subverted the patriarchal rule of Zeus/Jupiter.) Later in his career, Fuselier wrote two parodies of Homer for the *foire: Arlequin*

---

47. Charles Perrault, *Parallèle des anciens et des modernes en ce qui concerne les arts et les sciences* (1692–97; Geneva: Slatkine, 1979), 3: 286. These qualities were largely derived from the new feminine influence, exemplified in the conversation of the salons, as Mary Vidal has convincingly argued. For a discussion of salon conversation and a new galant style in music, see Barbara Russano Hanning, "The Iconography of a Salon Concert: A Reappraisal," in *French Musical Thought,* ed. Georgia Cowart (Ann Arbor: UMI Research Press, 1989; Rochester: University of Rochester Press, 1994), 129–48.

48. Hippolyte Rigault, *Histoire de la querelle des anciens et des modernes* (1859; Burt Franklin, n.d.), 455.

défenseur d'Homère of 1715 and (with Alain Le Sage and Jacques-Philippe d'Orneval) *La Penelope moderne* of 1728.[49] The second of these, in which a final divertissement of pilgrims once again invites the public as a "pilgrim" to the théâtre de la foire, brings together the pilgrimage to Cythera, Homeric satire, and the early eighteenth-century theater audience.

The world of art criticism had its own corollary to the quarrel of the Ancients and the Moderns, in its series of debates over line and color dating back to the seventeenth century. The champions of line, the Poussinistes, adhered to the "ancient" standards of draftsmanship and narrative form, while the champions of color, the Rubenistes, favored the "modern" liberation of the painterly signifier from the academic rules of imitation as they had been codified by Le Brun. Watteau moved among circles of the Rubenistes, and his acceptance into the Académie reflects an era of increased tolerance for painting outside the limits established by the Académie at the height of its power in the 1670s and 1680s. This tolerance may be associated with a natural evolution in taste; Antoine Coypel, the director of the Académie at the time of Watteau's acceptance, has been acknowledged for an eclecticism that reconciled or transcended the conflicting claims of Rubenistes and Poussinistes. It is also possible—given the antagonism between Louis XIV and the artistic community in his late years, the widespread nature of Cytherean protest, and the freer political atmosphere of the Regency—that it may be associated with a movement from within the Académie, a collusion of certain of its artists with the Cytherean forces of a new art.

When he had to choose a topic for a reception piece following his acceptance as a candidate in 1712, Watteau chose one drawn from the ballet that used the mythological trappings prized by academic painting to deliver a message reversing the typical academic *loci topici*—just as the opéra-ballet reversed those of the court ballet and opera. Only in his final version of the painting, produced for a private collector (perhaps Jean de Jullienne) in the years following his academic reception, did Watteau translate in detail the politicized imagery of the ballet to canvas. Clearly, he would have felt more comfortable revealing the details of this imagery in the privacy of a work undertaken for a personal friend and conceived in the safer political climate following the death of Louis XIV.

Watteau's paintings, like the genre of the opéra-ballet, bring together a number of modernist elements, foremost among them a freedom from the

49. *Le théâtre de la foire*, 1: 131–42 and 2: 152–73.

accepted academic topoi and rules and an unapologetic appeal to the physical senses. While an assessment of the political implications of the quarrel of the Ancients and the Moderns is still needed, it seems clear that the call for a freedom from the rules, the liberation of art from the outworn signified of royal propaganda, and the iconoclastic glorification of the artistic signifier in the service of Venus indicate at least some form of intersection between a modernist aesthetic and an oppositional ideology in the first two decades of the eighteenth century, akin to a similar intersection in the ballet. If so, the Cytherean and Venetian opéra-ballets, as well as Watteau's *Pilgrimage to Cythera,* all stand precisely at this point of convergence. Completed during the Regency, a six-year period of transition between the long-awaited end of Louis XIV's reign and the beginning of the reign of his great-grandson as Louis XV in 1721, Watteau's *Pilgrimage* may be seen as an expression of resistance to the politics and aesthetics of the old king, as well as a utopian blueprint for the regent and king-to-be.

Ironically, the utopian message of Watteau's paintings was lost to later generations. In the second half of the eighteenth century, the third estate, turning its rebellion on the aristocracy as well as the monarchy, began to view Watteau's fêtes galantes as outdated and Cythera as the libertine symbol of a degenerate upper class. Ironically, with Venus's association with this degeneracy, the goddess Minerva became the new symbol of a progressive, libertine Enlightenment.[50] Watteau's modern-day reception, like Campra's, has continued to be accompanied by a nagging, negative perception of his association with Regency frivolity. It is true that an iconography of cupids, lovers, water imagery, shells, fêtes galantes, and fêtes champêtres is associated with the hedonism of an aristocratic elite released from the constraints of life at court. But the bourgeoisie and to some extent the third estate, through the seventeenth and early eighteenth centuries dazzled like M. Jourdain by the glittering surface of aristocratic pleasure, adopted its playful, pretty pastimes as the means of fulfilling an obsessive desire for social status. Within this process, certain artists such as Lully and his sons, Molière, Campra, and Watteau were able to weave an ideological vision of a new society, based on an idealized view of the musical spectacle and its audience.

This vision was a private, encoded one, probably limited to a coterie of artists and writers, along with certain patrons and audience members. At the same time, it could be comprehended in more general terms by an audience

50. Jacob, *Radical Enlightenment,* 164.

sensitive to the nuances of image and iconography. Especially after the death of Louis XIV in 1715, it reflected and to some extent influenced the changing outlook and tastes of a more general public. The expansion and diffusion of a galant aesthetic in the early eighteenth century was fueled by the popularity of the opéra-ballet and by a cult of Watteau that spread to all of Europe after his early death. The art of Campra and Watteau marked an important turning point in the arts, as both these artists were supported mainly by the commercial marketplace as well as by private patrons, and neither enjoyed the direct patronage of Louis XIV. Their galant idiom,[51] elements of which were continued in the opéra-ballets of Rameau and the paintings of Boucher and Fragonard, represented a historical moment in which aristocratic elements were assimilated into a more general upper-class mystique that was disseminated via the commercial art market. At some points, this mystique

51. Daniel Heartz's discussion of a galant style (*Music in European Capitals: The Galant Style, 1720–1780*, 3–23) revives the notion of galanterie as a defining term for European art and music in the years between 1720 and 1780. The book opens with a chapter entitled "Watteau, Galant Cynosure," which traces the popularity of Watteau at the beginning of this period and demonstrates the impact of Watteau's *oeuvre* on the worlds of both art and music in the early part of the eighteenth century. Heartz's study attests to the extension, continuation, and even domination of a galant aesthetic that, despite a turn toward more serious trends in the 1760s, remained influential until the eve of the Revolution.

By the mid-eighteenth century the perception of a musical *style galant* was essentially an international one, comprising mainly French and Italian components. Heartz traces only the Italian branch of these terms' genealogy; the French connection is traced in David Sheldon's older study, "The *Galant* Style Revisited and Evaluated," *Acta musicologica* 47 (1975): 240–70. This connection exists not only in the association of these terms with the *galant homme de bon goût*, but also in their association with chamber music and the suite, particularly the French lute suite with its *style brisé*. Throughout the eighteenth century, the term *galanterie* could refer to free keyboard compositions, suites, and individual dances. In a more general sense, it referred to musical composition characterized by a lighter, homophonic style, and also by an expressive quality connected with melodic figuration and ornamentation. Along with the *style brisé* of the older lute suite, this aspect could be seen to originate in France with the expressive, ornamented *doubles* of the *air sérieux* as practiced by Lambert, and in general with the earlier French chamber music for which La Fontaine expressed such deep nostalgia (see chap. 4 above). In addition, Sheldon (257) notes that "the innumerable whims, inventions, and polite alterations associated here with *galanterie* suggest *galant* conversation, witticism, and repartee," social conventions traceable to the French salon. In the late eighteenth century these conversational, ornamental qualities fell out of fashion, giving way to the Enlightenment virtues of clarity and directness, in musical taste as well as in society. Such a trajectory may also be discerned in painting and the decorative arts as they move from the fête galante and the rococo style with which it is associated toward Neoclassicism in the later part of the eighteenth century.

intersected with political and social reform, which in preindustrial Europe was also linked with capitalistic enterprise.

In the period preceding the Revolution, the delicate ideal of galanterie was engulfed by a new brand of heroic idealism, appropriated to the uses of the Revolution and the new Republic. The Neoclassical canvases of Jacques-Louis David attest to the new civic virtues of duty and self-sacrifice, which bear some resemblance to the glorification of heroic duty and the self-sacrifice of the prince in the mythology of absolutism. During the Revolution, the grand choruses and heavy orchestrations of Louis XIV's glorious militarism were transformed into the new musical style of the *fêtes publiques* of a new citizens' republic. The music of the French Revolution was not lost on Beethoven, who responded to a renewed desire for the heroic, the lofty, and the abstract in the service of a new world order.

The ideals of galanterie continued to be eclipsed until the late nineteenth century when, partly as a way of affirming its French heritage, a fashionable wealthy class began to offer entertainments inspired by the ancien régime. The comte de Montesquiou-Fezensac and the comtesse Greffulhe (respectively reputed to be the models for Marcel Proust's baron de Charlus and duchesse de Guermantes) both began producing such fêtes in the 1890s. In 1908 and 1909, using dancers from the Opéra, the comtesse Greffulhe produced historical recreations of ancien-régime dances at the palace of Versailles and the Bagatelles gardens of the Bois-de-Boulogne. Also in the pre–World War I period, the fashion designer Paul Poirer hosted a series of historicizing concerts and in 1912 recreated *Les fêtes de Bacchus,* one of the earliest and most hedonistic of Louis XIV's court ballets. The influence of seventeenth-century France on the Ballets Russes de Monte Carlo, from their early Paris performance of *Le pavillon d'Armide* (1909), is likewise a strong one; Stravinsky's *Apollon musagète* (Apollo leader of the Muses) revived the "glories of the French classical past" as did Tchaikovsky's *Sleeping Beauty,* based on Charles Perrault's 1697 rendering of a folk tale for a stylish salon audience.[52] At the same time, a renewed fascination with the atmosphere of the ancien régime, if not the actual musical style, produced such

52. On the comtesse Greffuhle and music in the French Third Republic, see Jann Pasler, "Countess Greffulhe As Entrepreneur: Negotiating Class, Gender, and Nation," *Writing through Music: Essays on Music, Culture, and Politics* (Oxford: Oxford University Press, 2008), and *Composing the Citizen: Music as Public Utility in Third Republic France* (Berkeley: University of California Press, 2009). *Les fêtes de Bacchus* is described above, at the beginning of chapter 1. On Poiret and the convergence of an ancien régime galanterie with a twentieth-century neoclassicism, see Davis, *Classical Chic,* 38–47, 234–40.

works as Ravel's *Tombeau de Couperin* and Debussy's *Suite bergamasque* and *Fêtes galantes,* with their references to song and dance, lovers, parks, marble statues, and masked comedians. It is a testament to the artists discussed in this book that two centuries later, the French would have chosen their delicate imagery as a mark of cultural identification.

❋ Bibliography

MANUSCRIPT SOURCES

Bibliothèque nationale de France

Collasse, Pascal. *Ballet des saisons*. Vm2 57.
———. *La naissance de Vénus*. Vm2 58.

*Bibliothèque nationale de France, Collection Philidor
des Fonds du Conservatoire, F-Pc*

Campra, André. *Le carnaval de Venise*. Rés. F 1668.
Lully, Jean-Baptiste. *Ballet des fêtes de Bacchus*. Rés. F 505.
———. *Ballet des plaisirs*. Rés. F 506.
———. *Ballet royal d'Alcidiane*. Rés. F 507.
———. *Ballet royal de la raillerie*. Rés. F 508.
———. *Ballet royal de l'impatience*. Rés. F 509.
———. *Les noces de village*. Rés. F 510.
———. *Ballet des amours déguisés*. Rés. F 511.
———. *Ballet royal de la naissance de Vénus*. Rés. F 513.
———. *Ballet royal de l'Amour malade*. Rés. F 514.
———. *Ballet royal de Flore*. Rés. F 515.
———. *Ballet des Muses*. Rés. F 521.
———. *Le bourgeois gentilhomme*. Rés. F 578.
———. *Recueil de ballets de feu Monsieur de Lully*. F-Vm⁶ 1, vols. 1–6.

SOURCES BEFORE 1800

Benserade, Isaac. *Benserade: Ballets pour Louis XIV*. Ed. Marie-Claude Canova-Green.
   2 vols. Toulouse: Société de littératures classiques, 1997.
Boindin, Nicolas. *Lettres historiques sur tous les spectacles de Paris*. Paris: P. Prault, 1719.

Bourgeois, Thomas. *Les amours déguisés*. Paris: Ballard, 1713.

———. *Les plaisirs de la paix*. Paris: Ballard, 1715.

Cahusac, Louis. *La danse ancienne et moderne*. 3 vols. The Hague: J. Neaulme, 1754; Geneva: Minkoff, 1971.

Campra, André. *Les âges*. Paris: Ballard, 1718.

———. *Les amours de Mars et Vénus*. Paris: Ballard, 1712.

———. *Le carnaval de Venise* (Paris, 1699). Reprinted in *French Opera in the Seventeenth and Eighteenth Centuries*, vol. 17. Ed. James Anthony. Stuyvesant, NY: Pendragon Press, 1989.

———. *L'Europe galante*. Paris: Ballard, 1697. Farnborough, Hampshire: Gregg Press, 1967.

———. *L'Europe galante*. Paris: Ballard, 1697. Toulouse: Société de musicologie de Languedoc, n.d.

———. *Les fêtes vénitiennes*. Ed. Max Lütolf. Paris: Heuget, 1970.

———. *Les fragments de Monsieur Lully*. Paris: Ballard, 1702.

———. *Les Muses*. Paris: Ballard, 1703.

Collasse, Pascal. *La naissance de Vénus*. Paris: Ballard, 1696.

———. *Les saisons*. Paris: Ballard, 1695.

Constantini, Angelo [Mezzetin]. *La vie de Scaramouche*. Paris: À l'Hôtel de Bourgogne et chez Claude Barbin, 1695.

Dancourt, Florent Carton. *Oeuvres de théâtre*. 3 vols. Paris, 1760; Geneva: Slatkine, 1968.

De Brosses, Charles, le président. *Lettres familières sur l'Italie*. Ed. Yvonne Bezard. Paris: Firmin-Didot, 1931.

Desfontaines, Pierre-François Guyot, and Guillaume Plantavit de La Pause. *Mémoires pour servir à l'histoire de la Calotte*. New ed. N.p., 1732.

Desmarets, Henri. *Les amours de Momus*. Paris: Ballard, 1695.

———. *Les festes galantes*. Paris: Ballard, 1698.

Destouches, André Cardinal. *Le Carnaval et La Folie*. Paris: Ballard, 1704.

Durey de Noinville, Jacques Bernard. *L'Histoire du Théâtre de l'Opéra en France depuis l'établissement de l'Académie Royale de Musique jusqu'à present*. Paris: J. Barbou, 1753.

Félibien, André. *Relation de la fête de Versailles, les divertissements de Versailles*. Ed. Martin Meade. 1697; Paris: Dédale, 1994.

Fénelon [François de Salignac de la Mothe]. *Lettre à Louis XIV*. Ed. Henri Guillemin. Neuchâtel: Ides et calendes, 1964.

———. *Télémaque*. Paris, 1699.

Foigny, G. de. *La terre australe connue: c'est-à-dire la description de ce pays inconnu jusqu'ici, de ses moeurs et des ses coutumes*. Ed. F. Fachèvre. In *Les successeurs de Cyrano de Bergerac*. Geneva, 1676; Geneva: Slatkine, 1968.

Gherardi, Evariste. *Le théâtre italienne, ou le recueil général de toutes les comédies et scènes françoises jouées par les comédiens du roy, pendant tout le temps qu'ils ont été au service*. 6 vols. Paris: Cusson and Wittwe, 1717; Société des textes français modernes, Klinksieck, 1944.

Gilbert, Claude. *Histoire de Caléjava ou de l'isle des hommes raisonnables*.1700; Paris: Éditions d'Histoire Sociale, 1970.

Hatin, Eugène. *Manuel théorique et pratique de la liberté de la presse*. Paris, 1986.

La Barre, Michel de. *Le triomphe des arts*. Paris: Ballard, 1700.

———. *La Vénitienne*. Paris: Ballard, 1705.

La Beaune, Jacques de. *Panegyricus*. Paris, 1684.

Lacoste, Louis. *Aricie*. Paris: Ballard, 1697.

La Fontaine, Jean de. *Oeuvres complètes*. Ed. Louis Moland. 4 vols. Paris: Garnier frères, 1877; Nendeln: Klaus Reprints, 1973.

La Motte, Antoine Houdar de. *Oeuvres complètes*. 2 vols. Geneva: Slatkine, 1970.

Lecerf de la Viéville, Jean-Laurent. *Comparaison de la musique italienne et de la musique française*. 3 vols. Brussels, 1704–6; Geneva: Minkoff, 1972.

Le Sage, Alain René, and Jacques-Philippe d'Orneval [and Louis Fuselier]. *Le théâtre de la foire, ou l'opéra comique; contenant les meilleures pièces qui ont été représentées aux foires de Saint-Germain et de Saint-Laurent*. 10 vols. Paris: Graneau, 1737; Geneva: Slatkine, 1968.

L'Héritier, Marie-Jeanne. *Le triomphe de Madame Deshoulières, reçue dixième muse au Parnasse*. Paris, 1694.

Limojon de Saint-Didier, Alexandre-Toussaint. *La ville et la république de Venise*. Paris: L'Eillaine, 1680.

Loret, Jean. *La Muze historique*. Paris: C. Chenault, 1650–65. New edition in 4 vols. Paris: P. Jannet, 1857–78.

Lully, Jean-Baptiste. *Ballets*, ed. J. P. Cassaro, Albert Cohen, and Rebecca Harris-Warrick. In *Oeuvres complètes*, ed. Jérome de La Gorce and Herbert Schneider. Series 1. Vol. 1. Hildesheim: Georg Olms, 2001.

———. *Le bourgeois gentilhomme* (1670), ed. Herbert Schneider. In *Oeuvres complètes*, ed. Jérôme de La Gorce and Herbert Schneider. Series 2. Vol. 4. Hildesheim: Georg Olms, 2006.

———. *Isis* (1677), ed. Lionel Sawkins. In *Oeuvres complètes*, ed. Jérôme de La Gorce and Herbert Schneider. Series 3. Vol. 6. Hildesheim: Georg Olms, forthcoming.

———. *Oeuvres complètes*. Ed. Jérôme de La Gorce and Herbert Schneider. Hildesheim: Georg Olms, 2001–.

———. *Oeuvres complètes*. Ed. Henry Prunières. New York: Broude Brothers, 1966–74.

Lully, Louis. *Orphée*. Paris: Ballard, 1690.

Lully, Louis, and Jean-Louis Lully. *Zéphyre et Flore*. Paris: Ballard, 1688.

Marino, Giambattista. *L'Adone*. Ed. Giovanni Pozzi. Milan: A. Mondadori, 1976.

Menestrier, Claude-François. *Des ballets anciens et modernes selon des règles du théâtre*. Paris: R. Goignard, 1682; Geneva: Minkoff, 1972.

———. *Des représentations en musique anciens et modernes*. Paris: R. Goignard, 1681; Geneva: Minkoff, 1972.

Molière. *Oeuvres complètes*. Ed. Georges Couton. 2 vols. Paris: Gallimard, 1956.

———. Ed. Georges Mongrédien. 4 vols. Paris: Garnier-Flammarion, 1965.

Montpensier, Mlle de. *Mémoires*. In *Collection des mémoires relatifs à l'histoire de France*, vols. 40–43. Ed. M. Petitot. Paris: Foucault, 1824.

———. *La relation de l'isle imaginaire*. Amsterdam: François Changuion, 1723.

Noinville, Durey de, Jacques Bernard, and Louis Travenol. *Histoire du Théâtre de l'Opéra en France depuis l'établissement de l'Académie royale de musique jusqu'à présent*. Paris: Barbou, 1753; 2nd ed. rev., Paris: Duchesne, 1757; Geneva: Minkoff, 1972.

Parfaict, Claude, and François Parfaict. *Histoire de l'ancien Théâtre-Italien, depuis son ori-gine en France, jusqu'à sa suppression en l'année 1697.* Paris, 1753; Roget, 1767.

———. *Mémoires pour servir à l'histoire des spectacles de la foire.* 2 vols. Paris: Briasson; New York: AMS Press, 1978.

Pure, Michel de. *Idée des spectacles anciens et nouveaux.* 1668; Geneva: Minkoff, 1972.

Pure, Michel de, ed. *Recueil général des opéras représentés par l'Académie royale de musique depuis son établissement.* 3 vols. Paris: Christophe Ballard, 1703–45; Geneva: Slatkine, 1971.

Quinault, Philippe. *Livrets d'opéra.* Ed. Buford Norman. 2 vols. Toulouse: Société de litté-ratures classiques, 1999.

Regnard, Jean-François. *Oeuvres complètes.* Paris: Didot aîné, 1823.

Scudéry, Madeleine de. *Artamène ou le Grand Cyrus.* Paris, 1649–53; Slatkine, 1972.

———. *The Story of Sapho.* Translated and with an introduction by Karen Newman. Chicago: University of Chicago Press, 2003.

Segrais, Jean Regnault de. *"Relation de l'isle imaginaire* et *l'histoire de la Princesse de Paphlagonie."* In *Oeuvres diverses.* Amsterdam: F. Changuion, 1723.

SOURCES AFTER 1800

Abbate, Carolyn. *In Search of Opera.* Princeton: Princeton University Press, 2001.

Abraham, Claude. *On the Structure of Molière's Comédies-ballets.* Biblio 17, 19. Paris: Papers on French Seventeenth-Century Literature, 1984.

Adam, Antoine. *Histoire de la littérature française au XVIIe siècle.* 5 vols. Paris: Del Duca, 1962.

———. *Les libertins au XVIIe siècle.* Paris: Buchet-Chastel, 1964.

Adhémar, Hélène, and René Huyghe. *Watteau, sa vie, son oeuvre.* Paris: Pierre Tisné, 1950.

Albert, Maurice. *Les théâtres de la foire, 1770–1789.* 1900; New York: Lenox Hill, 1970.

Alm, Irene. "Dances from the 'Four corners of the earth': Exoticism in Seventeenth-Century Venetian Opera." In *Musica franca: Essays in Honor of Frank A. D'Accone,* ed. Irene Alm, Alyson McLamore, and Colleen Reardon, 233–58. Stuyvesant, NY: Pendragon Press, 1996.

———. "Theatrical Dance in Seventeenth-Century Venetian Opera." Ph.D. diss., Uni-versity of California, Berkeley, 1993.

Alter, Jean V. *L'esprit antibourgeois sous l'ancien régime.* Geneva: Droz, 1970.

Anderson, Benedict. *Imagined Communities: Reflections on the Origin and Spread of Nation-alism.* Rev. ed. London: Verso, 1991.

Anthony, James. *French Baroque Music from Beaujoyeulx to Rameau.* Rev. ed. Portland, OR: Amadeus Press, 1997.

———. "The French Opera-Ballet in the Early Eighteenth Century: Problems of Defi-nition and Classification." *Journal of the American Musicological Society* 18 (1965): 197–206.

———. "Lully's Airs—French or Italian?" *Musical Times* 128 (1987): 126–29.

———. "More Faces Than Proteus: Lully's *Ballet des Muses."* *Early Music* 15 (1987): 336–44.

———. "The Opera-Ballets of André Campra." Ph.D. diss., University of Southern California, 1964.

———. "Printed Editions of André Campra's *L'Europe galante*." *Musical Quarterly* 56 (1978): 54–73.

———. "Some Uses of the Dance in the French Opera-Ballet." *Recherches sur la musique française classique* 9 (1969): 75–90.

———. "Towards a Principal Source for Lully's Court Ballets: Foucault v. Philidor." *Recherches sur la musique française classique* 25 (1987): 77–104.

Antoine, Michel. "La monarchie absolue." In *The French Revolution and the Creation of Modern Political Culture*, ed. Keith Baker. Vol. 1: *The Political Culture of the Old Regime*. Oxford: Pergamon Press, 1987.

Apostolidès, Jean-Marie. *Le roi-machine: Spectacle et politique au temps de Louis XIV*. Paris: Minuit, 1981.

Astier, Régine. "Louis XIV, premier danseur." In *Sun King*, ed. David Lee Rubin, 73–102. Washington, D.C.: Folger Books, 1992.

———. "Pierre Beauchamp, the Illustrious Unknown Choreographer." Parts 1 and 2. *Dance Scope* 8 (1974): 32–42; 9 (1974–75): 30–45.

Atkinson, Geoffroy. *The Extraordinary Voyage in French Literature before 1700*. New York: Columbia University Press, 1920.

Attinger, Gustave. *L'esprit de la commedia dell'arte dans le théâtre français*. Paris: Librairie théatrale, 1950.

Auerbach, Nina. *Communities of Women*. Cambridge: Harvard University Press, 1978.

Auld, Louis. *The Lyric Art of Pierre Perrin, Founder of French Opera*. Musicological Studies, 42. Henryville, PA: Institute of Mediaeval Studies, 1986.

———. "The Unity of Molière's Comedy-Ballet." Ph.D. diss., Bryn Mawr, 1969.

Backer, Dorothy. *Precious Women*. New York: Basic Books, 1974.

Baker, Keith, ed. *The French Revolution and the Creation of Modern Political Culture*. Vol. 1: *The Political Culture of the Old Regime*. Oxford: Pergamon Press, 1987.

———. *Inventing the French Revolution: Essays on French Political Culture in the Eighteenth Century*. Cambridge: Cambridge University Press, 1990.

Bakhtin, Mikhail. "Discourse and the Novel." In *The Dialogic Imagination: Four Essays by M. M. Bakhtin*. Ed. Michael Holquist. Trans. Michael Holquist and Caryl Emerson. Austin: University of Texas Press, 1981.

———. *Problems of Dostoevsky's Poetics*. Ed. and trans. Caryl Emerson. Theory and History of Literature, 8. Minneapolis: University of Minnesota Press, 1984.

———. *Rabelais and His World*. Trans. Hélène Iswolsky. Boston: MIT Press, 1968; Bloomington: Indiana University Press, 1984.

Bannister, Mark. *Condé in Context: Ideological Change in Seventeenth-Century France*. Oxford: Legenda (European Humanities Research Centre, University of Oxford), 2000.

———. *Privileged Mortals: The French Heroic Novel, 1630–1660*. Oxford: Oxford University Press, 1983.

Barish, Jonas. *The Antitheatrical Prejudice*. Berkeley: University of California Press, 1981.

Barnes, Clifford. "The *Théâtre de la Foire* (Paris, 1697–1762), Its Music and Composers." Ph.D. diss., University of Southern California, 1965.

Barthélemy, Maurice. *André Campra, 1660–1744: Étude biographique et musicologique.* Paris: Picard, 1957; Arles: Actes sud, 1995.

Beard, Mary. *The Roman Triumph.* Boston: Belknap Press of Harvard University Press, 2007.

Beasely, Faith. *Revising Memory: Women's Fiction and Memoirs in Seventeenth-Century France.* New Brunswick: Rutgers University Press, 1990.

Beaussant, Philippe. *Louis XIV artiste.* Paris: Payot, 1999.

———. *Lully ou le musicien du soleil.* Paris: Gallimard, 1992.

———, and Patricia Bouchnot-Déchin. *Les plaisirs de Versailles: Théâtre et musique.* [Paris]: Fayard, 1996.

Beik, William. *Absolutism and Society in Seventeenth-Century France: State Power and Provincial Aristocracy in Languedoc.* Cambridge: Cambridge University Press, 1985.

Bell, David. "Recent Works on Early Modern French National Identity." *Journal of Modern History* 68 (1996): 84–113.

Benda, Frederick Joseph. "The Tradition of Menippean Satire in Varro, Lucian, Seneca and Erasmus." Ph.D. diss., University of Texas, Austin, 1979.

Bénichou, Paul. *Morales du grand siècle.* 1948; Paris: Gallimard, 1997.

Bevington, David. *Tudor Drama and Politics: A Critical Approach to Topical Meaning.* Cambridge: Harvard University Press, 1968.

Bevington, David, and Peter Holbrook. *The Politics of the Stuart Court Masque.* Cambridge: Cambridge University Press, 1998.

Bianconi, Lorenzo, and Thomas Walker. "Production, Consumption, and Political Function of Seventeenth-Century Opera." *Early Music History* 4 (1984): 209–96.

Biet, Christine. *Les miroirs du soleil: Louis XIV et ses artistes.* Decouvertes, 58. Paris: Gallimard, 2000.

Birberick, Anne L. *Reading Undercover: Audience and Authority in Jean de La Fontaine.* Lewisburg: Bucknell University Press, 1998.

Bitton, Davis. *The French Nobility in Crisis, 1560–1640.* Stanford: Stanford University Press, 1969.

Blanc, André. *Le théâtre de Dancourt.* Paris: Librairie Honoré Champion, 1977.

Blanning, T. C. W. *The Culture of Power and the Power of Culture: Old-Regime Europe, 1660–1789.* Oxford: Oxford University Press, 2002.

Bloechl, Olivia A. *Native American Song at the Frontiers of Early Modern Music.* Cambridge: Cambridge University Press, 2008.

Bluche, François. *Louis XIV.* Paris: Fayard, 1986.

Bohanan, Donna. *Crown and Nobility in Early Modern France.* Houndmills, Basingstoke, Hampshire: Palgrave Macmillan, 2001.

Börsch-Supan, Helmut. *Antoine Watteau, 1684–1721.* Cologne: Könemann, 2000.

Boucher, Thierry. "Un haut lieu de l'Opéra de Lully: la salle de spectacles du château de Saint-Germain-en-Laye." In *Jean-Baptiste Lully: Congress Report from the 1987 meeting in Heidelberg and Saint-German-en-Laye,* ed. Herbert Schneider and Jérôme de La Gorce, 457–67. Laaber, Germany: Laaber Verlag, 1990.

Brenner, Clarence D. *The* Théâtre Italien: *Its Repertory, 1716–1793.* University of California Publications in Modern Philology, 63. Berkeley: University of California Press, 1963.

Bridgeman, Nanie. "L'aristocratie française et le ballet de cour." *Cahiers de l'Association internationale des études français* 11 (1959): 9–21.

Brockett, O. G. "The Fair Theatres of Paris in the Eighteenth Century: The Undermining of the Classical Ideal." In *Classical Drama and Its Influence*, ed. Michael John Anderson. New York: Barnes & Noble, 1965.

Brooks, William. "Louis XIV's Dismissal of the Italian Actors: The Episode of *La fausse prude.*" *Modern Language Review* 91 (1996): 840–47.

———. "Lully and Quinault at Court and on the Public Stage, 1673–86." *Seventeenth-Century French Studies* 10 (1988): 101–21; supplementary note in *Seventeenth-Century French Studies* 11 (1989): 147–50.

———. "Seventeenth-Century Culture: Quinault and Lully Resurgent." *French Studies* 47 (1993): 17–19.

Bryson, Norman. *Word and Image: French Painting in the Ancien Régime.* Cambridge: Cambridge University Press, 1981.

Burgess, Geoffrey. "Ritual in the *Tragédie en musique:* From Lully's *Cadmus et Hermione* (1673) to Rameau's *Zoroastre* (1749)." Ph.D. diss., Cornell University, 1999.

Burke, Peter. *The Fabrication of Louis XIV.* New Haven: Yale University Press, 1992.

———. *The Historical Anthropology of Early Modern Italy.* Cambridge: Cambridge University Press, 1987.

———. *Popular Culture in Early Modern Europe.* New York: Harper & Row, 1978.

Cahuet, Albéric. *La liberté du théâtre.* Paris: Chevalier-Maresq, 1902.

Cairncross, John. *Molière: Bourgeois et libertin.* Paris: Nizet, 1963.

Calame, Alexandre. *Regnard: Sa vie et son oeuvre.* Paris: Presses universitaires de France, 1960.

Calhoun, Craig, ed. *Habermas and the Public Sphere.* Cambridge: MIT Press, 1992.

Camesasca, Ettore. *L'opera completa di Watteau.* Milan: Rizzoli, 1968. Rev. ed., 1983. Translated as *The Complete Paintings of Watteau.* New York: H. N. Abrams, 1971.

Campa, Cecilia. "The *Théâtre italien:* Parody and the *Querelles* of the Early Eighteenth Century." *Nuova rivista musicale italiana* 23, no. 3 (1989): 342–77.

Campardon, E. *Les Comédiens italiens du roi de la troupe italienne pendant les deux dernières siècles.* 2 vols. Paris, 1880; Geneva: Slatkine, 1970.

Campbell, Mildred, ed. *The* Utopia *of Sir Thomas More, including Roper's* Life of More *and* Letters of More and His Daughter Margaret. Princeton, NJ: D. Van Nostrand, 1947.

Canova-Green, Marie-Claude. "Ballet et comédie-ballet sous Louis XIV ou l'illusion de la fête." *Papers on French Seventeenth-Century Literature* 17 (1990): 253–62.

———, ed. *Benserade: Ballets pour Louis XIV.* 2 vols. Toulouse: Société de littératures classiques, 1997.

———. "Dances and Ritual: The *Ballet des nations* at the Court of Louis XIII." *Society for Renaissance Studies* 9 (1995): 395–403.

———. *La politique-spectacle au grand siècle: les rapports franco-anglais.* Biblio 17, 76. Paris: Papers on French Seventeenth-Century Literature, 1993.

———, and Francesca Chiarelli, eds. *The Influence of Italian Entertainments on Sixteenth- and Seventeenth-Century Music Theatre in France, Savoy, and England.* Lewiston, NY: Mellen Press, 2000.

Censer, Jack R. *The French Press in the Age of Enlightenment.* London: Routledge, 1994.

Chae, Donald B. "Music, Festival, and Power in Louis XIV's France: Court Divertissements and the Musical Construction of Sovereign Authority and Noble Identity,
1661–1674." Ph.D. diss., University of Chicago, 2003.

Chaline, Olivier. *Le règne de Louis XIV.* Paris: Flammarion, 2005.

Charbonnel, J.-L. *La pensée italienne et le courant libertin.* Paris: Champion, 1919.

Chartier, Roger. *The Cultural Origins of the French Revolution.* Trans. Lydia G. Cochrane.
Durham: Duke University Press, 1991.

Chaussinand-Nogaret, Guy. *The French Nobility in the Eighteenth Century.* Trans. William
Doyle. Cambridge: Cambridge University Press, 1985.

Christout, Marie-Françoise. *Le ballet de cour au XVIIe siècle.* Geneva: Minkoff, 1987.

———. *Le ballet de cour de Louis XIV, 1643–1672: Mises en scène.* Paris: Picard, 1967.

———. "Baptiste, interprète des ballets de cour." In *Jean-Baptiste Lully: Congress Report
from the 1987 meeting in Heidelberg and Saint-German-en-Laye,* ed. Jérôme de La Gorce
and Herbert Schneider, 209–22. Laaber: Laaber Verlag, 1990.

Cioranescu, Alexandre. *Le masque et le visage: Du baroque espagnol au classicisme français.*
Geneva: Droz, 1986.

Coeyman, Barbara. "Opera and Ballet in Seventeenth-Century French Theaters: Case
Studies of the Salle des machines and the Palais Royal Theater." In *Opera in Context:
Essays on Historical Staging from the Late Renaissance to the Time of Puccini,* ed. Mark
A. Radice, 37–71. Portland, OR: Amadeus, 1998.

———. "Theatres for Opera and Ballet during the Reigns of Louis XIV and Louis XV."
Early Music 18 (1990): 22–37.

———. "Walking through Lully's Opera Theatre in the Palais Royal," 216–42.

Cohen, Sarah R. "Antoine Watteau's 'Fête galante' and Its Relationship to Early
Eighteenth-Century Dance." Ph.D. diss., Yale University, 1988.

———. *Art, Dance and the Body in French Culture.* Cambridge: Cambridge University
Press, 2000.

———. "Un bal continuel: Watteau's Cythera Paintings and Aristocratic Dancing in the
1710s." *Art History* 17 (1994): 160–81.

———. "Body as 'Character' in Early Eighteenth-Century French Art and Performance." *Art Bulletin* 78 (September 1996): 454–66.

Colton, Judith. *The Parnasse François: Titon du Tillet and the Origins of the Monument to
Genius.* New Haven: Yale University Press, 1979.

Constant, Jean-Marie. *La noblesse française aux XVIe et XVIIe siècles.* Paris: Hachette,
1994.

Cook, Susan, and Judy Tsou. *Cecilia Reclaimed: Feminist Approaches to Music.* Urbana:
University of Illinois Press, 1993.

Cornette, Joël. *Absolutisme et lumières, 1652–1783.* Paris: Hachette, 1993. 4th ed., 2005.

———, ed. *La France de la monarchie absolue.* Paris: Seuil, 1997.

———. *Le roi de guerre: Essai sur la souveraineté dans la France du Grand Siècle.* Paris:
Payot et Rivages, 1993.

Cosandey, Fanny, and Robert Descimon. *L'absolutisme en France.* Paris: Seuil, 2002.

Cottret, Monique. *La vie politique en France aux XVIe, XVIIe, et XVIIIe siècles.* Paris:
Ophoys, 1991.

Couvreur, Manuel. "La collaboration de Quinault et Lully avant la *Psyché* de 1671." *Recherches sur la musique française classique* 27 (1992): 9–34.

———. *Jean-Baptiste Lully: Musique et dramaturgie au service du prince*. Paris: Marc Vokar Éditeur, 1992.

Cowart, Georgia. "Carnival in Venice or Protest in Paris: Louis XIV and the Politics of Subversion at the Paris Opéra." *Journal of the American Musicological Society* 54 (2001): 265–302.

———, ed. *French Musical Thought, 1600–1800*. Ann Arbor: UMI Press, 1989; Rochester: University of Rochester Press, 1990.

———. "Inventing the Arts: Changing Critical Language in the *Ancien Régime*." In *French Musical Thought, 1600–1800*, ed. Georgia Cowart, 212–38. Ann Arbor: UMI Press, 1989; Rochester: University of Rochester Press, 1990.

———. "Lully *enjoué: Galanterie* in Seventeenth-Century France." In *Actes de Baton Rouge*, ed. Selma A. Zebouni. Biblio 17, 25 (1986): 35–51.

———. "Of Women, Sex and Folly: Opera under the Old Regime." *Cambridge Opera Journal* 6 (1994): 205–20.

———. *The Origins of Modern Musical Criticism: French and Italian Music, 1600–1750*. Ann Arbor: UMI Research Press, 1981.

———. "Sense and Sensibility in Eighteenth-Century Musical Thought." *Acta Musicologica* 56 (1984): 251–66.

———. "Watteau's *Pilgrimage to Cythera* and the Subversive Utopia of the Opera-Ballet." *Art Bulletin* 83 (2001): 460-78.

Crow, Thomas. *Painters and Public Life in Eighteenth-Century Paris*. New Haven: Yale University Press, 1985.

Culpin, David. "*Raillerie, honnêteté*, and 'les grands sujets': Cultured Conflict in Seventeenth-Century France." In *Culture and Conflict in Seventeenth-Century France and Ireland*, ed. Sarah Alyn Stacey and Véronique Desnain. Portland, OR: Four Courts Press, 2004.

Dacier, Emile, Albert Vuaflart, and J. Herrold. *Jean de Jullienne et les graveurs de Watteau au XVIIIe siècle*. 4 vols. Paris: Imprimerie nationale pour la Societé pour l'étude de la gravure française, 1921–29.

Darnton, Robert. *The Literary Underground of the Old Regime*. Cambridge: Harvard University Press, 1982.

Dartois-Lapeyre, Françoise. "L'opéra-ballet et la cour de France." *Dix-huitième siècle* 17 (1985): 209–19.

Daston, Lorraine, and Katherine Park. "The Hermaphrodite and the Orders of Nature: Sexual Ambiguity in Early Modern France." *Gay and Lesbian Quarterly* 1 (1995): 419–38.

Davis, Nathalie Zemon. *Les cultures du peuple*. Paris: Aubier, 1979.

———. *Society and Culture in Early Modern France*. Stanford: Stanford University Press, 1975.

De Baecque, Antoine. *Les éclats du rire. La culture des rieurs au XVIIIe siècle*. Paris: Calmann-Lévy, 2000.

———. "Les éclats du rire: Le Régiment de la Calotte, ou les stratégies aristocratiques de la gaieté française (1702–1752)." *Annales: Histoire, sciences sociales* 3 (1997): 477–511.

Debord, Guy. *The Society of the Spectacle.* Trans. Donald Nicholson-Smith. New York: Zone Books, 1995.

Defaux, Gérard. *Molière et les métamorphoses du comique: de la comédie morale au triomphe de la folie.* Lexington, KY: French Forum, 1980. 2nd ed. Paris: Klinksieck, 1992.

DeJean, Joan. *Ancients against Moderns.* Chicago: University of Chicago Press, 1997.

———. *The Essence of Style: How the French Invented High Fashion, Fine Food, Chic Cafés, Style, Sophistication, and Glamour.* New York: Free Press, 2005.

———. *Fictions of Sappho, 1546–1937.* Chicago: University of Chicago Press, 1989.

———. *Libertine Strategies: Freedom and the Novel in Seventeenth-Century France.* Columbus: Ohio State University Press, 1981.

———. *Tender Geographies: Women and the Origins of the Novel in France.* New York: Columbia University Press, 1991.

Démoris, René. "Les fêtes galantes chez Watteau et dans le roman contemporain." *Dix-huitième siècle* 3 (1971): 337–57.

Denis, Delphine. *Le Parnasse galant: Institution d'une catégorie littéraire au XVIIᵉ siècle.* Paris: Champion, 2001.

Denis, Jacques-François. *Sceptiques ou libertins de la première moitié du XVIIe siècle.* Geneva: Slatkine, 1970.

Dewald, Jonathan. *Aristocratic Experience and the Origins of Modern Culture: France, 1570–1715.* Berkeley: University of California Press, 1993.

———. *The European Nobility, 1400–1800.* Cambridge: Cambridge University Press, 1996.

Dubost, Jean. *La France italienne, XIVe au XVIIe siècle.* Paris: Aubier, 1997.

Du Crest, Sabine. *Des fêtes à Versailles: Les divertissements de Louis XIV.* Paris: Aux Amateurs de Livres, 1990.

Ducrot, Ariane. "Les Représentations de l'Académie de musique à Paris au temps de Louis XIV (1671–1715)." *Recherches sur la musique française classique* 10 (1970): 19–55.

Dufourcq, Norbert, ed. *La musique à la cour de Louis XIV et de Louis XV d'après les mémoires de Sourches et Luynes: 1681–1758.* La vie musicale en France sous les rois Bourbons, 17. Paris: A. et J. Picard, 1970.

Du Gérard, N. B. *Tables alphabétiques et chronologiques des pièces représentées sur l'ancien Théâtre italien.* Paris, 1750; Geneva: Slatkine, 1970.

Duggan, Anne E. *Salonnières, Furies, and Fairies: The Politics of Gender and Cultural Change in Absolutist France.* Newark: University of Delaware Press, 2005.

Duhamel, Jean-Marie. *La musique dans la ville de Lully à Rameau.* Lille: Presses universitaires de Lille, 1994.

Duindam, Jeroen. *Myths of Power: Norbert Elias and the Early Modern European Court.* Trans. Lorri S. Granger and Gerard T. Moran. Amsterdam: Amsterdam University Press, 1994.

Dunlop, Ian. *Louis XIV.* New York: St. Martin's Press, 1999.

Dupont, Paul. *Un poète philosophe au commencement du XVIIIe siècle: Houdar de la Motte.* Paris: Hachette, 1898.

Duranton, Henri. "La très joyeuse et très véridique histoire du Régiment de la Calotte." *Dix-huitième siècle* 33 (2001): 399–417.

Durosoir, Georgie. *L'air de cour en France, 1571–1655.* Liège: Pierre Mardaga, 1991.

———. *Les ballets de la cour de France au XVIIe siècle, ou les fantaisies et les splendeurs du baroque*. Geneva: Papillon, 2004.

———. "Pastorales avec musique et pastorals en musique en France au milieu du XVIIe siècle." In *Théâtre et musique au XVIIe siècle*, ed. Charles Mazouer, 234–48. Paris: Klinksieck, 1994.

Duval, Sophie, and Marc Martinez. *La satire: Littératures françaises et anglaises*. Paris: Armand Colin, 2000.

Eisenstein, Elizabeth L. *Grub Street Abroad: Aspects of the French Cosmopolitan Press from the Age of Louis XIV to the French Revolution*. Oxford: Clarendon Press, 1992.

Elias, Norbert. *The Court Society*. Trans. Edmund Jephcott. Oxford: Basil Blackwell, 1983.

———. *The History of Manners: The Civilizing Process*. Trans. Edmund Jephcott. New York: Urizen Books, 1978.

———. *Power and Civility*. Trans. Edmund Jephcott. New York: Pantheon, 1982.

Elliott, John Huxtable, and L. W. B. Brockliss, eds. *The World of the Favourite*. New Haven: Yale University Press, 1999.

Ellis, Harold A. *Boulainvilliers and the French Monarchy: Aristocratic Politics in Early Eighteenth-Century France*. Ithaca: Cornell University Press, 1988.

Ellis, Meredith. "Inventory of the Dances of Jean-Baptiste Lully." *Recherches sur la musique française classique* 9 (1969): 21–55.

Elmarsafy, Ziad. *Freedom, Slavery, and Absolutism*. Lewisburg: Bucknell University Press, 2003.

Fabre, Daniel. *Carnaval ou la fête à l'envers*. Paris: Gallimard, 1992.

Fader, Donald. "The 'Cabale du Dauphin,' Campra, and Italian Comedy: The Courtly Politics of French Musical Patronage around 1700." *Music and Letters* 86 (2005): 380–413.

———. "The *Honnête homme* as Music Critic: Taste, Rhetoric, and *Politesse* in the Seventeenth-Century Reception of Italian Music." *Journal of Musicology* 20 (2003): 3–44.

Fajon, Robert. "La comédie-ballet: fille et heritière du ballet de cour." *Littératures classiques* 21 (1994): 207–20.

———. *Esthétique de l'identité dans le théâtre français (1550–1680): Le déguisement et ses avatars*. Geneva: Droz, 1988.

———. *Molière*. Paris: Bordas, 1990.

———. *L'opéra à Paris: du Roi soleil à Louis le bien-aimé*. Paris: Slatkine, 1984.

Farge, Arlette. *Subversive Words: Public Opinion in Eighteenth-Century France*. Trans. Rosemary Morris. University Park: Pennsylvania State University Press, 1995.

Feldman, Martha. *Opera and Sovereignty: Transforming Myths in Eighteenth-Century Italy*. Chicago: University of Chicago Press, 2007.

Ferrier-Caverivière, Nicole. *L'image de Louis XIV dans la littérature française de 1660 à 1715*. Paris: Presses universitaires de France, 1981.

Finch, Robert. *The Sixth Sense: Individualism in French Poetry, 1686–1760*. Toronto: University of Toronto Press, 1966.

Fleck, Stephen H. *Music, Dance, and Laughter: Comic Creation in Molière's Comedy-Ballets*. Biblio 17, 88. Paris: Papers on French Seventeenth-Century Literature, 1995.

Fleisher, Martin. *Radical Reform and Political Persuasion in the Life and Writings of Thomas More*. Geneva: Droz, 1973.

Foigny, Gabriel de. *La terre australe connue*. Ed. Pierre Ronzeaud. Société des textes français modernes, 191. Paris: Aux Amateurs de livres, 1990.

Fontaine, Léon. *La censure dramatique sous l'ancien régime*. Lyon: Rey, 1892.

Forestier, Georges. *Jean Racine*. Paris: Gallimard, 2006.

———. *Le théâtre dans le théâtre sur la scène française du XVIIe siècle*. Geneva: Droz, 1981.

Foucault, Michel. *Les mots et les choses: Une archéologie des sciences humaines*. Paris: Gallimard, 1966.

———. *L'usage des plaisirs*. Paris: Gallimard, 1984.

Fourcaud, Louis de. "Antoine Watteau: scènes et figures galantes." *Revue de l'art ancien et moderne* 16 (1904): 341–56; 17 (1905): 105–20.

———. "Antoine Watteau: scènes et figures théâtrales." *Revue de l'art ancien et moderne* 15 (1904): 135–50, 193–213.

Franko, Mark. *Dance as Text: Ideologies of the Baroque Body*. Cambridge: Cambridge University Press, 1993.

Freeman, Robert S. *Opera without Drama: Currents of Change in Italian Opera, 1675 to 1725*. Ann Arbor: UMI Research Press, 1981.

Fried, Michael. *Absorption and Theatricality: Painting and Beholder in the Age of Diderot*. Berkeley: University of California Press, 1980.

Friedrich, Paul. *The Meaning of Aphrodite*. Chicago: University of Chicago Press, 1978.

Frost, M. *L'opposition à l'absolutisme dans la littérature française au temps de Louis XIV*. Paris: Sorbonne, 1954.

Fumaroli, Marc. *L'école du silence: Le sentiment des images au XVIIe siècle*. Paris: Flammarion, 1994.

———. *L'inspiration du poète du Poussin*. Paris: Editions de la Réunion des musées nationaux, 1989.

———. "Nicolas Fouquet, the Favourite Manqué." In *The World of the Favourite*, ed. J. H. Elliott and L. W. B. Brockliss, 239–55. New Haven: Yale University Press, 1999.

———. *Le poète et le roi: Jean de La Fontaine en son siècle*. Paris: Fallois, 1997.

———. "Politique et poétique de Venus: L'*Adone* de Marino et l'*Adonis* de La Fontaine." *Le Fablier, revue des Amis de Jean de La Fontaine* 5 (1993): 11–16.

———. *Quand l'Europe parlait français*. Paris: Fallois, 2001.

Gallois, Jean. *Jean-Baptiste Lully, ou, La naissance de la tragédie*. Geneva, Switzerland: Papillon, 2001.

Gambelli, Delia, and Letizia Norci Cagiano. *Le théâtre en musique et son double (1600–1762): Actes du colloque "L'Académie de musique, Lully, l'opéra et la parodie de l'opéra."* Colloques, congrès et conferences sur le Classicisme, 5. Paris: Champion, 2005.

Gay, Peter. *The Enlightenment, an Interpretation: The Rise of Modern Paganism*. New York: Knopf, 1966.

Garlick, Fiona. "Dances to Evoke the King: The Majestic Genre Chez Louis XIV." *Dance Research: The Journal of the Society for Dance Research* 15 (Winter, 1997): 10–34.

Gebauer, Gunter, and Christoph Wulf. *Mimesis: Culture—Art—Society*. Trans. Don Renau. Berkeley: University of California Press, 1995.

Gelbart, Nina Rattner. *Feminine and Opposition Journalism in Old Regime France: Le Journal des Dames*. Berkeley: University of California Press, 1987.

Gethner, Perry. "Le divertissement dans la comedie de Dancourt." *Littératures classiques* 21 (1994): 103-12.

Gibson, Wendy. *Women in Seventeenth-Century France*. New York: St. Martin's Press, 1989.

Giesey, Ralph. *Cérémoniale et puissance souveraine: France, XVe-XVIIIe siècles*. Paris: Armand Colin, 1987.

Giraud, M. "Tendances humanitaires à la fin du règne de Louis XIV." *Revue historique* 209 (1953): 217–37.

Giuliani, Elizabeth. "Le public de l'Opéra de Paris de 1750 à 1760." *International Review of the Aesthetics and Sociology of Music* 8 (1977): 159–81.

Goodman, Dena. "Public Sphere and Private Life: Toward a Synthesis of Current Historiographical Approaches to the Old Regime." *History and Theory* 31 (1992): 1–20.

———. *The Republic of Letters: A Cultural History of the French Enlightenment*. Ithaca: Cornell University Press, 1994.

Gordon-Seifert, Catherine. "Heroism Undone: The Erotic Manuscript Parodies of Lully/Quinault Tragédies lyriques." In *Music, Sensation, and Sensuality*, ed. Linda Austern, 137–66. New York: Routledge, 2002.

———. "'Precious' Eroticism and Hidden Morality: Salon Culture and the Mid-Seventeenth-Century French Air." In *Eros and Euterpe: Eroticism in Early Modern Music*, ed. Massimo Ossi. Oxford: Oxford University Press, forthcoming.

———. "Strong Men—Weak Women: Gender Representation and the Influence of Lully's 'Operatic Style' on French *Airs sérieuses* (1650–1700)." In *Musical Voices of Early Modern Women: Many-Headed Melodies*, ed. Thomasin LaMay, 135–67. Aldershot: Ashgate, 2005.

Goubert, Pierre. *Louis XIV et vingt millions de Français*. Paris: Fayard, 1966. Translated by Anne Carter as *Louis XIV and Twenty Million Frenchmen*. New York: Pantheon Books, 1970.

Grasselli, Margaret Morgan, François Moureau, Pierre Rosenberg, et al., eds. *Watteau: 1684–1721*. Paris: Éditions de la Réunion des musées nationaux, 1984.

Greenblatt, Stephen. *Renaissance Self-fashioning: From More to Shakespeare*. Chicago: University of Chicago Press, 1981.

Grigson, Geoffrey. *The Goddess of Love: The Birth, Triumph, Death, and Return of Aphrodite*. London: Constable, 1976.

Grinberg, Martine. "Carnaval et société urbain, XIVe–XVIe siècles: le royaume dans la ville." *Ethnologie française* 4, no. 3 (1974): 215–44.

Grout, Donald J. "Music of the Italian Theatre at Paris, 1682–97." *Papers of the American Musicological Society* (1941): 158–70.

———. "The Origins of the Comic Opera." Ph.D. diss., Harvard University, 1939.

———. "Seventeenth-Century Parodies of French Opera." *Musical Quarterly* 27 (1941): 211–19, 514–26.

———. "Some Forerunners of the Lully Opera." *Music and Letters* 22 (1941): 1–25.

Grubb, James S. "When Myths Lose Power: Four Decades of Venetian Historiography." *Journal of Modern History* 38 (1986): 43–94.

Guillumette, Doris. *La libre pensée dans l'oeuvre de Tristan L'Hermite*. Paris: Nizet, 1972.

Gunn, J. A. W. *Queen of the World: Opinion in the Public Life of France from the Renaissance to the Revolution*. Studies on Voltaire and the Eighteenth Century, 328. Oxford: Voltaire Foundation, 1995.

Gustafson, Bruce. *A Thematic Locator for the Works of Jean-Baptiste Lully*. New York: Broude, 1989.

Habermas, Jürgen. *The Structural Transformation of the Public Sphere: An Inquiry into a Category of Bourgeois Society*. Trans. Thomas Burger. Cambridge: MIT Press, 1989.

Hall, Gaston. *Molière's* Bourgeois gentilhomme: *Context and Stagecraft*. Modern Language series. Durham, England: Durham Modern Language Series, 1990.

Harris-Warrick, Rebecca. "Ballroom Dancing at the Court of Louis XIV." *Early Music* 15 (1986): 41–49.

———. "Contexts for Choreographies: Notated dances set to the music of Jean-Baptiste Lully," *Jean-Baptiste Lully: Congress Report from the 1987 Meeting in Heidelberg and Saint-German-en-Laye*. Laaber: Laaber Verlag, 1990.

———. "Magnificence in Motion: Stage Musicians in Lully's Ballets and Operas." *Cambridge Opera Journal* 6 (1994): 189–203.

———. "*La mariée:* The History of a French Court Dance." In *Jean-Baptiste Lully and the Music of the French Baroque: Essays in Honor of James R. Anthony*, ed. John Hajdu Heyer, 239–57. Cambridge: Cambridge University Press, 1989.

———. "The Phrase Structures of Lully's Dance Music." In *Lully Studies*, ed. John Hajdu Heyer, 32–56. Cambridge: Cambridge University Press, 2000.

———. "Recovering the Lullian Divertissement." In *Dance and Music in French Baroque Theatre: Sources and Interpretations*, ed. Sarah McCleave, 55–80. London: University of London, 1998.

———. "Staging Venice." *Cambridge Opera Journal* 15 (2003): 297–316.

Harris-Warrick, Rebecca, and Carol G. Marsh. *Musical Theater at the Court of Louis XIV: The Example of "Le Mariage de la Grosse Cathos."* Cambridge: Cambridge University Press, 1994.

Harth, Erica. *Ideology and Culture in Seventeenth-Century France*. Ithaca: Cornell University Press, 1983.

Hatin, Eugène. *Gazettes de Hollande et la presse clandestine aux XVIIe et XVIIIe siècles*. Paris: R. Pincebourde, 1865; Geneva: Slatkine, 1964.

Haymann, Emmanuel. *Lulli*. Paris: Flammarion, 1991.

Hazard, Paul. *The European Mind, 1680–1715*. Trans. J. Lewis May. London: Hollis and Carter, 1953.

Head, Matthew. *Orientalism, Masquerade, and Mozart's Turkish Music*. London: Royal Music Association, 2000.

Heartz, Daniel. *Music in European Capitals: The Galant Style, 1720–1780*. New York: Norton, 2003.

———. "Opéra Comique and the Théâtre Italien from Watteau to Fragonard." In *Music in the Classic Period: Essays in Honor of Barry S. Brook*. Stuyvesant, NY: Pendragon Press, 1995.

Heller, Wendy. *Emblems of Eloquence: Opera and Women's Voices in Seventeenth-Century Venice*. Berkeley: University of California Press, 2003.

———. "Dancing Desire on the Venetian Stage." *Cambridge Opera Journal* 15 (2003): 281–95.

Hennet, Léon. *Le Régiment de La Calotte*. Paris: Librairie des bibliophiles, 1886.

Henshall, Nicholas. *The Myth of Absolutism: Change and Continuity in Early Modern European Monarchy*. London: Longman, 1992.

Heyer, John Hajdu, ed. *Jean-Baptiste Lully and the Music of the French Baroque: Essays in Honor of James R. Anthony*. Cambridge: Cambridge University Press, 1989.

———, ed. *Lully Studies*. Cambridge: Cambridge University Press, 2000.

Hilgar, Marie-France. "Théatricalité du travissement au XVIIe siècle." *XVIIe siècle* (January/March 1981): 53–62.

Hill, John Walter. *Baroque Music: Music in Western Europe, 1580–1750*. New York: W.W. Norton, 2005.

Hilton, Wendy. *Dance and Music of Court and Theater: Selected Writings of Wendy Hilton*. Dance and Music Series, 10. Stuyvesant, NY: Pendragon Press, 1997.

———. "A Dance for Kings: The Seventeenth-Century French Courante." *Early Music* 5 (1977): 161–72.

———. *Dance of Court and Theater: The French Noble Style, 1690–1725*. Princeton: Princeton Book Publishers, 1981.

———. "Dances to Music by Jean-Baptiste Lully." *Early Music* 14 (1986): 51–63.

Hobson, Marian. *The Object of Art: The Theory of Illusion in Eighteenth-Century France*. Cambridge: Cambridge University Press, 1982.

Hoffmann, Kathryn. *Society of Pleasures: Interdisciplinary Readings in Pleasure and Power during the Reign of Louis XIV*. New York: St. Martin's Press, 1997.

Hogwood, Christopher. *Music at Court*. London: Folio Society, 1977.

Hourcade, Philippe. "Louis XIV travesti." *Cahiers de littérature du XVIIe siècle* 6 (1984): 257–71.

———. *Mascarades et ballets au grand siècle (1643–1715)*. Paris: Éditions Desjonquères/Centre national de la danse, 2002.

Howard, Patricia. "The Influence of the *Précieuses* on Content and Structure in Quinault's and Lully's *Tragédies lyriques*." *Acta Musicologica* 63 (1991): 57–72.

———. "Lully and the Ironic Convention." *Cambridge Opera Journal* 1 (1989): 139–53.

———. "The Positioning of Women in Quinault's World Picture." In *Jean-Baptiste Lully: Congress Report from the 1987 meeting in Heidelberg and Saint-German-en-Laye*, ed. Herbert Schneider and Jérôme de La Gorce, 193–99. Laaber, Germany: Laaber Verlag, 1990.

———. "Quinault, Lully, and the *Précieuses*: Images of Women in Seventeenth-Century France." In *Cecilia Reclaimed: Feminist Perspectives on Gender and Music*, ed. Susan C. Cook and Judy S. Tsou, 70–89. Urbana: University of Illinois Press, 1994.

Howarth, William D. *Molière: A Playwright and His Audience*. Cambridge: Cambridge University Press, 1982.

———, and Merlin Thomas. *Molière: Stage and Study. Essays in Honour of W. G. Moore*. Oxford: Clarendon Press, 1973.

Huppert, George. *Les Bourgeois Gentilshommes: An Essay on the Definition of Elites in Renaissance France*. Chicago: University of Chicago Press, 1977.

Ikor, Roger. *Molière double*. Paris: Presses universitaires de France, 1977.

Isherwood, Robert. *Farce and Fantasy: Popular Entertainment in Eighteenth-Century Paris*. New York: Oxford University Press, 1986.

————. *Music in the Service of the King: France in the Seventeenth Century*. Ithaca: Cornell University Press, 1973.

Jacob, Margaret. "The Mental Landscape of the Public Sphere: A European Perspective." *Eighteenth Century Studies* 28 (1994): 95–113.

Jeanneret, Michel. *Éros rebelle: Littérature et dissidence à l'âge classique*. Paris: Seuil, 2003.

Johnson, James H. *Listening in Paris: A Cultural History*. Berkeley: University of California Press, 1995.

Jones, Dorothy F. *Jean de Campistron: A Study of His Life and Work*. Romance Monographs, 32. University, MS: Romance Monographs, 1979.

Jouhaud, Christian. *Mazarinades: La Fronde des mots*. Paris: Aubier, 1985.

Jouanna, Arlette. *Le devoir de révolte: La noblesse française et la gestation de l'état moderne (1559–1661)*. Paris: Fayard, 1989.

Jullien, Adolphe. *La comédie et la galanterie au XVIIIe siècle*. Paris: E. Rouveyre, 1979.

Kaiser, Thomas E. "The Monarchy, Public Opinion, and the Subversions of Antoine Watteau." In *Antoine Watteau: Perspectives on the Artist and the Culture of His Time*, ed. Mary D. Sheriff. Newark: University of Delaware Press, 2006.

Kantorowicz, Ernst Hartwig. *The King's Two Bodies: A Study in Medieval Political Theology*. Princeton: Princeton University Press, 1957.

Kapp, Volker. "Benserade, librettiste de Lully et panégyriste du roi." In *Jean-Baptiste Lully: Congress Report from the 1987 meeting in Heidelberg and Saint-German-en-Laye*, ed. Jérôme de La Gorce and Herbert Schneider. Laaber: Laaber Verlag, 1990.

Kettering, Sharon. *French Society: 1689–1715*. Harlow, England: Longman, 2001.

————. *Patrons, Brokers, and Clients in Seventeenth-Century France*. Oxford: Oxford University Press, 1986.

Kinser, Sam. *Rabelais's Carnival: Text, Context, Metatext*. Berkeley: University of California Press, 1990.

Kintzler, Catherine. *Jean-Philippe Rameau: Splendeur et naufrage de l'esthétique du plaisir à l'âge classique*. Paris: Le Sycomore, 1983.

————. *Poétique de l'opéra français de Corneille à Rousseau*. Paris: Minerva, 1991.

Kirkness, W. John. *Le Français du Théâtre italien d'après le Recueil de Gherardi, 1681–1697*. Geneva: Droz, 1971.

Klaits, Joseph. *Printed Propaganda under Louis XIV: Absolute Monarchy and Public Opinion*. Princeton: Princeton University Press, 1976.

Knapper, Stephen. "The Master and the Mirror: Scaramouche and Molière." In *The Cambridge Companion to Molière*, ed. David Bradby and Andrew Calder, 37–56. Cambridge: Cambridge University Press, 2006.

Kramer, Lawrence. "Carnival, Cross-Dressing, and the Woman in the Mirror." In *Musicology and Difference*, ed. Ruth Solie, 305–25. Berkeley: University of California Press, 1993.

Lacroix, Paul. *The Eighteenth Century: Its Institutions, Customs, and Costumes*. New York: Ungar, 1963.

La Gorce, Jérôme de. "L'Académie royale de musique en 1704, d'après des documents inédits conservés dans les archives notariales." *Revue de musicologie* 65 (1979): 160–91.

———. *Berain dessinateur du Roi Soleil.* Paris: Herscher, 1986.

———. *Carlo Vigarani, intendant des plaisirs de Louis XIV.* Paris: Perrin/Etablissement public du musée et du domaine national de Versailles, 2005.

———. *De la naissance à la gloire: Louis XIV à Saint-Germain, 1632–82.* Saint-Germain-en-Laye: Chapelle du Château, Musée des Antiquités Nationales, 1988.

———. *Féeries d'opéra: Décors, machines et costumes en France, 1645–1765.* Paris: Caisse nationale des monuments historiques et des sites/Éditions du patrimoine, 1997.

———. "Guillaume-Louis Pecour: A Biographical Essay." Trans. Margaret McGowan. *The Journal of the Society for Dance Research* 8 (Autumn, 1990): 3-26.

———. "Jardins et décors d'opéras français sous Louis XIV." In *Jardins d'Opéra.* Paris: Bibliothèque nationale de France, 1995.

———. *Jean-Baptiste Lully.* Paris: Fayard, 2002.

———. *L'Opéra à Paris au temps de Louis XIV: Histoire d'un théâtre.* Paris: Desjonquères, 1992.

———. "Opéra et son public au temps de Louis XIV." *Bulletin de la Société de l'histoire de Paris et de l'île de France* 108 (1981): 27–46.

———. "L'opéra français à la cour de Louis XIV." *Revue de la Société d'histoire du théâtre* 35 (1983–84): 387–401.

———. "Un proche collaborateur de Lully: Philippe Quinault." *Dix-septième siècle* 161 (1998): 365–70.

———. "Quelques rapports entre les dessins d'opéras français du regne de Louis XIV et l'architecture, la sculpture et la peinture." In *Iconographie et arts du spectacle,* ed. La Gorce, 135–54. Paris: Klincksieck, 1996.

———. "Watteau à l'Opéra (1702)?" In *Antoine Watteau (1684–1721): The Painter, His Age, and His Legend,* ed. François Moureau and Margaret Morgan Grasselli, 11–16. Paris: Champion; Geneva: Slatkine, 1987.

La Gorce, Jérôme de, ed. *Lettres sur l'Opéra à l'abbé Dubos.* Suivies de *Description de la vie et moeurs, de l'exercice et l'état des filles de l'Opéra (c. 1694).* [Paris]: Cicero, 1993.

La Gorce, Jérôme de, and Herbert Schneider, eds. *Jean-Baptiste Lully: Congress Report from the 1987 meeting in Heidelberg and Saint-German-en-Laye.* Laaber: Laaber Verlag, 1990.

———. *Quellenstudien zu Jean-Baptiste Lully/L'oeuvre de Lully: Études des sources. Hommage à Lionel Sawkins.* Hildesheim: Georg Olms, 1999.

LaGrave, Henri. *Le théâtre et le public à Paris de 1715 à 1750.* Paris: Klinksieck, 1972.

Lajarte, Théodore de. *Bibliothèque musicale du Théâtre de l'Opéra: Catalogue historique, chronologique, anecdotique.* Paris, 1878. Hildesheim: Georg Olms, 1969.

La Laurencie, Lionel de. "André Campra, musicien profane." *L'année musicale* 3 (1913): 153–205.

———. "Notes sur la jeunesse d'André Campra." *Sammelbände der Internationalen Musikgesellschaft* 10 (1908–9): 159–258.

———. *"L'Orfeo nell'inferi* d'André Campra." *Revue de musicologie* 9 (1928): 129–33.

Lancaster, Henry Carrington. *A History of French Dramatic Literature*. Baltimore: Johns Hopkins University Press, 1945.

———. *Sunset: A History of Parisian Drama in the Last Years of Louis XIV, 1701–1715*. Baltimore: Johns Hopkins University Press, 1945.

———. *The Comédie française, 1680–1701: Plays, Actors, Spectators, Finances*. Baltimore: Johns Hopkins Press, 1941.

Lapouge, Gilles. *Le singe de la montre*. Paris: Flammarion, 1982.

———. *Utopie et civilisations*. Paris: Weber, 1973.

Launay, Denise. "Les airs italiens et français dans les ballets et les comédies-ballets." In *Jean-Baptiste Lully: Congress Report from the 1987 Meeting in Heidelberg and Saint-German-en-Laye*, ed. Jérôme de la Gorce and Herbert Schneider. Laaber: Laaber Verlag, 1990.

———. "Les ballets franco-italiens de Lully: Leur importance pour la formation de son style." *Ars Lyrica* 8 (1994): 105–22.

Lawrence, Francis L. *Molière: The Comedy of Unreason*. Tulane Studies in Romance Languages and Literature, 2. New Orleans: Tulane University, 1968.

Lawrenson, T. E. *The French Stage and Playhouse in the Seventeenth Century: A Study in the Advent of the Italian Order*. 2nd ed. New York: AMS Press, 1981.

Lefebvre, Joël. *Les fous et la folie en Allemagne pendant la Renaissance*. Paris: Klinksieck, 1968.

Leibacher-Ouvrard, Lise. *Libertinage et utopies sous le règne de Louis XIV*. Geneva: Droz, 1989.

———. "Sauvages et utopies (1676–1715): l'exotisme-alibi." *French Literature Series* 13 (1986): 1–12.

Leiner, Wolfgang, and Michael Griffiths. "Names in Francion." *Romance Notes* 15, no. 1 (1973): 445–53.

Leppert, Richard D. *Arcadia at Versailles. Noble Amateur Musicians and Their Musettes and Hurdy-gurdies at the French Court (c. 1660–1789)*. Amsterdam: Swets & Zeitlinger, 1978.

Lever, Maurice. *Les bûchers de Sodome*. Paris: Fayard, 1985.

———. *Le roman française au XVIIe siècle*. Presses universitaires de France, 1981.

———. *Le sceptre et la marotte: Histoire des fous de cour*. Paris: Fayard, 1983.

Levey, Michael. *From Rococo to Revolution: Major Trends in Eighteenth-Century Painting*. New York: Praeger, 1966.

———. "The Real Theme of Watteau's *Embarkation for Cythera*." *Burlington Magazine* 103 (1961): 180–85.

Levinson, André. "Notes sur le ballet au XVIIe siècle: Les danseurs de Lully." *La revue musicale* 6 (January 1925): 44–55.

Levron, Jacques. "Louis XIV's Courtiers." In *Louis XIV and Absolutism*, ed. Ragnhild Hatton. London: Macmillan, 1976.

Lévy, J. "Une vie inconnue d'Antoine Watteau." *Bulletin de la Société de l'histoire de l'art français* (1958): 175–203.

Little, Meredith Ellis, and Carol G. Marsh. *La Danse Noble: An Inventory of Dances and Sources*. Williamstown, MA: Broude Brothers, 1992.

Lossky, Andrew. *Louis XIV and the French Monarchy*. New Brunswick: Rutgers University Press, 1994.

Lougee, Carolyn. *Le Paradis des femmes: Women, Salons, and Social Stratification in Seventeenth-Century France*. Princeton: Princeton University Press, 1976.

Lough, John. *Paris Theatre Audiences in the Seventeenth and Eighteenth Centuries*. London: Oxford University Press, 1957. Reprint, 1982.

———. *Writer and Public in France: From the Middle Ages to the Present Day*. Oxford: Clarendon Press, 1978.

Louvat-Molozay, Bénédicte. *Théâtre et musique: Dramaturgie de l'insertion musicale dans le théâtre français (1550–1680)*. Paris: Champion, 2002.

Lowinsky, Edward E. *Cipriano de Rore's Venus Motet: Its Poetic and Pictorial Sources*. Provo, UT: College of Fine Arts and Communications, Brigham Young University, 1986.

Lukowski, Jerzy. *The European Nobility in the Eighteenth Century*. Houndmills, Basingstoke, Hampshire: Palgrave Macmillan, 2003.

MacKee, David Rice. *Simon Tyssot de Patot and the Seventeenth-Century Background of Critical Deism*. Baltimore: Johns Hopkins University Press; London: H. Milford, Oxford University Press, 1941.

Maclean, Ian. *Woman Triumphant: Feminism in French Literature, 1610–1652*. Oxford: Clarendon Press, 1977.

MacPherson, Harriet Dorothea. *Censorship under Louis XIV, 1661–1715: Some Aspects of Its Influence*. New York: Publications of the Institute of French Studies, 1929.

Malachy, Thérèse. *Molière. Les métamorphoses du carnaval*. Paris: Nizet, 1987.

Mandrou, Robert. *Louis XIV en son temps, 1661–1715*. Paris: Presses universitaires de France, 1973.

Mannheim, Karl, Louis Wirth, and Edward Shils. *Ideology and Utopia*. New York: Harcourt, Brace, 1936.

Manuel, Fritzie Prigohzy. *Utopian Thought in the Western World*. Cambridge, MA: Belknap Press, 1979.

Marin, Louis. *Le portrait du roi*. Paris: Minuit, 1981. Translated by Martha Houle as *Portrait of the King*. Theory and History of Literature 57. Minneapolis: University of Minnesota Press, 1988.

———. *Utopiques: jeux d'espaces*. Paris: Minuit, 1973.

Massip, Catherine. *L'art de bien chanter: Michel Lambert, 1610–1696*. Paris: Société française de musicologie, 1999.

———. "Michel Lambert and Jean-Baptiste Lully: The Stakes of a Collaboration." In *Jean-Baptiste Lully and the Music of the French Baroque: Essays in Honor of James R. Anthony*, ed. John Hajdu Heyer, 25–39. Cambridge: Cambridge University Press, 1989.

Masson, Paul-Marie. "*Les fêtes vénitiennes d'André Campra*." *Revue de musicologie* 16 (1932): 127–46.

Mazouer, Charles. *L'âge d'or d'influence espagnole: La France et l'Espagne à l'époque d'Anne d'Autriche, 1615–1666*. Mont-de-Marsan: Editions InterUniversitaires, 1991.

———. "Les comédiens italiens dans les ballets au temps de Mazarin." In *La France et l'Italie au temps de Mazarin: 15e Colloque du C.M.R. 17*, ed. J. Serroy, 319–29. Grenoble: Presses universitaires de Grenoble, 1986.

————. "Comédies-ballets." In *The Cambridge Companion to Molière*, ed. David Bradby and Andrew Calder, 107–20. Cambridge: Cambridge University Press, 2006.

————. *Molière et ses comédies-ballets*. Paris: Klinksieck, 1993.

McBride, Robert. "Ballet: A Neglected Key to Molière's Theater." *Dance Research* 2 (Spring 1984): 3–18.

————. *The Sceptical Vision of Molière: A Study in Paradox*. London: Macmillan, 1977.

————. *The Triumph of Ballet in Molière's Theatre*. Lewinston, NY: Edwin Mellen Press, 1992.

McCarthy, Gerry. *The Theatres of Molière*. London: Routledge, 2002.

McClary, Susan. *Feminine Endings: Music, Gender, and Sexuality*. Minneapolis: University of Minnesota Press, 1991.

————. "The Dragon Cart." Paper delivered at Case Western Reserve University, October 2006.

————. "Temporality and Ideology: Qualities of Motion in Seventeenth-Century French Music." *ECHO: A Music-Centered Journal* 2 (Fall 2000): 8–14.

McGowan, Margaret. *L'art du ballet de cour en France, 1581–1643*. Paris: Éditions du Centre national de la recherche scientifique, 1963. 2nd ed., 1978.

McLeod, Ken. "Judgment and Choice: Politics and Ideology in Early Eighteenth-Century Masques." Ph.D. diss., McGill University, 1997.

————. "Narrating a Nation: Venus on the Late Seventeenth-Century English Stage." *Journal of Seventeenth-Century Music* 11. http://www.sscm-jscm.org/jscm/vii/noi/mcleod.html. Accessed 2007.

McQuaide, Rosalie. "The Crozat Concerts, 1720–1727: A Study of Concert Life in Paris." Ph.D. diss., New York University, 1978.

Mélèse, Pierre. *Le théâtre et le public à Paris sous Louis XIV (1659–1715)*. Paris: Droz, 1934; Geneva: Slatkine, 1976.

Melton, James Van Horn. *Politics, Culture, and the Public Sphere in Enlightenment Europe*. Cambridge: Cambridge University Press, 2001.

————. *The Rise of the Public in Enlightenment Europe*. New Approaches to European History, 22. Cambridge: Cambridge University Press, 2001.

Melzer, Sara E., and Kathryn Norberg. *From Royal to the Republican Body: Incorporating the Political in Seventeenth- and Eighteenth-Century France*. Berkeley: University of California Press, 1998.

Merlin, Hélène. *Public et littérature en France au XVIIe siècle*. Paris: Les Belles Lettres, 1994.

Mettam, Roger. *Power and Faction in Louis XIV's France*. Oxford: Basil Blackwell, 1988.

Meunier, Mario. *Sappho, Anacréon et Anacréontiques*. Paris: Grasset, 1932.

Michael of Greece. *Louis XIV: The Other Side of the Sun*. Trans. Alan Sheridan. New York: Harper & Row, 1983.

Michel, Marianne Roland. *Watteau*. Paris: Flammarion, 1984.

Minois, Georges. *Censure et culture sous l'Ancien Régime*. Paris: Fayard, 1995.

Mirimonde, Albert P. de. *L'iconographie musicale sous les rois Bourbons: la musique dans les arts plastiques (XVIIe–XVIIIe siècles)*. Paris: Picard, 1975.

————. "Statues et emblèmes dans l'oeuvre de Watteau." *Revue du Louvre et des musées de France* 1 (1962): 11–20.

———. "Les sujets musicaux chez Antoine Watteau." *Gazette des beaux-arts* 58 (1961): 249–88.

Mirollo, James V. *Marino: Poet of the Marvelous*. New York: Columbia University Press, 1963.

Moine, Marie-Christine. *Les fêtes à la cour du Roi Soleil, 1653–1715*. Paris: F. Lanore, 1984.

Mongrédien, Georges. "Molière et Lully." *XVIIe siècle* 98–99 (1973): 3–15.

Moraud, Yves. *Masques et jeux dans le théâtre comique en France entre 1688 et 1730*. Paris: Champion, 1977.

Moriarty, Michael. *Taste and Ideology in Seventeenth-Century France*. Cambridge: Cambridge University Press, 1988.

Mornet, Daniel. *La pensée française au XVIIIe siècle*. Paris: Colin, 1926.

Motley, Mark. *Becoming a French Aristocrat: The Education of the Court Nobility, 1580–1715*. Princeton: Princeton University Press, 1990.

Moureau, François. "Les comédiens italiens et la cour de France (1664–1697)." *XVIIe siècle* 33 (1981): 63–81.

———. *De Gherardi à Watteau: Présence d'Arlequin sous Louis XIV*. Paris: Klinksieck, 1992.

———. "Iconographie théatrale." In *Watteau, 1684–1721*, ed. Margaret Morgan Grasselli, François Moureau, Pierre Rosenberg, et al., 509–28. Paris: Éditions de la Réunion des musées nationaux, 1984.

———. "Lully en visite chez Arlequin: parodies italiennes avant 1697." In *Jean-Baptiste Lully: Congress Report from the 1987 meeting in Heidelberg and Saint-German-en-Laye*, ed. Jérome de La Gorce and Herbert Schneider. Laaber: Laaber Verlag, 1990.

———. "Watteau dans son temps." In *Watteau, 1684–1721*, ed. Margaret Morgan Grasselli, François Moureau, Pierre Rosenberg, et al., 471–508. Paris: Éditions de la Réunion des musées nationaux, 1984.

———. "Watteau libertin?" In *Antoine Watteau (1684–1721): Le peintre, son temps et sa légende*, ed. François Moureau and Margaret Morgan Grasselli, 17–22. Paris: Champion; Geneva: Slatkine, 1987.

———, and Margaret Morgan Grasselli, eds. *Antoine Watteau (1684–1721): Le peintre, son temps et sa légende*. Paris: Champion; Geneva: Slatkine, 1987.

———, and Alain-Marc Rieu, eds. *Éros philosophe: Discours libertins des lumières*. Paris: Honoré Champion, 1984.

Mueller, Marlies. *Les idées politiques dans le roman héroïque de 1630–1670*. Harvard Studies in Romance Languages, 40. Cambridge, MA: Department of Romance Languages and Literatures of Harvard University, 1984.

Muir, Edward. *Civic Ritual in Renaissance Venice*. Princeton: Princeton University Press, 1981.

Mukerji, Chandra. *Territorial Ambitions and the Gardens of Versailles*. Cambridge: Cambridge University Press, 1997.

Mulryne, James Ronald, and Elizabeth Goldring. *Court Festivals of the European Renaissance: Art, Politics, and Performance*. Aldershot: Ashgate, 2002.

Nagy, Peter. *Libertinage et révolution*. Paris: Gallimard, 1975.

Néraudau, Jean-Pierre. *L'Olympe du Roi-Soleil: Mythologie et idéologie royale au Grand Siècle*. Paris: Société d'Édition "Les Belles Lettres," 1986.

Nettl, Paul. "Notes sur la forlane." *La revue musicale* 14 (1933): 191–95.

Nicoll, Allardyce. *The World of Harlequin: A Critical Study of the Commedia dell'arte.* Cambridge: Cambridge University Press, 1963.

Norberg, Kathryn. "Prostitutes." In *A History of Women in the West,* vol. 3: *Renaissance and Enlightenment Paradoxes,* ed. Natalie Zemon Davis and Arlette Farge, 458–74. Cambridge: Belknap Press of Harvard University Press, 1993.

Norman, Buford. *Touched by the Graces: The Libretti of Philippe Quinault in the Context of French Classicism.* Birmingham, AL: Summa Publications, 2001.

———. "La tragédie lyrique, déca-danse ou apothéose? Le cas d'*Isis.*" In *La pensée de la danse à l'âge classique: Écriture, lexique et poétique,* ed. Catherine Kintzler, 35–46. Ateliers 11. Lille: Cahiers de la Maison de la recherche, Université Charles-de-Gaulle, 1997.

Norman, Larry. "Molière as Satirist." In *The Cambridge Companion to Molière,* ed. David Bradby and Andrew Calder. Cambridge: Cambridge University Press, 2006.

Orgel, Stephen. *The Illusion of Power: Political Theater in the English Renaissance.* Berkeley: University of California Press, 1975.

Packer, Dorothy S. "'La Calotte' and the Eighteenth-Century French Vaudeville." *Journal of the American Musicological Society* 21 (1970): 61–83.

Paquot, Marcel. *Les étrangers dans les divertissements de la cour de Beaujoyeulx à Molière (1581–1673).* Brussels: H. Vaillant-Carmanne, 1932.

Pekacz, Joanna. *Conservative Tradition in Pre-Revolutionary France: Parisian Salon Women.* New York: Peter Lang, 1999.

Pelous, Jean Michel. *Amour précieux, amour galant.* Paris: Klinksieck, 1980.

Peraino, Judith. *Listening to the Sirens: Musical Technologies of Queer Identity from Homer to Hedwig.* Berkeley: University of California Press, 2006.

Perrens, François Tommy. *Les libertins en France au XVIIe siècle.* Paris: Léon Chailley, 1896; New York: Burt Franklin, 1973.

Petitfils, Jean-Christian. *Louis XIV.* Paris: Perrin, 1995.

Phillips, Henry. *The Theater and Its Critics in Seventeenth-Century France.* Oxford: Oxford University Press, 1980.

Pintard, René. *Le libertinage érudit dans la première moitié du dix-septième siècle.* Paris: Boivin, 1943.

Pitou, Spire. *The Paris Opéra: An Encyclopedia of Operas, Ballets, Composers, and Performers.* 3 vols. Westport, CT: Greenwood Press, 1983–90.

Plax, Julie Anne. "*Gloire* Surrenders: Watteau's Military Paintings." In *Conflicting Visions: War and Visual Culture in Britain and France c. 1750–1830,* ed. John Bonehill and Geoff Quilley, 15–40. Aldershot: Ashgate, 2005.

———. *Watteau and the Cultural Politics of Eighteenth-Century France.* Cambridge: Cambridge University Press, 2000.

Posner, Donald. *Antoine Watteau.* Ithaca: Cornell University Press, 1984.

Powell, John S. "Appropriation, Parody, and the Birth of French Opera: Lully's *Les festes de l'Amour et de Bachus* and Molière's *Le malade imaginaire.*" *Recherches sur la musique française classique* 29 (1998): 3–26.

———. "*Le bourgeois gentilhomme:* Molière and Music." In *The Cambridge Companion to Molière,* ed. David Bradby and Andrew Calder, 121–38. Cambridge: Cambridge University Press, 2006.

————. "Musical Practices in the Theater of Molière." *Revue de musicologie* 82 (1996): 5–37.

————. *Music and Theatre in France, 1600–1680.* Oxford Monographs on Music. Oxford: Oxford University Press, 2000.

————. Music and Theater in Seventeenth-Century France. http://www. personal. utulsa.edu/~John-powell/theater

————. "The Opera Parodies of Florent Carton Dancourt." *Cambridge Opera Journal* 13 (2001): 87–114.

————. "Pierre Beauchamps, Choreographer to Molière's Troupe du Roy." *Music and Letters* 76 (May 1995): 168–86.

————. "Pourquoi toujours les bergers? Molière, Lully, and the Pastoral Divertissement." In *Lully Studies,* ed. John Hajdu Heyer, 166–98. Cambridge: Cambridge University Press, 2000.

————, with Claudia Jensen. "'A Mess of Romans Left Us but of Late': Diplomatic Blunder, Literary Satire, and the Muscovite Ambassador's Visit to Paris Theaters in 1668." *Theatre Research International* 24, no. 2 (1999): 131–44.

Prest, Julia. "Conflicting Signals: Images of Louis XIV in Benserade's Ballets." In *Culture and Conflict in Seventeenth-Century France and Ireland,* ed. Sarah Alyn Stacey and Véronique Desnain. Portland, OR: Four Courts Press, 2004.

————. *Theatre under Louis XIV: Cross-Casting and the Performance of Gender in Drama, Ballet, and Opera.* New York: Palgrave Macmillan, 2006.

Pruiksma, Rose. "'Dansé par le roi': Constructions of French Identity in the Court Ballets of Louis XIV." Ph.D. diss., University of Michigan, 1999.

Prunières, Henri. *Le ballet de cour en France avant Benserade et Lully.* Paris: Henri Laurens, 1914.

————. "La Fontaine et Lully." *Revue musicale* 398-99 (1987): 49-64. Reprint of an article appearing in August, 1921.

————. *Lully.* Paris: Laurens, 1909. 2nd ed., 1927.

————. *L'opéra italien en France avant Lully.* Paris: E. Champion, 1913.

————. "Les premiers ballets de Lully." *La revue musicale* 12 (1931): 1–17.

————. "Recherches sur les années de jeunesse de J.-B. Lully." *Rivista musicale italiana* 17 (1910): 645–54.

Ranum, Orest. *Artisans of Glory: Writers and Historical Thought in Seventeenth-Century France.* Chapel Hill: University of North Carolina Press, 1980.

————. *The Fronde: A French Revolution, 1648–1652.* New York: W. W. Norton, 1993.

————, ed. *National Consciousness, History, and Political Culture in Europe.* Baltimore: Johns Hopkins University Press, 1975.

————. *Paris in the Age of Absolutism, An Essay.* New York: John Wiley, 1968.

————, and Patricia Ranum, eds. *The Century of Louis XIV.* New York: Walker, 1972.

Ranum, Patricia. "Audible Rhetoric and Mute Rhetoric: The Seventeenth-Century French Sarabande." *Early Music* 15 (1986): 23–39.

————. "Les 'caractères' des danses françaises." *Recherches sur la musique française classique* 23 (1985): 45–70.

Reato, Danilo. *Histoire du carnaval de Venise.* Translated from the Italian by Claire Normand. Bordeaux: Oréa-Marco-Polo, 1991.

Reichler, Claude. *L'age libertin*. Paris: Minuit, 1987.

Roche, Daniel. *The Culture of Clothing: Dress and Fashion in the Ancien Régime*. Trans. Jean
Birrell. Cambridge: Cambridge University Press, 1994.

———. *Histoire des choses banales*. [Paris]: Fayard, 1997. Translated by Brian Pearce as
The History of Everyday Things: The Birth of Consumption in France, 1600–1800. Cambridge: Cambridge University Press, 2000.

Roland-Michel, Marianne. *Watteau: An Artist of the Eighteenth Century*. London: Trefoil,
1984.

Rollin, Sophie. "De la société de salon à la société de cour: L'ambivalence du processus de
civilization." *French Literature Series* 33 (2006): 1–15.

Ronzeaud, Pierre. "La femme au pouvoir ou le monde à l'envers." *XVIIe siècle* 108 (1975):
9–33.

———. *L'Utopie hermaphrodite:* La terre Australe connue *de Gabriel de Foigny (1676)*.
Marseille: CMR 17, 1982.

Rosand, David. "'Veneta figurata': The Iconography of a Myth." In *Interpretazioni venez-
iane: Studi di storia dell'arte in onore di Michelangelo Muraro*, ed. David Rosand. Venice:
Arsenal Editrice, 1984.

———. *Myths of Venice: The Figuration of a State*. Chapel Hill: University of North Carolina Press, 2001.

Rosand, Ellen. "Music in the Myth of Venice." *Renaissance Quarterly* 30 (1977): 511–537.

———. *Opera in Seventeenth-Century Venice: The Creation of a Genre*. Berkeley: University of California Press, 1991.

Rosenberg, Aubrey. *Tyssot de Patot and His World (1655–1738)*. The Hague: Martinus
Nijhoff, 1972.

Rosenberg, Pierre. *Vies anciennes de Watteau*. Paris: Hermann, 1984.

Rosow, Lois. "How Eighteenth-Century Parisians Heard Lully's Operas: The Case of
Armide's Fourth Act." In *Jean-Baptiste Lully and the Music of the French Baroque:
Essays in Honor of James R. Anthony*, ed. John Hajdu Heyer, 213–37. Cambridge: Cam-
bridge University Press, 1989.

———. "Lully's *Armide* at the Paris Opéra: A Performance History, 1686–1766." Ph.D.
diss., Brandeis University, 1981.

Rothkrug, Lionel. *Opposition to Louis XIV: The Political and Social Origins of the French
Enlightenment*. Princeton: Princeton University Press, 1965.

Rubin, David Lee. *Sun King: The Ascendancy of French Culture during the Reign of Louis
XIV*. Washington: Folger Shakespeare Library, 1992.

Rule, John, ed. *Louis XIV and the Craft of Kingship*. Columbus: Ohio State University
Press, 1969.

Sabatier, Gérard. *Versailles ou la figure du roi*. Paris: Albin Michel, 1999.

Sadie, Julie Anne, ed. *Companion to Baroque Music*. New York: Schirmer Books, 1990.

Saslow, James M. *The Medici Wedding of 1589: Florentine Festival as Theatrum Mundi*. New
Haven: Yale University Press, 1996.

Saunders, Harris Sheridan, Jr. "The Repertoire of a Venetian Opera House (1678–1714):
The Teatro Grimani di San Giovanni Grisostomo." Ph.D. diss., Harvard University,
1985.

Schalk, Ellery. *From Valor to Pedigree: Ideas of Nobility in France in the Sixteenth and Seventeenth Centuries*. Princeton: Princeton University Press, 1986.

Schmidt, Carl B. *The* Livrets *of Jean-Baptiste Lully's* Tragédies Lyriques: *A Catalogue Raisonné*. New York: Performers Editions (Broude Brothers), 1995.

Schmitter, Amy M. "Representation and the Body of Power in French Academic Painting." *Journal of the History of Ideas* 63 (July 2002): 399–424.

Schneider, Herbert. *Chronologisch-thematisches Verzeichnis sämtlicher Werke von Jean-Baptiste Lully (LWV)*. Tutzing: Hans Schneider, 1981.

Schwartz, Judith, and Christena Schlundt. *French Court Dance and Dance Music: A Guide to Primary Source Writings, 1643–1789*. Dance and Music Series, 1. Stuyvesant, NY: Pendragon Press, 1987.

Scott, Virginia. *The Commedia dell'arte in Paris, 1644–1697*. Charlottesville: University Press of Virginia, 1990.

See, Henri Eugène. *Les idées politiques en France au XVIIe siècle*. Geneva: Slatkine, 1978.

Seguy, J. "Monarchisme et Utopie." *Annales* 26 (1971): 328–94.

Seifert, Lewis. "Eroticizing the Fronde: Sexual Deviance and Political Disorder in the Mazarinades." *L'esprit créateur* (Summer 1995): 22–36.

Semmons, Richard. *The* Bals publics *at the Paris Opera in the Eighteenth Century*. Dance and Music Series, 13. Hillsdale, NY: Pendragon Press, 2004.

Shaw, David. *"Le bourgeois gentilhomme* and the Seventeenth-Century Social Revolution." *Modern Languages* 60 (December 1979): 211–18.

Sheriff, Mary D., ed. *Antoine Watteau: Perspectives on the Artist and the Culture of His Time*. Newark: University of Delaware Press, 2006.

———. *Fragonard: Art and Eroticism*. Chicago: University of Chicago Press, 1990.

Silin, Charles. *Benserade and His Ballets de cour*. Baltimore: Johns Hopkins University Press, 1940; New York: AMS Press, 1978.

Smart, Mary Ann. *Representations of Gender and Sexuality in Opera*. Princeton: Princeton University Press, 2000.

Smith, Gretchen Elizabeth. *The Performance of Male Nobility in Molière's Comédies-Ballets: Staging the Courtier*. Aldershot, Hampshire: Ashgate, 2005.

Smith, Jay M. *The Culture of Merit: Nobility, Royal Service, and the Making of Absolute Monarchy, 1600–1789*. Ann Arbor: University of Michigan Press, 1996.

———. "'Our Sovereign's Gaze': Kings, Nobles, and State Formation in Seventeenth-Century France." *French Historical Studies* 18, no. 2 (1993): 396–415.

Solnon, Jean-François. *La cour de France*. Paris: Fayard, 1987.

Sonnino, Paul, ed. *The Reign of Louis XIV*. Atlantic Highlands, NJ: Humanities Press International, 1990.

Souleyman, Elizabeth V. *The Vision of World Peace in Seventeenth- and Eighteenth-Century France*. New York: G. P. Putnam's Sons, 1941.

Spink, John Stephenson. *French Free-Thought from Gassendi to Voltaire*. London: Athlone Press, 1960.

Stanton, Domna C. *The Aristocrat as Art*. New York: Columbia University Press, 1980.

———. "The Ideal of 'Repos' in Seventeenth-Century French Literature." *L'esprit créateur* 15 (1975): 79–104.

Starobinski, Jean. *L'invention de la liberté, 1700–1789.* Geneva: Skira, 1964.

Stein, Louise. *Songs of Mortals, Dialogues of the Gods: Music and Theatre in Seventeenth-Century Spain.* Oxford: Clarendon Press; New York: Oxford University Press, 1993.

Storer, Maud. "Abbé François Raguenet, Deist, Historian, Music and Art Critic." *Romantic Review* 36 (1945): 283–96.

Storey, Robert F. *Pierrot: A Critical History of a Mask.* Princeton: Princeton University Press, 1978.

Strong, Roy. *Splendor at Court: Renaissance Spectacle and the Theater of Power.* Boston: Houghton Mifflin, 1973.

Sutton, Dana Ferrin. *The Greek Satyr Play.* Meisenheim am Glan: Hain, 1980.

Tanner, Marie. *The Last Descendent of Aeneas: The Hapsburgs and the Mythic Image of the Emperor.* New Haven: Yale University Press, 1993.

Tessari, Roberto. *La commedia dell'arte nel seicento: Industria e arte giocosa della civiltà barocca.* Florence: L. S. Olschki, 1969.

Thomas, Downing. *Aesthetics of Opera in the Ancien Régime, 1647–1785.* Cambridge Studies in Opera. Cambridge: Cambridge University Press, 2002.

Thompson, Geraldine. *Under Pretext of Praise: Satiric Mode in Erasmus' Fiction.* Toronto: University of Toronto Press, 1973.

Tomlinson, Robert. *La fête galante: Watteau et Marivaux.* Geneva: Droz, 1981.

———. *Metaphysical Song: An Essay on Opera.* Princeton: Princeton University Press, 1999.

———. *Music in Renaissance Magic: Toward a Historiography of Others.* Chicago: University of Chicago Press, 1993.

Tracy, James D. *The Politics of Erasmus: A Pacifist Intellectual and His Political Milieu.* Toronto: University of Toronto Press, 1978.

Van Kley, Dale. *Religious Origins of the French Revolution: From Calvin to the Civil Constitution, 1560–1791.* New Haven: Yale University Press, 1996.

Van Orden, Kate. "An Erotic Metaphysics of Hearing in Early Modern France." *Musical Quarterly* 82 (1998): 678–91.

———. *Music, Discipline, and Arms in Early Modern France.* Chicago: University of Chicago Press, 2005.

Viala, Alain. *L'esthétique galante (Paul Pellisson,* Discours sur les œuvres de M. Sarasin *et autres textes, réunis et annotés sous la direction d'Alain Viala).* Toulouse: Société de littératures classiques, 1989.

———. *Naissance de l'écrivain: Sociologie de la littérature à l'âge classique.* Paris: Minuit, 1985.

Vialet, Michèle, and Buford Norman. "Sexual and Artistic Politics under Louis XIV: The Persephone Myth in Quinault and Lully's Proserpine." In *Images of Persephone: Feminist Readings in Western Literature,* ed. Elizabeth T. Hayes, 45–74. Gainesville: University Press of Florida, 1994.

Vidal, Mary. *Watteau's Painted Conversations.* New Haven: Yale University Press, 1992.

Wade, Ira Owen. *The Intellectual Origins of the French Enlightenment.* Princeton: Princeton University Press, 1971.

Wadsworth, Philip. *The Novels of Gomberville: A Critical Study of Polexandre and Cythérée.* New Haven: Yale University Press, 1942.

Walkling, Andrew. "Court, Culture, and Politics in Restoration England: Charles II, James II, and the Performance of Baroque Monarchy." Ph.D. diss., Cornell University, 1997.

Webb, J. B. "Utopian Fantasy and Social Change, 1660–1666." Ph.D. diss., State University of New York at Buffalo, 1982.

Weber, William. "Learned and General Musical Taste in Eighteenth-Century France." *Past and Present* 89 (1980): 58–85.

———. *Music and the Middle Classes*. New York: Holmes and Meier, 1975.

Welsford, Eind. *The Fool: His Social and Literary History*. 1935; London: Faber and Faber, 1968.

White, Frederic R. *Famous Utopias of the Renaissance*. New York: Hendricks House, 1955.

Wild, Nicole. "Aspects de la musique sous la Régence. Les foires: naissance de l'opéra-comique." *Recherches sur la musique française classique* 5 (1965): 129–141.

Wildenstein, Georges. "Le goût pour la peinture dans le cercle de la bourgeoisie parisienne, autour de 1700." *Gazette des beaux-arts*, 6th ser., 48 (1956): 113–94.

Willeford, William. *The Fool and His Scepter: A Study in Clowns and Jesters and Their Audience*. Evanston, IL: Northwestern University Press, 1969.

Wine, Humphrey. *Grands peintres: Watteau*. London: Scala, 1992.

Witherell, Anne L. *Louis Pécour's 1700 "Receuil de dances."* Ann Arbor, MI: UMI Research Press, 1983.

Wolf, John B. *Louis XIV*. New York: W. W. Norton, 1968.

Wood, Caroline. *Music and Drama in the* Tragédie en musique, *1673–1715: Jean-Baptiste Lully and His Successors*. New York: Garland, 1996.

Yardeni, Myriam. *Utopie et révolte sous Louis XIV*. Paris: Nizet, 1980.

Yates, Frances. *Astraea: The Imperial Theme in the Sixteenth Century*. London: Routledge & Kegan Paul, 1975.

Zanger, Abby. *Scenes from the Marriage of Louis XIV: Nuptial Fictions and the Making of Absolutist Power*. Stanford: Stanford University Press, 1997.

Zaslaw, Neal. "The First Opera in Paris: A Study in the Politics of Art." In *Jean-Baptiste Lully and the Music of the French Baroque: Essays in Honor of James R. Anthony*, ed. John Hajdu Heyer, 7–23. Cambridge: Cambridge University Press, 1989.

Index

Abbate, Carolyn, 80n51

absolutism: aesthetic of, xvii, xxii, 67, 112, 122; and comédie-ballet, 133; and court ballet, 35, 47, 77, 181; and heroism, xxiii; myth of, xx–xi; and opéra-ballet, 165, 167–68, 170, 177, 179; vis-à-vis popular culture, 213n; propaganda of, xx–xxi, xxii, 47, 57, 83, 112, 116, 121, 156, 194; and tragédie en musique, 121, 124, 133, 146–47, 149, 160. *See also* Louis XIV; power; representation

Académie française, 83, 87, 195, 220, 246

Académie royale d'architecture, 83

Académie royale de danse, 6, 83

Académie royale de musique: as counter-court, 144, 162, 204, 210; in eighteenth century, 167–72, 176, 180–81, 189, 190, 192, 194, 196–97, 202, 206, 215, 221, 245–48; founding of, 83; and image making, 89, 155; in late seventeenth century, xxiii, 15, 143–44, 145–50, 156–59, 160, 162–67; before Lully, 120–21; under Lully, 116, 118, 121–50, 172; metatheatricality of, 146, 204, 208, 210–11; as refuge for libertinism, xviii;

taste set by, xxiii; and Watteau, 222, 224, 226. *See also* opéra-ballet; propaganda; tragédie en musique

Académie royale de peinture et de sculpture, 83, 224, 227, 246–48

Académie royale des médáilles et des inscriptions, 83. *See also* Petite Académie

Achilles, 142

acrobats, xv, 153, 196, 214, 221, 231

Adonis, 51, 52, 81, 82

aesthetics: changing systems of, xxii, 15, 48, 90–92, 95, 191–92, 102, 249; of comédie-ballet, 90, 92–94, 100; of court ballet, 33, 35, 65, 67–80, 86, 167, 191, 208; Cytherean, 52–53; of *fête galante*, 138, 170; of *galanterie*, xviii, xxii–xxiii, 6, 13–14, 16, 46, 125, 137, 224, 247–51; of La Fontaine, 136–37; of modernism, 168; modernist (eighteenth-century), 249; Neoplatonic, 48; neo-*précieux*, 194, 247; noble, xxii, 8, 13–15, 196; of opéra-ballet, 167, 192; of pastoral, 13, 169; of satire, 194; of tragédie en musique, 133, 160. *See also* arts; ideology

air de cour, 16, 18n27, 137

air galant, 193

air sérieux: in comédie-ballet, 95, 110; in
    court ballet, 8, 10, 63, 81, 117; *double*
    of, 17, 78–79, 81, 110, 210, 250n51; be-
    fore Lully, 16–18; in tragédie en mu-
    sique, 125, 149; praised by La Fontaine,
    136–38, 170
Alcina, 166–67
Alexander, 56, 66, 75, 76–77, 174, 214
allusion: in court ballet, 10–11; and inter-
    textuality, xvii; in opéra-ballet, 160,
    171, 182, 190, 201, 204, 213; at théâtre
    de la foire, 188; in tragédie en musique,
    145–46. *See also* intertextuality; parody;
    satire; tribute
Amadis, 124
Amazons, 19, 55, 214, 232
"Amori, volate," 207–10
"Amour, vole," 208. *See also* "Volez,
    amours"
Amours déguisés, Les. See Bourgeois,
    Thomas; frontispieces
Amours de Psyché et de Cupidon, Les (1669),
    137–38
Amphion, 137, 175
Anet, château de, 141–42, 145
Anne of Austria, wife of Louis XIII, 57;
    regent for Louis XIV, 1, 7, 49, 55, 115
Anthony. *See* Mark Anthony
antimilitarism, 50, 54, 223
antiquity: classical, 245–48; decline of, 162;
    Roman, 42, 43, 82
antitheatricalism, xvi, 176
Apelles, 175, 245
Apollo: in court ballet of 1650s, 1, 34, 35,
    82; and Muses, 36, 77, 120; in opéra-
    ballet, 165–66, 174, 176, 238–40, 242;
    ridiculed in Comédie-Italienne, 151, 154;
    surrogate of Louis XIV, 51, 77; in tra-
    gédie en musique, 133
Apostolidès, Jean-Marie, xx–xxi, 72, 74, 81
aria, da capo, 149, 153, 198, 200, 204, 206,
    212, 219
Aricie (1697). *See* La Coste, Louis de
ariette, 149, 198, 200, 221
aristocracy, 5, 6, 45, 94, 169

Arlequin (Domenico Biancolelli), 23, 77,
    110, 151, 151–52, 196, 198; as ballet role,
    212, 221; (costume of) at théâtre de la
    foire, 218
Armida (Armide), 59, 61–63, 81–83, 134,
    167, 211, 251
artists: alliance with Dauphin, 143; com-
    munity of, 51; of court ballet, 5–6, 11, 61,
    134; of fête, 93; glorification of, xvii; as
    image makers, xxi; of opéra-ballet, 171,
    174, 189, 208; personae in comédie-
    ballet, 92, 94, 102; personae in court
    ballet, 38, 66–80, 83, 160; personae
    in opéra-ballet, xxi, 178, 203, 210;
    personae in tragédie en musique, xxi,
    122, 126–28, 146, 148, 156, 160; of public
    sphere, 226; vision of, 172
arts: of absolutism, 196; artful life, 138;
    as blueprint for new society, 172–73,
    177, 180, 189, 249; centralization of,
    83; colonized by Louis XIV, 90, 112,
    191; commodification of, 15, 94–95, 98;
    at court, 83, 193; emblems of, 174, 235,
    238, 240–42; of fête, 93; glorification
    of, xvii; and ideology, xvii, 48, 66–83,
    173–79, 189, 242, 248–49; in late reign,
    127, 134, 157, 246; of opéra-ballet, 171;
    as regenerative force, 55; personifica-
    tion of, 59–62, 133; politicization of,
    83; portrayed in comédie-ballet, 92,
    94, 100, 102–3; portrayed in opéra-
    ballet, 165–66, 174–79, 189, 191–92,
    204, 235; portrayed in tragédie en mu-
    sique, 122, 133; portrayed in Watteau,
    234–45; of public sphere, 148, 191, 196,
    208, 226, 231, 238; triumph of, 172–81,
    231, 234–45. *See also* aesthetics; artists;
    triumph
Athena (Pallas Athena or Minerva), 15, 53,
    57–62, 82, 174–75, 181–83, 235, 247,
    249
Atys (1676), 124, 126–27
audience: of comédie-ballet, 84–85, 93,
    103–13; of Comédie-Italienne, 152; at
    court, 10, 15, 65, 110; diverse, 103–13;

dual, 84–85, 121; of opéra-ballet,
162–64, 168, 170–71, 176, 179, 180;
Parisian public, xxii–xxiii, xxiii, 51, 110,
111, 121–22, 125, 146, 170, 177, 190, 208,
213, 247–48; as societal model, xvii,
111, 115, 249; stage audience, 9, 103–13;
109–11, 122, 133, 146, 182, 188, 204,
211–12
augmentation, 153
Augustus Caesar, 56, 59, 82, 181–82

Bacchus: in court ballet, 1, 34; in opéra-
ballet, 191–92, 194, 235; in tragédie en
musique, 127; in Watteau, 235
Bakhtin, Mikhail, xviin2, 213n
Ballet: *à l'entrées*, 8, 166; ballet-within-
ballet, 9; move from court to public
sphere, 208; at Opéra in 1670s, 6; as
spectacle, xv. *See also* comédie-ballet;
court ballet; opéra-ballet
balls: costume, 9, 196; at court, 11, 14, 164;
masked, 209; in opéra-ballet, 170, 214.
See also masquerade
ballet de cour. See court ballet
Ballet d'Alcidiane (1657), 18n31, 26, 28–32,
44, 46, 98
Ballet de Cassandra (1651), 21
Ballet de Flore (1669), 80–82, 110, 123, 147;
parodied, 210, 213
Ballet de l'Amour malade (1657), 18n31,
21, 26
Ballet de la galanterie du temps (1656), 19,
26, 34
Ballet de la naissance de Vénus (1665),
65–66, 123, 164, 174
Ballet de la nuit (1653), 19, 35, 38, 40, 44,
57, 162
Ballet de la raillerie (1659), 21
Ballet de la revente des habits (1655), 21
Ballet de l'impatience (1659), 21, 22
Ballet des amours déguisés (1664), 57–65,
77, 81, 134, 167, 174, 181, 210
Ballet des arts (1663), 44, 174–75, 177, 240
Ballet des fêtes de Bacchus (1651), 1–5, 21,
26, 34, 35, 251

Ballet des Muses (1666), xvii, 66–83,
90–94, 120, 123, 208, 219; and opéra-
ballet, 174, 191–93, 208; parodied in *Le
bourgeois gentilhomme*, 100–12, 115, 191;
parodied in *Les fêtes vénitiennes*, 213–14;
and tragédie en musique, 121, 133, 148,
149, 156, 158
"Ballet des nations." See Lully, Jean-
Baptiste; Molière (Jean-Baptiste
Poquelin)
Ballet de Psyché (1656), 39–40, 47, 148
Ballet des plaisirs (1657), 18n31, 26, 35, 44,
219
Ballet des proverbes (1654), 11, 21
Ballet des saisons (1661), 164, 174
Ballet du temps (1654), 18n31, 34
Ballet du triomphe de l'Amour (1681), 148
ballet-mascarade, 163
Banville, Théodore, 225
Barthes, Roland, xvi
Bauge, M., 157
Bayle, Pierre, 151–52
Beauchamps, Pierre, 9, 26, 27n43, 75–76,
92, 104; *Les facheux*, 84–85
Beethoven, Ludwig van, 251
Bellerophon (1679), 134
Bellona (goddess of war), 127
Benserade, Isaac de: and court ballet
(1650s), 10, 14, 17, 27, 34, 38–39, 47, 57;
and court ballet (1660s), 40, 44, 66, 78,
81n54, 83, 94, 164, 202, 208; and liberti-
nism, 115–16; and Louis XIV, 47; publi-
cation of *livrets* (1698), 163, 189
Berain, Jean, 142; *L'isle de Cythère*, 227,
232–33, 237. *See also* Duflos, Claude;
Picart, Bernard
Bergerotti, Anna, 19, 63
Boësset, Jean-Baptiste, 16, 27, 136
Boileau-Despréaux, Nicolas, 175
Bononcini, Giovanni, 200
Boreas, 146, 160, 210
Bossuet, Jacques-Bénigne, xvi, 176
Boucher, François, 250
Boulay, Michel du, 145, 150
Bourbon dynasty, 52, 113, 121

Bourgeois, Thomas, 174, 181, 183, 201; *Les amours déguisés* (1713) 174, 181–90, 201, 226–27, 237, 243–45, 247

bourgeoisie: and comédie-ballet, 84–113; and Comédie-Italienne, 152; imitators of nobility, 15, 170, 249; and opéra-ballet, 162; scorned by nobility, 14

Bourgogne, duc de, 161, 163, 172, 179–80, 182, 221

Bourgogne, duchesse de, 163

bourrée, 21

Burke, Peter, xx

burlesque: in comédie-ballet, 77, 84, 89, 90, 92–113; in comedy of manners, 180; in court ballet, 10, 19, 21, 22–26, 27–30, 46, 85, 86, 89, 92, 96; and *galanterie*, 27–30; 92–113, 125; in opéra-ballet, 192; politics of, 86–89, 117; and *théâtre de la foire*, 183, 188; in tragédie en musique, 122, 123

Bussy, comte de, 88

Buti, abbé, 58n31

cabal, 143, 179n24, 180, 214

cabaret, 115–16

Caesar. *See* Augustus Caesar

Calliope (Muse of poetry), 76, 104, 133, 214

Cambefort, Jean de, 16

Cambert, Robert, 120

Campistron, Jean de, xviii, 139–44, 145, 150, 156, 160, 194

Campra, André: and Antoine Danchet, 192, 246; ideology and reception, 249; and opéra-ballet, xviii, 22, 167–69, 191–92, 196–217, 224; and patronage, xxii, 250; and satire, 160. *See also* opéra-ballet.
WORKS: *Les ages* (1718), 221; *Les amours de Mars et de Vénus* (1712), 215; *Le carnaval de Venise* (1699), 196–98, 201–8, 210–13, 217, 221; *L'Europe galante* (1697), 168; *Les fêtes vénitiennes* (1710), 196, 198, 207–21; *Les fragments de M. Lully* (1702); *Les Muses* (1703), 174, 191–94, 207–8, 213; "L'Opéra" (1710), 210, 214; "Orfeo nell'inferi" (1699), 200, 202–6; *La sérénade vénitienne* (1702), 196, 198

canaries, 21

cantata, 153, 198, 212, 219

capitalism: and culture, xvi; linked to political and social reform, 250. *See also* commerce

Le Carnaval, mascarade (1675). *See* Lully, Jean-Baptiste

Le Carnaval, mascarade royale (1668). *See* Lully, Jean-Baptiste

carnival: and burlesque, 86; and carnivalesque, 93, 112, 153, 191, 213, 213n; and comédie-ballet, 110; and court ballet, 10, 11, 41, 66; and opéra-ballet, 191, 196–217; and politics, 86, 87, 196–217, 213n; pleasures of, 44; and théâtre de la foire, 218; and tragédie en musique, 123

carnival of Venice: as counterutopia, xxii; in opéra-ballet, 196–219

Carnival (Le Carnaval; allegorical figure), 194, 211–12, 218

carpe diem, 194, 206

Casanova, 217

Castiglione, Baldassare, 13

castrato, 20

Cavalli, Francesco, 23; *Ercole amante*, 58n31

Caesar, 135. *See also* Augustus Caesar

censorship, xviii, 59, 87, 116, 118, 119, 143, 154, 165, 168, 179, 195, 211, 213, 246

Ceres: 164, 191–92, 127

chaconne, 20, 21, 212

chamber music: aesthetic of 17, 250n51; opposed to tragédie en musique, 136–38

Chambonnières, Jacques de, 136

Chambord, château de, 6

chanteuses (Opéra), 140, 210–11. *See also filles de l'Opéra*; Le Rochois, Marthe; Moureau, Françoise; Moureau, Louise

Chapelain, Jean, 51, 159

Chappuzeau, Samuel, xvi

charlatan, 26, 196, 211–13, 213n, 217–18, 221

Charlottenburg Palace, Berlin, 224

Chartres, duc de. *See* Orléans, duc de

Chaulieu, Guillaume de, 140, 142

choreography: 9, 9n7, 94, 169

chromaticism, 63–65, 100, 110, 194. *See also* Italian style

class identity, 12

classes, lower, 92–93, 181

classes, social, 6, 8, 23, 85, 94, 103–13, 168, 188–90, 211, 234

classicism (literary), 123n3, 168, 175, 219. *See also* Neoclassicism

Cleopatra, 59, 62, 81–83

Clio (Muse of history), 76, 104, 133, 157–58, 164, 214

Colbert, Jean-Baptiste, xix, 43, 45, 49, 101, 118, 159, 246

Collasse, Pascal: emphasis on pastoral, 169; member of libertine circle, 150. WORKS: *Achille et Polixène* (completed), 142, 156, 156n66; *L'Astrée* (1691), 138; *La naissance de Vénus* (1696), 164–68, 171, 174–75, 178, 190n39; *Les saisons* (1695), 164, 168–69, 171, 174

colonialism, 43

Columbine, 154, 196

comédie-ballet, 84–119: and burlesque, 21, 92–113; and court ballet, xvii, 77, 84–86, 89–92, 94–95, 98, 100, 103, 112, 117, 122; and *grands divertissements;* and libertinism, xviii; metatheatricality of, 89, 92; music of, 92–113; and opéra-ballet, 119, 160, 163, 194, 197; reception of, 117; and tragédie en musique, 121, 122

Comédie-Française: and Comédie-Italienne, 152–53; and Cythera, 224, 226, 232; and opéra-ballet, 172, 180, 190, 206

Comédie-Italienne: audience of, 152; and comédie-ballet, 90; and court ballet, 5, 21, 23; costumes of, xxii, 223; expulsion of, 154–55, 172, 194, 196–97, 219; in late seventeenth century, 172; metatheatricality of, 91, 153; music of, 152–53; new (after return in 1715), 188; and opéra-ballet, 196–217; petition to return, 204; as site of subversive satire, xvii, 220, 223; in 1660s, 77, 110, 214; as spectacle, xv; and tragédie en musique, 148,

150–55, 173, 189; and Watteau, 222, 224. *See also* commedia dell'arte

commedia dell'arte, 104, 191, 194, 196–98, 211–12, 213n, 214, 218, 220

comedy (as genre), 8, 9, 76, 90, 104, 156–58, 163, 168, 177, 192–93, 214, 226

commerce, xxii, 10, 15, 83, 191–92, 217, 250. *See also* capitalism; marketplace

Comus (god of entertainment), 141

Condé, prince de (Le Grand Condé), 32–33, 38, 43, 54, 87, 89

Conti, princesse de, 139

Corneille, Louis, 138

Corneille, Pierre, 57, 123, 138

costumes (costuming), xix, xxii, 2–4, 61, 94, 104, 134

Couperin, François, 110

Couperin, Louis, 136

court: court life, 45; critique of, 55, 91, 94, 166; in early reign, 1, 5–7, 10–16, 19, 26–33, 47; entertainments of, 5, 46, 84, 89; in late reign, 167, 139, 144, 221, 249; leisured society of, xvi, 5, 13; and music, 5; and opera production, xxiii, 7, 121; reflected in court ballet, 5, 35, 170; ritual of, xix; "shadow" court (countercourt) of Opéra, 144, 162, 204, 210; as taste setter, 95; theatrical productions of, 5

court ballet: aesthetics of, xxii, 48, 67–80, 86; and comédie-ballet, 77, 84–86, 89–92, 94–95, 98, 100, 103, 112, 114, 117; and forerunners of opéra-ballet, 163; of Louis XIII, 7–8; of Louis XIV (1650s), 1–40; of Louis XIV (1660s), 41–84, 94, 125, 174; of Louis XIV (1681), 148; metatheatricality of, 8–9, 89; music of, 9, 16–33, 59–81, 172, 190; and noble identity, 5–6, 11; and opéra-ballet,160, 163–65, 167–71, 173–74, 176, 181–82, 189–92, 248, 208; pdfs on Gallica Web site, 16, 78; publication of *livrets* (1698), 163; in Renaissance, 15; and representation, xvii, xxi, 102, 165; and tragédie en musique, 121, 123, 137. *See also* comédie-ballet; court; Louis XIV; opéra-ballet courtiers, xviii, xxiii, 8, 10, 12–13, 39, 45, 49, 85–86, 138. *See also* aristocracy; nobility

courtesans, 176

Coypel, Antoine, 248

Coypel, Charles-Antoine, 196

critique (of monarchy), 54–56, 89, 114, 118–19, 135, 141, 144, 160, 161, 164, 166, 167, 170, 172, 177, 189–90, 219, 246. *See also* protest; resistance; satire; subversion

cross-casting, 10, 11, 11n11

cross-dressing, 11n11

crotesque. See burlesque

Crow, Thomas, 222

Cupid (*l'Amour*), 15, 20, 59, 66, 78, 120, 126, 137, 149, 157, 166–67, 175–76, 179, 182, 208–10; in opéra-ballet, 192, 198, 211–12, 214, 217, 220–21; in Watteau, 234–38, 243

cupids (*les amours*): in court ballet, 57–59, 61–63; iconography of, xxii, 211; in opéra-ballet, 174–76, 179, 181, 183; in Watteau, 224–25, 232, 234, 235–36, 238, 242–43, 245

Cynicism, 193, 220

Cyrano (Cyrano de Bergerac), 87, 88, 113, 114, 116, 118, 141

Cythera, island of: as counterutopia, xxii, 51, 137, 165; equated with theater and art, 189; opéra-ballet, 161, 165–66, 173, 179, 181–83, 188; in Renaissance festivals, 15; in in Watteau, 222–45. *See also* island; utopia

dance: ballroom, 20–21; and comédie-ballet, 85–86, 100–1, 104, 112; and Comédie-Italienne, 153; at court, 5, 8, 86; and court ballet, xix, 8, 5, 9–11, 20, 76, 169; and opéra-ballet [carnival], 193, 196–98, 200, 202, 210, 219; and opéra-ballet [Cythera], 163, 163n, 164, 168, 175–76, 178, 182, 213, 235; as social phenomenon, 55–56, 95, 163, 170; as spectacle, xv; in tragédie en musique, 123,

125; in Watteau, 230, 236–37. *See also* Dance (La Danse); dancers; music and dance masters

dancing masters. *See* dancers; music and dance masters

Dance (La Danse; allegorical figure), 175–76

dancers: noble, 1, 5, 9–11, 35, 44, 47, 92, 98, 164; professional, 1, 16, 18–19, 26, 27, 98, 100, 128–29, 135, 169. *See also* Louis XIV, dancing roles; music and dance masters

Danchet, Antoine, 162, 174, 192–94, 196, 206, 211–13, 246. *See also* Campra, André

Dancourt, Florent Carton, 168. WORKS: *La comédie des comédiens* (1710), 217–18; *Le carnaval de Venise* (1690), 202, 213; *Les trois cousines* (1700), 172–73, 180, 183, 190, 226–27, 230–31, 237

D'Anglebert, Jean Henry, 136

Danneret, Elisabeth, 197

danseuses. See dancers; *filles de l'Opéra*

Dante Alighieri, 51

D'Assoucy (Charles Coypeau), 87, 141

David, Jacques-Louis, 250

Dauphin. *See* Louis, Dauphin de France

Dauphine. *See* Marie-Anne, Dauphine de France

Debord, Guy, xvi

DeJean, Joan, 55, 117

Democritus, 193, 214

desire, 63, 77, 100, 134, 183, 238

Desmarets, Henri, 140, 142, 150; *Les amours de Momus* (1695), 194

Destouches, André Cardinal: *Le Carnaval et la Folie* (1704), 194, 197; *Issé* (1708), 208

devout party, 115, 118, 125, 139, 168, 176, 188

dialectic: in comédie-ballet, 95–113; in tragédie en musique, 133

dialogue: xvii; dialogic, xvii, 220; "dialogue of theaters," 167, 180; Diogenes, 192; in tragédie en musique, 133

Discord (La Discorde; allegorical figure), 52

divertissement: in comédie-ballet, 92, 102–3; *grand divertissements*, 166–67, 167n7; *à l'italienne*, 198, 152–53; at Opéra, 163; in opéra-ballet, 198, 203, 217, 219; as site of subversion, xviii; social, 170; theatrical, 172, 180, 202; in tragédie en musique, xxii, 127, 133, 135, 169, 183. *See also* entertainment; fête

le docteur, 23, 151, 198

Donneau de Visé, Jean, 89, 118

double. See under air sérieux

double entendre, 154, 171

drums, 127–28, 136–37, 158, 240

Duflos, Claude, 227, 232, 234, 237

Dufresny, Charles Rivière, 152–53

Dupuis, Hilaire, 17–18, 19, 77, 95, 100, 110, 116, 135, 136

D'Urfé, Honoré, 13, 91, 138; *L'Astrée*, 13, 16, 91, 138

écriteaux, 218

Elias, Norbert, 12

L'embarquement pour Cythère (anon.), 227. *See also* Gillot, Claude; Watteau, Antoine

empire: of Arcadia, 192; of arts, 76, 90, 93, 112; cult of, 42; French, 43, 73–75, 126; imperial domination, 82, 114, 124; of love and folly, 212; and nobility, 56; of Venus, 165, 177, 181. *See also under* iconography

Enlightenment, xviii, xviii, 45, 114, 162, 168, 172, 178, 234, 250n51

entertainment: within comédie-ballet, 93, 111; at court, 8, 67, 161, 166, 212; within court ballet, 77; as power, xvi; private, 19, 55, 170; public, xv, xxii, 122–23, 163, 211–12; as societal model, xv, 112. *See also* comédie-ballet; court ballet; divertissement; fête; opéra-ballet; spectacle; tragédie en musique

entry, as term *entrée*, 8, 175

Epicureanism, xviii, 52, 87, 114, 179

Erasmus, 113–14, 191, 194, 213, 220; *Praise of Folly*, 113–14, 220

Erato (Muse of love), 35, 37, 76, 104, 214

eroticism, xviii, 82, 188

Ertinger, Franz, 239, 242

Euterpe (Muse of pastoral and music), 76, 104, 122, 157–58, 163–65, 193, 214, 240

everyman, 88, 151

exoticism, 82, 88, 111, 198, 213, 219–20

Facheux, Les. See Beauchamps, Pierre; Molière (Jean-Baptiste Poquelin)

Fame (La Fame, allegorical figure), 120, 128, 133, 135, 240, 242

fanfare, xxii, 127–28, 147, 231

faun, 30, 165, 169, 214

Favier, M., 100

Félibien, André, 166

feminism, 55. *See also* women

Fénelon, François de La Mothe, 161, 179–80; *Explication des maximes des saints sur la vie intérieure*, 179; *Télémaque* (1699), 179

festivals, Renaissance, 42

fête, 119, 138, 141, 156, 163, 171, 180, 182. *See also* divertissement; entertainment; *fête champêtre; fête galante;* spectacle

fête champêtre, 166, 192, 249

fête galante: aesthetic of, 138; in literature, 14, 54, 55; in opéra-ballet, 165–67, 175, 178, 182, 192; sacred ritual of, 175, 178; of Watteau, xxii, 222–24, 246, 249, 249, 250n51. *See also* aesthetics

Fêtes de Bacchus, Les. See Ballet des fêtes de Bacchus

Fêtes galantes, Les, 170

Fêtes parisiennes, Les 218

Feuillet, Raoul Auger, 9n7, 169n

Ficino, Marsilio, 15

filles de l'Opéra, 176. See also *chanteuses; danseuses*

fireworks, 167

fleur-de-lis, 80, 101, 242

Flora, 80, 110, 127, 133, 146, 149; in opéra-ballet, 191–92, 210 floridity. *See* ornamentation

flûte: iconography of, xxii, 59, 61, 136, 149; highlighted in opéra-ballet, 169, 183

Foigny, Gabriel de, 114, 119

Foire Saint-Germain, 196, 218. *See also* théâtre de la foire

Foire Saint-Laurent, 183, 196. *See also* théâtre de la foire

folly, 118, 191, 213

Folly (La Folie, allegorical figure), 111, 113, 191, 194–96; as counterpart of Louis XIV, 212–14

Fontainebleau, château de, 6, 164

Fontenelle, Bernard le Bovier de, 114, 140

fool: and carnival, 213; in comédie-ballet, 119; at court, 91; fool king, 94, 102–3, 110–13, 213; impunity of, 119; in opéra-ballet, 191–96, 199;

forgetfulness (opposed to memorial), 192, 194

forlane, 200, 200n13

Fortune (La Fortune, allegorical figure), 202, 210, 220

Foucault, Michel, xxn9

Fouquet, Nicolas, 49, 50–53, 54, 84, 89, 121, 136, 166

fragmentation, 85, 88, 103, 105, 112, 117, 192

Fragonard, Jean-Honoré, 250

Francion, 88, 105, 113. *See also* Sorel, Charles

Freemasons, 195, 234

free thought, xviii, 52, 87, 117, 151, 195, 222, 234

Fronde, civil wars of, 1, 7, 12, 19, 40, 45, 54, 47, 54, 55, 56

frontispieces: *Les amours déguisés,* 238, 243–45; *Les fêtes vénitiennes,* 216–17; *Panegyricus,* 238, *Le triomphe des arts,* 238–40, 242–43, 245

Fumaroli, Marc, 51–53

Fuselier, Louis, 174, 181–82, 106, 222, 237; and Watteau, 226–27, 247. WORKS: *Arlequin défenseur d'Homère* (1715), 247;

La Pénélope moderne (1728), 247; *Les pélerins de Cythère* (1713), 183–84, 188, 190, 227, 231. *See also* Bourgeois, Thomas

galanterie: assimilation by bourgeoisie, 94–95; associated with ballet, 41, 117, 251; changes in meaning, 13–14; chivalric, 8; cult of, 14–15, 246; ideology of, 38, 137, 224, 251; and king, 34, 66, 165; and libertinism, 116; and nobility, xviii, xxii, 8, 11, 13–16, 41, 94–95, 101, 105; in opéra-ballet, 162–63, 167–69, 175; and tragédie en musique, 134. *See also* aesthetics; *galant homme de bon goût; style galant*

galant homme de bon goût, 250n51

Gallica Web site, 16, 78

Gallot, Jacques, 18

Games (*les Jeux,* allegorical figures), 4, 35, 38, 127, 141, 146, 181

Gassendi, Pierre, xviii, 52, 87

Gatti, Theobaldi di: *Coronis, pastorale heroïque* (1691), 157

Gautier, Denis and Ennemond, 136

gavotte, 20

gazettes à la main. See pamphlet literature

gender, 11n11, 79

Germany, 50, 144

Gersaint, Edme, 222

Gherardi, Everisto, 153

gigue, 21, 194

Gilbert, Claude, 114, 120

Gilliers, Jean-Claude, 153

Gillot, Claude, 234; *L'embarquement pour l'île de Cythère,* 227–31, 237, 245

glory (*gloire*): in court ballet, 66–67, 72, 81, 83; identified with monarch, xxi, 161–62, 164; of Louis XIV in early reign, 39, 51; of Louis XIV in late reign, 57, 125–27; mechanisms of, xxi; mocked in opéra-ballet, 194, 196, 211; in tragédie en musique, 126, 133–34, 141, 158–60

Glory (allegorical figure), 127, 158–59, 164, 194

Gomberville, sieur de, 26, 30, 32, 33, 54;
   Polexandre, 26
les goûts réunis, 110
Graces (Les Graces, allegorical figures),
   35, 59, 120, 127
grand ballet, 11, 80, 174, 176
Grand Dauphin. *See* Louis, Dauphin de
   France
Grande Mademoiselle. *See* Montpensier,
   duchesse de
les grands seigneurs, 6, 12. *See also* aristocrats; nobility
grands violons, 80
guerre des théâtres, 172–73, 206
Guiche, comte de, 44
Guise, chevalier de, 18
guitar, 137, 153
gypsies, 21, 26, 198

harpsichord, 136
Heartz, Daniel, 200n12, 250n51
hedonism: aesthetic of, 35; of court ballet,
   1, 11, 35, 46; aristocratic, xix, 143, 249;
   ideology of, 52; and libertinism, xviii;
   of opéra-ballet, 162, 167, 169; of spectacle, 35
Henriette d'Angleterre, 35, 37, 65, 92, 174
Henry II, 80
Henry IV, 80
Heraclitus, 193, 214
Hercules, 124, 151
heresy, 52
hermeticism, 53. *See also* pantheism
L'Hermite, Tristan. *See* Tristan
heroism: in Beethoven, 251; in court ballet, 8, 33, 39, 44, 57, 66, 125, 165, 202; in
   eighteenth century, 163, 165, 167–69,
   192; in novel, 56; in tragédie en musique,
   121, 122, 124–28, 134, 159, 162–63,
   169; in Revolution, 251. *See also* mock-
   heroism
Hesselin, M., 26
"high" style, 180, 188–89
Hilaire, Mlle. *See* Dupuis, Hilaire

History painting, 246
Holland, campaign against (1652), 44
Homer, 53, 178, 247
Hôtel de Bourgogne, théâtre de: and
   comédie-ballet, 90; and Comédie-
   Française, 172; and Comédie-Italienne,
   150–51; and court ballet, 58, 77, 104, 193,
   214; at early court of Louis XIV, 5
humanism, 114
Huygens, Christian, 18

iconography: of arts, 235, 238, 240–42;
   of empire, 42–43, 73–74, 82, 126, 162,
   177–78; of kingship, xvii, xxi, 39,
   41–42, 46, 57, 80, 160, 162–63; of kingship deconstructed, xx, 51, 145, 165,
   168; of noble pleasure, 57; of spectacle,
   xv, xviii, xxiii, 123–24, 171, 249; of Venus and Cupid, 59, 59n34, 188, 224–25,
   234, 235, 242; of Watteau, 226, 234, 246,
   249
ideology: of arts, xvii, 48, 66–83, 173–79,
   242, 248–49; of comédie-ballet, 85–86,
   90–91, 103, 117; of court ballet, 30–33,
   62, 65, 83, 86, 117, 226; of Cythera,
   51–52; of *fête galante*, 138, 223; of nobility, 196; of opéra-ballet, xviii, 164, 167,
   171–74, 192, 212; oppositional, 52, 249;
   of royal memorial, 85, 192; shifts in,
   xv, 162, 192; and spectacle, xv–xviii; of
   tragédie en musique, 123–26, 160; utopian, 180. *See also* aesthetics; *galanterie*;
   politics
imagery. *See* iconography
image makers. *See* artists
image making, 6, 94. *See also* propaganda
imperialism. *See* empire
intertextuality: as dialogic system, xvii,
   210; as libertine strategy, 115, 145, 213; in
   galant coteries, 175n15
Isabelle (Françoise-Marie Apolline Biancolelli), 152, 196, 204
island, 1, 15, 32–33, 54–56, 165–67, 175,
   178–81. *See also* Cythera; utopia

Italian musical style: assimilated into French style, 136, 219n38; in comédie-ballet, 93, 110; in Comédie-Italienne, 153, 198; as counterdiscourse, xxii; in court ballet, 20, 22, 40, 63, 77, 81, 93, 117, 219; and cultural *italianisme*, xxii, 152, 196, 220; and libertinism, 221; in opéra-ballet, 169, 193–94, 198–200, 202–4, 208, 212, 219–21; in opposition to absolutism, xxii; in tragédie en musique, 122

Janequin, Clément, 30
Jansenism, 176
Jean, M. S., 158
Jeanneret, Michel, 115, 150n28
jester. *See* fool; Momus
Jordaens, Jacob, 227n19
Journet, Mlle, 211
Juno, 165
Jullienne, Jean de, 248
Jupiter, 77, 120, 124, 151, 157, 166, 217

king's two bodies, xix

La Barre, Anne de, 19
La Barre, Michel de: *Le triomphe des arts*, 172–83, 190, 192, 201, 226, 227–28, 230–40, 245; *La Vénitienne* (1705), 198–99. See also La Motte, Antoine Houdar de
La Beaune, Jacques de, *Panegyricus*, 240, 242
La Calprenède, seigneur de, 32, 54, 56, 181; *Cassandre* (1642–58), 56; *Cléopatre* (1647–58), 56
La Coste, Louis de: *Aricie* (1697), 165–67, 192
La Fare, Charles Antoine de, 140, 142
La Fontaine, Jean de, 51, 52, 82, 115, 121, 140, 170, 178, 250n51. WORKS: *L'Adonis* (1658), 52; *Les amours de Psyché et de Cupidon* (1669), 137–38, 163; *L'Astrée* (1691), 138; *Daphné* (uncompleted), 138; *Le Florentin* (1674), 138; *Galatée* (un-

completed), 138; *Lettre à M. Niert sur l'opéra* (1677), 135–38; *La songe de Vaux* (1671), 136, 138
La Gorce, Jérôme de, 18n32, 77n46, 85, 177n18
Lalande, Michel-Richard de, 142
Lambert, Madeleine, 19
Lambert, Michel: and *air sérieux*, 16–18, 117; associated with libertines, 116; *doubles* used in court ballet, 63, 78, 81; and La Fontaine, 135–37; and Lully, 19, 116; as performer in court ballet, 21, 26, 27n43; and *style galant*, 250n51
lament, 63–65, 77–79, 81–83, 146, 148, 156, 179
La Motte, Antoine Houdar de: and opéra-ballet, 162; and Régiment de la Calotte, 195; and Watteau, 226–27, 230, 238, 245, 247. WORKS: *Le Carnaval et la Folie* (1704), 194; *L'Europe galante* (1699), 168; *Le triomphe des arts* (1700), 173–80; *La Vénitienne* (1705), 198. *See also* Campra, André; Destouches, André Cardinal; La Barre
La Roque, Antoine de, 222–23, 227
laurel wreath, 66, 144, 225, 235, 238, 242
Léandre (Charles-Virgile Romagnesi de Belmont), 152, 196, 198, 204; impersonated at Comédie-Française, 217
Lebrun, Charles, xxii, 49, 246, 248
LeCamus, Sébastien, 136
Lecerf de la Viéville, 116, 142
leisure: as appurtenance of *galant* style, 15; associated with pleasure, 5, 124, 127, 137, 170; as marker of nobility, 8, 26, 124; Lenclos, Ninon de. *See* Ninon de Lenclos
Le Nôtre, André, 49
Le Petit, Claude, *Le bordel des Muses, ou les neuf pucelles putains*, 115
Le Rochois, Marthe, 142
Lesbos, island of, 175. See also Cythera; Sappho
Le Vau, Louis, 49
libertinism: and Comédie-Italienne, 151; and community of Temple, 139–50; of

Dancourt, 183, 217; literature and philosophy of, xviii, 87–89; and Menippean satire, 220; and Molière, xviii, 114–18; and novel, 87, 89; of Opéra, 176; of opéra-ballet, 166, 168, 178, 189; of Parisian society, 180, 195, 221, 226; of Parisian theater, 188; types of, 168, 189; and Venus, 53–54; and Watteau, xviii, 222–33, 236, 249. *See also* Benserade; Enlightenment; *libertins érudits;* Lully, Jean-Baptiste; Molière (Jean-Baptiste Poquelin)

libertins érudits, 52

Loret, Jean, 18, 26

Louis XIII, 17, 32, 47, 51, 52, 57, 80, 86, 87, 88, 89, 137

Louis XIV: and arts, 122, 246, 248; and chamber music, 137; and comédie-ballet, 94, 101–2, 117; court of, 68–69, 83, 88; and court ballet, 7, 33, 41, 68–69, 75, 85, 164, 181; dancing roles in early court ballet, xix, 1–2, 19, 33–36, 38, 40, 66, 148, 162, 171, 189; dancing roles in late court ballet, xix, 44, 66, 80–81, 164, 171, 176, 189, 235; death of, 221, 242, 248–49; early reign of, 41, 81n54, 84, 87, 91, 159, 218; identified with love, 57, 66, 83, 158; late reign of, xxiii, 115, 134, 142–44, 155–60, 161–63, 168, 179, 191, 204, 215, 242; long reign of, xv, xxiii, 114, 161, 191; and Lully, xviii, 139–44, 155–56, 172; and nobility, 45, 56; and opéra-ballet, 165–66, 179; representation of, xix, xx–xxi, 41, 50, 57, 73–75, 120, 146, 151, 240; and sacred music, 162; satirized, 101, 201–2, 206, 208, 210–11, 218; and theater, xvi; and tragédie en musique, xxiii, 121, 124, 127, 133–34, 145. *See also* critique (of monarchy); glory; militarism (of Louis XIV); propaganda; protest; resistance; satire; subversion; war

Louis XV, xxiii, 163n, 182, 195, 221, 249

Louis, Dauphin de France (Le Grand Dauphin): early life, 58; and Lully, 139,

143–48, 163, 172; and Opéra, 180, 182, 204, 215, 221. *See also* cabal

Louvre, palace of, 6, 26, 84; museum, 224–25

"low" style, 180, 188–89

Low Countries, campaign against (1667–68), 50, 50n13, 56n30, 144

love (*l'amour*): in comédie-ballet, 103, 111; cult of, 52, 138; in early court, 56; in early court ballet, 13, 38, 39; in late court ballet (1660s), 57–66, 78, 81, 124; in late reign of Louis XIV, 134, 188; in opéra-ballet, 165–57, 170, 189, 192, 194, 174–75, 179–81, 183, 194, 211, 235; opposed to glory, 57–63, 65, 66, 81, 83, 138, 211; Renaissance concept of, 15; as site of political opposition, 51–56, 82; in théâtre de la foire, 218; in tragédie en musique, 120, 124–27, 133, 149; in Watteau, 236, 238, 245. *See also* opposition (political)

Lucian, 114–15, 194, 220

Lucretius, 52, 89; *De rerum natura*, 89

Lully, Jean-Baptiste: and comédie-ballet (with Molière), xvii, 76–77, 84–85, 89–90, 92–113, 116–18, 191; and Comédie-Italienne, 152; and court ballet, 18–27, 63, 77–79, 117; death of, 162, 176, 246; ideology of, 249; as libertine, xviii, 79, 115, 139–44; and Louis XIV, xviii, 18, 47, 116, 148, 155–57, 172; and opéra-ballet, 163–64; as Orpheus, 77–80, 160, 208; and patronage, xxii; and tragédie en musique, 121–50, 151, 160, 162; as violinist, 77–80. WORKS: *Achille et Polixène* (1688), 142–43, 156–57; *Acis et Galatée* (1687), xxiii, 138, 139–42, 144–45, 150, 169; *Alceste* (1674), 126, 133; *Les amants magnifiques* (1669), 101; *Armide* (1686), xxiii, 134, 139, 144, 210; *Atys* (1676), 126–27, 208; *Le bourgeois gentilhomme* (1670), 92–113; "Le Ballet des nations" (1670), 103–13, 122, 168, 173; *Cadmus et Hermione*, 123, 126, 133; *Le Carnaval, mascarade* (1675),

Lully, Jean-Baptiste (*continued*)
163–64, 173, 174, 213; *Le Carnaval, mascarade royal* (1668), 164, 163, 174, 202, 206, 208, 211, 213, 218–19; *L'Égloge de Versailles* (1685), 163; *L'Idylle de Sceaux* (1685), 163; *Isis* (1677), 124, 128–33, 136, 156; *Les fêtes de l'Amour et de Bacchus* (1672), 121–23, 156; *Isis* (1677), 128–33; *Les noces de village* (1663), 21, 22, 26; *Phaéton*, 126; *Perséphone*, 124; *Les plaisirs de l'île enchantée* (1664), 166; *Roland* (1685), 134; *Le Sicilien* (1666), 76; *Le temple de la paix* (1685), 139, 163; *Thésée* (1675), 127, 133. See also *Ballet de . . .*
Lully, Jean-Louis, 145, 150, 160, 171, 201, 208, 210, 213, 215. WORKS: *Alcide*, 142, 150; *Zéphire et Flore* (1688, with Louis Lully), 145–50, 155, 160, 189, 207, 210
Lully, Louis, 143, 149–50, 155, 160, 171, 201, 208, 210, 213. WORKS: *Zéphire et Flore* (1688, with Jean-Louis Lully), 145–50, 160, 189, 207, 208, 210, 213; *Orphée* (1690), 145–50, 160, 189, 202–4, 213, 215
lute, 35, 136–37, 153
Luxembourg, palace, 55

machines, 9, 15, 122–23, 153, 172, 174; "machine king," xx; machine plays, 172
Maintenon, marquise de, 134, 139, 143, 154, 165, 176
maître de danse. See dancers, professional
Malplaquet, 223
Marais, Marin, 143, 149. WORKS: *Ariane et Bacchus* (1696), 158; *Alcyone* (1706)
marches, 128
Marie-Anne, Dauphine de France, 139, 148
Marie de Médicis, 51, 52, 55
Marie-Thérèse (wife of Louis XIV), xvi, 41
Marin, Louis, xix–xxi
Marino, Giambattista, 51, 82, 87, 178; *Adone* (1623), 51–52, *Orfeo*, 54
Mark Anthony, 59, 62–63, 81–82

marketplace, commercial, xxii, 114, 211–12, 250
Mars, 38, 55, 58, 127, 135, 144, 151, 182, 235
Marsyas, 165–66
mascarade, 11, 26, 27, 90–91
masks and masking: carnival, xxii, 10; of commedia dell'arte, 151, 218–19; in court ballet, 11–12, 21, 202, 219; in opéra-ballet, 198, 206, 208, 211; and representation, xxi; and spectacle, 213
Massip, Catherine, 16n24, 116, 116n33, 137
masque, xvii
masquerade, 8, 26, 90–91, 102, 104, 163–64, 206
matriarchal ideal, 124, 165, 213, 53
Mazarin, Jules, 7–8, 12, 32, 41, 47, 49, 50, 54, 56
Mazarinades, 7
Mazuel, Michel, 16
McClary, Susan, 17n26, 80n51
Medici family (Florence), 43
Melpomene, 76, 104, 122, 123, 126, 127, 133, 156–58, 163–65, 193, 214
memorial (memorializing), xix, xx, 77, 158, 194
Memory (Mnemosine; allegorical figure), 67, 77, 79, 104, 192, 214. *See also* Muses, of Memory
Mercure galant, 222
Mercury, 58, 157
Mezzetin (Angelo Constantini), 153–54; impersonated at Comédie-Française, 217
militarism: in court ballet, 44, 57, 76, 174; critiqued in opéra-ballet, 164, 166, 168, 203, 206, 214; critiqued in Watteau, 223; of Louis XIV, 47, 53, 125, 128, 144, 163, 246; in music, xxii, 48; in Revolution, 251; in tragédie en musique, 124, 126–27, 135–36, 146–47, 163
Minerva. *See* Athena
minuet: in comedy-ballet, 101; in opéra-ballet, 169–70, 175, 183; in Watteau, 236

Mirth (*un ris*; allegorical figure), 2

Mnemosine. *See* Memory

mock-heroism, 150–55

modernism (eighteenth-century), 168, 178, 183; and Watteau, 227, 246–48

Molière (Jean-Baptiste Poquelin): and comédie-ballet, xvii, 23, 49, 77, 84–114, 121, 122, 123, 176; and Comédie-Italienne, 151, 191; and egalitarianism of theater, 188; ideology of, 249; as libertine, xviii, 114–19; and opéra-ballet, 168, 171, 174. WORKS: *Les amants magnifiques*, 101; *Le bourgeois gentilhomme* (1670) 84–115, 117–18, 121, 122, 156, 168, 171, 173, 191, 207–8, 213–14; "Le Ballet des nations" (1670), 103–13, 122, 168, 173; *Dom Juan*, 89; *Les fâcheux*, 84–85; *Les précieuses ridicules*, 95, *Tartuffe*, 89; *Le Sicilien* (1666), 76, 104

Mollier, Louis de, 16

Momus, 191–94, 198–99

Montaigne, Michel de, 52, 113

Montesquieu, baron de, 102

Montpensier, duchesse de (La Grande Mademoiselle), 18–19, 55–56; *La princesse de Paphlagonie* (1658), 55; *La relation de l'isle imaginaire* (1658), 55–56

More, Thomas, 113, 114, 220; *Utopia*, 113

Morpheus, 3

Moureau, Françoise, 142

Moureau, Louise, 142

Muses: as artist personae, xxi, 122, 160; in court ballet (1650s), 1, 34, 35, 37, 38; in court ballet (1660s), 67, 75–79, 164, 213; in comédie-ballet, 84, 90, 100, 104, 112–13, 214–15; in Comédie-Italienne, 154; of Folly, 191, 196; of Memory, 41, 66, 72, 112, 126; in opéra-ballet, 163–66, 192–95, 214–15; in opposition to Louis XIV, 51, 155–59, 191; of pleasure, 1, 8, 12, 195; in royal propaganda, 51, 75, 77, 83, 120, 122; in tragédie en musique, 121, 127, 133, 135, 156–58. *See also* artists; *Ballet des Muses*; Campra, André, *Les Muses*; Sappho (tenth Muse)

musette: iconography of, xxii, 166; in opéra-ballet, 170, 183, 193

music and dance masters, xxi–xxii, 100, 104, 208, 214–15

music. *See under* arts; comédie-ballet; court ballet; opéra-ballet; tragédie en musique

Music (La Musique, allegorical figure), 175–76

Musique de la Chambre du Roi, 67

Musique de la Chapelle du Roi, 67

Neoclassicism, 250, 250n51

Neoplatonism, 15, 48, 57, 79, 82

Neptune, 133

Nerval, Gérard de, 225

Niert, Pierre, 17, 135–36

Ninon de Lenclos, 116, 140

nobility: as audience at Opéra, 162–63; changing status, 13, 13n16, 15, 17; and comédie-ballet, 84, 101; and Comédie-Italienne, 152; and court ballet (1650s), 6, 8, 10, 12–13, 23, 26–33, 163; and court ballet (1660s), 44; identity with pleasure and *galanterie*, 12–13, 23, 39, 41, 44, 45, 47, 84; in late reign, 141, 143, 172, 180; lesser, 12; and monarchy, xvii, xxii, 26, 40, 43, 45, 56; and opéra-ballet, 170; and Watteau, 225; satirized by Comédie-Italienne, 152. *See also* aristocracy; courtiers; *grands seigneurs*; noble dancers

Les noces de Pélée et de Thétis, 35

Les noces de village (Lully, 1663), 21, 22, 26

noise, 135, 158

nostalgia, 13, 136

novel: burlesque, 88, 117; chivalric, 14, 26–27, 32, 51, 54–57, 104, 125, 214; libertine, 87–88; pastoral, 13, 90, 125, 138; utopian, 56, 113, 224

nymph, 78, 165, 169

oboe, 127, 136, 169

Olympus, 51, 82, 111, 121, 156

opera: comic, 188, 204; Italian, 5, 7, 47, 153; term, 123, 164. *See also* tragédie en musique

Opéra. *See* Académie royale de musique

opéra-ballet: and comédie-ballet, 119, 160, 163, 194, 197; as counterutopia, xxii; and court ballet, 160, 163–65, 167–71, 173–74, 176, 181–82, 189–92, 248, 208; and Cythera, 172–90, 249; as *fête galante*, 167; forerunners of, 163–67; as genre, 167–73; and libertinism, xviii, 167–68; metatheatricality of, 210; music of, 169, 182–87, 193, 198–200, 202–10; parodied by Dancourt, 173; reception of, 249; and representation, xxi; as societal model, 172, 177; and Venetian carnival, 196–217, 249; and Watteau, 222–24, 234–50. *See also* court ballet; tragédie en musique

opéra comique, 196

opposition (political), 55, 57, 82. *See also* critique; love; resistance; subversion

Orlando (Roland), 124

Orléans, duc de (regent for Louis XV), xxiii, 142, 182–83, 221, 248

ornamentation: in *air*, 17, 19, 149; in court ballet, 17, 78, 80, 81; extravagant style, 87, 195; in lute and harpsichord music, 136; in opéra-ballet, 194, 206, 208, 210, 219–21; in tragédie en musique, 149; in *style galant*, 250n51

Orpheus, xxi, 53, 77–83, 137, 146–50, 203, 208, 242

otherness, 167, 194, 219

overture, French, 20, 27, 156

Ovid, 181–82

pacifism, 50, 165, 179. *See also* peace

paganism, 87, 178, 234

Palais-Royal: as home of Comédie-Italienne, 151; as home of Molière's theater, 84; as home of Paris Opéra, xxiii, 123, 142; Place du, 128; residence of duc d'Orléans, xxiii; venue for court ballet, 6

pamphlet literature, 49–50, 118, 144–45, 155, 165, 211

panegyric, 157, 177, 240–42

Pantalon, 23, 26, 151, 198, 212, 218

pantheism, 53, 234

pantomime, 104

Paphos, temple of, 66

parade, xvii

Paris: as center of operatic production, xxiii; comédie-ballet performed in, 84, 85, 89; depicted in comedies, 183; masked as Venice, 196, 208, 210, 212, 218; as public sphere, xv, 208; and Watteau, 222, 236

Parnassus, 35, 51, 67, 83, 115, 121, 137, 137, 156–58

parody: in comédie-ballet, 89, 93, 100, 121, 191; at Comédie-Française, 180, 217, 226; in court ballet, 26; of Homer, 247; as intertextuality, xvii, 83, 172; in opéra-ballet, 193, 201, 206; at théâtre de la foire, 183, 188, 189, 190, 217, 226; opera parodies, xvii, 145, 150–55, 173, 189, 196. *See also* allusion; intertextuality; parody; satire

part: as term *partie*, 8

pastiche, 123, 163–64, 197

pastoral: in comédie-ballet, 90–91, 100, 104, 111; at Opéra, 120–21; ; in court ballet, 9, 35, 76, 61, 62, 66; in opéra-ballet, 163, 166, 169–70, 192–93, 214; in opposition to absolutism, xxii; in tragédie en musique, xxii, 121, 122, 127, 128, 137–38, 141, 157–58, 182

patriarchy, 54, 81, 124, 167, 181, 212, 219, 247

Patroclus, 142

patronage: of bourgeoisie, 94, 113, 208; of Fouquet, 49–50; of Louis XIV, xxii, 35, 46, 77, 153, 121, 124, 128, 177, 202, 208, 250; private, 56, 139, 250; public, xxii, 101, 112, 177; Venus as patron goddess, 174. *See also* Louis XIV; power

peace: in court ballet, 5, 33, 66, 164, 174; in Europe, 182; in literature, 54, 137; in opéra-ballet, 163, 175–76, 181–83; in tragédie en musique, 126–28, 133, 156, 158, 160; in Watteau, 247 peasantry, 170, 175–76, 235–36

Pecour, Louis, 9, 169, 169n

Les peines et les plaisirs de l'Amour (1672), 120, 133

Pellison, Paul, xix, 51, 52, 159

performance, xvi, 80, 88

Perigny, abbé de, 58

Permessus (river of Muses), 158

Perrault, Charles, 159; *Parallèle des anciens et des modernes* (1688), 247

Perrin, Pierre, 17, 120–21

Perseus, 124

Petite Académie, 83, 159, 246

Petit-Bourbon, theater of, 88

petits violons, 19, 59, 80

Philidor, André (*l'aîné*), 128

Pic, Jean, 164–65, 167, 174

Picart, Bernard, 227, 227n19, 233–34, 237

Pierrot (Giuseppe Giaratoni), 151, 154, 196, 198; impersonated at Comédie-Française, 217; impersonated at foire, 218

pilgrimage, 172, 180, 183, 188

pilgrims: theatrical, 180, 188, 227n19, 247; in Watteau, 225–26, 234

pleasure: in antitheatricalist discourse, xvi; of carnival, 44; consumption of, xxii; discourse of, xv–xxiii, 53; identified with ballet, 41, 168; identified with king, 48, 202, 218; identified with pastoral, 183; identified with theater, 188; and noble identity, 6, 15, 26, 39, 47, 48, 124, 170; in opéra-ballet, 17, 192; opposed to discourse of power, xv, 54–57, 67, 86, 133, 138, 177; philosophies of, xviii, 52; prerogative of, xv, xxii–xxiii, 47–48; public, 191–92, 206, 211–13; staging of, xxii, 222, 224; in tragédie en musique, 126–28, 133

Pleasures (les Plaisirs, allegorical figures), 35, 59, 126–28, 133, 141, 146, 157, 181, 202, 211–12

Les poètes. See Quinault, Philippe

politics, 5, 85

Polymnia (Muse of rhetoric [lyric poetry]), 76, 104, 122, 165, 214

Polyphemus, 141, 160

Pont neuf (bridge), 211, 218

Pluto, 58–59, 146–48, 151, 203–6, 210

Plutus, 191–92, 217. *See also* commerce

Poiret, Paul, 251

Polexandre. See Gomberville, sieur de

Polichinelle, 196, 198, 212, 218, 221

politics: of comédie-ballet, 91; of court ballet, 33; in literature, 88. *See also* ideology

popular culture, 102

Port Royal, 176

Posner, Donald, 246

power: centralization of, 87; cult of, 16, 191; depicted in court ballet, 35, 39, 41, 202; depicted in opera, 124, 126; discourse of, 54, 57; limits of, xx, 118; of music, 48, 134; of nobility, 12, 47; opposed, 54, 195; and patronage, xxii, 46; politics of, xv–xvi; and representation, xvii, xxi, xxii, 43–44, 160; satire of, 95, 155; of spectacle, 33; staging of, xix, 224; of state, xix, 162; undermined, 121, 218, 220

précieuses, 14, 94

prologue: of "Ballet des nations," 103; of court ballet, 58; of opéra-ballet, 181, 197, 212, 240; of pastoral, 120–21; of tragédie en musique, 120–27, 133, 145–46, 156–58, 162, 165, 177

propaganda: and arts, 67, 79; of court ballet, 8, 63, 66, 72, 73, 7779, 86, 100, 116, 165, 202; of empire, 42; of love and glory, 39; of pleasure, 48; of social harmony, 6; of sovereign power, xvii, xx–xxi, 6, 41, 43, 47–48, 67, 85, 125, 151, 159, 168, 170, 177; and spectacle, xvii; as term, xxi, 48; in tragédie en musique, 122; undermined, 51, 77–80, 151, 160–62, 174, 178, 189–90, 246. *See also* absolutism; iconography; representation

prostitution, 53, 115, 177, 226

protest: aristocratic, 45, 47; Cytherean,
    248; literature of, 49, 51, 144; of Muses,
    133; utopian, 114, 114n29
Psyché (1671), 138, 163
public sphere, Paris: and image war, xxiii;
    and arts, 95, 112, 121, 191, 208; and
    Opéra, xxiii, 166–67, 213
Pygmalion, 175–76, 236, 242–43, 245

quarrels over ancient and modern music,
    149–50
quarrels between the Ancients and the
    Moderns, 73, 180, 227, 246
quarrels over line and color (between
    Poussinistes and Rubenistes), 248
querelles des théâtres, 176
Quietists, 179
Quinault, Philippe: and ballet, 174; and
    comédie-ballet, 91; orations by, 159–60,
    246; parodied by Dancourt, 173; pref-
    aces, 126, 133; *Les poètes* (1666), 76,
    90–92, 102, 104, 193, 208, 214; and tra-
    gédie en musique, 121–24, 133–34, 151,
    156, 162. *See also* Lully, Jean-Baptiste,
    works

Rabelais, François, 52, 113, 114, 213n, 220
Racine, Jean, 115, 123, 141
raillerie, 91
Rameau, Jean-Philippe, 250
Ranum, Orest, 7n3, 217n34
récit: in comédie-ballet, 95, 100; in court
    ballet of 1650s, 8, 10, 16, 20, 35, 137; in
    court ballet of 1660s, 62, 63, 77, 79, 81;
    definition, 8; in opéra-ballet, 200; paro-
    died, 104, 214
recitative: in comédie-ballet, 100, 108; in
    court ballet, 47; in opéra-ballet, 193,
    198, 212; in tragédie en musique, 122
reform, political and social, 114, 250
Regency. *See* Orléans, duc de; Anne of
    Austria
Régiment de la Calotte, 195, 195n7
Regnard, Jean-François, 152–53, 197–98,
    202–4, 206

Renaissance, 42–43, 53, 115, 178, 211, 220,
    236, 245
representation: of artists, xxi, 79; changing
    systems of, 48, 162; controlled by artists,
    xxi, 47; of kingship, xvii, xxi, 44, 162; of
    power and pleasure, 48; of tyranny, 160;
    semiotic emptiness of, xx. *See also* art-
    ists; Louis XIV
republic, 182, 250–51
republicanism, 234
resistance (political): aristocratic, 45, 47;
    artistic, 49–51, 54, 85, 86, 160; and bur-
    lesque, 86; libertine, 87–89. *See also* cri-
    tique; protest; subversion
reversals: and comédie-ballet, 92; at
    Comédie-Italienne, 150–55; and Menip-
    pean satire, 220; at Opéra, 144–150, 217;
    in opéra-ballet, 165, 171, 173, 208, 210,
    213, 217
revisionism, xx
Revolution, 162, 165, 225, 250–51
Richelieu, Cardinal, 7, 32, 47, 56, 84, 89
Rinaldo (Renaut, Renaud), 59, 61–63, 124,
    134, 151, 210–11
rococo, 250n51
roles: in comédie-ballet, 93, 101n20, 102;
    in court ballet, 1–2, 8, 10, 19–21, 26–27,
    30, 33–35, 44, 76n44, 189; in tragédie en
    musique, 123. *See also* Louis XIV, danc-
    ing roles
rose. *See* Venus, rose as attribute of
Rossi, Luigi, 23; *L'Orfeo*, 58n31
Rousseau, Jean-Jacques, 87, 246
Rubens, Peter Paul, 227n19

Sacrati, Francesco, 23
Saint-André, M., 100
Saint-Aignan, comte de. *See* Saint-Aignan,
    duc de
Saint-Aignan, duc de, 10, 44, 91, 92, 104
Saint-Germain-en-Laye, château de, 6, 66
Sainte-Colombe, Jean de, 18
Saint-Cloud, 188
Saint-Evremond, seigneur de, 118
Saint Mark's Square (Venice), 211, 217–18

Saint-Simon, 140

salons, Parisian: and court, 15; ideology of, 55; in late seventeenth century, 125; and music, 16–18, 170; as site of *galant* aesthetic, xxii, 51, 94, 138; in 1650s, 13–15, 17, 17; society of, 136. *See also* women

Sapho, 54, 55, 56, 175

Sappho, xxi, 54, 161, 175, 178, 179, 182; as tenth Muse, 175, 178, 182–83, 236

sarabande, 20, 21, 59, 77, 169

Sarasin, Jean-François, 14, 17

satire: carnivalesque, 191, 200; in comédie-ballet, 84, 86, 92–94, 102, 111, 115, 117–119; at Comédie-Italienne, 150–55, 160, 189, 197; in court ballet, 38; in literature, 115, 145, 179, 211; Homeric, 248; Menippean, 219–21; in Molière, 89; in opéra-ballet (carnival), 192–95, 200–1, 207, 217; in opéra-ballet (Cythera), 160, 163, 165, 171, 189, 197; in théâtre de la foire, 189; in tragédie en musique, 122, 141, 145–50, 160. *See also* allusion; intertextuality; parody

Saturnalia, 192

satyr, 165, 169, 217

Scaramouche (Tiberio Fiorelli), 23, 26, 77, 151, 154, 196; as ballet role, 26, 197–98, 212; at Comédie-Française, 217; at foire, 218

Scarlatti, Alessandro, 200

Scudéry, Madeleine de, 14–15, 18, 32, 51, 52, 54, 56, 90, 94, 138, 175, 178–79; WORKS: *Clélie* (1654–61), 56; *L'histoire de Sapho* (1653), 54–56, 138, 170, 235

Scudéry, Georges de, 51

Segrais, Jean Renaud de, 14, 17

Seine, river, 165, 183, 218

self-representation. *See* artists (personae)

Sensuality, 17

Servien, abbé, 215

Sévigné, Mme de, 18, 159, 171

Sicilien, Le, 90, 92, 100, 102, 103

silence: as libertine ploy, 78–79; of Louis XIV, 161

singers, 17–18, 19, 20, 77, 95, 98, 100, 110, 116, 135–37. *See also chanteuses*

Snuff takers' chorus, 24–25

society: alternative, xviii, 47, 87, 112, 114, 121, 138, 172, 174, 177, 179, 188, 190, 210, 221, 223; changes in, xv, 5, 191; libertine, 168, 221; pleasure-centered, 13; reflected in spectacle, xv, 113–14; regeneration of, xxii, 235, 245–46; shaped by arts, xxii

Society of Pleasures, 42, 46, 218

sodomy, 79, 115, 117, 140, 142

sonata, 153, 198, 219

song, 8, 55, 196, 202, 210, 213

Sorbonne, 177

Sorel, Charles, 87, 88, 105, 113; *Francion*, 88, 105, 113

Spanish theater, 90, 92

spectacle: allure of, xv–xvi; and comédie-ballet, 86; and Comédie-Italienne, 152–53; contested ground of, xv–xvii; and court ballet, 6, 8, 62; and Cythera, 231; as dialogue, xvii; illusory nature of, xvii; opposed to textuality, 81; as mask for subversion, 213; and opéra-ballet, 170–71; as predecessor of opéra-ballet, 163; superficial, xvi, xviii; as term, xv; and tragédie en musique, 122. *See also* entertainment; utopia

Spenser, Edmund, 42

stage design, 9, 109, 123

stage-within-a-stage, 204

state, xix, xx, 126

statues, 174–75, 193, 197, 199, 206, 224, 232, 239–40, 242–43, 245

style brisé, 250n51

style galant, 200, 200n12, 250n51

subjectivity, 29

subversion: and cabaret, 116; in comédie-ballet, 102; in Gomberville, 33; in late reign of Louis XIV, 118, 145, 149–51, 155, 211, 214, 223; in late works of Lully, xviii, 160; and libertinism, 87; of Louis XIV's artists, xxi, 89; in Lully sons, 146, 160; in salon, 116

Tallemant des Réaux, 33

tambourines, 200

Tasso, Torquato, 16n21

Temple: of Cupid, 174–76, 178–79; libertine community of, xviii, 140–45, 246; of Raillery, 192–93; of Venus, 175–76, 230, 232

Terpsichore, 76, 104, 156–58, 214

textuality, 81

Thalia (Muse of comedy), 76, 104, 122, 133, 156–57, 163, 193, 214

theaters, Parisian, xxii, xvii, 113, 115, 119, 122, 146, 148, 155–56, 168, 176, 188, 189, 221, 222, 224, 230, 176, 204; wars of (*guerres de*), 172–73, 188, 190

théâtre de la foire: mock heroism of, 151; and opéra-ballet [carnival], 191, 194, 196, 198, 201, 206, 218; and opéra-ballet [Cythera], 172–73, 181, 183, 188–89; rise of, 172; as spectacle, xv; and subversion, xvii; and Watteau, 222, 224, 226, 247. *See also* Foire Saint-Germain, Foire Saint-Laurent

Theater Guénégaud, 172

Théophile (Théophile de Viau), 87, 115, 117

theorbo, 136

Theseus, 124

third estate, 249

tightrope, 153, 196

"timelessness," 17

Torelli, Giacomo, 9

tragédie en musique: 1669–87, xxii, 116, 120–50; 1687–99, xxiii, 150–55, 158, 162, 189, 210; 1700–10, 163; critiqued by La Fontaine, 135–38; foreshadowed in court ballet, 81; music of, 128–33, 147, 149, 183; and opéra-ballet, 167–68, 170, 182, 201, 248; as representation, xvii, xxi. *See also* court ballet; opéra-ballet; parody

tragédie-ballet, 138

tragedy: in court ballet, 76; parodied in comédie-ballet, 104, 119; parodied in opéra-ballet, 192, 194, 201, 214; in tra-

gédie en musique, 121–23, 126, 127, 128, 156–58, 163, 165, 189

transformation, 121, 174–79

Treaties, Spanish succession (1698–1700), 179

Treaty of Ryswick (1697), 172

Treaty of Utrecht (1713–14), 182

Trianon, palace of, 145–46

Tribute: in comédie-ballet, 115; in opéra-ballet, 160, 204, 213; as type of intertextuality, xvii. *See also* allusion; intertextuality

Tristan (Tristan L'Hermite), 53, 54, 87, 117, 141, 148; *Orphée*, 54

Le triomphe des arts. See frontispieces; La Motte, Antoine Houdar de; La Barre, Michel de

triumph: of artists, 179; of arts, 172–81, 231, 234–45; of Folly, 212, 221; of glory, 57; imperial, 42; of love, 120, 161, 177, 247; of pleasure, 121; triumphal arch, 128, 231, 240, 245; triumphal entry, 231

Trivelin, 23, 26

Trojan War, 183

trumpet, 127–28, 136–37, 147, 158, 240

Tuileries, palace of, 6, 19, 127

Turkish scene: of *Le bourgeois gentilhomme*, 102–3, 105, 110, 112–13; of *Le Sicilien*, 93

underground press. *See* pamphlet literature

Urania (Muse of astronomy), 76, 104, 133, 214

utopia: of arts, 231, 237; of court, 114, 168; of court ballet, 6; of Cythera, 165, 175, 179, 226, 234; of folly, 112, 113; libertine, 176, 188; of love, 137, 180; of opéra-ballet, 165, 168, 170, 172, 174, 177–78, 181, 224; of pleasure, 170; of public culture, 95, 114, 202; of spectacle, xvii, 84, 111–12, 118, 121, 122, 167, 173, 210, 231; utopianism, 119; of Watteau, xviii, 224, 237, 249. *See also* novel, utopian; imagery, utopian

Utopia. See More, Thomas

Valois dynasty, 51

Vanni, Giulio Cesare, 115

Vaux-le-Vicomte, château of, 47, 84, 136–37

Veiras, Denis, 114, 119

Vendôme, duc de, 139–45, 149, 215

Vendôme, Philippe de (le grand Prieur), 139, 141–42, 145, 149–50

Venice, 196–218

Venus (Aphrodite): and art, 52–53, 249; in court ballet of 1650s, 1, 15, 33, 35, 38; in court ballet of 1660s, 57–60, 65, 66, 81–83; cult of, 175; iconography of, 59, 59n34, 188; in opéra-ballet, 165–68, 175–81, 183, 192, 230, 247; opposed to Athena, 57–60, 181–82; rose as attribute of, 224–25, 234, 235, 242; as symbol of political opposition, 51–54, 82; in théâtre de la foire, 189; in tragédie en musique, 120, 127, 133, 146; in Watteau, 224–25, 234–38, 242–43, 245

vers de personnages: for court ballets of 1650s, 10, 34, 38, 40; for court ballets of 1660s, 44, 57, 66, 78, 149, 202, 206, 208

Verpré, M., 16

Versailles: courtiers at, xxiii, 152; and Grand Dauphin, 163; and *grand divertissements*, 166–67; and tragédie en musique, 127

Vigarani, Carlo, 9

Vigarani, Gaspare, 9

Vigarani, Ludovico, 9

Vignon, Pierre, 149

village, 180–81, 231

violon, 16, 19, 27, 59, 67, 77–80, 128, 136, 149

vingt-quatre violons du roi, 19

Virgil, 42, 53

voice (opposed to logos), 80n51

Voiture, Vincent, 14, 17

"Volez, amours," 211

Voltaire (François-Marie Arouet), 195

war: and comédie-ballet, 104; and court ballet, 15, 30, 38, 40, 62, 66, 174, 176, 181, 202; with Holland (1672–78), 126, 136; iconography of, 57; of League of Augsburg (1688–97), 148, 157; in literature, 54, 56, 113; music of, 128, 137; and nobility, 12; and opéra-ballet, 165, 177, 182–83, 214; of Spanish Succession, 223; of theaters (*guerre des théâtres*), 172–73; and tragédie en musique, 127, 133, 134, 146, 156–58; warriors, 83; and Watteau, 223, 240, 247. *See also* Holland, campaign against; Low Countries, campaign against; militarism

Watteau, Antoine: and Campra, xxii–xxiii, 249; costumes in, 225, 225n11; forerunners to *Pilgrimage*, 227–34; and *Le triomphe des arts*, 227–40; and *Les amours déguisés*, 235; and libertinism, xviii; and Louis XIV, 223, 238, 240–42; and nostalgia, 225; and patronage, xxii; reception of, 249–51. WORKS: *Departure of the Italian Comedians*, 223; *L'isle de Cythère*, 226, 231, 233; *Pilgrimage to Cythera*, xviii, 173, 222–27, 234–45, 248–49; *Plaisirs d'amour*, 224. *See also* opéra-ballet

women: and aesthetic of *galanterie*, 13–14; as audience of court ballet, 10; in opposition to Louis XIV, 55; as participants in court ballet, 11, 164; and *querelles des théâtres*, 177n18; as victims in court ballet, 81–83. *See also* salon

woodwind instruments, 183, 240

Zephyrus, 145–48